Monographs of the
Hebrew Union College,
Number 5

From Reform Judaism
to Ethical Culture:
The Religious Evolution
of Felix Adler

An I. Edward Kiev
Library Foundation Book

Monographs of the Hebrew Union College

From Reform Judaism to Ethical Culture: The Religious Evolution of Felix Adler

by

Benny Kraut

Hebrew Union College Press
Cincinnati, 1979

Library of Congress Cataloging in Publication Data

Kraut, Benny.
    From Reform Judaism to ethical culture.

    (Monographs of the Hebrew Union College ; no. 5)
    "An I. Edward Kiev Library Foundation book."
    Revision of the author's thesis, Brandeis University.
    Bibliography: p.
    Includes index.
    1. Adler, Felix, 1851-1933—Biography. 2. Ethical
culture movement—Biography. 3. Reform Judaism—
United States. 4. Jews in New York (City)—Biography.
I. Title. II. Series: Hebrew Union College-Jewish
Institute of Religion. Monographs ; no. 5.
BP605.E84K72 1979   296.8'346'0924 [B]   79-14441
ISBN 0-87820-404-0
ISSN 0190-5627

Designed by Noel Martin
Manufactured in the United States of America
Distributed by KTAV Publishing House, Inc.
New York, New York 10013

To my beloved parents
Miriam and Pinchas Kraut
‏ותפארת בנים אבותם . . .‏
(Proverbs 17:6)

I. Edward Kiev Library Foundation

In memory of Dr. I. Edward Kiev, alike distinguished as Rabbi, Chaplain and Librarian of the Hebrew Union College-Jewish Institute of Religion in New York, his family and friends have established in September 1976 a library Foundation bearing his name, to support and encourage the knowledge, understanding and appreciation of books, manuscripts and other efforts of scholars in Judaica and Hebraica. In cooperation with the Faculty Publications Committee of the Hebrew Union College-Jewish Institute of Religion the Foundation offers the present volume as the first I. Edward Kiev Library Foundation Volume.

Felix Adler

Table of Contents

Table of Contents

xi

Preface

Felix Adler (1851–1933), the Jewish-born social and religious reformer, educator, and philosopher, underwent a decisive religious transformation during the 1870s. Influenced by the modern trends of religious liberalism, neo-Kantianism, and the general scientific spirit of critical inquiry, Adler was unable to maintain his adolescent adherence to Reform Judaism. In the 1870s, therefore, he propounded a unique, eclectic religious ideology which he deemed more meaningful and more consistent with the temper of the modern age. And by the end of that decade, he left the Jewish socio-religious consensus completely, having created his own universal socio-religious fellowship, the New York Society for Ethical Culture.

This study traces the history of Felix Adler's religious evolution and his emergence out of Judaism. It reveals the factors precipitating Adler's religious departure, and exposes both the controversies which his break from Judaism engendered within the American Jewish community and the significant impact which it had on American Jewish religious life. In addition, this work examines Adler's relation to Judaism and the Jewish community following his break, and outlines his views on the two major Jewish issues of international prominence from the 1880s on, anti-Semitism and Zionism.

While other aspects of Felix Adler's life and thought have been evaluated by American historians and philosophers, his life as a Jew and his emergence out of Judaism have never been the objects of serious study. For reasons not altogether apparent, Jewish historians, in fact, seem to have neglected Felix Adler. He receives but fleeting attention in studies of American Jewish history and is often totally ignored in the broader works of modern Jewish history. Indeed, it is curious that with the exception of one brief article by Rabbi Levi Olan (see the Bibliography), no Reform Jewish scholars or scholars of Reform Judaism have attempted any sort of critical analysis of Adler's changing religious life. This book, it is hoped, will fill this gap in Jewish historical investigation.

This book is a revised version of a study initially prepared as a doctoral dissertation in the Department of Near Eastern and Judaic Studies, Brandeis University. I should like to express my deepest appreciation to my graduate advisor and doctoral thesis director, Professor Ben Halpern, who in no small measure helped to train me as a historian. His meticulous supervision of the thesis and incisive critical comments contributed significantly to the production of a tighter, better balanced work. I also benefited from the comments of Professors Marvin Meyers and Marshall Sklare, both members of my dissertation committee.

As editor of the Hebrew Union College Press, Professor Michael A.

Meyer devoted considerable time and effort in helping me to transform this work from thesis to book. His observations, probing questions, and suggestions forced me to rethink and reevaluate a number of issues which might otherwise have remained unclear. I cannot sufficiently express my enormous gratitude to him.

I should also like to express my deepest gratitude to the late Professor Horace Friess, son-in-law and literary executor of Felix Adler, and to his wife, Mrs. Ruth Adler Friess. Professor Friess's passing in 1975 was a very great loss to his many colleagues, students, and friends. While I only came to know him in the last years of his life, his warmth, dignity, and generosity quickly endeared him to me. He permitted me to browse freely through the Adler archives; he offered for my inspection numerous unseen Adler manuscripts in his personal possession; and he allowed me to read some chapters of his own biography of Felix Adler, which he had been preparing for publication. During our many discussions together and in his reading of my work, Professor Friess offered invaluable advice and constant personal encouragement. Mrs. Friess consented to personal interviews relating to her father which helped put certain issues into clearer perspective.

While a student, I benefited from a number of scholarship grants which allowed me to study and to do the needed research free from all financial burdens. I acknowledge sincerely awards from the Canada Council, the · Quebec Ministry of Education, the Canadian Foundation for Jewish Culture, and the Memorial Foundation for Jewish Culture. I would also like to thank the Memorial Foundation for Jewish Culture and the University Research Council at the University of Cincinnati for having awarded me grants to defray the expenses involved in the revision of this study.

I extend my thanks to Mr. Kenneth A. Lohf, Librarian of the Rare Book and Manuscript Library of the Columbia University Libraries, for having permitted me to research the Felix Adler Papers at Columbia, and to Mr. B. Crystal of the Columbia Libraries, who was extremely helpful in giving me practical access to the material. I extend my thanks as well to Dr. Gould P. Colman, University Archivist of Cornell University, for having permitted my use of university archival material pertaining to Adler. I am grateful to Dr. Herbert C. Zafren, Director of Libraries at Hebrew Union College–Jewish Institute of Religion, Cincinnati, Ohio, Dr. Jacob R. Marcus, Director of the American Jewish Archives, Cincinnati, and Dr. Stanley F. Chyet, former Associate Director of these Archives, for having allowed me to use material housed in their respective collections. Fannie Zelcer of the American Jewish Archives was especially kind in expeditiously forwarding all material requested during the initial stages of research. My thanks to Temple Emanu-El, New York City, for having permitted me to study the "Minute Book of the Emanu-El Trustees" in their archives. Mr. Fred Garel's willing cooperation facilitated my use of the Adler archives at the New York Society for Ethical Culture. I am grateful to the late Dr. I. Edward Kiev and his staff at the Hebrew Union College–Jewish Institute of Religion, New York, for having opened their library resources to me.

I am indebted to Prof. Hyman Grinstein, Professor of History at Yeshiva University, for having alerted me to a number of important newspaper sources. I acknowledge with deep gratitude the assistance of my aunt, Mrs. Sophie Gunzburg, in the deciphering of near-illegible German manuscripts, and the editorial comments of my father-in-law, Rabbi Morris J. Besdin. Ms. Barbara Pomerantz read the manuscript and offered very helpful stylistic suggestions. Mrs. Alvena Stanfield did an excellent job in typing the manuscript.

To my parents go my love and heartfelt gratitude for their constant encouragement and devotion, and for having granted me all the educational opportunities which I have enjoyed. And *acharon acharon chaviv,* my deepest thanks go to my dear wife, Penny, for having edited my manuscript. But words alone cannot express my feelings of appreciation for her more subtle—perhaps even more significant—contributions. Without her gentle prodding, her calming patience, and her unflagging confidence in my ability, this book might never have been written.

University of Cincinnati   Benny Kraut
September 1977

Chapter I

Growing Up as a Reform Jew

From Old World to New

Born on August 13, 1851 in Alzey, a small town in Rhenish Hesse, Southwest Germany, Felix Adler was reared in the profoundly religious home of a family steeped in a rich rabbinic tradition. His mother, Henrietta, was the daughter of Rabbi Feibisch (Phoebus) Frankfurter of Friedberg. His father, Samuel, was the son of Rabbi Sirig (Isaac) Adler, dayan (rabbinical judge) of Worms, and cousin to Rabbi Nathan Adler, leader of the prestigious rabbinical academy in Frankfurt am Main during the last decades of the eighteenth century. Nathan Marcus Adler, who became chief rabbi of the British Empire in the nineteenth century, was also a relative.

Samuel Adler attended traditional yeshivot in Germany and, like his two brothers, Jacob and Abraham, was ordained as a rabbi in the Orthodox Jewish faith. Due to the secular and liberal impact of his university studies, however, he gradually turned from Orthodoxy; and, after considerable intellectual wrestling and religious soul-searching, he concluded that Reform Judaism was for him the most acceptable form of religious faith and doctrine. He soon became a Reform rabbi in a German Jewish community, thus preserving the rabbinic office in the Adler family, although not in its traditional character.[1]

Upon his appointment as district rabbi of Alzey in 1842, Samuel quickly established himself as an energetic and learned exponent of the Reform movement. He promptly instituted several significant reforms, including the removal of the rampart segregating men and women in the synagogue and the introduction of confirmation ceremonies for boys and girls of the religious school. Samuel also participated actively in the three German rabbinical conferences between 1844 and 1846 and was a prominent member of several crucial religious subcommittees. Utilizing his extensive knowledge of rabbinic sources, he upheld the right of the contemporary rabbinate to reform Judaism in accordance with changing times and ideologies.[2]

Following the rabbinical conferences, Samuel was one of the few rabbis able to introduce into his rabbinic district some of the most striking reforms suggested by the conferences' resolutions, such as the omission from the liturgy of all hopes for Jewish national restoration; the establishment of a triennial cycle of Torah readings; and the abolition of the second day of Jewish festival celebrations. It was not long, therefore,

1

before he gained prominence as a scholarly, enterprising, and innovative rabbi in the Reform movement. Abraham Geiger, the most eminent of European Reform rabbis and theologians, held Samuel in great esteem, and in 1854 endorsed him for the position of rabbi of the Lemberg synagogue; but Samuel regretfully had to decline the offered position because of his mother's illness. Samuel Adler's distinguished reputation soon reached the shores of America, however, and led to his election to the prestigious pulpit of Temple Emanu-El in New York City.

On February 22, 1857 Rabbi Samuel Adler, his wife, Henrietta, and their two sons, Isaac (b. 1849) and Felix, set sail for America. The rabbi left his rabbinical parish in Alzey with a "heavy heart," but he felt his decision to assume the Emanu-El pulpit to be both wise and necessary. "It had to be done," he noted in his autobiography, "both out of consideration for my family, to provide them with a better future, and not less to gain for myself a more extended field of action."[3] America, he believed, would not only provide greater opportunity for the general advancement of his family but also would grant him freedom from the political pressures and religious restrictions which hampered him in Germany. No longer would the state interfere with his innovative religious reforms, impede his rabbinic career, or stifle his open avowal of democracy.[4]

In emigrating to America, the Adler family joined the millions of Central and Western Europeans who, between 1840 and 1880, sought either refuge from the severe economic depressions ravaging Europe or asylum from the political repression that followed the failure of the European revolutionary movements in 1848 and the early 1850s. The especially harsh conditions in the rural areas of the Southern German states precipitated, in the period between 1848 and 1860, a considerable exodus to America, which had gained a reputation as a land of economic opportunity and a haven for the oppressed.

German Jews emigrated in large numbers as well. Not only did they share in the general economic and political situation, but they also suffered from the humiliating restrictions imposed specifically on them. These disabilities—the Judengasse, the Jewish oaths and "moral patent," capricious government intrusion in Jewish communal affairs—all of which Samuel Adler had personally experienced or witnessed[5]—were an added spur to German Jewish emigration. By 1865 approximately one hundred thousand German Jews, most from the Southern German states, had joined the emigration to America.

Besides the unique discriminations against Jews to which the Adler family was subject, the climate of political repression touched Samuel's family directly. His brother Abraham was imprisoned for his participation in the revolutionary movement of 1848 and subsequently died in

1856 from an illness contracted during his prison term. Samuel himself was implicated for his outspoken democratic sympathies, and he later became a victim of harassment and obstruction by state functionaries.[6] He soon realized that the advancement and fulfillment of his rabbinic career could always be checked by government whim. Thus, when he received the invitation from America, he accepted the post after only a few days of deliberation and with the enthusiastic approval of his wife, devoutly affirming that the offer from Temple Emanu-El illustrated "the rule of God in this world."[7]

Like other immigrants arriving before the Panic of August 1857, the Adlers found the country in a state of strong economic growth and prosperity. Manufacturing, commerce, railroads, and other aspects of the economy were expanding at an accelerated pace, and the process of urbanization had been well on its way since the 1840s. While much of America was still agrarian, the course of industrialization was proceeding rapidly, providing wide opportunities for profit and wealth even as it also created pockets of poverty and slums.

American economic advances, however, could not mask the raging national conflict over slavery, which came to engage the Adlers' attention as well. During the 1850s the nation seethed in social and political ferment; the debate over slavery divided American national life and found expression in economic, political, social, and religious thoughts and actions. Further, while the conflict over slavery served to deepen social idealism, to some extent it also tended to absorb reforming energies. With the later outbreak of the Civil War, concern with most other social and religious issues receded into the background; the social-religious conscience was preoccupied with the problem of slavery.

American society in the 1850s was essentially religious in character and conservative in its theological orientation. Liberal religious groups, such as the Universalists, Unitarians, and Transcendentalists, did exist in the New England states, but they were a small minority whose national influence was not significant. On the whole, religious liberalism was the exception rather than the rule.

Nevertheless, one could already discern a subtle under-current of intellectual challenge and religious skepticism that would, in the following decades, shake the religious serenity of America. This current had its source in the new and often radical temper of European academic thought and culture. The surge of scientific knowledge, the publication of Darwin's *On the Origin of Species by Means of Natural Selection*, the iconoclastic trend in the study of the history of religion, the ascendance of a materialistic, this-worldly philosophy, and above all, the analytic dissection of the Bible by the exercise of Higher Biblical Criticism all tended to question the faith and subvert the dogma of Christianity. Americans studying abroad and exposed to the new intellectual methods and conclusions returned home to disseminate the new thinking to their countrymen. Octavius Brooks Frothingham, founder of the Free Religious Association, William James Potter, and John Fiske among others eventually helped to bring America under the influence of the intellectual Weltanschauung of Europe and to foster a variety of forms of liberal religious expression.

While the overall American social, political, and religious climate constituted the general atmosphere in which the Adlers lived, the American Jewish community framed the more immediate environment and background of concerns of the Adler family. The American Jewish community, which the Adlers joined in 1857, was still young, relatively small, and energetically engaged in the process of adjustment to the economic and socio-religious conditions of its new environment. The German Jewish immigrants who comprised the great bulk of American Jewry quickly established social and economic roots and generally sought to preserve their Jewish identity and to transplant their religious heritage.[8] They built synagogues, religious schools, Jewish hospitals and orphanages, cultural and philanthropic fraternities, and founded Jewish newspapers and magazines.

And yet the Jewish quest for socio-economic integration in America—Americanization—significantly affected and dramatically colored the character of American Jewish religious life. Economic motives, in particular, provided the primary impetus for Jewish religious laxity and compromise. Often religious laxity was perceived to be a practical economic necessity. The observance of the Sabbath and Jewish dietary laws, for example, posed extreme hardships for numerous Jewish peddlers traveling in isolated areas of the Midwest as well as for Jews in towns and cities who, prohibited from working on Sundays because of Sunday Blue Laws, would have lost a full day to their economic competitors. Eventually, religious compromise led some Jews to religious indifference, to secularism, and even to atheism.

The Jewish desire for Americanization also helped to sustain the poor quality of religious education in America and militated against its improvement. The masses of South German Jewish immigrants of the late 1840s and 1850s were uneducated and Jewishly ignorant. Most were ritually observant when they arrived, but as their commitment to religious observances weakened, Jewish education beyond a basic familiarity with Jewish rituals was not regarded to be a high priority. The failure of these American Jews to establish an institution of higher Jewish learning before the 1870s reflected their low level of concern for, and awareness of the need for, sound Jewish education in general and American-trained rabbis in particular. Indeed, this educational neglect mirrored the general poverty of American Jewish religious-intellectual life at this time.

The Jews' anxious pursuit of socio-economic acceptance in American society, resulting in religious compromise and a diminished concern for religious education, also stimulated the rise and development of the predominant Jewish religious trend from the mid-1850s through the mid-1880s: the trend of religious reform. Some Jews may have sought a more acceptable interpretation of Judaism than was offered by Orthodox Judaism on the grounds of religious and intellectual principles; most Jews, however, sought both a religious justification for the lessening of their religious observance and a religion more compatible with the American social environment. Since religious reforms were geared to reduce Jewish ritual obligations, to remove many obstructions hindering social respectability and economic advancement, and to Americanize the forms of Judaism so that the Jewish religion could become an acceptable weave in the total fabric of American religion, reforming Judaism became increasingly popular among upwardly mobile Jews who, relatively quickly, joined the middle class.

While the early stirrings of American Jewish religious reform had already occurred in 1824 and in the 1830s, the seeds that were to flower into the American Jewish Reform Movement were not actually planted until the 1850s, and they did not really blossom into a coherent organized movement until the 1870s, when Rabbi Isaac M. Wise orchestrated the creation of the Union of American Hebrew Congregations (1873) and the Hebrew Union College (1875), and when the Eastern and Western factions of Reform united (1879). Thus, when Samuel Adler assumed the pulpit of Temple Emanu-El in 1857, American Reform Judaism was still in its infancy. The direction of ritual changes was gradually being established, but the ultimate fate and character of Reform Judaism had by no means been determined.

At Temple Emanu-El Samuel Adler intensified his efforts on behalf of Reform Judaism, and he soon became a dominant rabbinic figure and intellectual leader of the burgeoning Jewish community. He had the triennial cycle of Torah reading instituted and the partition separating men and women removed. In 1860 he revised the *Seder Tefilah,* the prayerbook compiled by his predecessor, Leo Merzbacher, and founded a short-lived school for the training of Reform rabbis, the Emanu-El Theological Seminary.[9] In 1864, in concurrence with the temple trustees, Samuel had the practice of praying with uncovered heads made mandatory.[10] And, long interested in Jewish education, Samuel himself taught at the Emanu-El Sunday School.[11] He also upgraded the religious school curriculum by writing and revising educational materials that were widely used in the Sunday schools of Emanu-El and other Reform temples.[12]

Samuel's practical activities were paralleled by his scholarship. He contributed scholarly articles to the *Jewish Reformer,* Stade's *Zeitschrift,* the *Hebrew Review,* Graetz's *Monatsschrift,* Brüll's *Jahrbücher für Jüdische Geschichte und Literatur,* and *Johnson's New Universal Cyclopedia.*[13] Moreover, as a recognized scholar, his advice was often sought in the establishment of new Reform congregations. The American Jewish Archives in Cincinnati contains much material in the form of rabbinic responsa in which Adler answered requests for guidance and assistance from Reform groups and congregations. On November 24, 1858, for example, the Jüdische Reformverein of Chicago sought advice on how to proceed to establish a Reform temple. Other letters with similar requests were received from such places as New Orleans, Buffalo, and Curaçao.[14]

Samuel Adler also contributed to the formulation of Reform Judaism's ideology and theology in America. In 1869, together with Rabbi David Einhorn, he convened the Philadelphia Reform Conference, which met at the home of Rabbi Samuel Hirsch and saw the adoption of the Philadelphia Platform. In concert with Einhorn and Hirsch, Adler advanced this seven-plank platform enunciating basic Reform principles. In reality, the platform merely served to ratify in America the fundamental Reform ideology already crystallized in Germany. Nevertheless, though formulated in the crucible of German socio-political reality, this ideology was readily applicable to the American socio-religious context.

Essentially, the Philadelphia Platform affirmed that the messianic mission of Israel was, not to restore the old Jewish state and divide the Jews from other nations, but rather to spread monotheism around the world and unite all people under God; that the Jewish dispersion was not a punishment for past sins, but rather a manifestation of Divine Will to enable the Jews to fulfill their mission; and that inner devotion and ethical sanctification comprised the essential components of religion. All of these ideas tended to minimize the theological, logical, and psychological necessity of practical ritual observances and furnished both an impetus and a rationale for continued religious reform in American Jewish life. Reform Jewish theology as proclaimed by the rabbis also seemed to offer an attractive religio-cultural identity for acculturating American Jews groping for some type of synthesis between the demands of Judaism and of American life. This theology afforded Jews the opportunity to affirm their status as Americans in the full socio-national sense of the term; as Jews they differed from other Americans only in their adherence to a particular religious creed.

Not surprisingly, then, by the 1870s Reform Judaism had established itself as the preeminent and most prestigious form of Jewish religion in America. Prior to 1860 only a handful of synagogues had committed themselves to Reform, but by 1870 there existed few congregations in

America in which substantial reforms had not already been instituted and in which the process of radical reform had not been initiated.[15] Samuel Adler shared in this meteoric rise of Reform Judaism in the 1860s and in large measure contributed to its impressive growth and achievement.

Felix Adler's Adolescence

Both in family background and home environment, young Felix Adler was set apart from the overwhelming majority of German and American Jewish children. His father was neither a trader, an artisan, nor a petty merchant as were the fathers of most Jewish Americans in the 1850s. While the bulk of Felix's peers during the explosive decade of the 1860s gingerly walked the tightrope of religious traditionalism and practical ritual reforms in seeking a meaningful religio-cultural identity, he was assimilating the fundamental beliefs and fully articulated Reform ideology of his father.

A strong and vital religious atmosphere pervaded the Adler home.[16] By personal example, family ritual observances, and the religious instruction of his children, Samuel sought to inculcate his children—Isaac, Felix, and Sarah (b. 1858)—with the values and principles of Reform Judaism. His prestigious position as rabbi of Temple Emanu-El enhanced his personal stature and the persuasiveness of his religious beliefs in their eyes.[17] Beyond this, Samuel's constant devotion to Jewish and general scholarship, his diligent study, and his impressive library inspired his family with an intellectual zeal for both Jewish and secular areas of knowledge.[18]

As youngsters both Isaac and Felix were sent to the Temple Emanu-El Sunday School for religious instruction; later both served as instructors in the school. Samuel, however, personally supplemented his sons' religious education. Evidence exists that Samuel taught Felix parts of the Talmud, Bible, and other Jewish subjects.[19] He channeled his sons' readings into recent works of Jewish scholarship as well. As a teenager Felix had already read selections, or substantial parts, of the works of Jost, Zunz, Graetz, Munk, Riesser, the *Monatsschrift* of Frankel, the *Zeitschrift* of Geiger, the *Itinerary of Benjamin of Tudela,* and issues of *HaMeassef* and *Bikkure Halttim.*[20]

While no records on this matter remain, undoubtedly Samuel also instructed his elder son, Isaac, in Jewish religious and scholarly subjects. He hoped that Isaac, as the oldest, would continue the Adler rabbinic tradition and succeed him as rabbi of Emanu-El.[21] However, influenced by Isidor Walz, an older cousin living with the Adlers in the 1860s, as well as by his studies at Columbia College, Isaac devoted his full attention to science during his undergraduate years. In 1868 he returned to Germany to pursue medical studies at Berlin and Heidelberg universities, and ultimately became a well-known specialist of clinical medicine in New York City.[22] In the 1860s Samuel may well have been ambivalent, if not very disappointed, about his son's preference for science, despite his own personal commitment to the furtherance of knowledge. He soon anchored his hopes on young Felix to succeed him at Emanu-El.

Both Isaac and Felix received their secular education at the Columbia Grammar School, a private institution which concentrated heavily on the Greek and Latin classics, mathematics, and English.[23] Upon their graduation, they continued their studies at Columbia College. Both the elementary school and the college were fairly exclusive middle- to upper-class Christian institutions having almost no Jewish students. Samuel's position as rabbi of Emanu-El undoubtedly helped in gaining admission for his sons.

Besides providing young Felix with a stimulating educational and cultural environment, and a comforting sense of security in the faith of Reform Judaism, Samuel and Henrietta Adler, by their own practical ethical deeds, instilled in Felix the ethical idealism that was to be the spiritual leitmotif of his life. Samuel Adler's commitment to Reform Judaism went beyond abstract theological doctrines. It imbued him with a sense of religious duty to implement the moral and ethical precepts of Judaism in his personal life as well as in his rabbinic office. The tradition of ethical benevolence which he had inherited from his father, Sirig, also heightened his resolve to fulfill his perceived religio-ethical duty.[24] Thus, together with Rev. Samuel Isaacs, for instance, he was chiefly responsible for the founding of the Hebrew Orphan Asylum of New York in 1859. From its inception, Samuel guided the trustees of Emanu-El to support the institution, and when, on October 14, 1859, a special meeting of Emanu-El's trustees was held to consider the propriety of making a collection in the temple on the holiday of Shemini Atseret in aid of the projected asylum, Samuel strongly advocated the holiday appeal.[25] From that time forward, the "Minute Book of the Temple Emanu-El Trustees" records the continuing and growing support of the temple members for the asylum.

The "Minute Book" also records the temple's numerous charitable donations for diverse causes. Among the beneficiaries of Emanu-El's money were the martyred Jews of Morocco and Gibraltar in 1860, the injured and seriously ill Union soldiers in 1862, the poor Irish left desolate in the wake of the famine of 1863, the Jewish victims of yellow fever in New Orleans and Galveston in 1867, the suffering Jews of Russia in 1869, and the victims of the Avondale boat tragedy of 1869. No doubt Samuel Adler's stress on the practical application of Jewish religious ethics helped to steer his temple on a charitable course. Samuel himself set an inspiring example for his temple when, in February 1864, together with a Mr. Moses Schlofs, he accepted the guardianship of the orphaned children of Emanu-El's sexton, Mr. Abraham Mayer.[26] The lessons of the ethical character and practices of his father were not lost on young Felix, who later cited the "profound ethical influence of his father" as one of two "Chief Influences" on him as a young man.[27]

Felix's mother, Henrietta Adler, also set an inspiring example of religious piety and practical ethical activity. Like her husband, she endowed the home with an atmosphere of spirituality and ethical sensitivity. Felix remembered his mother as a warm, gentle, and very generous person who contributed to the development of his ethical consciousness. He noted in a later autobiographical sketch that the second "Chief Influence" on him as a young man was the "early training of [his] mother in visiting and helping poor families in the tenements of New York,"[28] and he cited her "strong sense of practical righteousness. Her charities— training in practical charity by errands to the poor, paralyzed doctor, etc."[29] According to Eleanor Adler, her grandmother Henrietta was extremely concerned about the general welfare of the community and always invited some poor individuals to dinner. Henrietta insisted that her sons come in personal contact with the poor so she sent them "regularly into the tenements with baskets of food. In this way, Felix was given his first lasting impression of the destitute and had his first indignation stirred by their misery."[30]

Henrietta Adler also assumed a somewhat different role from her husband in the Adler home. Unlike Samuel, who "was a much more distant figure in the life of the household, [she] carried most of the burden of the family thinking it part of her duty to shield her husband's scholarly life from daily friction with the outside world."[31] Felix himself compared his mother to "G.'s characterization of his mother,"[32] evidently referring to Goethe's portrait of his own mother in his *Dichtung und Wahrheit.*[33] The comparison is rather fitting, for like Goethe's mother, Henrietta Adler was a kind, gentle, yet dependable and practical human being, a loving mother who mediated between her husband and the outside world, and who complemented her husband's more stern intellectual posture with her own example of warmth and personal goodness.

Felix's adolescence was fortunate in that his family did not know the strain of poverty and privation. Temple Emanu-El amply provided for the rabbi and his family. The pressure of economic integration—so critical a factor in molding the religious habits and ethical attitudes of most American Jews—did not affect the Adler family. Economics was not a motive force in Felix's religious development.

Despite the attractiveness of the Adler home, Felix's close bonds with his parents, and the favorable circumstances in which the family lived, one cannot depict the period of Felix's youth as altogether happy and cheerful. According to the late Professor Horace Friess, Felix Adler's son-in-law and literary executor, Felix spoke very little of his younger days.[34] This reticence may have been due, as some autobiographical sources suggest, to the fact that his boyhood memories included feelings of considerable unhappiness caused by periods of painful loneliness and the trials of social adjustment.

As a youngster, "Felix was quiet, shy and dreamy." His personality and nature stood in marked contrast to that of his older brother, Isaac, "a handsome, energetic dominating boy [who] was apt to overshadow his younger brother."[35] Isaac must have been held up by his parents as a model for Felix to emulate, for while still a teenager Felix recorded his critical view of this practice. Selecting a very pointed excerpt from Bacon's essay "Of Parents and Children," Felix noted that "men have a foolish manner (both *Parents* and schoolmasters and servants) in creating and breeding an emulation between Brothers during *childehood* which many times soweth to Discord when they are men, and disturbeth Families."[36] In a later autobiographical sketch entitled "Character Traits of X," Felix wrote about himself: ". . . In early youth he had the sense of being overshadowed or disprized, being judged by the standards of others." The reference to "others" probably referred to his brother Isaac and possibly to his cousin Isidor Walz as well. At any rate, in these excerpts one may detect a tinge of resentment which probably caused some tension between Felix and his brother (and cousin) and prevented the forging of close bonds of friendship between them during their youth.

Nor did Felix seem to make any other close friendships during his adolescence; loneliness and the lack of close friends plagued him throughout his adolescent years. In part, this lack was caused by social and educational circumstances beyond his control. At age fourteen Felix passed the demanding examinations of Columbia College, and in October 1866, at fifteen, he entered Columbia's freshman class. He was obviously a bright and able student and academically qualified for college study. But his relative youth and lack of social confidence hindered his adjustment to his older classmates.

Felix was one of the youngest students in his class; virtually every other student was at least two to three years older.[37] Quite probably Felix was also the only Jew in his class. The student paper, *Cap and Gown*, records that Felix's 1870 graduating class consisted of thirteen Episcopalians, five Presbyterians, two Baptist, two Unitarians, one Methodist, one Catholic, and one Moslem; no Jews are mentioned, which is surprising since Felix remains unaccounted for. At that time Columbia College was still closely affiliated with the Episcopal Trinity Church, and the composition of the student body as well as the faculty reflected this relationship.[38] Attendance at chapel services was still compulsory. One wonders what Felix felt while sitting through these compulsory services.

The behavior of his brother, Isaac, at chapel services, in fact, seems to have been the source of some irritation for Columbia's trustees. In his diary entry of November 6, 1865, George T. Strong noted: "Barnard [president of Columbia] brought up a curious correspondence about a contumacious Hebrew Sophomore named Isaac Adler (I think), Isaac of New York, whose conscience compels him to decline standing up with the rest during service in chapel, and who wants to be a martyr like his forebears in Maccabees. Barnard offered certain resolutions affirming the College to be a Christian institution."[39]

As a Christian college catering mainly to Protestant youths from well-to-do homes, Columbia hardly offered an inviting social atmosphere for a retiring, shy, and underaged Jewish youth. The Jewishness of the Adler boys must have been very much noticed during their years at Columbia, and Felix, for one, felt ill at ease. In an autobiographical note, he wrote: "Education—Inharmonious setting from the first. A Jewish boy largely German among typically American boys of the wealthy class (Shepard, Low, Kelley, etc.)"[40] In another autobiographical sketch, he noted one aspect of his nature as displaying "a strong desire for social assimilation."[41] The memory of painful social tension while a young student at Columbia lingered on.

In addition to his social problems at Columbia, Felix was also dissatisfied with the college's intellectual offerings. He found its curriculum to be narrow, and he later complained about the inadequate instruction in philosophy.[42] Indeed, if one looks at the catalogues of Columbia at that time, one finds the college's curriculum heavily stressing the Greek and Latin classics, mathematics, and English—continuing the emphasis of Felix's Columbia Grammar School education—and including the study of philosophy only in the senior year.

The subject of philosophy was included in the general Department of Philosophy, History, Political Economics and Belles Lettres chaired by Charles M. Nairne. The method of philosophical inquiry was restricted to the students finding answers to previously formulated questions. It was further circumscribed by a distinct psychological orientation to which even some of Columbia's trustees objected; Hickok's *Empirical Psychology* was the standard text used.[43] Moreover, to the extent that the educational outlook of the college reflected the policies of its president, Columbia had a built-in bias against philosophy. In his inaugural address in 1864, President Frederick A. P. Barnard contrasted the religiously beneficial results of the study of science with the religiously malevolent results of philosophical inquiry:

Philosophy may no doubt be pursued in a Christian spirit, but it has had in point of fact too often the fatal effect to undermine, subvert, and destroy in its devotees all belief in the personality of God, and so to obliterate every sentiment of fear or reverence for Him in the human heart.[44]

For an inquisitive youth like Felix, neither the quality of the study of philosophy at Columbia nor the institution's attitude to the subject adequately met his needs.

Felix was intellectually disposed already as a youngster, and he spent many enjoyable hours reading at the Cooper Union library. He ranked sixth in a class of thirty graduates from Columbia in 1870, no mean scholastic achievement for one of the youngest students in the class. But perhaps even more indicative of his intellectual orientation was the scope of his scholarly interest in the readings of Columbia's courses. In his book of jottings, Felix quoted from and made reference to Alexander von Humboldt's *Cosmos*, Robert Chambers' *Book of Days,* Robert Burton's *Anatomy of Melancholy*, F. C. Schlosser's *History of the 18th Century and the First Half of the 19th Century,* Sir A. H. Layard's *Discovery of the Ruins of Nineveh and Babylon*, and Edward Gibbon's *Decline and Fall of the Roman Empire.* Felix's apparent interest in von Humboldt's *Cosmos*, in particular, placed him among a select group of rising intellectuals and scholars, since knowledge of this work was a mark of advanced education and learning. As John Fiske, primary American exponent of Darwin and Spencer, wrote at the beginning of the Civil War at age nineteen, "what's a war when a fellow has 'Kosmos' on his shelf and 'Faust' on his table?"[45]

Knowledge and the attainment of wisdom were primary values to Felix. He rejected superficial education as vulgar and expressed disdain for intellectual quackery. So great was his veneration of knowledge and the intellect that he sometimes assumed a posture of intellectual elitism, a trait of which he was also accused—not unjustifiably—in later years. Young Felix displayed little tolerance for the superstitions of the ignorant, whose misplaced faith often restrained them from showing "true reverence for what is sacred. Their minds are too uneducated to comprehend the distance between them and perfection," he wrote. "They are like children that cannot yet distinguish physical distances."[46]

Intellectual excellence to Felix, however, did not imply intellectual abstraction. On the contrary, he favored specifically that knowledge which produced practical good for mankind. For this reason, he greatly admired the writings of Francis Bacon and devoted three pages in his book of jottings to a description of Bacon's philosophy of practical wisdom and virtuous conduct. He referred to Bacon as "one of the greatest intellects the world ever saw."

[In contrast to] the Ancient philosophers from the time of Socrates [who] had wasted their time in striving after an end which could not be obtained, in fruitless discussions about virtue which could not aid the cause of virtue . . . [and who] despised everything practical and devoted themselves wholly to the abstract, Bacon revolutionized philosophy by advancing the proposition that the aim of all philosophy must be first—practical good to mankind. This is the cornerstone of the Baconian system. To arrive at near truths—his aim—he made use of the inductive system in opposition to the syllogistic. . . . Bacon pointed out the way for the great achievements which have since been made and numberless benefits have and will result to mankind from his system.[47]

Felix's concern for the practical good of ideas illustrated the enduring influence of the practical moral and ethical idealism of his parents, in which righteous action complemented religious teaching and ideology. To Felix, the ultimate value of religious doctrine and ethical philosophy was to be measured by the human good and welfare which they generated. This principle, expressed in his early writings, was a cornerstone of his life's teaching and activity.

His sensitive social conscience was also directed inward and inclined him to constant self-analysis and self-evaluation by the same high standards and objectives that he set for others. He was highly introspective, with a heightened sense of self-awareness. His youthful writings of this period, as well as his later autobiographical notations, indicate cognizance of these traits in his personality.

Felix's serious and introspective nature also contributed to his lack of close friends and nurtured his loneliness; in turn, the lack of close friendships intensified further his introspection and penchant for self-appraisal. His advanced intellectual attainment—both his strong intellectual capacity and his exceptional status as a very young Jew in the restrictive Columbia College—exacerbated the problem and was not apt to win him many close Jewish friends in his neighborhood and in the Temple Emanu-El community. Few Jewish youths shared his intellectual pursuits, and this hampered him in forming intimate social bonds. While Felix may have been friendly with some of his fellow teachers at the Emanu-El Sunday School, such as Emil Salinger and Henry Cohn, no record exists of any really close relationships between him and his Jewish contemporaries. Too young for his Columbia peers, Felix probably seemed "too old" in mien to his Jewish acquaintances, resulting in a not very happy social situation.

Felix's social tensions, however, did not precipitate anti-social behavior on his part. On the contrary, his intense self-awareness helped to make him highly sensitive to the needs of others; and, following parental examples, he rejoiced in the performance of ordinary acts of kindness. He later recalled how he had "melted with tenderness when as a boy I helped a little stray child find her way." He noted that "that sort of thing has at times recurred." And elsewhere he reminisced on his character: "Tenderness, certainly, especially towards children, the incident of the little girl."[48] His tender-hearted nature manifested itself on the occasion when he generously gave almost one year of his own savings, earmarked for a silver watch, to an Emanu-El Sunday School teacher who claimed to be in dire financial need. The money was never returned, and his father, Samuel, "sternly refused to come to his help feeling that Felix was too tender-hearted, and hoping that the incident would prove a lesson to him."[49]

Felix's natural sympathy and concern for others was a notable factor in his performance as a teacher in the Temple Emanu-El Sunday School. He was very sensitive to the educational needs of his students, and the educational references which he chose to include in his book of jottings probably reflect his own successful pedagogic philosophy. "Education is from *educo*—to bring out. It does not mean to stuff in—but to bring out, i.e. the talents" (p. 17). Elsewhere he cited the Talmud (*Berachot* 28a): "Said Rabbi Joshua to R. Gamliel, 'Woe to the generations over whom you preside that know not the toils and trials of the student' " (p. 44).

His respect for the educational process and appreciation of the "toils of the student" contributed to his proficiency as a teacher, which was acknowledged publicly.[50] But Felix was not simply proficient; he excelled as a teacher because his instruction was prompted by a love for his students and the desire to extend his good deeds by teaching them. This fact earned him the appreciative response of his students and the praise of his superiors. On July 5, 1867, in describing an examination taken by Emanu-El Sunday School students "to give proof of their progress in Biblical history and catechism," the *Hebrew Leader* also depicted the teachers of the various classes. The paper cited Felix's "pleasing manner [which] evinced a love that actuated him to do good, to teach and instruct—a matter well appreciated by the audience as well as his students." Only Felix, not quite sixteen at the time, received such a warm personal approbation from the paper. In describing other teachers, the paper resorted to either vague platitudes or to impersonal accounts of their intellectual ability.

Interestingly, the paper's description of Felix's brother illuminated further the distinctly contrasting natures of the Adler boys. Isaac Adler taught the highest class, the sixth, and was depicted as "a man of thought and erudite learning who indeed put questions in such a style and manner, that many in the audience felt austere towards the questioner and sympathizing [*sic*] with the students; but there was no failing; answers given so correct that it convinced the most skeptical that it was not a mere matter of memory, but one of true and firm conviction." Isaac, rigorous and austere, gained the students' respect, but Felix's "pleasing manner" gained their esteem and admiration.

Felix endeared himself not only to the students and their parents, but also to the School Committee and Emanu-El's Board of Trustees. The "Minute Book" records that prior to his departure for Europe the School Committee requested "the appropriation of certain sums" from the board "towards a testimonial for Felix Adler who is about departing [*sic*] for Europe." The board responded that it lacked the power to grant this request, "but [that it] would assist a private subscription started by the School Committee, liberally."[51]

The board was true to its word. Following the Emanu-El Sunday School examinations of Sunday, June 12, 1870, Felix was honored at a special ceremony tendered in his behalf. As reported by the *Jewish Times*, June 17, 1870, he received "a set of resolutions, beautifully engrossed, expressive of the high appreciation of his eminent services rendered to the school, the regret at his withdrawal and the kind wishes for his success and prosperity" from Mr. S. Frankenheimer, the chairman of the School Committee. He also received a valuable gold watch from Mr. Lewis May, the president of Emanu-El, on behalf of the trustees and the School Committee, and an "elegant dressing case" from his postbiblical history class. Felix was "deeply affected," the paper noted, "but succeeded in controlling his feelings and made a most eloquent response."

No other teacher in the school was so honored. Other young teachers had departed for Europe before him—Bernheimer, Cohn, and his own brother, Isaac—but Felix alone was feted. His understanding, sensitivity, and affection for his students had left a strong and positive imprint on Emanu-El and the broader New York community. For Felix, the classroom served as a valuable social outlet and stimulated his dedication to his students. In the classroom, he could give expression to the "intense sociability" which he harbored within him.

Felix's exposure as an adolescent to the desperate plight of the many urban poor of New York City both during and following the Civil War aroused his social conscience and sensitivity to the needs of others. He was deeply disturbed and agitated by the painful realities confronting so many New Yorkers. The Civil War brought great economic hardship to the majority of New York's residents. Businesses failed, unemployment rose drastically, prices soared, and wages dropped significantly. The laboring class was hardest hit by the inflation and unemployment, and countless strikes dotted New York's economic landscape during the war. Following the war, large-scale urban industrialization boosted the laborers' wage scale, but also caused numerous increases in the prices of basic com-modities and living necessities. Labor's plight had improved, but not substantially enough; disaffected workers began to organize trade unions, such as the Knights of Labor in 1869, to protect their interests.

The economic woes brought on by the war created much social misery long after the war's end. Accompanying his mother on regular charity trips to New York's slums, Felix encountered first-hand the substandard housing, the neglected sewage systems, and the myriad other dangerous health hazards of the filthy tenement environs. This intense exposure to the wretched existence of the poor helped to shape his life-long resolve to improve their social, physical, and spiritual state of existence. Felix's zealous regard for social reforms to alleviate the suffering of the tenement dwellers later became the keynote of the practical activities of his Society for Ethical Culture. The first activities which it undertook included the establishment of the Free Visiting Nurses in America and the first Free Kindergarten in 1878; the Society also lobbied for the creation of the first model tenement in the crowded Cherry Street section of New York, which opened in 1887.

The bleak socio-economic conditions of New York's laboring poor contributed significantly to the worsening race relations in the city. New York's mostly German and Irish laborers feared that Negroes would serve as strike-breakers and even take their jobs. Often their fears were not groundless: for example, Negroes were employed to replace striking longshoremen in 1863. At times violence erupted, and Negroes were attacked by roving mobs of the white laboring class. The Negro became the scapegoat for labor's intense frustrations and discontent.

The Conscription Act of 1863 triggered the deep-felt emotions of the laboring poor. The enrollment of draftees set off the notorious Draft Riots of New York, and full-scale rioting lasted for days. The riots, which began as a protest against the draft, quickly degenerated into anti-Negro outbursts. The staggering burden of inflation, high taxes, and the draft's interference with personal liberty were all blamed on the Negro. The rampaging mobs sacked the homes of anti-slavery advocates and burned the Colored Orphan Asylum to the ground.[52]

Felix was not unaware of the great suffering caused by the Draft Riots. As Eleanor Adler wrote, "he remembered looking down at the riots in the streets after the draft laws had been passed, and seeing the red glow in the sky when the Negro Orphan Asylum was burning."[53] That Felix was sympathetic to the plight of the Negro is indicated in a later autobio-graphical sketch in which he noted, "the moral sting of the Civil War I felt myself as a boy."[54] His later outspoken addresses supporting basic Negro freedoms and condemning slavery testified to his earlier concern for their unfortunate situation.[55]

In his feelings for the Negroes, Felix was influenced by his father, an ardent Republican who wept openly for days following Lincoln's assassination. The Adler "house was in mourning for many days afterwards as if a member of the family had died," and Samuel Adler eulogized the slain president in grand fashion at several special services.[56] Samuel's profuse emotional outburst was more than an expression of grief for the beloved person of Lincoln. His pious and ethical orientation, as well as his commitment to political liberalism and human freedom, led him to view the death of Lincoln as a calamitous loss of moral and political leadership. He did not, however, use his pulpit for the cause of abolition; deferring to the wishes of his congregation, he maintained a conspicuous silence. As Eleanor Adler commented, Samuel's "sympathies were actively with Lincoln, though this was not a popular side, cutting across the business interests of many New Yorkers as it did."[57] Economic interests tied many New York businessmen to the South, particularly those in the dry-goods trades, who were primarily Jewish. Many Emanu-El members, therefore, did not favor the Republican party and its political position. In fact, until the South's attack on Fort Sumter, New York as a whole was strongly Democratic and anti-Republican.[58] Samuel Adler's public silence on abolition perhaps even contributed to Felix's "moral sting."

In addition to horrible socio-economic conditions and racial and class conflicts, the Civil War also fostered widespread moral laxity and an atmosphere of diminished respect for law and authority. The incidence of gambling, prostitution, and especially drinking increased dramatically in New York. The massive and rapid industrialization which followed the war led to aggressive growth on the one hand, but also to widespread public and private corruption on the other. Speculation and graft to obtain government contracts grew; civic responsibility and morality declined. Scandals in economics and politics rocked the city and were the order of the day.[59] Felix was not oblivious to the amoral and lawless climate of the city. His later successful efforts on behalf of moral and political reform—he was the chairman of the Committee of Fifteen, which first investigated the red-light district on the Lower East Side and which helped to defeat Tammany and to elect Seth Low as Mayor in 1891—also drew their original inspiration from some of these boyhood experiences.

The immediate effects on young Felix of the socio-economic and moral conditions which he witnessed as an adolescent were twofold. On the one hand, his contact with New York's wretched conditions intensified, if they did not help to create, the somewhat dark, mournful strain in his personality. The power and inevitability of death was an oft-repeated theme in his youthful writings. The two poems he chose to translate for the *Jewish Times,* for example—"The Dreamer" and "Elegy on the Death of Moses Mendelssohn"—both portray death's unwanted intrusion into human life. The sadness and even futility of life is sharply limned in "The Dreamer," which compares the futile aspirations of man to the equally unattainable hopes of the dreamer; both man and the dreamer awake, unable to realize their dreams. The poem ends:

> Thus, in this world of strife,
> This restless, stormy life
>   When in our race
> The goal seems nearing fast
> Ever he wakes at last
>   In Death's Embrace.[60]

Apparently, Felix found the poem's image of a "world of strife" and a "restless, stormy life" to mirror some of his own impressions of life in this world. Allusions to or images of death seem to have attracted him in a rather haunting way, for a number of cryptic references to death also appear in his book of jottings.

On the other hand, Felix's introspective and pessimistic impulses, stirred by the impact of social evils, seem to have been offset by the fervor of his activist response. As he wrote in later years, "I think I was always sensitive to suffering . . .";[61] he was, therefore, attracted to the "powerful Isaiah motive, go tell them to cease to do evil."[62] Practically, Felix's youthful activism was limited by his circumstances to some small efforts, such as bringing baskets of food to the poor. But the rivulets of charitable activity in which he participated as an adolescent grew into the tidal wave of social reform and reconstruction which he led as a man.

The Appeal of Religion and Reform Judaism

From early childhood Felix was sensitized to religion, particularly to the faith and ideals of Reform Judaism as taught and practiced by his father. In later years Felix called his father one of the three greatest intellectual influences on him, along with Abraham Geiger and Heymann Steinthal.[63] Young Felix's intense affinity for Samuel Adler's religious beliefs reflected not simply a rabbi's son aping his father's views but, more significantly, his genuine personal affirmation of his father's religious ideals. Felix possessed a passion for religion which he termed an "unquenchable thirst for the Infinite";[64] until his late teens, his father's Reform Judaism quenched his spiritual thirst and responded to the demands of his ethical conscience.

Samuel Adler's religious ideals attracted Felix so strongly because they addressed themselves directly to his vital human and societal concerns. To Samuel,

Temple Is... ...

the belief in God is the highest and holiest treasure which man can possess; it is the source of all moral life, the fountain of innumerable joys, and the strongest support and comfort in sorrow and trouble.[65]

By serving as the ground for morality and the source for human happiness, and by providing solace for the oppressed and the grieving, religious faith was viewed by Samuel as "indispensable for human life."[66] Samuel taught that religion aided both man and society by teaching the need for proper ethical relations between people;[67] herein lay religion's mighty appeal for his son Felix.

The impact of Samuel's religious outlook on Felix manifests itself throughout the first third of Felix's book of jottings—the part written sometime in the fall of 1868—in which Felix echoes his father's concept of religion as an aid to human existence. Like Samuel, he appreciated the soothing qualities of religion in time of death and sorrow.

> Religion [is] like the sun. Where the clouds and the darkness of death close around, its light will break through and will form a rainbow, a bridge between heaven and earth for the departing soul.[68]

He also acknowledged religion as the source of human happiness and strength, which reason and the intellect—however valid and useful in matters of science—were unable to provide.

> And thus he [Bacon with his scientific-philosophic work] affords another sad instance of the little power which the intellect possesses, however right and distinguished it may be, to make the life of a man a happy one if the cultivation of the heart be missing. . . . A higher motive power must be called in if the happiness of mankind would be secured.[69]

From the context, the "cultivation of the heart" mentioned seems to suggest religious faith. This passage may also have reflected the ongoing sibling rivalry between Felix and Isaac, for Felix may have been criticizing his more austere brother's consuming passion for science.

How does religion engender human happiness? By guiding man to lead a moral life, Samuel asserted. In his opinion, the belief in God provided man with a meaningful purpose in life—to sanctify and purify himself,[70] which could only be accomplished by means of proper moral behavior: practicing truthfulness in word and deed, administering justice to all, and exhibiting kindness and love to all, especially to the unfortunate.[71] With this moral elevation of life, man could "walk with God," and "attain a purity of conscience," a "tranquil soul," and happiness on earth.[72]

Felix concurred with his father on the purpose of religion: "This [prayer] of itself aids us in the purification of our lives—the aim of all Religion."[73] He further defined the moral-ethical goals of religion by asserting that "religion is the stirring after the good—the highest good, the advance towards perfection."[74] Like Samuel, he also acknowledged that religion is indispensable to human existence because belief in God is the ground for ethical behavior.

> If man were not restrained by the consciousness that God's eye is upon him at all times, he would say "my small affairs are too insignificant for this great God. I will follow my senses. . . ." And thus the very foundation of society, its morality and values would be destroyed.[75]

One clearly detects the religious influence of Samuel Adler, who himself wrote that

> without it [belief in God] there would be neither right nor duty, and man devoid of the Belief in God, would be nothing more than the most cunning, the most dangerous and the most unfortunate amongst all created things.[76]

Until the middle of his eighteenth year, Felix believed that man is guided by a Divine Providence which really cares for him, a personal God relating to the affairs of man. Samuel had written that "the relation of man to God is that of a child to his father," and that as a result of this relation, God bore a special love for man.[77] Felix elaborated:

> It is sometimes contended that there is indeed a providence for the great affairs of the human race, but for the petty incidents of individual life there is none. But do not great effects spring from slightest causes, and are not those very affairs which seem to us most trivial oftentimes the prime origin of great events? The providence of God is great enough to embrace all things, all things coming under its laws. . . . What are all the affairs indeed of the universe in comparison with His greatness; and from His distance, the distance between the great and small affairs of man are lost and they appear like stars in close proximity to each other.[78]

The promise of greater happiness and social justice held out by religion had a particular appeal for Felix. Religion offered him a meaningful mode of expression as well as a source of hope for the amelioration of the anguish of human life and the wretchedness of extant social conditions. He regarded religious faith as both a tool and a mechanism by which people could overcome their suffering irrespective of its intensity.

Felix's adolescent writings clearly reflect the extent to which he had internalized some of the fundamental attitudes and concepts of the German Reform Jewish tradition conveyed to him by his father. Reminiscent of nineteenth-century Orthodox-Reform polemics in Germany, as well as reflecting his father's own objections to the lack of progressiveness of Orthodox Judaism,[79] Felix sharply reproached Jewish religious Orthodoxy. "Religion is the stirring after the good—the highest good, the advance towards perfection," he declared. "How then can those who stand still (the Orthodox) be religious?"[80] He contrasted sharply what he felt to be unwarranted Orthodox traditionalism with Reform innovations. For example, Orthodox opposition to the use of the organ during synagogue services, he maintained, was logically inconsistent.

The shophar is allowed. What is the shophar? A reed instrument. To many, [use of the] shophar [brings] no objections. What objection then can there be to having a number of reed instruments only more polished and melodious? One organ.[81]

In justifying Reform's adoption of the triennial cycle of Torah reading over the Orthodox annual cycle, he implied that Orthodox Jews did not take the Torah, or at least the Torah reading, very seriously. "In the orthodox synagogue where the word of instruction is of none or only secondary importance, they can read the Torah in 1 year," he concluded. "In reform synagogues, however, where it forms the chief part of the service we need more time."[82]

In addition to his critical appraisal of Orthodox Judaism, Felix also assimilated the position on the *mitzvot,* the commandments, which the consensus of Reform Judaism had reached at that time. The status and authority of the *mitzvot* were among the most crucial theological issues confronting nineteenth-century German and American Reformers. Feeling themselves unable to accept many biblical precepts, and especially postbiblical rabbinic ordinances, the Reformers sought an ideological formulation by which to invalidate the authority of the onerous *mitzvot.* Biblical commandments such as circumcision and Sabbath observance posed a particular theological challenge to the Reformers: how could they annul the religious authority of rituals and ceremonies prescribed by the biblical text, the divinity of which they accepted? Indeed, Samuel Adler and even men such as the more radical Einhorn still accepted the divine authorship of the Bible in 1856.[83]

To solve the dilemma, the Reformers of this period created a workable intellectual dichotomy: that which is *divine* in origin need not be *eternal* in binding authority. They distinguished between the essential ethical-religious Higher Truths of the Bible and the divine-in-origin yet temporal biblical forms, the ritual commandments. They suggested that the essential truths were clothed in the temporal forms of the *mitzvot* to insure their preservation. In the course of time, they contended, man became more sophisticated. He became able to distinguish the eternal essence from the temporal form on his own; he no longer needed the forms. Conditions had changed, Reformers asserted, and therefore, in this day, many of the biblical forms—the *mitzvot*—were no longer applicable.

Of these essential truths, Samuel Adler wrote:

> The objects embraced within the covenant of God and Israel are: the acknowledgement of certain Higher Truths and the observance of certain Precepts corresponding with these truths and intended to promote the sanctification of man. These Truths and Precepts are contained in general outline in the Ten Proclamations.[84]

In looking at the Ten Commandments, one finds that the first few concern the existence and oneness of God and that the last six are all moral injunctions. Sabbath observance alone is the one ritual practice commanded. But consistent with his general approach to biblical law, Samuel interpreted the Sabbath in terms of its essential and eternal validity. To him, Sabbath observance was a critical precept because it proclaimed the existence of the creator and thus corresponded to a Higher Truth.[85]

Samuel taught his son to distinguish between the temporal commandments and the eternal truths or principles. Paraphrasing a talmudic text, Felix noted: "Israel compared to a dove. As the dove rises on its wings, so are the commandments (*the principles* which it bears) its wings."[86] In translating the word *mitzvot* (commandments), Felix underlined in parentheses "*the principles* which it bears," thus giving the talmudic statement the modern Reform interpretation: the *principles* of Judaism, rather than the body of commandments, are the essential ingredients of the Jewish religion.

Samuel Adler also believed, as did other Reformers, that the inapplicability and invalidation of biblical laws result specifically from changes in historical circumstances. Thus, the loss of Jewish nationhood following the Roman dispersion made many biblical laws lose their "practicality," their "animating power," and consequently their religious-legal authority.[87] Paralleling Samuel's thinking, Felix recorded in his jottings: "Rabbi Joshua states that with regard to Ammonites circumstances had changed and that the ordinances of the Tora were, therefore, no longer applicable. (the reform view)."[88] By adding "(the reform view)," Felix attempted to extend a talmudic decision in a particular instance in which a historical event had changed the facts of the case, but not the law, into a general statement of Reform on the validity of *mitzvot.*[89]

As for the authority of postbiblical laws, Samuel contended that just as the rabbis of the Talmud interpreted biblical laws, contemporary rabbis had the equal right to do so.[90] He respected the rabbis of the Talmud, but imputed to their legal decisions no higher religious authority and sanction than to those of contemporary rabbinic leaders. "The men of the Talmud, however exalted they may have been, in intellect and character, were nonetheless children of their age," he averred, "and they cannot be expected to have remained altogether free from its influence."[91] Consequently, neither the talmudic sages nor their promulgated rabbinic laws stood above criticism; certainly he could not consider their rabbinic legislation to be binding. While no explicit statement exists regarding Felix's views on this matter, one may assume that he accorded no greater acceptance to rabbinic laws than to biblical ritual forms; both were subject to the test of circumstances and applicability.

Though renouncing the Talmud's legislative jursidiction over Jews, Samuel Adler held the work in great esteem. In general, the Reform position on the Talmud was ambivalent. While its claim to divine origin and commanding authority was rejected, the Talmud's historical status as a compendium of Jewish religious law and teaching could not be denied. The respect and deference accorded to it varied among individual Reform rabbis and in different periods in the development of the Reform Movement's ideology.

In the initial stages of Reform, the first three decades of the nineteenth century in Germany, religious and liturgical reforms were most often justified by reference to the rabbinic sources of the Talmud and later codes of law. In the more scholarly and theologically radical second stage of German Reform, men like Geiger, Einhorn, Holdheim, and Samuel Adler came to regard the Talmud as no more than a human document, a record of the religious beliefs and thought of a particular historical era. They therefore did not hesitate to overrule its legal decisions whenever it was deemed necessary.

But even within this group of Reformers, there was no consensus as to the moral value of the Talmud. To Einhorn, the Talmud's "morals are narrow-minded, the high universal sense of the Bible is strange to it."[92] To Samuel Adler, however, "to characterize the moral height on which the Talmud stands, it is sufficient to point to the single sentence, 'the good of all nations participate in the bliss eternal,' in which the main emphasis of religion is laid not on belief, not on ceremonial observances, but on morality alone."[93]

In his scholarly article "Talmud," written originally for *Johnson's New Universal Cyclopedia,* 1876–77, and published later in his *Kovets al Yad* collection, Samuel Adler wrote an extremely approbatory article on the Talmud. He admitted that the Talmud contained "much that is lifeless," but claimed that "innumerable pearls and much priceless treasure is hidden in its depths." The "treasures" hidden in the Talmud included material on science, mathematics, medicine, botany, zoology, astronomy, technology, law, history, geography, and pedagogics. But Samuel hailed the ethical significance of the Talmud as "the crowning portion of the whole work." Despite "isolated passages which must be rejected by a pure morality," he noted that "what is laid down as moral law in the Talmud can still defy scrutiny at the present day."[94]

To praise the *moral* level of the Talmud was rare for an exponent of Reform in Adler's generation; usually, when seeking examples of Jewish ethics and morality, Reformers pointed to the Bible, especially to certain prophetic texts. Admittedly, Samuel wrote the article for a non-Jewish *Cyclopedia,* and no doubt he consciously attempted to show the Talmud—a work largely unknown to Christians and often maligned by theological bias—in its best light. But even if his article was somewhat colored by this consideration, it nevertheless represented his genuine views, for he was honest and conscientious in his scholarship.

Samuel did not hide the talmudic "treasures" from his sons. Throughout his jottings, Felix cited talmudic sources of a homiletical, educational, or moral-ethical nature, materials reflecting favorably on the Talmud. Often his selections consisted of moral aphorisms, such as "He who gladdens the bridegroom at the marriage feast will have the reward of five *kolot*."[95] One talmudic excerpt mentioned points to a moving ethical custom: following the lowering of his loved one into the grave, the mourner passes through the ranks of his attendant friends while they utter, "May God console thee in the midst of those who mourn for the loss of Jerusalem."[96] In other instances, Felix's talmudic citations offer some valuable or instructive lesson on human behavior, such as the reference to Rabbi Eliezer's formula for "a life leading to happiness hereafter."[97]

Young Felix's early writings also faithfully reflect the "mission theory" of his father and of contemporary Reform Judaism, a central doctrine in Reform ideology. Developed in Germany, the mission theory proclaimed the Jews to be chosen by God for a religious mission and charged with the task of teaching certain truths to mankind: the unity of God, the need for moral sanctification in preparation for the messianic day of universal peace, and the union of all mankind. According to Samuel Adler, the reason God chose the Jews for this mission was that their progenitor, Abraham, was "the first restorer of the Belief in One Sole God." God made a convenant with Abraham and pledged to preserve his descendants on condition that they keep the doctrine of the "One Sole God and His Law."[98] By virtue of this convenant, the "Israelite tribe" became a "kingdom of priests," whose historic function it was to teach the nations of the world the divine truths of their religious heritage. The Jews could fulfill their role only by remaining loyal to the ideals of Judaism, and through the mediation of Israel, mankind would gradually free itself of all vestiges of idolatry and achieve the spiritual and moral perfection inherent in ethical monotheism. The existence of the "Israelite tribe," which inherited the pure belief in God from its progenitors, served as a means to educate and elevate the human race.[99] On the ultimate goal of this "education," Samuel wrote:

> The time of universal knowledge of God and moral purity is approaching, slowly but surely coming nearer and nearer.—On some future day, its light will break forth in its full brightness over all the earth: such is the aim of mankind. Everlasting peace will then dwell on earth, all men and nations will live happily in the service of God and His Holy Will.[100]

The mission theory was crucial to German Jewish Reformers because it provided a raison d'être for Jewish existence. As long as this religious mission had not been accomplished, the Jews and their religion served a vital and meaningful purpose; Jews were justified in preserving their separate identity. And many German Jews did seek precisely such a justification; some began to assimilate because the retention of their Jewishness seemed to make little sense in the new age. Spurred by the ominous threat to Jewish existence which the rapid dissolution of Jewish ties caused, Reform thinkers in Germany developed the mission idea to justify continued Jewish existence and identification and to stave off the trend of Jewish defection, which often took the form of voluntary conversion. This rationale was equally germane for the Jews in America, where the potential for assimilation was even greater owing to the lack of restrictive political and economic measures.

The mission theory was also significant for German Jews because it helped to furnish a Jewish ideology geared to making them politically and socially more acceptable in the German states. Stressing a raison d'être only in terms of Jewish religious identification, it provided German Jews with a philosophy of Jewish history which divested them of their Jewish nationality and nationhood. Reformers and other Jews who maintained that the Jews had ceased to be a nation following the Roman destruction of Jerusalem, and who emphasized that Jews were "duty bound to regard and love that land wherein they live, as their home and country,"[101] sincerely felt that their national identification as Germans of the Israelite religion would gain for them the political and social acceptance which they craved. The essential drift of this thinking was transferred to America on an ideological level by immigrating German Reform rabbis between the 1850s and 1880s, including David Einhorn, Samuel Adler, Samuel Hirsch, and Kaufmann Kohler.

The Reform mission theory held concomitant theological implications necessitating a basic reinterpretation of God's historical relationship to the Jewish people, both past and future. The *galut,* Jewish dispersion, was no longer seen as Jewish exile and a punishment for Jewish sins. As Article II of the resolution of the Philadelphia Conference of 1869 asserted, "we do not consider the fall of the Second Commonwealth as a punishment for the sinfulness of Israel." Rather, the Jewish dispersion was regarded as a tool which God employed to enable the Jews to fulfill their mission. The same article affirmed that

> the fall of the second Jewish Commonwealth [was] a sequence of divine intent . . . to send the members of the Jewish nation to all parts of the earth so that they may fulfill their high priestly task to lead the nations in the true knowledge and worship of God.

The Jewish messianic goal, therefore, was no longer expressed in the hope for a national rebirth and the physical return of the Jews to Zion, but rather in the spiritual fulfillment of the goal to disseminate the idea of the Oneness of God. Jewish nationality and Jewish nationhood of the past were viewed as but incidental factors of the Jews' religious mission. In this radical shift of Jewish messianic meaning lay the underlying rationale of classical Reform's vehement ideological and theological opposition to Zionism and the Jewish national renaissance which emerged in the last decades of the nineteenth century.

This theological reorientation made certain practical ritual reforms urgent, particularly liturgical reforms. All the liturgical references to the return to Zion, to the reconstruction of the Temple, and to the "antiquated," "primitive" sacrificial rites had to be ferreted out. This process, initiated by the Hamburg prayerbook of 1819, lasted for decades. Prayerbook reform was almost always the first activity of Reformers wherever Reform Judaism arose because the prayerbook professed the old ideology. In addition, ritual observances, such as Jewish holidays, were interpreted as spiritual-religious occasions; the national aspects of Passover, Shavuot, and Sukot were discarded as irrelevant to modern times.

The significance of the mission idea was not lost on Felix, who referred to aspects of the mission theory on a number of occasions. In his Orphan Asylum Address, delivered only one month following the Reform Philadelphia Conference, he cited "Israel's priestly mission to humanity."[102] In his book of jottings, he alluded to the basic Reform notion that Jewish nationhood in the past was but a tool to help man attain a pure idea of the true God.[103] He renounced the notion of a messianic return to Zion and, like other Reformers who had dismissed the prospect of the rebuilding of the Temple and the reinstitution of the sacrifices, he, too, steadfastly opposed this idea.

He was especially disturbed by the sacrificial practices of the bibilical Jews, and his apologetic posture concerning the Bible's heavy emphasis on them appears evident.

> The great space which the Torah devotes to the sacrificial rites may seem to some an argument for the love and esteem with which they are said to be regarded by Judaism. It is, however, quite to the contrary. The true reason why so much space is devoted there is because our Religion wished [to] narrow down within strict and marked limits this heathenish custom which it was impossible at once to eradicate.[104]

While the basis for this thought is found in Maimonides' *Guide for the Perplexed,* the manner in which Felix expressed it—"this heathenish custom" which cannot be eradicated immediately—illustrated his strong aversion to the Bible's sacrificial ritual. In contrast to biblical Judaism, Felix also pointed with pride to the lack of sacrifices in modern Judaism. "It [Judaism] has no solemn mysteries, no gorgeous temples, no stately priests, no pompous ceremonies."[105] And in his book of jottings, he recorded at great length a sermon by his father which attempted to prove by talmudic interpretation that the *prayers* which accompanied the sacrifices were the *essential* devotional elements in the sacrificial ritual.[106]

Of the stated goals of the Reform mission theory, Felix was most attracted to the idea of the Jewish mission to teach the unity and oneness of God to mankind. His father's views, which heavily accented the Jewish mission to teach God's unity, no doubt had a significant impact.[107] Apart from Samuel's influence, however, Felix's own intellectual proclivities drew him to the concept of the unity of God and the Jewish mission to promulgate that idea. Man, he contended, was intellectually predisposed to reduce everything to a unity, including religious beliefs.[108] But ultimately the idea of God's unity still must be taught by living example; Israel was privileged to be given this educational-religious mission and was faithfully discharging its responsibilities.

> The Unity of God is a sublime and noble thought; yet simple though it be, it cannot be attained in its completeness but by long and deep reflection. More than five thousand years have passed since the race of man first saw existence, and the majority of men have not yet arrived at a clear conception of the Supreme. . . . It was Israel's high privilege to be the bearer of the belief in the one sole God, and knowing the loftiness

of its mission, and imbued with the truth of its convictions, it remained true to it with unrivalled faithfulness.[109]

Personal psychological factors also contributed to his ready acceptance of the mission doctrine. The doctrine's specific focus on the Jewish mission to disseminate the concept of God's unity furnished Felix with a meaningful religious identity, a justification for his identification as a Jew, and a rationale for the invincible force of Jewish martyrdom with which he identified himself with deep emotion.

In an autobiographical sketch, Felix noted that he found himself "attracted early in life to certain types of martyrdom," and especially to the ability in man to transcend suffering.[110] Psychologically, the root of this attraction lay in his tendency to imagine painful situations and their happy outcome: "From early boyhood it seems to me that my mind dwelt on more or less dark situations and their happy solutions."[111] Beyond this, Felix's attraction to martyrdom stemmed from his personal reaction to Jewish history and from his unfortunate social experiences while at Columbia College.

Felix was fully cognizant of the heroic display of Jewish martyrdom throughout history. His readings in the scholarly German Jewish works of Zunz, Graetz, and Geiger—with their "Kultur- und Leidensgeschichte" orientation to Jewish history—certainly made him conscious of it. His familiarity with his father's personal experiences in Germany and with Samuel's opinion about the Jewish "history of sufferings" confirmed it.[112]

His total awareness of Jewish martyrdom was reflected in the frequent appearance of this theme in his youthful writings. He was alive and responsive to the historical sufferings of the Jewish people. In his essay "The Christmas Tree," Felix declared Christmas to be a day of Jewish "martyrdom, persecution and suffering," a day on which Jews were brutally slaughtered. This martyrdom showed itself "on every page [in history], a hundred times repeated."[113] In the first of his two Orphan Asylum Addresses, he compared the life of the orphans to that of Jacob and the Jewish people. The life of the Jewish people began at "night," in darkness and sorrow, he emphasized; only following numerous trials and suffering did the Jews see "morning," light and happiness.[114] His second Orphan Asylum Address, describing the martyrdom of Castro-Tartas, a young Marrano, was dedicated almost in its entirety to the martyrdom of the Jewish people and its ability to transcend its suffering.

Felix's sensitivity to the martyrdom of the Jewish people in some measure sprang from his own youthful experiences of "martyrdom." Reference has already been made to his profound unhappiness while attending Columbia College. Feeling completely out of place in the Protestant atmosphere of the school, and socially isolated from his older

Christian classmates, Felix himself depicted his educational setting as "totally inharmonious from the first," often resulting in a "strong desire for social assimilation." His social isolation at Columbia intensified his sense of suffering and martyrdom; he too belonged to the martyred Jewish religious community and was sharing in its experience. Given Felix's highly sensitive nature, his being stirred by the emotional impact of past Jewish persecutions, and his being oppressed by his own unhappiness, it is not strange that he linked his own painful situation to the long chain of martyrdom in Jewish history.[115]

How did the Jews overcome their persecutions, pain, and travail? Felix felt that the answer lay in the Jewish mission. The Jews were the bearers of the belief in "the one sole God"; they testified "to the holiness of the Eternal God." Because of this mission and the truth which it proclaimed, Jews were tortured and killed. But they died "in the cause of truth," and this truth—the oneness and unity of God—was their constant source of inspiration and strength.

> Whenever the storms raged around the ship of its [Israel's] fortunes, when the seas went high and the ocean of destruction was yawning to devour it, then their belief was to them a life boat, which rode the angry waves and brought them safely through tempest-tossed [seas] to some haven where they might rest a while, until they again went forth on their weary toilsome voyage. The Shema Yisroel was their watchword and in its clear, inspiring tones they found strength and courage, strength to combat and strength to die.[116]

In his tale of the young Jewish martyr Castro-Tartas, it was the latter's awareness of his mission of truth which allowed him "to walk like a conquerer [before the inquisitors] to offer up his young life to God and to Truth."[117] Thus, Felix averred, it was the Jews' faith in the one sole God and their consciousness of their mission to spread this truth despite all personal consequences which sparked both their resolve to overcome their anguish and their ability to suffer martyrdom.

Setting himself in the continuum of Jewish history, Felix felt that his own sense of martyrdom, born from his distressing social experiences at Columbia, could be overcome in the same way. Despite whatever pressures he may have been subjected to at Columbia, he apparently resolved to bear the historical Jewish yoke and to accept the responsibility of testifying to the supreme truth—that God is one—just as his ancestors had. He manifested this resolve in his firm and passionate commitment to the continued existence of both Jews and Judaism.

Nowhere is Felix's intense concern for the perpetuation of the Jews and Judaism more evident than in his article "The Christmas Tree." Published in the *Jewish Times* on December 31, 1869, one week after Christmas, the article severely criticized the custom which had arisen among some New York Jews to bring a Christmas tree into their homes during the Yuletide season. This practice was clearly motivated by the Jews' desire to acculturate their families by making their homes and religious differences less conspicuous during the Christmas season. Felix resented this form of Americanization, which he regarded as nothing less than the undermining of Judaism. He reacted with unmitigated anger, and in his article he unleashed a furious direct assault against the Jewish adoption of this custom. None of his other youthful writings approximate the passionate tone, the bitterly ironic humor, the savage sarcasm, and the almost lyric quality of the prose found in "The Christmas Tree." His intense emotional involvement in the issue virtually bursts forth from the words, and the reader can sense the rage within him. His vital concern for the integrity of the Jewish past and the survival of a Jewish future reached no better literary expression in any of his subsequent writings.

Felix contends in the article that Christmas is a festival and holiday for Christians; for the Jews, however, it represents nothing other than a day of mourning and a memorial of religious martyrdom. In the first half of the article, he describes a Christmas scene in fourteenth-century Europe: the ghetto Jews shutting themselves in their homes, trembling in fear of the consequences of Christian religious frenzy; the town's priests stirring up a mob's religious fanaticism to a fever pitch; the mob burning Jewish homes and murdering Jewish women and children; finally, the mob taking the elite leadership of the Jews and burning them on a gigantic funeral pyre. He sarcastically remarks that repeatedly in Jewish history Jews were brought "as a great Christmas sacrifice on the altar of love."

Shifting the scene to an American Jewish home in the nineteenth century, Felix sneeringly observes that the lights of the Sabbath candles have been replaced by those of a Christmas tree. And he vigorously objects:

> A strange sight meets the eye. They call it a Christmas tree. What means the tree? Is it the stake at which our fathers died they would commemorate? Are the lights that burn so numerously on it, are they in memory of the martyred dead who perished by the flame by countless thousands in honor of him whose birth they celebrate today, the prophet of charity, or do they worship at the shrine of the stranger and thus avow in deed that which the heart denies? Surely this is carrying our liberality too far.

His anger leaps through his biting sarcasm as he continues:

Let us speak plainly and without metaphor. To celebrate a day which has cost us so much pain, so much blood, so many sorrowful experiences with joy and merriment—is this not a bitter and cruel mockery? However much we may esteem our Christian neighbors, however highly we may honor their institutions, we are Jews and we have our own history, our own remembrances of the past. The day brings with it no pleasing recollections to the Jewish mind. Centuries of persecution and suffering were the Christmas gifts which Israel received at the hands of all nations. But they tell us that legend and tradition have written their fanciful garb, and that the "tree" being meaningless is harmless and can effect no wrong. There can certainly be no more genuine pleasure than to witness the pure joy of children. But, we ask, is the joy of our children to be bought at the price of honor of our name and the integrity of our faith? Are there no festivals in the Jewish calendar on which our gifts might be bestowed (and depend on it they would not be refused)? Is there not Purim, which has even now become a recognized institution in our city, or the New Years day, if you must invent some new holiday? The Christmas tree is meaningless, you say? Why, the very name proves the contrary. We might as well erect a crucifix in our houses and call it mere wood and meaningless! It has a meaning which we have not given it, which, with all our arguments, we cannot take from it. It is to be presumed that with most parents, good-nature and thoughtlessness rather than evil inclination lead them to comply with the usage of their neighbors and the wishes of their children. But there are times when good-nature becomes culpable weakness, and thoughtlessness, a crime. *Let them beware! the fruits of the tree they are nursing can bring them little good. Let them beware! for they are planting in the tender soil of the child's heart a poisonous root. The day will come when it shall multiply and cover the fair garden of Judaism with a foul and noxious growth, the day will come when they shall gather in the harvest,*

> "And they that have sown the wind
> Shall reap the whirlwind."[118]

Religious Problems

Felix's fervent devotion to Judaism and his anxious concern for the continued existence of Jews and Judaism did not shield him from grave religious doubts and tensions, which he came to experience particularly in his late adolescent years. Intellectually oriented and introspective, he took his religious faith very seriously and subjected it to constant review and critical judgment. This was bound to induce doubts and issues that unsettled his religious state of mind.

The holiday of Yom Kippur, the Jewish Day of Atonement, seems to have been the major ritual observance that troubled young Felix. In her biographical notes, Eleanor Adler records that one Yom Kippur Felix forgetfully drank a glass of water. He fully expected immediate divine punishment for his indiscretion, but it did not come. When he later confessed to his father, Samuel's response, "well, well, don't do it again," bewildered the boy, for his father's reaction seemed to condone the breaking of the law.[119]

This incident may be related to an excerpt in Felix's book of jottings in which he points to the possible rabbinic circumvention of the biblical command to fast on Yom Kippur.

> Those who taste food the size of a *rimon* and allow the time consumed in eating a *peras* to pass between the different times they partake of foods do not according to the Talmud transgress the law of *Yom Hakipurim*. Does this imply that the Rabbis deemed the taking of food in a moderate measure not prejudicial to the purpose of the day?[120]

The fact that Felix dwelled on this text perhaps reflects his personal uneasiness with Yom Kippur's demand of total abstinence from food and drink. In both this rabbinic approach and his father's seeming lack of concern over his transgression of the biblical law of fasting, he may also have found some measure of vindication for his religious problems with the Day of Atonement.

Sometime in the last half of 1868, Felix wrote in his jottings:

> Prof. McVickar maintained that Judaism could never become the religion of the whole world because it commands its votaries to fast one day in the year from sunset to sunset, and as in the northern regions the sun sets for half a year, this could never be accomplished.[121]

McVickar, a professor at Columbia University, tried to use the biblical commandment to fast on Yom Kippur to illustrate that Judaism could not become a universal religion. Significantly, Felix did not respond in his jottings in defense of Judaism as he did on other issues which he felt threatened Judaism. While this by no means demonstrates that he was convinced of the merit of McVickar's argument, the professor's observation may well have struck a responsive chord in him, adding a new dimension to his already existing problems with the day.

What precisely annoyed Felix about the Day of Atonement is not certain since the sources provide no explicit clues. He may have considered fasting to be a negative mode of religious expression or of no religious value at all; he may have regarded the prescribed fasting and somber solemnity of the day to be onerous and oppressive. These types of feelings would certainly have been consistent with his understanding of the role of religion to help people overcome suffering, not to increase their suffering, if only for one day. Very conscious of human suffering, Felix may well have objected in principle to this paradigmatic ascetic ritual.

In his later addresses on Yom Kippur, Felix interpreted the meaning of the day in terms of his conception of the Priest-Prophet conflicts of the first and second Jewish commonwealths. He ascribed the fast, sacrificial rituals, and the day's atmosphere of mourning to the priestly tradition within Judaism, a tradition which he rejected. He imputed what he believed to be the true and correct sense of atonement—acting to extirpate societal evil—to the Prophets.[122] In the late 1870s, he came to define "atonement" in terms of his own vision of social reform. His later explicit rejection of the traditional solemn atmosphere of the Day of Atonement with all of its accompanying rituals should be seen as an outgrowth of his earlier religious wrestling over the character and meaning of the day.

It is probable that Felix was equally critical of other less honored Jewish ritual observances which he may have discarded without the qualms occasioned by the Yom Kippur issue. Except for his rejection of daily prayer, however, no other conflict with Jewish ritual is mentioned in his writings.

The Bible posed vexing religious questions to Felix, particularly the biblical episodes which he thought to be immoral. In one of his later autobiographical sketches, he listed some of the moral problems which arose when he studied the biblical text with his father: the story of Lot and the Sodomites;[123] Judah's sexual relations with his daughter-in-law;[124] the near sacrifice of Isaac by Abraham;[125] "the disgusting ordeal of the bitter water."[126] "At various times," Felix wrote, "an inward protest was aroused and suppressed." He was deeply perplexed: how could the inspired biblical text contain such morally reprehensible content? How could an ethical, righteous God tolerate such morally objectionable actions on the part of honored biblical figures? Moreover, how could He himself act unjustly and unethically?

> Among other statements that aroused a moral protest was the one that God hardened the heart of Pharaoh. I remember feeling about for some way of reconciling this with the idea of a righteous God, and not succeeding, and letting it go,—a sort of foreign unassimilated body in my soul.[127]

Felix's religious struggles with the moral-ethical character of the Bible explain two very curious omissions in his youthful writings: the rare use of

any biblical references and the total absence of any specific reference to
biblical moral teachings; and the lack of emphasis on the Jewish mission to
teach morality and ethical living to the world. With Felix having been
brought up in a Reform Jewish home in which the Bible was accepted as
the central theological and ethical text of Judaism, one would not have
expected these omissions. Felix was well aware of the preeminent moral
greatness ascribed to the Bible by his father, and one might have expected
his writings to have reflected this awareness.

To Samuel Adler, as to all Reformers, the Bible was the source and basis
for the concept of Jewish chosenness to fulfill a religious mission, a
mission which included the task of teaching and cultivating ethical behavior among men. The Bible, therefore, was regarded as the sourcebook
for human morality. Felix himself noted in his writings that religion was
the ground for morality; but he did not refer to the Bible as its source and
sanction, because, to him, the reality of the biblical text did not correspond
to the high moral standing that was accorded to it. While Felix was
certainly cognizant of the exalted ethical teachings of the Prophets, the
existence of other biblical texts which he conceived to manifest outrageous moral teachings restrained him from accepting the Bible as the
absolute moral arbiter of mankind. The Bible in its entirety was supposed
to be divine; even one example of biblical acquiescence to or approval of
apparent immoral behavior would have totally impugned biblical ethical
authority, and Felix felt that he had found several. It is not strange,
therefore, that on the few occasions when he alluded to Jewish ethical
teachings, the references are talmudic, not biblical. Because Felix did not
regard the Talmud as divine but human, shortcomings were to be
expected in this literature; the "ethical treasures" pointed out to him by
his father, however, could still be appreciated.

The skepticism Felix evinced toward the ethical standards of the Bible
as a whole rendered difficult a belief in Jewish chosenness for the moral
education of mankind, and this is reflected in the absence of any mention
of this aspect of the mission theory in his early writings. The monotheistic
aspect of the Jewish mission doctrine was most—or alone—appealing to
him. That monotheism rather than morality basically distinguished
Judaism from trinitarian Christianity may also have contributed to his
formulating his Jewish identity in terms of the monotheistic mission. And
this early disinclination for the concept of a Jewish ethical role may well
have been the point of origin for his later explicit renunciation of the idea
of a greater Jewish moral endowment than was apportioned to the rest of
mankind.

As to the divinity of the Bible, Felix's youthful views on the matter are
not recorded. His father, who accepted the Bible's divine origin, must
have sought to convey this belief to his son. If Felix did begin to question

the divine origin of the Bible at this time, his later studies of biblical criticism in Germany—ultimately leading to his rejection of the Bible as a divine document—could have been built upon this already established base.

Of all the religious issues and tensions that beset young Felix, the most critical one related to his essential belief in the existence of God. Could he retain his faith in God in spite of his objections to the Bible and religious rituals, in spite of the theological question raised by the continuing misery of New York's poor, and in spite of his academic introduction to science? Felix grappled long and hard with this question, and by the time he left for Germany in June 1870, he had reached a partial resolution of his dilemma. He still affirmed his belief in the existence of one God, but forsook his belief in a personal God, in Providence. In one of his later autobiographical sketches, he noted, "the anthropomorphic conception of God had already disappeared while I was at college. I stopped praying one day."[128]

This later reference suggesting Felix's loss of faith in Providence is also supported by his earlier writings. In the early sections of his book of jottings, written during the first semester of his junior year of college, he defended the concept of Providence against its detractors. Still under the influence of his father's religious teachings, he wrote of God and religion helping mankind and of religion's promise of happiness through moral living. Toward the end of the jottings, however, written sometime in the spring of 1869, the second semester of his junior year, Felix's attitude to God and religion appears to have changed. He no longer speaks of religion's contributions to human welfare, or of God's closeness to man and His concern for human affairs, but rather stresses the spiritual limitations of man, the distance between man and God, and the concept of the God of "mysteries." The possibility of man's cognition of God and His ways is no longer taken for granted, as evidenced by the following passage:

> We can observe the heavens in the zenith directly above us with certainty and precision. The nearer we approach the limits of our horizon the more do the disturbing influences of our terrestrial atmos-phere disturb our vision till at last all is lost in an uncertainty and doubt. So in religion. The zenith of its bright horizon is the God! but when we would explore the unutterable mysteries of the remaining heavens, the secrets of the spirits, the disturbing elements of earth obscure our vision and we soon reach the limits of our horizon.[129]

In his Orphan Asylum Address of the following winter, 1869, Felix continued the theme of the unknowable and "inscrutable God," the God who in "His inscrutable wisdom" took the parents away from young children thus making them orphans.[130] Apparently, sometime during his junior year at Columbia, at age seventeen, Felix began to believe that God was neither as reachable nor as close to man as he had once assumed.

Basically, two factors weakened, if not uprooted, his belief in Providence and changed his religious outlook: his religious doubts, provoked by the dire socio-economic condition of New York's poor, and his beginning of the study of science. As a highly sensitive adolescent exposed by personal contact to the plight of New York's poor, a maturing Felix could not help but wonder how a just, moral, and ethical God could permit so much human suffering. If, as his father taught, Divine Providence meant that God regulated all events and actions in the world with wisdom and justice, and that His works were perfect,[131] wherein was His perfection manifest in the dismal living conditions of the urban poor? This question alerted Felix to the theological problem of theodicy. As he wrote later, "the primordial tendency of my nature [was] to work out the solution of pain and evil, the transcendence of it."[132]

The problem of theodicy was an immediate practical concern and not simply of theoretical significance to Felix, and it gnawed at his belief in Providence. For just as he perceived a contradiction between the ascribed supreme morality of God and that of the biblical text, so too he recognized the contradiction between the religious promises held out by the concept of Providence and the social realities of the age. As he wrote later of his adolescent years, "the belief in the Father, . . . experience fails to correspond."[133]

What is particularly striking and significant in his concern over the theodicy issue is that as an adolescent, Felix was not *theologically* oriented (as distinct from being *religiously* oriented, which he clearly was). One finds nothing in his early writings on such topics as the attributes of God or the events and process of revelation, despite his having been undoubtedly exposed to these ideas by his father.[134] He was left unmoved by speculative theology; one need only recall his glorification of Francis Bacon's stress on the practical import of intellectual ideas to confirm this contention.[135] Theological problems arising from *concrete social problems,* however, did trouble him, and apparently engendered his religious soul-searching and concern.

What solutions did Felix find for his religious struggle over Providence and theodicy? Toward the end of the book of jottings, Felix refers to Graetz, who described R. Simlai's apparent reduction of the 613 laws of Moses to the one principle expressed by the prophet Habakkuk—"the just shall live by faith alone."[136] Felix did not elaborate this point in his jottings, but it is known that Habakkuk prophesied at the height of Babylonian power (608–598 B.C.E), and like Job, he was profoundly disturbed by God's silence while evil men swallowed up the righteous (Hab. 1:13). God's response to this problem of theodicy is that He is sovereign, and that in His own time and in His own way, He will deal with the wicked. In the meantime, the just shall live by faith (Hab. 2:4). This reference to Graetz's account of R. Simlai indicates Felix's awareness of both Habakkuk's problem and his final response to it. Whether he deemed this response adequate is not clear. In all probability he did not, because he did not elaborate on this point in his jottings, a usual procedure in regard to crucial religious issues discussed in the book. But more significantly, Felix's study of natural science introduced him to a then-current alternative view that obviated the need of positing the existence of a divine Providence governing the world.

As the discovery and knowledge of the physical sciences rapidly grew in the course of the nineteenth century, some religious quarters became increasingly wary of scientific progress, fearing that science would uproot traditional religious beliefs. Some religious scientists, themselves theologians, tried to reconcile religious views with some of the new scientific conclusions.[137] But fears and suspicion were not allayed, and scientists, particularly in the 1860s and the 1870s, felt the urgent need to defend their profession against the charges of their religious-theological critics.

In so doing, however, scientists formulated an ideology which, on the one hand, acknowledged the existence of God the creator, the designer of the wondrous natural harmony in the universe, the author of natural law, but which, on the other hand, opposed or, at best, neglected the concept of a personal God and of Divine Providence. At least by implication, if not by open admission, the emergent scientific Weltanschauung, which still adhered to the religious belief in God, from the 1860s on made the concept of Providence unnecessary. Scientists proclaimed the supreme transcendent God; they consciously skirted or unconsciously forgot the Providential aspect of a God intimately involved in the daily workings of the world.

Nowhere was this attitude more visible than in President Frederick A. P. Barnard's well-known inaugural address at Columbia College in 1864. Barnard, an eminent scientist himself, was a vigorous proponent of the claim of the harmony between science and religion. With his 1864 address, he established the tone and posture that Columbia was to adopt in regard to the relation between religion and science. He himself taught a course in "Evidences of Natural and Revealed Religion" to Columbia seniors, and Felix was a student in his class in 1869–70.[138]

Barnard proclaimed that no conflict between science and religion existed: "Nature and revelation, so far from being at variance, are entirely at harmony with one another."[139] Almost by definition, in fact, the conclusions of science and religion could not contradict each other because both study God's revelations.

> These physical causes, these powers of nature as they are called [which are the object of scientific study], what are they? . . . They are only modes through which God sees fit to manifest His own energy; the truths to which we are led by their attentive study are nothing less than revelations. They demand our acceptance not merely upon the authority of imperfect human reason, but as being directly vouched for by God himself.[140]

Moreover, Barnard affirmed, natural science enhanced and provoked religious faith and belief rather than uprooted it.

> Physics . . . by constantly presenting new and ever varying examples of power and forethought and design in the adaptations of means to ends, fosters and cherishes into ever-increasing strength the conviction that God is, that God reigns, that He works perpetually before us now, that by Him all things were made, and without Him was nothing made that was made.[141]

But what type of religious belief did science enhance? What was the character of the God about whom Barnard spoke? Barnard's God was the God of nature, the transcendent creator of the world and the universe. Nowhere did Barnard suggest the concept of a personal, Providential God. In the "class of truths that revelation has been confined," Barnard omitted all mention of Providence. God's revelation was confined to

> the great truths which relate to the being and attributes of God, to the origin of sentient life, to the purposes of God toward his intelligent creatures, to the duties they owe to Him, and to their possible destiny hereafter.[142]

Then, too, in regard to all other truths and affairs of life, man was left on his own; he would have to depend on himself and on his knowledge.

> He has been left to secure the benefits of knowledge, or to suffer the evils of ignorance, according as he may exercise the powers or improve the opportunities which he is here permitted to enjoy.[143]

To a large degree, Barnard's views on God and religion were highly reminiscent of those expressed by the eighteenth-century deists. Their point of origin differed, however, for the deists reached their conclusions on religion on the basis of speculative philosophy, while Barnard and other scientists grounded their views on inductive observation.[144]

Felix seems to have encountered difficulty with the idea of Providence during 1868–69. Barnard was his professor the following year, and, therefore, could not have had a direct influence in the initial phases of Felix's problem with science. Felix was, nevertheless, quite probably introduced indirectly to Barnard's scientific views in his junior year, for Barnard's views on the relation between religion and science held sway at Columbia from his appointment in 1864. In addition, his views reflected the most popular form of intellectual reconciliation between science and religion of the day; men like Rood (physics), Joy (chemistry), and Peck (astronomy, mechanics, and mathematics), who taught the sciences at Columbia from the junior level up, may well have held similar views. At home Felix also became acquainted with the scientific pursuits of his brother, Isaac, and of his cousin Isidor Walz. While Isaac left for Germany upon his graduation from Columbia in the summer of 1868, Walz, a chemist, probably aided Felix in his scientific studies and discussed with him the "new" ideas on the relation between science and religion as well.

One of the clearest examples of the scientific view of Providence to which Felix was exposed is found in Alexander von Humboldt's *Cosmos,* probably required reading in Rood's natural philosophy (physics) course in 1868–69. *Cosmos,* one of the most influential books of the mid-nineteenth century, was a compendium and synopsis of all the known human sciences of the physical world and attempted a systematic presentation of the natural order and a naturalistic panorama of the universe. As a handbook of natural science its reputation was unsurpassed; its authority and popularity were so universally acclaimed that scarcely any other text on these subjects was necessary or used at the time. Felix quotes quite liberally from it in the second half of his book of jottings.

In the *Cosmos,* von Humboldt affirms the magnificent harmony of forces and laws existing in the natural world and the universe. He describes in detail the various terrestrial and cosmic phenomena of the universe, such as volcanoes, magnetism, meteors, comets, and the like. But what of his view of God? In a speech in Central Park during the centennial celebration in honor of von Humboldt, Professor Doremus claimed that von Humboldt "unfolded the Supreme Intelligence controlling the universe in all its vastness."[145] Yet while von Humboldt found order, law, and cosmic harmony in the universe, he was, nevertheless, somewhat vague about the existence of an author of this natural harmony. He did allude to nature testifying to the "majesty and greatness of creation," thus implying the existence of a creator.[146] But when discussing the progression of organisms from the simplest cell to higher structures, he judiciously avoided the issue of who created the first cell.[147] Indeed, even if Doremus were correct, while God the transcendent creator may be present in von Humboldt's work, God as Divine Providence is not. The entire natural world is described without reference to a God who relates directly to the affairs of the world and of man—to Providence. Just as Barnard had indicated, man seemed very much on his own in the scientific world-view; God did not seem to impinge upon his existence, let alone control his fate.

Felix's introduction to the disciplines of science and to the *Cosmos* prepared him for the views of John Fiske, which caused an uproar one year later. Fiske, primary American exponent of Darwin and Spencer along with Edward L. Youmans, had been invited to deliver several lectures at Harvard University in the fall of 1869 by its president, Charles W. Eliot. Youmans arranged to have the lectures published serially by the *New York World.* The first articles, appearing in the paper on November 13 and 15, 1869, precipitated a major controversy that reached beyond the academic community.[148] Fiske sought a new approach or philosophy that would simultaneously recognize the truths of science and transcend the suppositions of dogmatic theology. He affirmed belief in an Infinite Power, but a Power that could only be known through its manifestations, that is, through natural phenomena and their laws. Man, he contended, could not know the Absolute. Fiske's attempted harmony of science and religion provoked theists, who felt their belief in a Providential, anthropomorphic deity challenged, and many Americans labeled him an agnostic and even a heretic.[149] Whatever his label, Fiske's views again illustrated to Felix the needlessness of positing the existence of a Divine Providence.

This emerging scientific view of the relation between God and man and God and the universe, as reflected in the *Cosmos,* in the opinions of Barnard, and in the opinions of at least some of the other science teachers at Columbia, as well as in the lectures of John Fiske, greatly distressed young Felix. To a young man brought up by his father to believe in Providence, to a boy who wanted the "infinite to impress itself on the finite," the lack of personal relation between man and God which science seemed to posit was the source of much religious tension. At the outset of his junior year, Felix still contested the scientific dismissal of the idea of Providence and the scientific claim that God did not intrude into the affairs of man; as the junior year progressed, however, he acclimated himself to the scientific view of God's role in the world. God exists; He created the heavens and the earth, but He is distant and removed from the routine daily affairs of man.

Interestingly enough, after having ranked among the top six in his class in his first two years at Columbia, Felix plummeted to eighteenth and sixteenth ranking in his junior and senior years respectively. In particular, his grades in the sciences over the last two years were—with one exception—almost abysmal. He attained a respectable 75 out of 90 in Rood's first-semester physics course, for juniors, but only a 24 out of 120 in the second semester.[150] These low grades—especially the radical contrast between semester physics grades—reflect not simply Felix's low aptitude in science, but perhaps also the religious turmoil within him and his anxiety over his diminishing faith in Providence due to science in general and physics in particular.

The scientific view of God's relation to the world, in part, alleviated one aspect of Felix's problem with theodicy. For if God was not immanent in the direction and government of the universe, but rather left man to use his own reason to control his affairs and destiny, then man, and not God, was responsible for much of the extant social evils. With increased scientific knowledge and with greater application of human intelligence, man could respond more readily to the needs of his fellow man and improve social conditions. On one level, this conception of God shifted more of the blame for socio-economic ills from God to man.

But this philosophy could not dispel the fundamental moral dimension of the theodicy problem, and it was this dimension that made Felix question his own faith in the very existence of God. Was the God who, in His "inscrutable wisdom," took parents from children a moral God? This was but one example of a tragic situation caused not by man, but by God. Moreover, if God's Bible contained immoral and unethical sections, and if God in His transcendence refrained from entering the world of man, then in what sense was God the guarantor of the moral behavior of man? Who was this God in whom man was asked to believe—did He in fact exist?

Felix had grown up to believe that religion and God helped man by bidding him to live morally so as to insure his happiness. But these early religious ideals, attractive at first, now came under severe scrutiny. His later eager avowal of Kantian ethics while in Germany testified to his adolescent difficulty in grounding ethics in the traditional theistic absolute—Providential God. In Germany he sought an ethical ground in another absolute power or law to replace the old discredited source of ethical legitimacy.

On the one hand, Felix must have wanted to maintain his belief in God; after all, he was Rabbi Samuel Adler's son, and he was venturing to Europe to study for the rabbinate in order to succeed his father at Emanu-El. On occasion, Felix did publicly express the view of God as the creator of law and cosmic harmony.[151] It was in this same Orphan Asylum speech, in fact, that he vigorously affirmed the Jewish mission of testifying to the existence of the one God. In light of the scientific emphasis on God as the sole creator of the universe, this Jewish mission could well have made even more sense to Felix: the Jews were charged with the task of constantly reminding the world of what scientists were now loudly proclaiming.

On the other hand, Felix had to struggle with his personal religious doubts. In this struggle, perhaps he found some comfort in the faith of Moses Mendelssohn, a Jew who had absorbed and mastered the most advanced ideas of his age and yet had retained his faith. Could Felix have been unmindful of the powerful words of the sixth stanza of Wessely's "Elegy on the Death of Moses Mendelssohn," which he himself translated as follows:

> The light dispelled the terrors of the tomb,
> Vanished like mist the cold sepulchral gloom,
> As a dark cloud before the sun passed.
> "There is a King, a God above the skies,"
> The doubter echoed back with glad surprise,
> And in the "Hours of Morn" found peace at last.[152]

Mendelssohn not only had sustained his own faith in light of the challenges of his age, but also had imbued others with faith in God so that doubters might utter, "There is a King, a God above the skies." Mendelssohn may well have illustrated the type of resolute religious faith to which Felix himself aspired but was struggling to reach.

On the eve of his departure for Europe in June 1870, young Felix Adler was still fundamentally tied to his Jewishness. Ideologically, he maintained his belief in the Reform mission theory, or at least one aspect of it; emotionally and psychologically, he showed a powerful attachment to the continued existence of both Jews and Judaism; and institutionally, while he severed his affiliation with the Emanu-El Sunday School and the Hebrew Orphan Asylum of New York, he continued his association with Jewish institutions by later pursuing his Jewish studies at the Hochschule für die Wissenschaft des Judentums in Berlin. To all who knew him, he was a model young Jewish man, as evidenced by the party given in his honor by the Emanu-El School Committee.

And yet, Felix was a religiously troubled young man, and he carried his religious doubts with him to Europe. He still believed in a transcendent Infinite God, but at the same time he engaged in a continuous battle with the severe challenges to his religious convictions. Retrospectively, it was this struggle which paved the way for his ultimate departure from Judaism and theistic religion.

In this state of mind, his departure for Europe specifically to pursue rabbinic studies could only have made his religious quandary even more vexing. Indeed, whether he wanted or ever expected to enter the rabbinate is not known; he may simply have acceded to his family's prodding and particularly to this father's ardent desire to have the Adler family's rabbinic tradition continued. Certainly the members of Emanu-El and New York Jewry expected him to enter the rabbinate, for on June 17, 1870, the *Jewish Times* reported, on the occasion of his being honored by Emanu-El, that Felix was departing for Europe to "finish his education for the Jewish ministry." Still, despite possible reservations, Felix must have anticipated the journey abroad with great relish. The promise of studying with the great Abraham Geiger and of pursuing advanced doctoral work in a field related to rabbinics at a German university must have fired his interest. His brother's enthusiastic letters during the previous two years, portraying the stimulating intellectual life of Germany, must also have excited his imagination.

On June 27, two days before his graduation exercises at Columbia, Felix sailed to his native German land to take up a course of study which seemed destined to lead him to a rabbinical career.

Chapter II

Return to Germany: 1870–1873

Student Years

On July 5, 1870, Felix arrived at the port of Cherbourg, France, aboard the steamer *St. Laurent*. Excited by the prospect of exploring a new land, he took the first train to Paris and settled down at the home of a cousin outside the city. Having nothing particular to do until classes began in the fall, he toured the country with great zest. Unfortunately, owing to youthful exuberance, he overexerted himself and contracted bronchitis. On doctor's orders, he was sent to a therapeutic spa in Hamburg for six weeks to be supplemented by a walking tour of Switzerland.[1]

This walking tour through the Swiss Alps and the subsequent ones which followed during his three-year stay in Europe etched an indelible mark on young Felix. The awesome mountains and the mountain-climbing experiences heightened his sensitivity to the grandeur of nature, a sensitivity which came to the fore in later years in countless lectures. The Swiss Alps also had an exhilarating spiritual impact on him, engendering feelings of deep reverence for the sublimity of nature.[2] And as he progressively lost faith in religious dogmas and rituals while in Germany, he discovered the direct experience of nature to be more moving to him and of greater value than the institutionalized forms of religious worship.[3]

While Felix passed the summer recuperating and walking through the Alps, Europe was astir with political and military activity. The Franco-Prussian War erupted soon after his arrival (July 19, 1870), and by September 2 the French army had surrendered and the government of Napoleon III had fallen. The Republic-oriented Paris Commune, which controlled Paris for a brief four months, soon capitulated under a German siege. On January 18, 1871, in the chateau of Versailles, Bismarck proclaimed the establishment of the German empire and consolidated his position as ruler of Germany.

The war prevented Felix from spending time with his brother during the summer of 1870 and delayed their reunion until the early fall.[4] Isaac, a medical student at Heidelberg and Berlin universities, had been appointed an assistant to the surgeon-general and was put in charge of the wounded soldiers in the Heidelberg Hospital. He spent the summer faithfully discharging his medical duties and had no opportunity to meet with Felix.

At war's end, Felix was personally introduced to the military might of

Bismarck's Germany. He witnessed the triumphant entry of the German troops through Berlin's Brandenburg Gate and up the broad Unter den Linden, led by the emperor, the crown prince, Moltke, and Bismarck. By virtue of his friendship with George Bancroft, the foremost American historian of the day and American minister to Berlin, Felix obtained a privileged seat which positioned him very close to the municipal council-lors who received the emperor. Bismarck was within two feet of Felix, so near that Felix "could see his eyes shoot out lightning flashes of anger at the poor burgomaster, whose address was far too long."[5] Felix was awed by the forceful bearing of Bismarck and the powerful empire which he had created. But it was this same experience which made him thankful for the "self-government and real liberty" of America, a country which could not be ruled by the caprice of one man.[6]

In the autumn of 1870, Felix arrived at Berlin to commence his studies. He had ventured to Germany to pursue rabbinic studies at the Hochschule für die Wissenschaft des Judentums and to obtain a doctorate in a related field from a German university. Due to the outbreak of the Franco-Prussian War, however, the Hochschule was forced to postpone its projected opening in late 1870. Abraham Geiger was appointed professor of Jewish history and literature only in the fall of 1871, and the institution began formal classes on May 6, 1872. As a result, not only was Felix's study of Jüdische Wissenschaft restricted in his first two years abroad, but also his exposure to the spiritual atmosphere of a rabbinical seminary was delayed. By the time the Hochschule opened, Felix's relig-ious problems with Reform Judaism seem to have taken firm root, and his intellectual interests had become deflected from specifically Jewish to more general concerns. In fact, he studied at the Hochschule less than a year. He enrolled at its opening in May 1872, but moved to Heidelberg in early 1873 to obtain a doctorate in semitics at the University of Heidel-berg.

Some aspects of Felix's relation to the Hochschule remain somewhat obscure. Considerable debate exists in the literature as to whether or not Felix was sent to Germany by Temple Emanu-El with his expenses paid. The earliest charge of this sort was leveled by one Judah Sequor in a letter to the editor of the *Reformer and Jewish Times* on March 23, 1877, but Felix resolutely denied the truth of Sequor's allegation in a response to a reporter of the *New York World* published one week later, March 30, 1877.[7] Also, no record seems to exist of Felix's having gained a rabbinical degree from the Hochschule. While the founders of the Hochschule did not intend it to be a theological school, in reality its main function came to be the training of Jewish theologians and ministers. The Hochschule con-ferred degrees at three levels. In descending order of authority, they were Rabbiner (rabbi), Prediger (preacher), and Religionslehrer (teacher of religion). Which degree Felix received, if any, is not known. Temple Emanu-El considered him for the position of assistant rabbi in September 1873, thus suggesting that he probably held some degree, unless the temple considered individuals without any ministerial degree for a rabbinic position. And yet, not only does no record of Felix's rabbinical degree remain, but legitimate doubt can be cast on his ever having been awarded one. He stayed at the Hochschule less than a year and he appears to have neglected his talmudic studies at the time.[8] Furthermore, while letters exist expressing the Adler family's joy at Felix's having attained his doctorate, no such letters in regard to a rabbinical degree are extant. And finally, from the time of his return to New York in September 1873, Felix was almost always referred to as *Dr.* Adler, never as *Rabbi* Adler. At present, the question of his rabbinical degree remains somewhat of a mystery.

Felix enrolled in Berlin University in the fall of 1870 with avid enthusiasm and thrilled at the prospect of learning from some of the world's most renowned scholars. And with the delay in the opening of the Hochschule, he devoted all his time and energy to his university studies. In fact, his habit of studying fourteen and fifteen hours a day prompted a number of letters from his parents pleading for a reduction in his work load. On February 16, 1871, Samuel wrote his son that "the only thing that disquiets us is that you have undertaken too much. . . . I made the same mistake in my youth, and speak from experience when I tell you that all work done with a tired mind and a sleepy head is worth less than nothing." Henrietta Adler added to her husband's concern: "I am worrying myself about your working too hard."[9]

Felix's total immersion in school work was neither unusual nor atypical. Diligent American students all felt intellectually liberated and challenged in Germany, and they applied themselves accordingly.[10] Years later, in public addresses, Felix often recalled his joyous intellectual experiences while at the German universities and sharply contrasted the freedom of expression which he found there with the authoritarian theological dogmatism of their American counterparts.[11]

At Berlin University it was his good fortune to sit at the feet of some of the outstanding scholars of the day. He studied natural science with Helmholtz, Greek philosophy with Hermann Bonitz and Eduard Zeller, modern philosophy with Eugen Dühring, philosophy of education and pedagogy with Friedrich Trendelenburg, Bible criticism with Emil Roediger and August Dillmann, semitics with August Petermann, and linguistics, philology, and psychology with Heymann Steinthal. All these men were major exponents of their respective fields of expertise. Steinthal, in fact, collaborated with his brother-in-law, Moritz Lazarus, in the development of the new field of ethno-psychology, which stressed the study of the development and manifestations of the spirit of peoples in addition to that of individuals.

Supplementing his formal university education, Felix studied Arabic, Aramaic, and halachic literature in a private class with Moritz Steinschneider, then an assistant at the Royal Library of Berlin.[12] He also studied Kantian philosophy privately with Hermann Cohen. Cohen had been pursuing postdoctoral studies at the University of Berlin, all the while anticipating an appointment to the university which never came. Nevertheless, having recently published his initial work on Kant's *Theory of Experience,* he had already been heralded as a philosopher to be reckoned with. Together with Friedrich Albert Lange at the University of Marburg, he was instrumental in launching the German neo-Kantian revival.

Felix recorded his impressions of some of his teachers in later autobiographical reflections. He particularly enjoyed Bonitz's "brilliant and inspiring lectures on Hellenic life."[13] Of Bonitz himself, he wrote:

There are those who served us partially at one period of our growth, opening a new vista—in my own experience, e.g. Bonitz. They served their turn. We remember them with pleasure and even gratefully, but we scarcely feel the desire to see them again.[14]

Of Zeller, Trendelenburg's successor in the chair of Fichte and Hegel, Felix caustically remarked:

He gives one the impression of treating great men and great historic phenomena like objects in a mineralogical cabinet. One does not feel that he himself experienced vitally the things whereof he speaks.[15]

Felix called Steinthal one of the three greatest influences on him along with Abraham Geiger and his father, Samuel,[16] but he resented Steinthal's "intellectual arrogance" and "the air of finality with which he expresses his judgments and opinions."[17] Of Hermann Cohen he noted, "then there are those who serve us partially, but whose nature, fixed in a different mental setting, was . . . antagonistic to our own."[18] By "different mental setting" Felix may have referred either to Cohen's avowal of socialism and lack of religious orientation at the time, a position he strongly opposed—"for us there can be no religion except socialism," Felix quoted Cohen as saying[19]—or to Cohen's great pride in his own intellectual ability, which Felix felt precluded him from treating human beings as ends in themselves.[20] Nevertheless, he respected the great intellectual ability of both Steinthal and Cohen. In regard to both he commented:

There was respect for eminent mental ability, for a stricture of standard in which I found myself deficient. . . . There was a kind of reverence from afar, coupled with determination to make good in my own way.[21]

Despite the personal shortcomings of those teachers noted in Felix's later reflections, the impact of their teachings on him, as well as that of his other instructors, was nothing short of revolutionary. Felix was trained in rigorous intellectual method and was introduced to the main currents of contemporary scholarly thought. Through these men he became fully exposed to the imposing views of Darwin and Spencer in science; the methodology of Vatke, Strauss, and Baur in Old and New Testament criticism; the ideas of Pestalozzi, Froebel, and Herbart in pedagogy and education; and the thoughts of Kant, Fichte, Hegel, Feuerbach, and other leading philosophers. Intellectually, Felix broadened his horizons immeasurably; he utilized the knowledge and intellectual thoroughness which he gained in Germany throughout his lifetime.

The available sources do not fully indicate to what extent Felix pursued his Judaic studies while the Hochschule was closed. During this time, he studied halachic literature, biblical criticism, semitics, and particularly Arabic, which his father considered to be an "important adjunct to Jewish theology."[22] But whether he studied any other area of "Jewish theology," such as Bible and Jewish philosophy, in private sessions with Geiger, Steinschneider, or others, cannot be determined. What is known, in fact, is that Felix's intellectual interest was deflected from Judaic to general scientific pursuits. In a letter of February 28, 1872, more than two months before the Hochschule's opening, Samuel did not object to his son's request to take up scientific studies with Wilhelm Wundt in Leipzig; he did, however, remind Felix that he must return to Berlin in the fall because "you have only at most another year in Germany. Therefore, you cannot waste your time in scientific studies, but must limit yourself to the Talmud which is the kernel of your future career."[23]

When the Hochschule opened in May 1872, Felix was one of its ten students. He studied Bible and the Prophets with Geiger and Steinthal, religious philosophy with Steinthal, Mishna and Talmud with the staunchly Orthodox Isaac Lewy, and the history and literature of the Second Commonwealth with the moderate Conservative David Cassel. He became particularly attached to Geiger, not simply because of the latter's friendship with his father, Samuel, but because he and Geiger shared a common interest of fundamental religious concern: the study of the evolutionary development of biblical literature and its implications for religion in general and Judaism in particular. Moreover, Felix was deeply fond of Geiger as both a teacher and a human being.

My relation to Dr. G. in Berlin. The attraction for me was respect for his great scholarship, his appreciation of the poets, which relieved his personality of the suspicion of narrowness, and his treatment of the younger man as one who had a career before him, and might take up the torch. The young are particularly grateful to an older person of superior standing who perceives possibilities in them before they have made good. This honor paid to the young by the old is the source of the greatest attraction.[24]

Apparently Geiger reciprocated the warm feelings, for when Felix received his doctoral degree from Heidelberg, Geiger gave him a personally inscribed vellum-bound copy of the *New Testament in Syriac* (1667).[25] Later, in a letter to Bernhard Felsenthal, September 16, 1874, Geiger expressed his disappointment over the lack of correspondence from his former pupils Kaufmann Kohler, Max Landsberg, and "Young Adler."[26]

Felix's esteem and even love for Abraham Geiger is evident in his two Geiger memorial lectures.[27] In his writings and addresses, particularly those of the 1870s, Felix repeatedly resorted to Geiger's teachings, especially to his identification of the Pharisees and the Sadducees and his revolutionary interpretation of their disputes, and his elaboration of the relationship between Priest and Prophet before and after the destruction of the First Temple in 586 B.C.E.[28]

At Geiger's suggestion, Felix traveled to Heidelberg early in 1873 to become a doctoral candidate in semitics. Such a student transfer was quite normal in German university circles, for universities specialized in particular areas and it was to the students' advantage to receive instruction from the top men in each field.[29] Felix studied diligently at Heidelberg and, in the spring of 1873, was rewarded with a doctoral degree, summa cum laude.

The Adler family was overjoyed at the good news. It suddenly dawned on each of them that, intellectually, Felix was unusually gifted. Isaac, long presumed the brighter of the two sons, had only graduated magna cum laude from Heidelberg. Felix's success in Arabic was especially gratifying to Samuel, for his son's mastery of an "important adjunct to Jewish theology" renewed his hope that Felix would succeed him at Emanu-El. On May 13, 1873, Samuel wrote:

I was overcome with surprise and delight and gave thanks to the Almighty. Now, indeed the time has come to think of your future career. I believe you know that my dearest wish is to gradually retire, enjoy my old age in peace and see you take my place.[30]

Not even Felix's neglect of his talmudic studies, studies on which his father had insisted in the early spring of 1872, could inhibit Samuel's utter happiness at the thought of his son taking his place. On June 23, 1873, Samuel wrote:

> Do not worry about what I expect of you in the way of Talmud studies. I know how much work it takes to master the Talmud and how far students of your type can be expected to go in that field. Moreover, Berlin is not the entire world and if you really want to continue your work you can find a way to do so in New York.[31]

Unfortunately for Samuel, his joyous expectation was not to be realized.

Greatly invigorated by German intellectual life, Felix found his social life, however, extremely disappointing. The situation was reminiscent of his Columbia years. He was often alone and lonely, and he found the social setting at Berlin University uncongenial.[32] He was repelled by Protestant and Jewish theologians and theological students.[33] His brother's medical school friends and "other students with whom I had acquaintance had not the least sympathy with my private aspirations,—my private dreams."[34] He was "forced back upon [himself] by this lack of companionship."[35] Even the weather contributed to the unhappy atmosphere, for Felix "disliked the lowering grey Berlin skies, bitter weather, and endless flurries of snow."[36]

His principal social outlets consisted of Bancroft's Sunday evening receptions, and walking trips, picnic outings, and correspondence with his brother and his brother's fiancée, Frieda Grumbacher. Frieda had been a Red Cross nurse stationed at Heidelberg during the Franco-Prussian War and Isaac had met her at the city's hospital. They became engaged in the winter of 1871, and Felix maintained a regular correspondence with his future sister-in-law.[37]

Felix made few new friends. For a time, in Berlin, he enjoyed the close friendship of a fellow New Yorker, Edward T. Rosenfeld. Rosenfeld, a youthful acquaintance from the Temple Emanu-El circle, came to the Hochschule against the wishes of his family, which had wanted him to enter his father's banking firm. Rosenfeld shared both Felix's attic lodging and his ethical idealism. Together they visited and aided some of the poor of Berlin. Within a year, however, Rosenfeld contracted typhus in a city epidemic and passed away shortly thereafter. His close friend's tragic death shook Felix deeply. His depressed state caused his mother to write, "I hope that you let your mind rule your sensitive and generous heart and did not let your feelings run away with you."[38]

Another of his friendships ended in tragedy as well. Being lonely himself, Felix tried to assist other students in unfortunate circumstances. He befriended a young Russian émigré who had fled Russia because of his radical views. Upon his return to America, Felix sent him money for many years until the Russian, despairing of ever returning home, committed suicide.

Particularly galling to Felix during his stay in Europe was his perception of the moral depravity and sexual debauchery of European life, with its crude debasement of women.

> I was a student in Berlin and Paris and Vienna, and I found that most of my associates had no scruples in regard to the social evil. Why should not the woman be the food of man's lust. If we are animals, we are animals—why not?[39]

To an extent, his perception of European morality was colored by his excessive zeal for sexual purity. In earlier years, he had never been quite comfortable with the subject of sex, due partially to his shy and retiring nature. As he matured, the reverence for women and sexual purity became a dominant motif in his lectures. In fact, his later addresses on women's role in society and on the subject of divorce reflect perhaps the most conservative of all his opinions.[40]

Felix's moral discomfort and social isolation did not dampen his active concern for human welfare so evident already during his adolescent years. During the Franco-Prussian War, he helped a women's committee to organize and to care for disembarking prisoners at the railroad station in Strasbourg.[41] He contributed to the financial support of his impoverished Russian friend. But his most energetic social activity was directed toward the alleviation of the misery of the emerging German industrial proletariat. The three-year period of Felix's stay in Germany, the *Gründerjahre* of 1870–73, witnessed a veritable explosion in the establishment of varied industrial plants, factories, large companies and corporations, and major banking firms. To some, these numerous enterprises brought unprecedented prosperity; a much larger part of the German populace, however, suffered from the multitude of social and economic ills generally associated with industrial revolutions.[42] Young Adler had ample opportunity to be of practical assistance to the urban poor. Before Rosenfeld's arrival, and later, together with him, he frequently visited the Berlin slums to lend a helping hand and to give what comfort and encouragement he could.[43] These experiences in Germany nourished his social awareness and sustained his life-long determination to have justice and opportunity granted to the victims of modern industrialization.

Religious Change

When Felix Adler arrived in Europe, he brought with him the religious doubts of his late adolescent years. His introduction to the study of science and its laws and his perception of divine injustice in the persistence of New York's urban squalor had led him to reject the concept of a personal Providence and to question the very existence of God. His studies and experiences in Germany only deepened his religious disquiet.

Young Adler was not alone in his religious struggle; Western Europe convulsed with religious turmoil from the second half of the nineteenth century on, and America followed suit in the 1870s. As Octavius B. Frothingham remarked in 1873, "By general admission the religious question is still foremost in modern society. It agitates Germany, convulses Italy, perplexes France, troubles England and threatens perpetual disturbance in America."[44]

Caught in the maelstrom of world religious upheaval while in Germany, Adler confronted the fundamental religious questions of the age: could religion meet the challenges of natural science, particularly Darwinism, of Bible criticism, comparative philology, anthropology, comparative religion, and the general freethinking atmosphere which these disciplines engendered? Could the meaning of religion and the integrity of the religious enterprise be salvaged, and if so, how? Moreover, as an intellectual Jew, Adler was compelled to come to terms with his own religion: could he maintain his Judaism in good conscience in light of the ideas of the modern age?

Adler recognized natural science as among the most serious threats to religious belief: "I believe that reflecting persons generally agree in attributing the decay of religious belief primarily to the influence of the natural sciences and their indulging conceptions."[45] His conclusion was understandable. By explicitly denying the concept of a personal Providence, natural science struck at the central core of all theism. Predicated on the regular operation of law in the universe, natural science rejected the supernatural suspension of nature by a superintending intelligence. By circumscribing the province of divine action, natural science circumscribed the very nature of divinity itself: since the idea of Providence was superfluous, God was either denied or reduced to a mere First Cause. Moreover, since the nature of God was called into question, so too were the dogmatic and creedal propositions about God. Religious creeds and mysteries grounded in theology were either dismissed outright or reinterpreted where possible to conform to scientific knowledge.

While neither the scientific method nor science's rejection of Providence was new to Adler—he had been introduced to both in his late adolescence—the radical conclusions drawn by many German scientists posed striking new challenges to his faith and idealism. Virtually no American scientist in the 1860s had espoused atheism and denied the existence of God; at the very least some form of deism prevailed in scientific circles. Drawing conclusions implicit in Darwin's theory of natural selection, German scientists on the other hand—men like Karl Vogt, Ludwig Büchner, Jakob Molesschott, and Ernst Haeckel—denied God as the creator of the world and rejected the entire conceptual category of the supernatural. They repudiated the notion of order and purpose in the world, mocked the other-worldly concerns and teleolgy of religion, and advanced Feuerbach's philosophy of materialism to impugn the meaning and value of any spiritual and moral ideals.

Young Adler was also introduced to the most advanced studies in the disciplines of history, Bible criticism, Near Eastern studies, philology, anthropology, and comparative religion, and these, too, undermined traditional conceptions of religion and theology. Broadly speaking, by incorporating the concepts of "progress" and "evolution," these disciplines effectuated the historicization of religion begun in earnest by Voltaire.[46] Adler was exposed to the predominant scholarship in religion, which viewed each specific religion as an evolving process unfolding *within* secular history, a process with a history of its own that was subject to the same critical scrutiny as all constituents of history. He learned that scholars no longer regarded religions as sacrosanct, definitive bodies of dogma with unimpeachable sacred histories. While Herder, Lessing, and Hegel had refined the historicization of religion philosophically, the most recent scholarship which he read brought this historicization to fruition scientifically.

Among the works that most influenced Adler were those by F. Max Müller, Heymann Steinthal, E. B. Tylor, and John Lubbock. Müller, the celebrated linguist, orientalist, and philologist, correlated the developmental levels of human language and thought with the levels of sophistication of religious conceptualization. In his comparative studies of language, Steinthal, Adler's own teacher, was led to the idea of a national folk-psychology inherent in all nationalities. He concluded that the disparate forms of religion were manifestations of unique national spirits which in turn reflected the psychic patterns of the discrete nations. Adler also read the anthropological studies of Tylor and Lubbock, which opined that religions and religious impulses mirrored the cultures in which they originated. Religion, these scholars contended, was a cultural manifestation, and the level of religion reflected the progress of civilization in any particular culture, from the most primitive to the most exalted.[47]

Adler thoughtfully digested the crucial religious implications of these historical studies, which both universalized the appearance of religion among human phenomena and yet, paradoxically, relativized the value of all positive religions. They suggested to him that the religious impulse was a universal historical phenomenon rooted in man's need to understand and to relate to the world and its mysteries. All religions, therefore, could be seen as emanating from a common motivational base, their singular forms reflecting only the different stages of man's intellectual, psychological, and cultural growth. Consequently, particular religions could not claim to have absolute religious truth, but at best only "relative" truth. The thrust of comparative religious studies was to grant each religious faith an impartial examination for whatever excellences it might have.[48]

Of even greater significance was Adler's recognition of the logical extension of these conclusions, which questioned the very existence of religious "truth": could religions claim any religious "truth" whatsoever, and if so, what was the nature of this "truth"? For if religions were human in origin and by-products of human evolution rather than divine inspiration, then perhaps God was but a man-made concept existing only in the mind of man. And if that were the case, what "truths" could religion offer? Could religion retain any value and meaning? Similar to the challenges of natural science, the critical historical perspective of the discipline of comparative religion caused Adler to realize the extent of the drastic curtailment, if not total obliteration, of the supernatural dimension of religion. The specter of Feuerbach's anthropological inversion of God and man hovered in the background.

The threat of history to religion was exacerbated for Adler because he found that organized religions could no longer point to their Scriptures to validate their religious claims. The textual and historical criticism of the Old Testament by men like Wilhelm Vatke, Wilhelm M. L. De Wette, Karl Heinrich Graf, and his own teacher Geiger, and the criticism of the New Testament by David Friedrich Strauss, Ferdinand Christian Baur, and the Tübingen school discredited the divine authenticity and authority of ancient Scriptures for him. He came to regard the Testaments as historical documents written by men over a period of centuries rather than as divinely revealed documents of eternally binding dogmas and creeds.

The combined force of natural science and the various disciplines which had historicized religion and had sent the leaders of organized religion and religious people everywhere reeling, had no less of a jolting impact on young Adler. His views on religion changed profoundly, and he hinted at this religious volte-face to his father, who replied:

> In your last letter you write of "your complete change of thought," without saying in what the change consists. That would make me a bit uneasy if I had not myself gone through something similar in my period

of spiritual development, and believe that "the change" will change back again, that it is only a stage in the spiritual growth that every thoughtful human being must go through in order to reach spiritual ripeness.[49]

But Adler's "change" did not "change back again." The impact of the modern knowledge which he gained in Germany was deep and lasting. From later sources, it is evident that while in Germany, he rejected theism completely.

... The curtain that had intervened between my eyes and the world, on which was painted the image of an individual man-like God slowly drew aside and I looked upon the world with fresh eyes.[50]

Adler suspended the question of the world's creation in time; it could neither be proven nor disproven, and he deemed the issue religiously insignificant. He adopted Darwin's theory of natural selection as the operating mechanism of nature, and he enthusiastically endorsed the principle of scientific progress in the world.[51] He accepted the canons of scholarship of Bible critics, anthropologists, philologists, and historians. Indeed, during his lectures in the 1870s, he often referred to himself as a historian of religion,[52] and his lectures were replete with references to Baur, Strauss, Renan, Müller, Lubbock, Tylor, Geiger, and others. While he maintained his independence of judgment from all these men, perhaps best reflected in his original ideas on the origin of monotheism,[53] he fully imbibed their critical-scientific method of research. Moreover, Adler accepted the historicization of religion generally and of organized religions in particular. He acknowledged that sociology and anthropology superseded theology as the basic categories of religious explanation.

The religious change which Adler underwent led him to attempt to synthesize a religious outlook in consonance with the scientific temper to which he subscribed. In doing so, he found his own religion, Reform Judaism, to be of no avail. On the contrary, his own religious beliefs were slipping away, precipitating an inner religious struggle which shook him to his roots.

I look back with dread to that time when everything seemed sinking around me, when the cherished faith which seemed at one time dearer than life itself was going to pieces under me, and it seemed to me that I could save nothing out of the wreck of all that seemed holiest to me.[54]

Adler accepted the historicization of Judaism. Because of his scientific studies, he came to consider Judaism as but one particular manifestation of the universal phenomenon of religion, and thus he could not acknowledge Reform Judaism's claims of religious singularity. He also concluded that Bible criticism and the insights of comparative religion undermined the uniqueness and, therefore, authority and significance of the Hebrew Bible and religion. For if the Old Testament was only a literary mosaic, written and compiled by men over generations of religious evolution rather than divinely authored or inspired religious Scripture, then it reflected but temporal human thinking and not eternal divine will.[55] As a textbook of religion, therefore, it carried no more weight than the New Testament of the Christians, the Vedas of the Hindus, or the Koran of the Moslems. Biblical institutions such as the Sabbath, festivals, and circumcision—that is, even those rituals preserved by Reform Judaism— lost their force when perceived as human institutions, let alone as institutions modeled after those of other Near Eastern cultures.

Of even greater import to Adler, the relativization of the Old Testament implied that biblical moral injunctions lost their absolute authority and legitimated his adolescent doubting of biblical ethical supremacy. While he still exalted and personally embraced prophetic ethics through the 1870s, he nevertheless sought a source or principle outside of the historicized Scriptures which could provide absolute validation for their ethical teachings. Only in the 1880s did he realize that the historicization of the Bible logically implied the historicization of biblical ethics as well, and that, therefore, a new ethical system was required which would not simply substantiate biblical ethics, but rather transcend them.[56]

Adler also conceded that contemporary science undermined the cardinal tenets of his religious faith: monotheism, and the chosenness of the Jews to teach ethical monotheism to mankind. In rejecting theism because of his studies in natural science, comparative religion, and Steinthal's folk-psychology, Adler subverted the cornerstone of Jewish theology— the belief in a personal, Providential deity. In embracing the methods and results of Bible criticism, he undercut Reform Judaism's belief in the divine selection of the Jews to teach ethical monotheism to the world: a historicized Bible implied that the Jewish mission theory was only a human conception arising from specific historical circumstances rather than a divinely ordained mandate binding on all future Jewish generations.

During the 1870s Adler came to the conclusion that the undermining of Reform Jewish theology destroyed the intellectual basis for the Reform Jew's continued existence as a Jew, since his raison d'être as a Jew hinged on his theological affirmation of Reform beliefs. While there is no direct evidence of his thoughts during 1870–73 on the problem of his own continued existence as a Jew, it is inconceivable that he did not grapple with the issue at this time. He reached no definite decisions in Germany, however, for he seems to have made at least an initial attempt to remain within the Jewish consensus upon his return to America. Until the mid-1870s he may still have been emotionally tied to American Jewry, as evidenced by his warm appraisals of Judaism before non-Jewish audiences and readers.[57] Still, it is clear that the conceptual grounds for Adler's departure from the Jewish socio-religious fellowship were laid in Germany, for they were founded on his break in Germany with Reform Jewish theology.

Geiger and Steinthal: Unacceptable Models

In his confrontation with Reform Judaism, Felix had access to the teachings of two of the most illustrious liberal Jewish scholars of the age, Abraham Geiger and Heymann Steinthal. He studied with both men at the Hochschule, and by his own admission benefited greatly from their courses. Abraham Geiger was without doubt the spiritual and theological leader of European Reform Judaism, and in a sense of American Reform Judaism as well. Bible scholar, philologist, community rabbi, and teacher at the Hochschule, Geiger from the 1830s until his death in 1874 was probably responsible more than any other man for the intellectual and religious evolution of Reform Judaism in the nineteenth century. His understanding of Reform and his attempted synthesis of Reform Judaism with modern scholarship was echoed repeatedly by his Reform contemporaries. In later years, outstanding Reform thinkers such as Kaufmann Kohler, Emil Hirsch, and Julian Morgenstern appropriated his religious rapprochement with modernity. Geiger's religious ideology, therefore, was the fundamental paradigm of Reform Judaism, and Felix's rejection of it was extremely significant, for it implied his inability to accept the general ideology of Reform Judaism as a whole.

Heymann Steinthal (1823–1899) was one of the outstanding philologists of the nineteenth century, as well as a renowned psychologist and philosopher. He wrote distinguished books on the origin of language and on the history of philology, and he was appointed lecturer in philology and mythology at the University of Berlin. Steinthal was also extremely loyal to the German Jewish community and to Reform Judaism. In 1883 he became one of the directors of the Deutsch-Israelitischer Gemeindebund, and he frequently lectured to Jewish audiences and wrote newspaper articles popularizing Judaism.

Advocates of critical biblical scholarship and comparative philological research, both Geiger and Steinthal were fully cognizant of the modern challenges to the Jewish religion; nevertheless, both remained loyal adherents of Reform Judaism. Potentially each was a model of a modern, intellectual religious Jew worthy of Adler's emulation. Yet Adler did not pattern himself after either man, for he deemed Geiger's religious ideology unsatisfactory and disapproved even more of Steinthal's lack of religious rapprochement with modern thought. Not surprisingly, he wrote, "in not one of these [two] instances was I able to become a disciple in the sense of accepting the teachings of the master."[58] Ultimately, his dissatisfaction with the approaches to Judaism of the modern-thinking Geiger and Steinthal heightened his awareness of the inability of Reform Judaism to meet his spiritual needs.

Geiger conceived of Judaism as an evolving religion; in fact, he equated Jüdische Wissenschaft with the understanding of the historical evolution of the Jewish religion. In this sense, his views were a direct product of modern scholarship's emphasis on progress and evolutionary development. Adler agreed with Geiger's evolutionary conception of Judaism; he concurred with his teacher's account of the religious evolution of the Jews from a barbarous horde to a prophetic, moral people.[59] He lauded Geiger's application of historical criticism to the Jewish religion, in particular to the Old Testament, and he ranked Geiger's achievements in Old Testament studies with those of Strauss in New Testament research. In Adler's opinion, both men correctly interpreted their respective biblical histories as works reflecting the diverse levels of consciousness of the people which had created them. Adler also assented to Geiger's method of judging the values of each historical generation only by its own standards of ethical development, for he too affirmed that ideals and religions evolved over the course of generations rather than having originated at a specific point in time.[60]

But Adler could not make Geiger his religious model because he deemed his teacher's application of the principle of religious evolution to Judaism inadequate for contemporary religious needs; he felt it both too timid and too conservative. Geiger was not only a scholar of religion but also a communal religious leader. In meeting his communal responsibilities, he attempted to translate his principle of continuous religious evolution into practical religious reform, for he saw the constant gradual change in Judaism over the centuries as legitimating the deliberate application of practical religious reforms to contemporary life. The ultimate goal of the evolution was the removal of all superfluous accretions from Judaism and the transformation of Judaism—prophetic ethics and pure theism—into the universal religion of humanity. As Adler quoted Geiger: "Judaism must be raised to become the expression of universal religious ideas."[61]

According to Adler, however, Geiger compromised the ultimate goal of Judaism by continuing to institute only gradual religious change in order to uplift the masses from their religious morass.[62] Geiger always adapted his measures of reform to the peculiar needs of his surroundings, first

Breslau, then Frankfort, and finally Berlin.[63] And herein Adler discerned the fatal flaw in Geiger's approach to Judaism in the modern age: Geiger's accommodation to the masses resulted in a historically unacceptable chasm between his scholarly theory of Jewish religious evolution and the practical implementation of its worthy goal, the universalization of Judaism.

> Here was the fatal weakness of his system. He hesitated to apply the axe, regardless of the consequences; and, when the masses were looking to him for guidance, he kept on practicing what he believed it expedient to practice, whereas the advanced of his time were drifting down the stream.[64]

Adler keenly felt the inadequacy of Geiger's approach. Instead of overhauling Judaism to bring about its final goal, he perceived Geiger to be slowly altering its forms. Adler reiterated that the historical age in which they lived simply made that process untenable.

> The continuous development of the slow change of tradition in the spirit of the new is an excellent principle of historical investigation, but there are times when it becomes dangerous to apply it without reserve to the actualities of real life. —There are times when history seems to take a sudden leap forward; times of reevaluation, when the progress of development is not indeed broken off, but new influences flowing in suddenly and with collected force swell the tide of events, and a single hour performs the work of years. Thus toward the middle of this century, the teachings of philosophy, the revelation of natural science bore down in tremendous current upon the doctrines of the prevailing religions, and while Geiger was slowly picking away the smouldering stones of ancient ruins, the resistless flood was already sweeping away far and wide the landmarks of the olden time.[65]

To Adler, Geiger's conscious attempt to fashion both the direction of reform and the actual religious reforms themselves confronted his teacher with an insoluble problem of historical logistics: the use of a principle which explained the past to determine with certainty the proper course of action in the present. Adler considered this goal to be unattainable, and he remained unsympathetic to Geiger's procedure. In fact, in rejecting Geiger's slow reforming enterprise, he actually suggested that Geiger lost claim to the title of religious reformer.[66] Adler was impatient; he insisted on immediate action and he urged the rearing of a new religion.

> In such a state of things [as found in this century] there is but one hope

of safety, to accept the inevitable, to cut loose from the moorings of tradition, even though it be to cut your own heartstrings; to recognize the just claims of science and on the broader ground, which her greatest and best grant you, urge upon you to begin the rearing of the new religion.[67]

Historical hindsight reveals to us an astonishing irony in Adler's critique of Geiger's religious views and practice. In his youth, suffused with the temper of religious universalism and sensing the dawn of a new age, Abraham Geiger exhibited the same uncompromising spirit, the same impatience, and the same eagerness for radical change in Judaism which his young pupil was now demanding. During his stay in Wiesbaden (1833–38), the radical young Geiger affirmed virtually the identical belief which so agitated young Adler: the world is changing so rapidly that unless Judaism is drastically overhauled it will deservedly perish.[68] Over the years Geiger's various congregational activities and regular preaching deepened his commitment to the unity of the Jews and the need for religious compromise in liturgy and community organizational structure.[69] It was this older Geiger who served as Adler's teacher, not the radical young man of former days. One is left to wonder to what extent, if at all, the two men discussed Adler's felt need "to cut loose from the moorings of tradition," and whether or not the elderly Geiger might not have caught a glimpse of his former self in the person of his idealistic student.

While Adler's call for a new religion was expressed in the winter of 1874, more than a year following his return home, it underlined the basic conclusion on religion which he had reached while still in Germany. For a time, he seemed to identify part of Geiger's vision of the final goal of Judaism—the universalization of prophetic ethics (though not of monotheism)—as his new religion. Upon his return to America, he actually espoused this ideal in the name of Judaism in his sermon at Temple Emanu-El in October 1873. He reasserted this ideal in his first Lyric Hall address one month later, but for the last time. Following this speech, he no longer advanced this ideal in the framework of Judaism, but rather in the guise of his new religion, which in the mid-1870s he termed Ethical Culture. By the mid 1880s, Adler publicly repudiated prophetic ethics as universally and eternally valid, thereby signifying his outright dismissal of the possible universality of the Jewish religion.[70]

Geiger was quoted by Adler as having proclaimed that "our strength thus far lies rather in criticism than in creation,"[71] and "we are still in the stage of criticism; we have not yet advanced toward the creative stage."[72] In light of these statements, Adler suggested that criticism was Geiger's forte and his historical role, and that it would be foolish to lament his inability to create a new religion; "criticism" paved the way for "creation," and thus Geiger's achievements were of the utmost significance.[73] Nevertheless, upon reading the typescript of his two lectures on Geiger, one cannot help but feel that already in Germany Adler saw himself as Geiger's successor, as the man completing the unfinished religious task; certainly, this self-perception is found explicitly in some of his later Sunday addresses to the Ethical Culture Society. Adler came to conceive of himself as a religious "creator" and, in subsequent years, perceived his religious creation, Ethical Culture, to be the next logical stage in the evolutionary unfolding of religion.[74]

The second major reason for his inability to accept Geiger as a religious model was Geiger's theology, with which he roundly disagreed. "These [the younger generation] he did not help by his positive religious conceptions. They could not accept them."[75] Adler did not disclaim Geiger's theology in his public lecture of 1874, and for good reason. Had he controverted Geiger's opinions, he would have aroused a major religious outcry from American Jews. Of necessity, he would also have had to publicly proclaim his own views on theology, and at that time he was either unprepared or unwilling—or both—to do so.

But without question Adler rejected Geiger's theology. Despite Geiger's forward-looking views on the evolution of the Jewish religion and despite his advocacy of biblical criticism, he still subscribed to the fundamental classical Reform theology: belief in monotheism and the Jewish mission to teach ethical monotheism to the world. Even Geiger's vision of the final form of Judaism embodied this theology, for the universal religion of humanity into which Judaism was slowly evolving consisted of pure theism and prophetic ethics. And despite the universalist orientation of Judaism's religious goal, Geiger insisted on the separate existence of the Jewish people to bring it to fruition. As Wiener wrote, Geiger conceived of a Judaism "which aspires to realize humanity in itself. But it is precisely in order to serve the humanistic conception that it must stress its own reality and individuality."[76]

Adler turned his back on these theological ideas. He denied theism, and while he embraced prophetic ethics as his own in the 1870s, the human origin of the Bible necessitated a source other than the Bible to validate their absolute claims. Furthermore, he rejected Geiger's theological response to the threat which a humanly contingent Bible posed for Reform Judaism and the rationale for continued Jewish existence. Engaging in biblical criticism himself, Geiger no less than Adler recognized that a humanly authored Bible imperiled the integrity of Judaism: the discrediting of biblical divinity dissipated the force of Jewish traditions and moral values, toppled Reform theology, and with it the basis of Jewish existence. As Morgenstern noted later, if the Bible was not the accepted word of

God, then what was the use of reading it? Moreover, if it was not the word of God, why should one remain a Jew?[77]

In attempting to salvage both the relevance and the "divinity" of the Bible in light of historical research, Geiger revealed perhaps the most significant aspect of his theology. He resorted to the method utilized by all later Jewish Reformers confronting the same issue: the theological reinterpretation of the concept of revelation. According to Geiger, biblical revelation did not denote a one-time miraculous manifestation of God at Sinai at which time God dictated a document to Moses; rather, it embodied an on-going, progressive, non-verbal illumination "proceeding from a higher mind and spirit which cannot be explained . . . .[78] It is the point of contact of human reason with the fundamental force of all things."[79] The Jews, in particular, have a special genius for religion and revelation. Their genius consists in "an aboriginal power that illuminated its [the Jewish people's] eyes so that they could see deeper into the higher life of the spirit, could feel more deeply and recognize more vividly the close relationship between the spirit of man and the Supreme spirit, that they could more distinctly and clearly behold the real nature of the Moral in man, and then present to the world the result of that inborn knowledge."[80]

On this theological foundation, Geiger structured his approach to the Bible. By interpreting revelation as the religious instinct or inclination of Israel guided by Providence, Geiger proclaimed the Bible to be the product of joint human and divine creation. While the Bible was written by men at different times, it was nevertheless composed by *Jewish* men— with a singular religious genius—under the inspiration of God. As human literature, therefore, the Bible is subject to the canons of modern historical investigation; as literature written with divine inspiration, however, the Bible in some way relates to the divine, and its spiritual significance stands above criticism. In effect, Geiger's resolution attempted to preserve a semblance of divinity for a totally historicized document.

While Geiger's theological interpretation of revelation foreshadowed in various degrees those of Kohler, Morgenstern, and Buber,[81] it is not original; its basic approach rests almost exclusively on that of Lessing.[82] Nonetheless, Geiger rendered a great service to Reform Jewish theology. By positing a special revelatory relation between the Jews and God resulting in the composite human-divine character of the Bible, he substantiated the Reformers' right to reject rituals deemed anachronous and lent some reason for the retention of prophetic ethics deemed of eternal value.[83] Moreover, Geiger not only reclaimed the "divinity" of the Bible to some degree, but he also restored the claim of *uniqueness* for both the Hebrew Bible and the Jewish religious community in the face of dissenting comparative religious studies. The Jews alone were endowed with a special religious genius, and their Scriptures alone reflect that bequest. Geiger's theological interpretation of revelation vindicated the purpose of continued Jewish existence.

But Geiger's theological ingenuity left Adler unaffected, for his denial of the existence of Providence negated the possibility of revelation, theological interpretations notwithstanding. And by negating revelation, he undercut Geiger's entire theology with all its implications. To Adler the Bible remained solely human literature; its concepts and creeds were considered products solely of human initiative, and its ethics, while exemplary, were grounded in the contingent rather than in the absolute. The continued existence of the Jews remained problematic, and Geiger's ideology really furnished no rationale for Adler's continued separate existence as a Jew. In the mid 1870s Adler concluded that the universalization of prophetic ethics need not restrict him to the Jewish socioreligious fellowship; on the contrary, he felt that only by stepping out of this religious fellowship could he realize his religious goal.

Whether Adler already had arrived at this conclusion while in Germany cannot be determined. What is demonstrated, however, is that he discovered no reasons in Germany which would have halted his departure not only from Judaism but from the Jewish fellowship as well. Clearly Geiger provided none; he could neither serve as a Jewish religious model nor mitigate Adler's problem with Judaism and religion in general. If anything, David F. Strauss's stepping out of Christianity provided Adler with a more lasting impression of how one ought to relate to one's religion and religious fellowship in the modern world. Strauss's book *The Old Faith and the New* caused a sensation in Europe and strongly influenced Adler, who later used it as his primary text for a private Saturday class which he led at Cornell University.[84]

Dissatisfied with Geiger's synthesis of Judaism and modern thinking, Adler was even more disturbed by the lack of any synthesis in the thinking of Steinthal. He suggested that Steinthal's adherence to the Jewish religion sprang from his dire need of "emotional self-preservation" rather than from any decisive intellectual conviction. "Steinthal is a highly sensitive nature, adheres to Orthodox habits, not from theoretical conviction, but from what might be called emotional self-preservation. He encloses himself in habits that smooth out and soften his feelings."[85] In a letter to Stephen S. Wise, January 10, 1920, he reiterated this thought. He pointed to "one conspicuous defect" in Steinthal, "a certain curious dogmatism—curious I say because it springs from the feelings rather than from the intellect. He was so deeply penetrated with the emotional values of his affirmation that he expressed them with an air of finality surprising in so fine a scholar."

Adler's perception appears to have been justified, for Steinthal was an academician incapable of bridging the gap between contemporary scholarship—including his own—and his religious beliefs. Steinthal's literary output reveals an extraordinary psychic compartmentalization: his own scientific thinking seems oblivious to his religious beliefs; his scholarship seems to have neither interacted with nor impinged upon his basic religious commitment to the Jews and to Judaism. As Adler correctly noted, "there is no constructive principle in his thinking" to integrate the domains of science and religion.[86] Without such a principle, perhaps only the need for "emotional self-preservation" underlay Steinthal's pious devotion to a faith whose authority was being undermined by his own scientific research.

In his collected essays, *Über Juden und Judentum*, Steinthal vigorously declared his belief in Providence;[87] he professed faith in the Bible as a holy source of values and Jewish traditions;[88] he avowed his love for the Jewish religion and its rituals, such as the Sabbath and festivals;[89] he affirmed his unswerving love for the Jewish people and his commitment to its perpetuation;[90] and he invoked the history of Providential concern for the Jews to espouse the doctrine of their divine election.[91] Much in the tradition of rabbinic homiletics, and with the same animating religious verve, he exhorted Jewish parents to raise their children as Jews proud of their ancestral traditions and heritage. He pleaded with these parents to instruct their children in the basic Jewish text, the Hebrew Bible.[92]

In these essays, however, Steinthal offered no reasons for his beliefs nor did he attempt to sustain them. Nowhere in these essays did he pose the critical issues confronting Adler: How is Judaism—its theology and values—vindicated in light of modern thought? Why should one adhere to Judaism and Jewish existence in the modern era? Moreover, the religious ideals which Steinthal took for granted were seriously compromised by his own scientific research, to say nothing of other aspects of modern research. Steinthal, for instance, proposed that the concept of monotheism developed among the Jews from their national psyche and collective conscience.[93] But if this monotheistic conception was the product of Jewish national conscience and spirit, if deity was what "we esteem as the ideal of highest perfection,"[94] the actual existence of a perfect being remained unproven. Steinthal's extensive research into the mythologies and religions of ancient peoples presented him with innumerable images of gods and goddesses, and yet he—and other scholars—did not for a moment entertain the possibility of their actual existence. They were understood as products of human invention—of religious merit, perhaps, but human inventions nonetheless. Steinthal's assumption that the monotheistic concept evolved by the Jews corresponded to reality was, therefore, not grounded in logic but in an intellectually inconsistent faith.

Such faith did not satisfy the intellectually probing Adler, who accepted Steinthal's research in religion and applied its implications to Judaism with a rigorous consistency wanting in his teacher's own thinking.

As for the Bible, Steinthal's avowal of its holiness seemed to contradict his own studies in comparative mythology, which had prompted his declaration that "not only Genesis, but also the narrative portion of the other Books of Moses, of Joshua, Judges and unrelated passages in all other books of the Old Testament . . . are mythical."[95] But if the Bible was but a human document illustrating ancient rites and beliefs, if Moses and Samson were to be regarded only as sun-gods,[96] if Abraham only personified the "ancient national god of the Semites,"[97] then how could biblical holiness be upheld? Steinthal tried to mitigate the thrust of this problem in his other book of collected essays, *Zu Bibel und Religionsphilosophie*. In this work he advocated an ethical and aesthetic approach to the biblical text.[98] But this stand could not dispel the fundamental challenges to the authority of historicized Scriptures: If the Pentateuch was to be treated like the works of Homer,[99] then in what sense were biblical strictures and traditions relevant for contemporary Jews? Geiger resorted to the theological reinterpretation of revelation to salvage biblical authority; ultimately, Steinthal resorted to faith alone.

Steinthal offered no viable Jewish ideology to Adler. Like Geiger, he too spoke of "Das ewige Judentum" and equated it with "moral humanism,"[100] but that expression did not suffice. Steinthal did not extend the results of his scholarship in religion to their logical conclusions for Judaism; Adler did. Egged onward by his unwavering demand for intellectual consistency and his unflagging zeal for coherence between one's accepted ideas and religious beliefs, Adler found Steinthal's dichotomous intellectual posture in regard to Judaism impossible to adopt. Steinthal's religious affirmations seem to have reflected the survival of a religious psychic habit in the face of his own scientific research, which undermined all theistic premises.[101] The price Steinthal paid for his religious attachment was a price Adler was unwilling to pay: the fragmentation of his intellectual and psychological-emotional existence.

It is not unlikely that Steinthal's failure to justify Judaism and continued Jewish existence was, to some extent, prompted by the anti-Semitic social environment of Germany. He asserted that in German eyes, nothing the Jews did—even conversion—would conceal or expunge their Jewish origins. "All your conversions, all your activities to free yourselves from your religion make you a laughing stock in the eyes of the Germans. . . . whatever you do, you will remain 'sons of Shem'; whatever you do, you are still Jews."[102] In such a social atmosphere, the vindication of Judaism and of Jewish existence was superfluous. The fundamental question became not why to remain Jewish, but how best to live as a Jew. To this issue

Steinthal unequivocally proposed a return to the heritage of the Jewish past.[103]

If this explanation is tenable, then one sees an additional reason for Adler's inability to concur with Steinthal's attitude toward Judaism. For not only did Steinthal not respond to the questions agitating the young Adler, but Steinthal's approach emerged from a social situation entirely irrelevant to him. Except for the first six years of his life, Adler grew up in America; he was an American, and America was his home. The base forms of German anti-Semitism were nonexistent in America, where a Jew could melt into the mainstream of society with much greater ease than in Europe. Steinthal's commitment to Judaism, if motivated in some measure by a lack of choice to be anything but a Jew, could not appeal to Adler, who lived in a land in which freedom of religion prevailed.

A New Religion

Rejecting Jewish theology and cognizant of the grave threat to the meaning of religion in general, obtaining no satisfaction from either Steinthal's schizophrenic intellectual position or Geiger's unacceptable theology, Adler sought a new religion consistent with modern thinking to fulfill his spiritual needs. He found it in a religious synthesis which he himself created, an eclectic religion of ethics whose ethical authority lay grounded in Kant, whose ethical models were represented by the Prophets, whose concept of God was derived from Matthew Arnold, and whose socially activist orientation was shaped by Lange and the German social-aid tradition.

Adler repeatedly acknowledged his debt to Kant and often recounted the decisive impact which Kantian ethics had on him.[104] His life-long interest in Kant manifested itself in countless lectures and in his keeping up to date with the latest scholarship in Kantian philosophy. Toward the mid-1880s he initiated a critical investigation of ethical systems. With greater philosophical maturity and independence, Adler came to consider Kant's ethical views inadequate; ultimately he superimposed his own ethical theory on that of Kant to formulate an ethical approach more to his liking.[105] Nevertheless, his introduction to Kant while in Germany completely molded his ethical outlook for more than a decade; in the 1870s his ethical statements merely echo those of Kant.

Adler's attraction to Kant stemmed from his desperate need to justify his belief in the special significance of the human being and human values in light of the scientifically based philosophy of materialism. A philosophy of materialism was very prevalent in Germany during 1850–80. In fact, it gained such international currency that select German works such as

Büchner's *Kraft und Stoff* (1855) were translated into numerous languages. As a result, most idealists in the last third of the nineteenth century returned to Kant to substantiate either ethical humanism or some form of ethical religion in the face of the intellectual onslaught of materialism. Adler's affinity for Kant was not unique, but rather indicative of a general neo-Kantian revival in Europe.

Based on natural science, philosophical materialism denied the existence of any unknowable reality behind natural phenomena and affirmed man's subjugation—like all other elements of nature—to its laws. These postulates undermined both ethics and religion: by asserting man's subjugation to nature, materialism implicitly denied human freedom, thereby nullifying the foundation of ethical judgments; and by rejecting all conceptions of "unknowable reality," materialism demolished the basic framework of all religions.

Kant's distinction between the phenomenal and the noumenal world repulsed the materialist thrust. Positing a noumenal world, Kant plausibly suggested an unknowable reality. He conceived of man from two points of view: as part of nature, man is a determined being subject to its laws; but as part of the noumenal world, he acts freely in accordance with laws prescribed by reason. Kant, therefore, could accept the claims of scientific determinism and simultaneously maintain the idea of human free will, thus escaping the dilemma of eighteenth-century materialist doctrines.[106] One century later, idealists employed the same escape route to thwart the challenge of nineteenth-century materialism.

Kant's ethical system became the fundamental component of Adler's new religion, and for good reason: it provided him with a satisfying principle by which to validate the absoluteness of ethical behavior; it helped provide him with a new concept of God to replace the idea of personal Providence of theism; and it also served as the ideological basis for the implementation of practical social reforms which he craved.

Adler wholeheartedly adopted Kant's notion of "practical reason," that is, of the existence of an innate moral faculty in man capable of apprehending the moral law. According to Kant, man's inward experience proved the existence of this moral faculty, which obligated and directed him to fulfill his duty and to do the right for the sake of right alone.[107] Adler's own idealistic drive to live morally, to institute social justice, and to follow his conscience at all costs, confirmed Kant's contention for him.[108] He found his personal moral inclinations substantiated by Kant's philosophical assertions. He was overjoyed by Kant's universalization of the moral law as formulated in the categorical imperative, for the universalization of the moral law suggested its absolute authority. He accepted Kant's principle of moral action—the doing of one's duty according to one's conscience—as absolute justification for ethical behavior. To Felix, the absolute ethical authority of the historicized Bible was superseded by the ethical absoluteness found in Kantian philosophy.

At least through the 1870s and part of the 1880s, however, Adler still extolled the sublimity of prophetic ethics. His study of the prophetic books in the original texts while in Germany,[109] when they were not "forced" upon him as they were in his youth, inspired him to see their "freshness" and human greatness.[110] In fact, on the surface his praise of prophetic ethics raises a considerable paradox: as a professing Reform Jewish adolescent, young Adler never acknowledged the high moral tone of biblical ethics despite their significance for Reform Jewish theology; now, however, having dismissed Reform theology, he repeatedly affirmed his love for prophetic ethics. But the paradox is readily resolved. In earlier years, the Bible posed serious moral problems because Adler had been taught that *all* of it reflected divine truth, and he could not reconcile that teaching with some of the apparently immoral sections of the Scriptures. Consequently, biblical morality *in toto* was impugned. In viewing the Bible as human literature reflecting the different moral levels of the evolving Jewish nation, however, Adler could conceive of the supposed immoral portions as but historical remnants. He could, therefore, regard the prophetic texts as the crowning jewel of the Jewish evolutionary process; they could be appreciated independently of the rest of the Hebrew Bible.

Adler's appreciation of the Prophets, however, stemmed from his perception of the conformity of their ethical deeds with Kantian ideals. He conceived of them as historical exemplars of the Kantian ethical system whose ethical actions were validated by Kantian principles. Consequently, he described the Prophets' acts of righteousness as flowing from a free moral will grounded in their consciences and motivated by a sense of duty to do the right for the sake of right alone.[111] Both Kant's terminology and his ethical approach are conspicuous in Adler's positive evaluation of prophetic ethics.

Yet in praising the Prophets, Adler ignored Kant's deprecation of Judaism with its accompanying claim of Christian ethical superiority grounded in the humanized figure of Christ.[112] Although he gradually severed his bonds with the Jewish community during the 1870s, Adler's preference of the Prophets to Jesus at this time clearly indicates that his departure from Judaism in the 1870s was not motivated by Christological concerns. He honestly believed in the greatness of the Prophets.

Kant's analysis of "practical reason" furnished Adler with a basis for believing in the transcendental origin of ethics. But the religious implications which he drew from Kant's position were even more profound. As he wrote:

The transcendental origin of the moral law replaced the anthropomorphic, the individual deity, so that there was no lacuna left. The god of theology was gone, but something else that was very real had taken his place. Because the moral law was not conceived as an abstract thing, but as a power actually working in the world.[113]

Adler's belief in theism was supplanted by his belief in the moral law, a moral law which "corresponds to a reality deeper than all other reality—a reality wiser than we can tell, truer than we can ever demonstrate."[114] He discovered in Kant's concept of the moral law a great power actively at work in the world insofar as something inherent within human nature drives man to fulfill it.[115] The moral law thus conceived was the foundation stone out of which was hewn Adler's new religious faith and his new conception of God.

Rooted in Kant, Adler found Matthew Arnold's understanding of God as a moral power particularly congenial; from his lectures in the later 1870s, it is clear that he appropriated Arnold's notion of God as "the Eternal Power, not ourselves, that makes for righteousness" as his own.[116] In adopting Arnold's formulation of moral-theological reality, Adler stood in good company, for a number of recognized thinkers and religious leaders had borrowed Arnold's conception.[117] Arnold's notion of God, in fact, was but one of a whole litany of attempted reinterpretations intended to salvage some meaning for "divinity" in the modern world: Strauss put forward his "All" or "Cosmic God," Spencer had his "Unknowable," Fiske propounded his "cosmic theism," and John Stuart Mill put forth his "limited liability God."[118] These latter views and others of this type became known to Adler either during his stay in Germany or shortly after his return to America. None appealed to him, however, because each concept of God was formulated as a response to the challenges of modern science and not to the moral challenges of the modern world; the various notions of God propounded by these men did not satisfy his ethical idealism. Arnold, on the other hand, prescribed an acceptable moral concretization of God built on the ethical-religious groundwork already laid by Kant.

Kant's analysis of the universe in moral terms furnished not only the intellectual foundation for Adler's new religion, but together with the examples of the Prophets, also provided a motivating rationale for practical reform activity. For, as Adler observed,

I slipped on easily from Theism to Kantian Ethicism because of the predominance at that time of element no. 3 ["the practical side of me . . . rooted in a will, especially the kind of will that is peculiar to moral reformers"]. A vague power for righteousness in the background was enough, the main thing being to exert the power in will effort.[119]

The implementation of practical social reforms became the fundamental goal of Adler's new religion, for he was driven by his idealism to translate his "vague power for righteousness" into practical good. As he himself recounted, he developed an "apostolic, prophetic consciousness" whose essential task lay in the concretization of the moral law in society.[120]

It was Friedrich Albert Lange, however, and not Kant, who in the main charted both the course and the method which Adler's social activity was to follow in the 1870s. Lange was one among many influential individuals who contributed to the intense social discussion in Germany about the condition of the industrial proletariat. In general, reaction to the widespread discontent of the industrial laboring class was much more immediate in Germany than either in England or in the United States.[121] From the 1860s on, socialists, liberals, social reformers, and religious leaders promulgated concrete social, political, and cultural programs to ameliorate the dehumanizing effects of massive German industrialization. The writings and activities of men such as Hermann Schulze-Delitzsch, V. A. Huber, Bishop Emanuel von Ketteler, Leopold Sonnemann, Ferdinand Lassalle, August Bebel, Wilhelm Liebknecht, Rudolf Gneist, Lujo Brentano, and Lange led to the creation of such vital institutions as trade unions, workers' cooperatives, the Verein für Sozialpolitik, dedicated to the scholarly study of socio-economic problems, and the Social Democratic political party. During the 1860s and Adler's three-year tenure in Germany, national debates on the labor issue captured the imagination of thousands.

Invigorated by this passionate climate of social concern, Adler's idealistic temperament drew him particularly to Lange and to his writings. As a democratic humanitarian and a man of action, Lange served as a welcome model. Adler read Lange's *The Labor Question* with "burning cheeks" and was equally captivated by his *History of Materialism*.[122] Lange's work convinced him that the orderly continuity of civilization depended critically on the dissipation of labor unrest by social justice and assistance to the working poor. Lange's solution to labor's plight, which "favored productive co-operation and [which] seemed to point a way to immediate action which socialism did not,"[123] deeply impressed Adler and furnished him with a practical guide for his own activities. Repeatedly in the late 1870s, Adler applied Lange's principle of labor cooperation in the projects of the Ethical Culture Society, such as the Cornell Iron Works, the Working Man's Lyceum, and others.

Lange and the socially conscious German climate had a formative impact on Adler. His experiences in Germany made him, upon his return to America, conscious far earlier and far more concretely than other Americans of the urgent necessity to solve the multifarious problems arising in the wake of extensive American industrialization. In his adolescence, young Adler had genuinely aspired to help New York's tenenment dwellers but realistically found that he could do very little; the broad practical aspects of his German education, however, provided him with concrete social direction, goals, and methods—with a social vision—which he hoped one day somehow to implement on a grand scale. Only a few years later, Adler's constant lectures on the need for social justice and the many social projects which he initiated with his society represented his attempt to fulfill that vision of social reform.

To Adler, social reform on behalf of labor was not only an issue of morality or social justice; rather, he conceived of social justice and reform for labor as a *religious* concern. Already in Germany he had mapped out a program to cure the misery of the manual laborer, and of this activity he wrote, "I told the boys that I had felt that religion had flowered out in my breast and that I was the first convert to my religion."[124] By the mid to late 1870s, Adler's concern with social justice for the industrial workers constituted the concrete manifestation of his religious ideology.

One may well wonder, however, why he characterized his social concern as religious. In fact, one may rightfully ask the more general question of why Adler conceived of his new ideology as a religion altogether, rather than as an ethical humanist outlook. Certainly, he had secularist ethical models after which to pattern himself, such as were found in Charles Bradlaugh's National Secular Society in England and among freethinking societies in Germany. Further, whether Adler distinguished ethics and moral behavior from religion while in Germany cannot be ascertained. In his early years, he composed no forthright analysis of the relation between ethics and religion, for his lectures in the 1870s, and even some in the 1880s, present rather muddled thinking on this topic. Sometimes he equated ethical behavior with being religious: "To be moral and to be religious is substantially the same thing."[125] On other occasions he clearly distinguished between the two realms, and ethical action was perceived as only one important ingredient in the overarching religious concern of gazing at the universe to seek the meaning of life.[126] Ultimately he adopted the latter view; but his designation of his ideology as religious at the very outset requires some explanation.

Fundamentally, Adler's identification of his ethical ideals and social activism with "religion" resulted from the latent influences of his father, Samuel, and the new influences of Kant. Samuel inculcated his children with the idea that values, morals, and good deeds lie in the domain of religion, ultimately validated by a Providential God. While Felix discarded his father's theology, he retained Samuel's intellectual framework.

Samuel's ideas had left a marked emotional imprint on his son, for young Adler was emotionally committed to saving religion in the modern age; his crucial problem was to determine what type of religion was viable. It is likely that Adler portrayed ethics and social action in a "religious" framework by dint of an intellectual and emotional predilection induced by his father.

But it was Kant's ethical ideology which sanctioned his "religious" orientation, for Kant himself had outlined his moral system in religious terms. Kant seemed to subsume ethics under religion: "Morality leads to religion";[127] moral religion "must consist not in dogmas and rites but in the heart's disposition to fulfill all human duties as divine commands."[128] What "divine commands," "religion," and "God" all meant to Kant is open to scholarly debate.[129] Indeed, the relation between ethics and religion in Kant is not altogether clear, which may help to explain Adler's own confusion on the matter. That Kant did place his ethical system in a "religious" framework, however, is beyond all question. Adler followed suit.

Adler's pursuit of Kantian philosophy did not sit well with his family, especially since he had specifically been sent abroad to study for the rabbinate. When his letters arrived home, broadly hinting at a "complete change of thought" and revealing his penetrating and time-consuming philosophic investigations, the family first requested clarification of his views. On April 27, 1872, his cousin Isidor Walz wrote:

> As to yourself, I would like sometime to be favored with something like a lucid intelligible statement of the religious and philosophic principles at which you have arrived. For a year past, your letters have teemed with allusions to something remarkable in that line and you have certainly succeeded in being very mysterious. For neither Pa [Samuel Adler] nor myself have been able to form the slightest idea of what you mean. Let us have it in plain English, Felix; I have thought a good deal on those topics, you know, have been, like every son of Adam thus far greatly puzzled, and like many, at best, disappointed, and have given up in despair. Or rather have concluded to turn my attention to something practical and useful, rather than devote my life to pondering over insoluble problems.

As a practical scientist, Walz had little patience with philosophical ruminations. In a May letter, Walz again expressed his perplexity in regard to Adler's metaphysics. He even suggested to Felix to "look into Herbert Spencer a little. . . . I can promise you a rich intellectual field."

By September 1872, Samuel Adler's impatience with his son's

philosophic studies came to the fore. In a letter dated September 16, he tried to dissuade his son from pursuing them any further.

> As to the difficult and exhausting philosophic courses you spoke of in your last letter, I earnestly advise you to let them be. To know the history of philosophy, its chief systems and their development is useful. More than that is effort without a goal and leads to just one conclusion—namely, that the deepest and most profound in the universe is not to be plumbed.

But young Adler's acquaintance with modern thought convinced him that the universe's depths could and must be plumbed, for to do otherwise implied the forfeiting of his intellectual integrity. He felt that a true religion could only be based on a true understanding of the universe; his father's advice did not deflect him from his course of study.

The Adler family continued to exhort Felix to cease his philosophical studies. On November 22, 1872, Isidor Walz wrote a scathing letter in which he rebuked both metaphysics and Felix's pursuit of it. "Metaphysical studies, or rather speculations, have thus far proved exceedingly barren and altogether unproductive of any practical results," he proclaimed. "I challenge you to adduce a single [point] on which philosophers agree without exception. You say Kant is the rock of modern philosophy; I am aware that it is the rock on which his immediate followers split." Walz defied his younger cousin to "cite a single principle, whether of ethics or logic or aesthetics, or psychology, etc. which had advanced the world practically an inch! And I challenge you further to produce the solution of a single metaphysical problem which agitated the ancient philosophers 3000 years ago."

Having dismissed the value of any metaphysical study, Walz then reproached Felix for living in a "poetical and ideal world" and with deluding himself that "it is an actual reality." He scorned young Adler's avowed goal of developing a comprehensive ethical theory to enable him the "better to obtain the ends of practical morality." To Walz, the scientific positivist, this quest was utter foolishness. "Let me assure you," he mocked Felix, "that if you cannot practice morality till you have discovered its nature, theory, and essence, you will die a very amoral man." With biting sarcasm, he berated what he considered to be his cousin's intellectual arrogance. Thousands of giant intellects have grappled with Felix's problems and all have failed, he wrote, "but Felix Adler, *student philosopher,* in the blessed year of 1872, entertains a just hope of finding the philosopher's stone." Walz was convinced that Felix over-rated his powers and that if he persisted he would be "doomed to utter failure and disappointment."

Radically different from Felix in temperament and intellectual outlook, Walz was completely out of sympathy with Felix's most fervent aspirations and displayed neither sensitivity nor real understanding of his cousin's quest. He claimed to be writing for Samuel Adler as well, and no doubt his letter echoed some of Samuel's sentiments; the elder Adler was bitterly disappointed with the direction of Felix's studies. But Samuel could never have written such harsh words to his son.

Isaac Adler also expressed his disapproval of his brother's course of study. In his letter of January 3, 1873, he judged his brother's pursuit of philosophy to be "much more dictated by a phantastic [*sic*] chase after an ideal never to be reached than by solid practical good sense and love of solid substantial science." Like Walz, Isaac Adler had a strong personal bias for empirical rather than speculative science that prevented him from appreciating and understanding an approach to science and to life other than his own.

In a letter of January 6, 1873, Henrietta Adler counseled her son in the same way as did the rest of the family. "Take my advice," she recommended, "leave Berlin, its philosophy, and prepare yourself for life with good practical knowledge and common sense. That will be of more use to you in your calling than all the philosophy in the world." Her advice also went unheeded. By 1873 Felix Adler had fully immersed himself in Kantian philosophy and had formulated a religious ideology essentially at odds with the Reform Judaism of his parents.

For a short time, the Adlers' fears for their son's future abated. Felix's summa cum laude degree in semitics from Heidelberg rekindled their hopes that his "practical" course of study would culminate in his assisting and one day replacing Samuel at Emanu-El. Young Adler also complied with his family's wishes to return home in September 1873, rather than December, in order to assume some of the "heavy load of office" resting solely on his father's shoulders.[130] The family's fondest dreams, however, were shortlived.

During his stay in Germany, Felix Adler broke with Reform Judaism. He rejected theistic theology, yet struggled to sustain the integrity of religion for himself. Committed to the preservation of religion, the idealistic Adler discerned that no one was reconstructing religion on a foundation suitable for practical living; no one propounded a synthetic view of the value and meaning of religion in light of all the challenges of the modern age. Jews and Christians alike were still bound in varying degrees to their respective creeds. Even liberal Jews, such as Geiger and Steinthal, could not escape their commitment to the belief in God and to Jewish tradition. Lange, for whose social concerns Adler had a great affinity, conceived of religion as poetry.[131] Adler could not accept this view because, for him, religion dealt with reality, not fantasy. The Jewish philosopher Hermann Cohen at this time espoused socialism rather than religion.[132] Matthew Arnold's outlook was overly aesthetic and cultural; he had no social program. Kant, the master, provided the basic principles, but he too offered no social program for society. Conceptions of divinity such as the "All" or the "Unknown" by Strauss, Spencer, and others offered no guide for practical religious activity. Even the scholars of religion afforded little or no assistance to Adler in his religious quest. Bible critics were too involved in textual criticism to furnish direction for contemporary religion. Anthropoligists, philologists, and those pursuing studies in comparative religion were concerned with the history of religion rather than with present-day religious reform. And the materialists and scientific positivists simply mocked the entire religious enterprise. In short, no one person, movement, or group fulfilled Adler's need for a meaningful religious ideology.

Consequently, he devised an eclectic religion of his own against the backdrop of modern scholarship. His religion affirmed belief in the reality of a moral power operating in the universe and demanded practical social action to implement justice and social reform in the world. He was among the first in Europe, if not the first, to promulgate a religion which combined the rejection of theism with a redefinition of the purpose of religion in terms of social reform. He was definitely the first to do so in America, soon initiating the shortlived social direction of the Free Religious Association in 1878. Upon his return to the United States in September 1872, Adler did not yet know how to implement his "evangelical mission" to "enact the moral law."[133] It took a few years for him to get his bearings on the American religious scene and to define precisely his vocation. Only in 1876–77, with the founding of the New York Society for Ethical Culture, did Adler assemble the necessary social base and establish the institutional structure within which to carry out his religious plans.

Chapter III
Setting the Scene: 1873–1876

The Temple Sermon

Adler returned to New York on September 15, 1873 with a new religious outlook but uncertain about the direction of his future career. Should he accept the position of junior minister awaiting him at Emanu-El and fulfill his parents' most fervid dream? Would his acceptance of Emanu-El's pulpit be consistent with his religious views? He was soon granted the opportunity to resolve the uncertainties which tormented him. On October 6, 1873, the president of Temple Emanu-El, Lewis May, was "appointed as Committee to invite Reverend Dr. Felix Adler in the name of the Board, to preach in the Temple on Saturday next."[1] Adler's upcoming temple sermon was simply the trial run preceding his expected appointment as his father's successor. This appointment, however, was never made. The sermon angered Samuel's associated rabbi, Gustav Gottheil, and some of Emanu-El's congregants; their reaction in turn convinced Adler that his religious outlook precluded his ministry at American Reform Judaism's leading congregation.

On Saturday, October 11, 1873, on the Festival of Sukot, Felix Adler delivered his first and only sermon at Temple Emanu-El, entitled "The Judaism of the Future."[2] The temple was crowded: "There was of course much anxiety to hear him [Adler] in his father's pulpit—as an American rabbi is somewhat of a novelty."[3] Few people, however, could have anticipated his address, for Adler's Temple Sermon essentially propounded the new religion which he had devised in Germany. While he identified this new religion with "the Judaism of the future," the sermon's new religious orientation and innovative homiletical format surprised the audience.

The Temple Sermon delineated the first public expression of Adler's fundamental religious message born from his educational experience abroad: contemporary religion lies in danger but it can be saved. With youthful ardor Adler presented both his conception of the problem and its antidote. In doing so, he foreshadowed the basic early program of the Society for Ethical Culture organized a few years later; even the society's motto—"not the creed but the deed"—found its first utterance in this sermon.

Adler enunciated his concern for the integrity and continued meaningfulness of religion.

76

On all sides, we hear the end of religion predicted, and no wonder, considering the sorry condition in which it finds itself. The question for us to answer now is, not this form or that form, this reform or that reform. The question is—life or death—is religion about to perish?[4]

In response to his own question, he contended that "it is not religion which is old; it is [our] mode of cultivating it which is antiquated." As the genius of mankind awakens, new religious forms will supplant the old, and "new institutions [will] call forth the religious powers of the human heart more intensely than ever before." The history of religion teaches us, he asserted, that while "religions may pass away, religion shall endure."[5]

To guarantee the perpetuity of religion, Adler called for the establishment of a religion permitting its union with "life," a practical religion intimately involved in all aspects of societal concern.

[This religion shall have] institutions . . . bearing on all conditions and relations of life. [This] religion, not confined to church and synagogue alone, shall go forth into the marketplace, shall sit by the judge in the tribunal, by the counselor in the hall of legislation, shall stand by the merchant in his warehouse, by the workman at his work. In every department of life, wherever man's activity is unfolded its quickening influences shall be felt; religion and life shall be wedded once more in inseparable union.[6]

To prepare the way for this union, he proposed to educate the masses,

to create among them an enlightened judgment which shall teach them to discriminate between the passing form and the immortal idea [the moral law]. Lest in abandoning the ancient forms they lose also the ideal element which they contained, and sink back into repulsive sensualism, which, under the specious cover of materialistic philosophy, in reality proclaims the reign of mental indolence and of unbridled passion.[7]

Essentially, Adler advanced his own eclectic form of religion, a humanitarian religion highlighted by practical social activity and the moral and educational elevation of labor, and identified it as "the Judaism of the Future." Three years later he named this religion "Ethical Culture." But now he asserted that Judaism, with its great humanitarian, prophetic doctrines, would become this religion of the future. The implementation of these moral principles would precipitate the rise of the "Temple of the Future, [with] Justice its foundation, Peace and Goodwill its columns, and the vast firmament of heaven itself its high dome."[8] Then and only then, Adler proclaimed, "shall religion in truth become a cause not of strife, but of harmony, laying its greatest stress not on the believing in but the acting out, a religion such as Judaism ever claimed to be—not of the creed but of the deed."[9] He equated Judaism with his own vision of universal humanitarian religion.

> We discard the narrow spirits of exclusion, and loudly proclaim that Judaism was not given to the Jews alone, but that its destiny is to embrace in one great moral state the whole family of man. . . .[10] The genius of religion . . . is the genius of Judaism; . . . again shall it proclaim its great humanitarian doctrine, its eternal watchword: One Truth, One Love, One Hope in the Highest, One great brotherhood of men on Earth.[11]

Adler's message of the universality of Judaism was by no means new. On the contrary, all the major exponents of Reform Judaism preached the same idea, for it constituted the basic teleological vision of Reform ideology. The congregation could not have been overly alarmed by his idealistic portrait of the religion of the future, for despite its specific suggestions, it was sufficiently general in tone to conform in broad outline to the final goal of Judaism advanced by most Reformers. The novelty in the sermon, however, lay, first, in its stress on social action for religion, on the deed in the marketplace rather than on the creed in the temple, and second, in the total absence of any theological affirmations. Not once did Adler refer to "God," "deity," or a "divinity" of any sort. Such a glaring omission in a sermon was unheard of at that time. While Adler did not deny theism in this sermon, he appeared to have ignored it.

Despite this omission, Adler's sermon was generally well received by Emanu-El congregants, especially by the younger members. On October 17, 1873, the *Jewish Messenger* reported:

> The young speaker was listened to with close attention and after the service a larger number of his friends congratulated him upon the success of his maiden discourse. He was in excellent voice being distinctly heard in every part of the building. He spoke without notes and betrayed no nervousness, but a seeming earnestness that won him admiration, despite the generalities of his discourse. . . . The lecturer created a favorable impression as an eloquent and enthusiastic speaker, and his next appearance in the pulpit will be welcomed.

The *American Israelite* of November 17, 1873 contained a similar declaration of the favorable impression which Adler had created. Eleanor Adler also noted the "admiration and praise" which Adler had received.[12]

Nevertheless, the sermon did elicit criticism, the foremost critic being Samuel Adler's associate rabbi, Gustav Gottheil. By threatening to resign,

Gottheil galvanized opposition to young Adler among the older, more conservative elements of the temple, particularly among the Board of Trustees. The lack of any motion in the trustees' "Minute Book" to thank Adler for his sermon—a customary courtesy for a guest speaker—reflected the board's displeasure. The existence of this opposition helps to explain later references to the "severe criticism" which Adler received despite contemporary reports to the contrary.[13]

According to Richard Gottheil, his father, Gustav, was most disturbed by the non-Jewish tone of the sermon: "The Temple was a Jewish place of worship and the Deity had not once been mentioned in the address."[14] Recognizing that Emanu-El seemed "well pleased" with Adler, Gottheil tendered his resignation and intended to return to his congregation in Manchester, England; he refused to share the pulpit with him. Apparently Gottheil's threat of resignation prompted a delegation of the Board of Trustees to visit Adler and request clarification of his religious views. The temple had just gained Gottheil's services (he arrived in September 1873), culminating years of fruitless search for an English-speaking rabbi of stature; it was not about to lose him now.[15]

The committee came to Adler and inquired whether or not his omission of God was intentional and whether he, in fact, believed in God. Adler acknowledged that, superficially, the omission was unintentional; he had read the sermon to his father earlier and neither had noticed the oversight. Nevertheless, he informed them that the exclusion of God reflected a new religious departure, and while he did believe in God, it was not their God.[16] At that moment Adler understood that he could not lead Emanu-El. He sensed that in clinging to theological dogmas which he had forsaken, the temple officials could not appreciate the religious message which he bore. They remained at Geiger's contemporary state of Jewish religious development; he had progressed beyond it. Years later he wrote:

Is it right for a teacher of religion who adheres to the New to enter the Old Pulpit for the purpose of gradually preparing men to accept the New? I say, no, because he would be entering under false pretenses. . . . The teacher who under such circumstances accepts or retains his position may have the best ends in view, but the means are dishonest and the best ends do not justify such means.[17]

His cognizance of the unacceptability of his religious orientation and his intellectual honesty militated against his succeeding his father at Emanu-El. He withdrew his candidacy for the rabbinical position, which at the very least was tacitly assumed to be his, if it had not already been formally offered to him.

Gottheil and the Emanu-El board were not the only ones to note the lack of reference to God in the sermon. In a letter to the *Jewish Messenger,* October 24, 1873, "C.L." of Philadelphia expressed his disappointment that Adler's sermon was "simply a pretty and eloquent speech, such as we might expect from a college graduate on Commencement Day, or from a youthful and enthusiastic speaker before a Lyceum lecture audience." "C.L." was particularly disturbed, however, that the speech contained "no doctrine in it, no allusion to religion as such, no invocation of the Deity, or reference to Him and His power and glory."

> It seemed quite strange to read a sermon by a Jewish preacher in which no reference to God was made. As little expect a Fourth of July orator to give a spread eagle address without mention at least once of America, as for a clergyman, who is not an atheist, to preach for an hour to his congregation without once introducing God in a reverent way. . . . The omission struck me as rather peculiar, and I cannot forebear calling your attention to it.

Interestingly enough, this letter to the editor seems to have been the only printed reaction of the Jewish public to the sermon. Both the *Jewish Messenger* and the *Jewish Times* printed the text in full, and the *American Israelite* reported on it; but no further accounts of the sermon and its aftermath were recorded by the Jewish press at that time. It seems that both the preaching of the sermon and the reaction to it remained a fairly private affair within Emanu-El.

Adler's lack of reference to God, which initially disturbed Gottheil and some members of his congregation, may have been the most serious factor inciting criticism, but it may not have been the only one. Many aspects of the sermon conceivably could have provoked unfavorable reactions. It is difficult to imagine that some people did not take offense at certain remarks of the young would-be rabbi as well as at the sermon's style.

Adler's sermon represented a radical departure from the typical homiletical format of the day. Besides constantly referring to God, pulpit sermons at that time almost always elucidated biblical or midrashic texts. The prime function of these sermons was religious exhortation, and with the exception of some of Einhorn's sermons, they almost never addressed topical or timely issues. This temple sermon departed from the accepted homiletical style. As Richard Gottheil recounted, "it was not a sermon; it was an address."[18] The *Jewish Messenger* and the *Herald* reached the same conclusion: "We can hardly style his effort a sermon. If it were a sermon, it flung aside time-honored rules. It may more properly be styled an address on the prospects of Reformed Judaism."[19] While some congregants may have enjoyed this departure from traditional homiletical form, it is not unlikely that others may have been startled by this innovation and may have preferred the more orthodox sermonic style.

Of far greater significance, however, especially to Gustav Gottheil, was Adler's none too subtle critique of contemporary Reform Judaism. Utilizing Geiger's idea of the evolution of Judaism, Adler lauded the transformation of medieval Judaism in the modern era initiated by the scholarly research of European Reformers. Indeed, he praised their reforming activity: "They have done their work bravely, and History will record of them that 'they have deserved well' of the cause of religion."[20] But, he asked, "What now? The field is cleared, the ruins are removed, but what remains?—Vacancy unmeasured. The Old has been torn down, but the New has not been reared in its stead. Looking to Europe, where the movement of Reform took its origin, what a spectacle meets the eye! Stagnation everywhere; hopes that were once so high, changed into hopeless indifference."[21] In the course of the sermon, it became increasingly obvious that Adler intended his portrait of religious stagnation to depict the situation not only in Europe but in America as well, and Adler proclaimed the end of the stage of Reform Judaism that stressed the scholarly criticism of religious rituals and the institution of religious reforms. He found that stage wanting and declared that something new must take its place. While some members of Emanu-El concurred, especially the youth, and others may have imputed his judgment to youthful exuberance, the European-trained Reformer Gottheil may well have interpreted Adler's sermon as a fundamental attack on the cherished faith of which he was a minister. This could help explain the vehemence of Gottheil's reaction to Adler and the reason his letter of resignation to the board suggested, in Richard Gottheil's words, that "Dr. Adler's views on religious matters differed from his so widely, it would be manifestly impossible for the two to work together."[22]

Gottheil's vigorous opposition to Adler may have been further fueled by his perception that Adler's adumbration of the Judaism of the future was really intended as a universalist, humanitarian religion in the present. After all, his proposals of taking religion to the "marketplace" and assisting labor were advanced as the blueprint for *contemporary* religious concern. Adler repeatedly underscored the need for such activity *now:* "*Let us* then strive . . . to educate the masses"; "let it [the martyrdom of his friend Edward Rosenfeld, stricken by typhus while aiding the poor of Berlin] show us that *we can do it . . .*"; "let it inspire *us* with courage to meet danger and difficulty"; "*we can not stand still . . . we must progress.*"[23] Gottheil was probably less than enthusiastic about Adler's vision of the "Temple of the Future" arising before him now;[24] such an admission, in his eyes, was tantamount to tolling the death knell for continued Jewish existence.

Classical Reformers always ascribed the coming of the universalist era to an undefined *future*, never to the present. In reality, these Reformers were unwilling to sacrifice Judaism and continued Jewish existence to the fulfillment of their ideology's teleological aims.

Adler's concrete social proposals for the resuscitation of religion must also have stirred some opposition among Temple Emanu-El's laymen, for Myer Stern correctly noted that "the views he expounded were much broader than those that prevailed at the time."[25] Like American Protestantism, American Reform Judaism catered overwhelmingly to the middle class. It is not surprising, then, that for a good many years the leaders of each denomination remained silent on labor issues; the Social Gospel movement among Protestants and the social reform movement among Reform Jews did not really begin in earnest until the 1880s–1890s and the first decade of the twentieth century respectively, despite the prevalent industrial ills following the Civil War.[26] The adherents of the various Protestant denominations and of American Reform Judaism were primarily concerned with maintaining their own economic status. Immigrant Jews who had prospered in the new land were particularly motivated to preserve their economic achievements. Adler's suggestion that Jews assist labor must have appeared rather odd to some and even outlandish to others.

Then too, his remarks came at a particularly unpropitious moment in history. The third week of September witnessed the disastrous Panic of 1873 and the beginning of a depression with international repercussions. Stocks plummeted, banks and other financial institutions closed, and thousands lost their jobs. Businessmen were eagerly engaged in minimizing or recouping their financial losses, and Emanu-El's businessmen were no exception. It is reasonable to assume that some individuals could not have been overly sympathetic to Adler's socio-religious message. That a brash young man of "unrealistic" idealism should dictate social direction to experienced men of affairs could have appeared to some as a personal affront.

Finally, Adler may well have insulted some congregants, for he actually challenged Emanu-El's financially successful Jews to transcend their economic pursuits, to release "the ideal powers . . . slumbering within you. . . . Not in the marketplaces above but in the field of letters in high places of the political and social world, above all, in the great arena of religion shall you be leaders, and lead to great and noble ends."[27] He seems to have pleaded with the congregation to heed the humanitarian doctrines of their prophetic religion. So far, he noted, it is not they but the Free Religionists who have paved the proper religious path: ". . . Listen to the clear, metallic notes that ring from the pulpits of the Free Religionists here and elsewhere [Germany]. Do you not hear the great humanitarian doctrines of Judaism re-echo in their words."[28]

In reality, Adler's reference to the "humanitarian doctrines" of the Free Religionists appears to have reflected a misconception of the nature of the Free Religious Association. He probably followed the developments of the association's first convention in New York in September 1873, which was widely covered by both the Jewish and non-Jewish press, and concluded—erroneously—that its religious goals mirrored his own. On the surface, the convention speech of the association's president, O. B. Frothingham, seemed to conform in broad outline to his very own religious ideals:

> Religion is to be the social science. It is to be the aspiration of society after a perfect social condition, and it is to be free. . . . It is to include all men, whether they profess anything or nothing; if they are seekers after the truth they belong to the religion of humanity.[29]

But Frothingham's definition of religion as the "aspiration of society after a perfect social condition" belied the actual religious concerns of his society. From the association's inception in 1867, its leaders were almost exclusively preoccupied with the idea of individual religious liberty and the availability of a free religious platform rather than with concrete social reform. Periodic statements expressing a commitment to humanitarianism and the furtherance of the social good found their way into the speeches of Free Religionists, but such expressions were most often only vague intellectual affirmations which viewed humanitarianism as an intrinsic constituent of the ideology of religious liberalism; such "humanitarianism," however, was not tied to practical social proposals or activity. Not until Adler himself replaced Frothingham as president of the association in 1878 did the organization publicly commit itself to practical social reform as a matter of ideological policy. But Adler was certainly not satisfied with a mere intellectual affirmation of "humanitarian doctrines" in 1873; he, therefore, probably misunderstood the religious direction and the nature of the FRA. Having returned from Germany only one month previous, Adler more likely than not identified the American association with its more socially oriented German counterparts.

He repeated his identification of the universalist humanitarian religion which he advocated with the "Judaism of the future" for the last time in a Lyric Hall lecture a month later: "Religion is for humanity," he declared, "Judaism is for mankind."[30] This identification was the product of sincere conviction and was not an expedient fabrication for the benefit of Emanu-El. He felt that he heralded the imminent arrival of the universal religion explicitly affirmed by Reform Jewish theology. Geiger's conception of an evolving Judaism furnished him with the dynamic historical principle justifying his belief in the potential realization of Reform teleology. While Adler criticized Geiger for not recognizing the urgency of fulfilling his own vision of the future now, while Adler's conception of the universalization of Judaism differed theologically and socially from that of Geiger and all Jewish Reformers—theism was an unnecessary vestige of the Jewish past and social reform was the religious program of the future—the substantive message of his religion still drew much of its inspiration from the universalist ethical doctrines of the Prophets. He could, therefore, still conceive of his universal religion as the culmination of the evolutionary development of Judaism in history—the "Judaism of the future."

But did he actually believe that Temple Emanu-El would subscribe to his views? Richard Gottheil observed that Dr. Emil Hirsch, son of Rabbi Samuel Hirsch and a classmate of Adler's at the Hochschule, was informed by Adler in Berlin that "when he [Adler] returned to New York he would 'make things hum' in the religious world."[31] If this statement is true, then Adler anticipated provoking a religious commotion at Emanu-El. While he may have hoped to receive approval for his religious ideas, it is difficult to imagine him expecting it. Geiger, the most eminent Reform thinker alive, did not endorse his progressive religious views. Could he have expected the leadership and lay membership of Emanu-El to prove more understanding? In later years he related that he had been consciously aware, even at the time of his sermon, of the new religious departure which he had advanced: "I sketched the idea of a new type of religious organization."[32] In historical retrospect he was certainly correct. Of necessity, however, the new organization—the Society for Ethical Culture—emerged outside the bounds of Temple Emanu-El and Reform Judaism: both the formal Jewish religious establishment and Reform Judaism as propounded by American Reform leaders could not assimilate his universalist religious views into their extant communal and ideological framework.

In a sense, Adler's sermon presented the guidelines under which he could have remained within the Jewish consensus. But Gustav Gottheil, Emanu-El's Board of Trustees, and some of the more conservative congregants rebuffed them. The Temple Sermon and its aftermath contributed significantly to Adler's ultimate alienation from his Jewish identity. Perceiving that the Temple Emanu-El leadership continued to adhere to beliefs which he had discarded and a theology which he considered outmoded, he reassessed his relation to the Jewish community and his own Jewish identity. He wondered whether his Jewishness could signify anything to him other than his racial-ethnic origin. His appreciation of the Free Religious Association—however misguided—only exacerbated his dilemma, for in its religious goals he believed he found support for his own religious orientation outside the Jewish religious and institutional framework.

In the course of the 1870s, Adler departed from both Judaism and the Jewish community. He never formally or publicly renounced his Jewish identity; he himself described his passing out of his Jewish affiliation as a "gradual, smooth transition" of which he "was hardly aware . . . until it was fairly consummated."[33] It is impossible to date precisely when he privately abjured the Jewish socio-religious fellowship; at the very latest, this transition was consummated a few years following the organization of the New York Society for Ethical Culture in 1876–77.

That Adler did not succeed his father at Temple Emanu-El bewildered and gravely disappointed the Adler family. Eleanor Adler depicted the family mood.

At home things were no easier [for Felix]. His mother was sad and quiet. Isaac [Adler] undertook to persuade Felix to change his stand, and when he found his usually quiet and amenable brother fixed in his resolve, he was outraged and forbade his fiancee and his sister to have any relations with him. Even his father's determined cheerfulness could not lift the clouds at home.[34]

Samuel Adler was amost heartbroken: the long-standing rabbinic tradition in the Adler family was broken; three years of preparatory education seemed to have been wasted; and the final drift of his son's religious views appeared unclear. And yet, despite his personal sense of pain, Samuel neither reproached nor restrained his son; he permitted Felix to continue his religious quest and, in the later 1870s, even he grew more appreciative of his son's religious goals. Samuel must have recalled his own youthful religious groping, which ultimately led him away from his father's Orthodox Judaism. Consistent with his honesty and intellectual integrity, he granted Felix the same religious freedom which he himself had enjoyed. Samuel's parental understanding and respect for his son's religious search helps to explain Felix's almost reverential feelings for his father long after his personal break with Judaism. In 1901, ten years after Samuel's death, Felix wrote to Rabbi Bernhard Felsenthal, "it is just ten years since the noble one passed away, and the void which he left behind has not been filled by anyone."[35] Ten years later he reiterated the sense of admiration and intimate caring that marked his bond to his father. In a letter to his daughters, Eleanor and Margaret, February 25, 1911, Felix Adler commented: "At many turns of life the image of my father stands out very vividly before me in reference to what would have been his standard of judgment and attitude."

Lyric Hall Lectures

While opposition to his Temple Sermon arose within Emanu-El, Adler, nonetheless, struck a responsive chord in quite a number of its congregants. Impressed with his superb oratorical skills, with his religious idealism, and with his scholarly credentials, these members provided him with a lecture platform during the winter of 1873–74. On October 21, 1873, they wrote him a letter inviting him to address them in the coming months.

> Impressed with the merits of your late address and believing that we represent the wishes of many of your audience on that occasion, we cordially invite you to deliver during the coming winter a course of lectures on subjects congenial to and connected with your line of studies. We are confident that such a course would prove both interesting and instructive, and therefore hope that you will be pleased to signify your acceptance of this invitation.

Forty-seven men signed the letter, including the three Seligman brothers and a few of the younger men, such as Julius Rosenbaum, Jacob Stettheimer, Jr., S. Frankenheimer, Adolph S. Sanger, and Edward Lauterbach, who later formed the nucleus of the Society for Ethical Culture.[36] To an extent Adler must have polarized families, for the fathers of Sanger, Stettheimer, and Frankenheimer were all important leaders of the Emanu-El congregation. This polarization foreshadowed the more sharply focused and bitter dissension within Emanu-El and its families with the later inception of the Ethical Culture Society.

Adler accepted the invitation, and he delivered a series of six public lectures at Lyric Hall (6th Avenue and 43rd Street) in New York: "The Fall of Jerusalem," November 24, 1873; "Brahma," December 29, 1873; "Martyrs and Martyrdom," January 19, 1874; "The Life of Buddha," February 9, 1874; "The Triumph of Mohammed," March 2, 1874; and "A Sign of the Times," March 25, 1874.[37] In "The Fall of Jerusalem," Adler declared that the rise and spread of the democratic, republican movement of the prophetic class of Pharisees was the historical cause of the destruction of the Temple and Jerusalem, a destruction of which he wholeheartedly approved. In "Brahma," "Buddha," and "The Triumph of Mohammed," he traced the psychological, national, and natural factors which sparked the genesis and evolution of these particular religious forms. In "Martyrs and Martyrdom," he opined that sacrifice is essential for all human progress, and he advanced a new perspective by which to define martyrdom. Finally, in "A Sign of the Times," he posited a theory to explain the revival of spiritualism in America—particularly in upstate New York—in the supposed "rational" age of the nineteenth century.

These lectures granted Adler his first opportunity to demonstrate the knowledge which he had gained in Europe. He made the most of the opportunity; the Lyric Hall lectures are replete with the methodological and intellectual insights to which he had been exposed. The names and ideas of men such as Kant, Feuerbach, Herbart, Trendelenburg, Müller, Tylor, Lubbock, Renan, Arnold, Helmholtz, Steinthal, and Geiger reappear throughout. One can identify the original sources of the recurrent themes underlying the six topics without undue difficulty: Feuerbach— religions and conceptions of gods are created in the image of man;[38] Steinthal—the character of religions and their fundamental ideas reflect the national spirit of their adherents;[39] Tylor, Lubbock, Herbart—the progressive evolution of religions conforms to the laws of human psychological and conceptual refinement;[40] Karl Ritter and H. Riehl— man and his religions develop within the limits that geographic, climatic, and natural factors allow.[41] Adler's very concern with Oriental religions reflected the fascination with Near Eastern and Far Eastern civilizations prevalent in European and American intellectual circles. His understanding of religion as the "feeling of the sublime"[42] was appropriated from the "philosopher of Königsberg," Kant, and his disdain for the priestly-aristocratic class in all religions stemmed primarily from Geiger.[43]

As a series in the history of religions, the Lyric Hall lectures bore great significance because they represented Adler's initial attempt to wean Jews away from their creedal religion on the basis of modern scholarship. Adler conceived of himself as a historian of religion who "sought out thoughts and beliefs of Palestine, India, and the Arabian desert . . . to discuss questions of religious history . . . with a view to the[ir] general bearings as understood by the philosophy of history."[44] By "general bearings" he did not here imply the usefulness of the pursuit of comparative religion for "practical" purposes; as he himself noted, he sought to avoid "practical" issues at present.[45] Rather he desired to educate the Jewish population—and any other interested listeners—toward a fuller understanding of the universal phenomenon of religion, and by virtue of the insights of history and comparative religion, to direct them to a more critical view of their own religious beliefs. That Adler ultimately wished the Jews to free themselves from their creeds and ritual forms is already evident from his temple sermon. Introducing his Jewish audiences to the fundamental premises and conclusions of Bible criticism, science, and comparative religion, he furnished them with the intellectual foundation for their own radical reevaluation of the Jewish religion. No American rabbi or Jewish preacher to date had attempted this task, and Adler seems to have been the first American Jew to engage in, to take seriously, and to elaborate publicly on the modern scholarship in religion.

Adler's invitation to the Jews to reassess their religion was subtle; he did not formally express this sentiment in these lectures nor did he himself criticize Judaism directly. Nevertheless, by denying the existence of absolute truth, including absolute religious truth,[46] by further relativizing all religious claims through an analysis of the anthropological, pyschological, and natural causes engendering religions and conceptions of deities,[47] by attributing to fetishes the same ability as that of higher religions to induce feelings of religious sublimity,[48] by pointing to the shortcomings of the *other* religions (see the MS of each lecture), by criticizing the doctrines of immortality, the divinity of supposed revelatory texts, and the notion of a Messiah in the context of *other* religions,[49] and by generally objecting to the dogmas of all religions,[50] he left the door wide open for a perceptive listener to infer the susceptibility of Judaism to the same criticism to which all religions were exposed and to follow him in applying critical contemporary scholarship to Judaism.

At this time, indeed throughout the three-year period of 1873–76, few seemed to perceive his veiled message or its implications. Few people realized that Adler's opposition to creeds included his dissent from Jewish monotheism. His public silence on the matter, in fact, precipitated heated debates as to his belief or disbelief in a Providential God even after the creation of the Ethical Culture Society. Only later did the Jewish community realize that the Lyric Hall lectures foreshadowed almost completely the conceptual groundwork of the Ethical Culture Society, which attracted thousands of Jews in the late 1870s. Even one of the society's primary social goals—the cultural and religious elevation of the masses—is intimated. In his final lecture, "A Sign of the Times," Adler rebuked the dastardly snobbery and self-serving attitude of David F. Strauss and others who disassociated themselves from the religious struggles of the less enlightened.

> Ye men that stand on the heights of knowledge and glory in the light that shines upon you while below all is dark, it is a mountain of ignorance ye stand upon. Do you not know that the mountain on which you rise so high is volcanic, eruptive, can destroy all your civilization as it has done of old. Do you not see that there is danger in your high position. You say what form of religion can there be more for us. If there were none beside, behold is not this a form worthy of your effort? To open your souls to those who are far from it, to help them work off the base superstitions which they have inherited from time immemorial

and thus to prevent these eternal relapses, to revel in the consciousness of grand sympathies, of widely beneficent action, to exalt yourself by raising them, to win redemption by redeeming. *But I am touching on a practical question of the day and this as yet I avoid. The time will come when the lips may utter of what the heart is full.*[51]

The Lyric Hall lectures also provided the first tentative hints that Adler had already stepped out of the Jewish consensus, or, at the very least, that he was cognizant of the necessity of having to break with his Jewish past. But again, no one understood his personal allusions, nor did they discern his inner struggle with his Jewishness. In his "Martyrs and Martyrdom," Adler defined the martyr as the man who seeks truth for its sake alone and who is willing to sacrifice his life for that truth, a man who dies for a truth not out of simple obedience to divine fiat, but for a truth in accord with his own conscience.[52] History teaches, he averred, that human civilization progresses with ongoing friction between proponents of enlightened change and advocates of continued conservatism. The former struggle to overcome their adversaries, and in so doing they signified to him the paradigm of human martyrdom.

> Therefore, whenever in a given state of society there be a man who feels the want of a [*sic*] higher conditions, of a greater good than can be accomplished under the system that prevails, a twofold consequence must by necessity result. The tendency for change struggles to overcome the conservative tendency which is maintained within him by the force of example, early recollections and the feelings which are bound up with them; he must quell those fond feelings, cut off those clinging memories and in the often violent struggle which this calls forth, he bares his inner self and brings a sacrifice so great as those only who have once brought it can understand.[53]

These last lines in particular pointed to Adler's own self-conception as a martyr by his standards; he felt the pangs of martyrdom in leaving the faith of his parents, and ultimately in having to leave their socio-religious fellowship as well. In his adolescent years, he had identified himself intimately with the martyrdom of the Jewish people; his new sense of martyrdom now emerged precisely because of his sense of alienation from his Jewish attachments of the past.

Adler's respectful portrayal of Jesus is a further indication of his emotional reorientation with respect to former Jewish ties. Whereas in his adolescent years he had vilified the Christian Church for its treatment of Jews and contemptuously referred to Jesus as the "prophet of charity,"[54] he now visualized Jesus as a true religious reformer "whose illustrious name we mention with all the reverence which is due to it."[55] The revolutionary metamorphosis of his former passionate bitterness toward Jesus—the historical symbol justifying persecution of the Jews—reflected not simply a new attitude picked up from his education in Germany but also probably indicated the loosening, if not rupture, of his emotional and intellectual bonds to Judaism and the Jewish people.

In the Lyric Hall lectures, Adler also exhibited the high degree of self-awareness manifested throughout his life. Instinctively, he sensed his future mission as a seeker of change even without yet comprehending the form it was to take. In forecasting the appearance of religious change, his historical intuition foretold the deprecation which those in the vanguard of change would experience. And sensing his own future role as a religious reformer, he predicted precisely the abusive aspersions to which he would be subject.

> They tell us that there is room for social improvement; however that may be, religious changes are surely imminent. The world is wearied to the death of shrivelled formalism of the past and demands something new, something that will refresh the springs of life, give new vigor to the energies of society, something that will rouse the deepest and warmest sympathies and appeal to the heart. But because this something will and must come, do you, therefore, believe that those who guard the old will stand quietly to see the change consummated? They dare not, they cannot.—Let those who would devote their lives to that much needed reformation well know the dangers they are incurring. They will be cut off from opportunity, their characters will be defamed, their purest motives vilified. Happily [we] do not burn heretics any more at the stake, but there are other modes of torture and other deaths more terrible.[56]

The later vigorous rebuke of Adler by the established New York Jewish community and its leaders fulfilled his prophetic prognosis.

As reported by the *Jewish Times* and the *Jewish Messenger,* Adler's lectures attracted hundreds of people, primarily Jewish, excited his listeners, and received great public approval.[57] Frequent references alluded to his profound scholarship,[58] eloquent oratorical style,[59] and extemporaneous speaking ability.[60] The lectures covered topics unheard in traditional pulpit sermons. His intellectual offerings in these addresses presented new models of religious thinking for the Jewish community, and supplemented in scholarship his homiletical innovation at Emanu-El.

The Jewish press provided fairly extensive coverage of the lectures. The *Jewish Times* offered very complete abstracts of the second and third lectures, and only because of technical difficulties did it omit an abstract of the first.[61] The *Jewish Messenger* reported on and briefly summarized all six lectures, paying particular attention to the two lectures which it felt related most to Judaism: "The Fall of Jerusalem" and "Martyrs and Martyrdom."

As might have been expected, the reactions of these two newspapers to the Lyric Hall series reflected their divergent attitudes to Judaism. The Reform *Jewish Times*, edited by leftist Reformer Moritz Ellinger, approved of the lectures which it covered. There was no hint of criticism. Perhaps Ellinger felt that Adler's idealism and scholarship were in the interest of Reform Judaism; Ellinger himself had proclaimed the compatibility of science with Judaism, the nonauthority of biblical miracles, and the lack of dogmas in Judaism.[62] Still, he devoutly affirmed belief in one God who created the universe as the basis for Jewish union, but considered monotheism to be self-evident and not a dogma.[63] Believing as he did, and not perceiving Adler's nontheistic point of view, at least at first, he endorsed the first three Lyric Hall lectures.

The *Jewish Messenger*, edited by the Orthodox Reverend Samuel Myer Isaacs and his son, generally reported with favor on Adler's lectures,[64] yet it did not hesitate to criticize opinions which it felt were detrimental to Judaism and which veered too far from accepted Jewish theology. It was also sensitive to some of the ramifications for Judaism of Adler's scholarly methodology. For instance, his description of the downfall of Jerusalem caused by republican prophetic forces overthrowing the aristocratic priestly dominance of the Sadducees elicited this comment from the paper:

> His views however at times smacked of paradox, and it was difficult then to understand where history ended and philosophy began. The pertinancy of some of his utterances, too, might be doubted, as, for instance, when he said that Jerusalem fell, not through Divine chastisement, but through the efforts of republicanism to crush aristocratic power. He seemed to make popular currents the cause of political upheaval; but currents are blind forces obedient to the laws created by a higher intelligence, who maketh the minds his messengers. The tendency of the lecturer to revert everything to historical laws and the philosophy of history, is an excellent trait of the mind when not carried to excess. But laws are merely methods of creation, not creators; and too often the philosophy of history is the unphilosophical mysticism and sophistry of the historian.[65]

One detects the paper's attempt to reemphasize Providence and Providential involvement in Jewish history to counter Adler's secular philosophico-historical method of analysis.

The *Jewish Messenger* disapproved even more strongly of Adler's conception of martyrs, for it felt that the long tradition of Jewish martyrdom—Jews dying for the sanctification of God's name—had by implication been severely and unfairly slighted.

> . . . His theories were upheld at the expense of injustice to the ancient Hebrews, and to the unnecessary depreciation of one of the highest motives that can sway mankind. We regret that we cannot assent even tacitly to his expressions and deductions upon purely religious questions, and feel confident that, to be useful to the community as his friends desire, he will, as he gains experience and knowledge of men, recognize weakness and danger where he now heads boldly and without fear.[66]

The paper felt that his ostensible religious radicalism would mellow as he matured, and never entertained the possibility that he would one day stand outside of the Jewish world. It was very much mistaken.

The paper also mistakenly understood Adler to have equated religion with superstition, and it took him to task: "Affirming rather strongly that 'where knowledge ends religion begins,' he seemed to make religion accountable for all the vagaries of the spirit and the delusions of the ignorant."[67] Actually, the clause "where knowledge ends, religion begins" should have represented a problem for a neo-Kantian like Adler as well. At any rate, the paper vigorously defended the integrity of religion as a whole primarily to prevent the identification of Judaism with superstition.

From the nature of its criticism of Adler, it is evident that the editors of the *Jewish Messenger* were aware of some of the implications of contemporary scholarship for religion and for Judaism. Yet, like virtually all dedicated Jewish intellectual leaders at that time, they did not apply the conclusions of modern learning to Judaism. While the paper assented to Adler's critical examinations of Brahma, Buddha, and Mohammed, it took exception when it perceived critical methods of investigation and ideas applied even slightly to Judaism.

Despite finding fault with some of Adler's views, the *Jewish Messenger*, on the whole, treated him with respect. It saw him much in the same light as did the *Jewish Times:* an idealistic, scholarly Reform Jew of valuable educational worth to the Jewish community. The *Jewish Messenger* lauded his lecture series and on several occasions proposed the institution of other such lecture series in the community. It concluded that "if Dr. Adler could hold the unflagging attention of his audience for nearly two hours on such diverse topics as the relation of capital to labor, metaphysics, and the qualities of the Ego, then it proved that our New York coreligionists are lecture loving after all and we are ready to encourage talent, when agreeably presented."[68]

Two weeks later, three days before Adler's "Martyrs and Martyrdom" lecture, a *Jewish Messenger* editorial recommended the following:

> The success which has attended Dr. Felix Adler's courses of historical lectures makes feasible a plan which would be adopted with the happiest results. It is simply this: to start a course of lectures on Jewish history and literature to be given in rotation by some of our prominent rabbis. Not our Jewish citizens only would be benefited by such lectures, but the general public, too, would be enlightened on subjects of which they do not possess too much knowledge. Such a course started by Reverend James Freeman Clarke has met with success in Boston where the lecturers are prominent clergymen of all denominations. Among ourselves the task is much easier.[69]

The paper repeated this proposal in its editorial page at the conclusion of the Lyric Hall series.

> Dr. Adler concluded his lectures this week; and besides instructing his audiences in matters concerning which they were not too well informed before the season, he has demonstrated that the public will encourage every laudable effort of this kind, and will welcome him or any colleague, in the same path. We are now favored with a half dozen Jewish clergymen, who can enlighten the public in good English on topics of interest, who are esteemed in their pulpits by their respective congregations, but who would lose none of that esteem if they consented to appear at intervals on the lecture platform and discourse, unrestricted by the presence of the pulpit and prayer making, on Judaism in its relations to science and history and kindred topics.[70]

The paper recognized that Adler filled a void in New York Jewish communal life, and it sought to rectify the religio-cultural deficiency.

The outcome of the wide public acceptance of Adler's lectures and the lobbying effort by the *Jewish Messenger* was the inauguration of a public lecture series in the fall of 1875 by the newly formed New York YMHA (1874). While not actually realizing the *Jewish Messenger*'s goals—its subjects were generally too secularly oriented—the lecture program of the YMHA nevertheless filled the cultural void of New York Jewry. In the next two years, the YMHA invited such nationally prominent figures as

Carl Schurz, Hon. Simon Wolf, S. S. Packard, O. B. Frothingham, Joseph Seligman, Rabbi de Sola Mendes, and others to address the public on diverse issues.[71] Topics ranged from matters of Jewish religion and Jewish wit and humor to modern architecture, Shakespeare, and business.

Curiously, Felix Adler, perhaps the man most responsible for inspiring Jewish-sponsored public lectures in New York, was not invited to speak at the YMHA. This exclusion puzzled the Jewish newspapers, which commented on his absence from the speakers' roll.[72] On September 24, 1875, Phil Point, New York correspondent to Cincinnati's *American Israelite,* wrote that the YMHA had displayed an excellent sign of liberalism in extending an invitation to O. B. Frothingham, the "most eloquent of liberals." But the lack of an invitation to Adler, he commented, was "a strange and unaccountable omission. The learned and fervidly eloquent Cornell Professor is heard too seldom in this city of his adoption and where so many of his friends wish to listen to him."

Actually the reasons for Adler's exclusion from the YMHA speaker's list were not so "strange and unaccountable"; in fact, they appear rather obvious. The first president of the YMHA was none other than Lewis May, president of Temple Emanu-El. Another central member of the YMHA's board was Myer Stern, secretary of Emanu-El.[73] Following the "temple sermon" incident, these men were probably not too eager to have Adler employ the YMHA as a public platform, being aware of his candid rebuff of the Emanu-El trustees. To one or both of these men, not inviting Adler to speak may well have been a personal matter of honor and, perhaps, even vengeance. One year later, on October 6, 1876, Phil Point reported in the *American Israelite* on "excellent authority" that while many members of the YMHA desired to hear Adler lecture, the board will not invite him "owing to the antipathy toward that gentleman by one of the directors."

Of immediate personal significance to Adler, the Lyric Hall lectures established his reputation as an excellent lecturer and transformed him into a scholarly Jewish celebrity. His appointment at Cornell University in the spring of 1874 only enhanced his public stature. He was invited to address New York's Liberal Club, the American Geographical Society, and the American Oriental Society.[74] And President Barnard of Columbia College, acknowledging "the strongly favorable impression which you have already produced upon the mind of the country," requested that he contribute three scholarly articles to *Johnson's New Universal Cyclopedia,* of which Barnard was editor.[75] Adler accepted the invitation and published articles on "Jewish Literature," "Jewish Sects," and "Jews" in the *Cyclopedia.*[76] Barnard, like most everyone else, regarded Adler as a Jew, as a member of the Jewish community, and as an expert on Judaism.

The Cornell Experience

One of the more significant consequences of Adler's Lyric Hall lectures was his appointment as nonresident professor of Hebrew and Oriental literature at Cornell University in the spring of 1874. President Andrew D. White of Cornell had attended two or three of the Lyric Hall lectures, had been deeply impressed, and moved to hire him.[77] For Adler, the teaching offer came at a particularly propitious time. Having rejected the rabbinate, the profession to which his educational training had supposedly been geared, he was now without a job and a profession. A college-teaching career seemed to be an attractive alternative and a solution to the immediate problem of finding suitable employment.

The appointment emerged from an agreement between President White and some of Adler's friends, principally Joseph Seligman.[78] Owing to the lack of Cornell funds, Adler's patrons agreed to fund a visiting professorship in Hebrew and Oriental literature with Adler the appointee. He was to receive a stipend of fifteen hundred dollars for his annual three-month teaching tenure, plus an apartment on the university grounds when at Cornell.[79] On April 9, 1874, on behalf of the trustees, President White formally invited Adler to assume the position, promising "to do all in my power to cooperate in making your instruction in all respects successful and your residence satisfactory."[80]

White's active pursuit of Adler for the Cornell faculty was motivated by a number of factors. He was extremely impressed by Adler's scholarly credentials. Men such as he, trained rigorously in European learning, were still rather scarce in America; he clearly felt that Adler would make valuable academic contributions to Cornell. As he wrote Seligman concerning the early fiscal difficulties involved in employing Adler, "it seems to me . . . a very great pity for so valuable a scholar as Dr. Adler not to have the opportunity to bring his knowledge to bear upon the young men of the nation."[81] It was no doubt expected that Adler's knowledge of Hebrew might bolster Cornell's already highly developed program in linguistics, semitics, and Near Eastern languages.[82] In addition, Professor William C. Russel, vice-president of Cornell, suggested that Adler could dispel some of the vast ignorance of the student body in the diverse aspects of Hebrew literature.[83] Then too, many Cornell students and residents of Ithaca assumed that, as a Jew, Adler would introduce them to the basic doctrines and beliefs of the Jewish religion.[84] That he did not fulfill these last expectations, however—he did not regard his professional role to be that of a teacher of Judaism—contributed greatly to the emerging friction between him and members of the local community.[85]

In appointing Adler to the faculty, White—ever defending Cornell's novel, controversial, and tenuous status as a "nonsectarian Christian" institution—appears to have been also interested in achieving other more ideological goals. In his letter to Seligman, he wrote:

> Cornell is one of the first institutions established on the basis of complete equality between men of every shade of religious ideas and of complete liberty in the formation and expression of thought. Dr. Adler if I am not mistaken is a man calculated by his lectures as well as by his influence in other ways to promote those studies calculated to break down all unfortunate barriers of creed which so long afflicted mankind. And this it was that led me at the outset to take a real interest in the case.[86]

It seems probable that White wished to promote the nonsectarian character of his school by hiring a Jew on the staff. Apparently he even suggested having services led by Hebrew preachers at Cornell.[87] Given White's personal religious liberalism and profession of a sort of evolutionary deism, Adler's appointment was in keeping with his intellectual temperament and religious proclivities. Evidently White sensed that Adler was a Jew seeking to remove all religious, creedal barriers now; unlike Gustav Gottheil, he heartily endorsed that goal.

Russel, confidant of White, and acting president during White's years abroad, may also have played a part in bringing Adler to Cornell. He proposed to White that Adler would attract Jews to the university. "How many will come on account of Adler? We cannot do better than encourage them."[88] He himself eagerly awaited the influx of Jews to Cornell because he sensed a spiritual affinity among them, Cornell University, and Cornell's graduates.

> Think of it—Where do our graduates go to church when in New York? To Frothingham's. Who compose half of his congregation? Hebrews. The old seekers after truth have travelled from Mt. Sinai up the Sixth Avenue and there they meet the Cornell boys. Will they not likely push on further and find what they want where the Cornell boys found their starting point? Yes, from the beginning it has been in my bones that we should find great support among these men whom none of [our] sects will recognize.[89]

Adler's appointment to Cornell thrilled his friends and supporters. In a letter of congratulation, Joseph Seligman wrote to him:

> I have no doubt but what your friends will find their expectations realized and that you will continue to render your lectures interesting

and instructive. . . . With the prospect of a long life of usefulness before you and with your known habits of industry, I am satisfied that your own hopes and those of your friends will be realized. I shall be glad to hear frequently from you.[90]

Abraham Geiger, responding to two letters from Adler informing him of the appointment, congratulated the young man, wished him "God's speed" and noted the "good fortune" Adler had at his "youthful age to commence a most honorable career."[91]

The joy at Adler's appointment was not restricted solely to his family and friends. Rev. S. M. Isaacs, editor of the *Jewish Messenger,* hailed the event as a "grand concession to the liberality of the age," benefiting the American Jewish community as a whole. So happy was Isaacs that on April 11, 1874 he discussed Adler's appointment in his Sabbath sermon. He published his thoughts in the next issue of his paper on April 17, 1874.

It is significant of the progress of culture in this country, when a thriving educational institution—such as Cornell University—adds to its faculty a young and talented Israelite to fill the professorship of Hebrew and Oriental Literature. Ezra Cornell intended from the first that there should be no religious distinctions in his college; that its advantages should be open to men of all creeds, and to men of no creed, and that its officers and professors should be equally unrestricted by doctrinal ties. It was therefore proper that to the Baptist, the Unitarian, the Catholic, the Episcopalian, the Freethinker, and the Methodist, a Jew should be added, to fully prove the consistency of Mr. Cornell's plan and action. We hail the appointment of a Hebrew professor as a grand concession to the liberality of the age, and congratulate the faculty of Cornell University in having thus demonstrated their freedom from prejudice.

Viewed in a personal aspect, the selection of Dr. F. Adler as Hebrew professor is exceedingly happy and timely. . . . His opening address at the Temple will be remembered as an eloquent effort, and his more recent lectures on Oriental literature and philosophy stamped him as an orator and thinker of rare merit. . . . They [Adler's supporters who financed the position] have the satisfaction of having not only placed their friend-protege in an honorable position, but elevated the Jewish name and Jewish interests in the opinion of the world, again demonstrating that the Jew has higher ideas than mere moneymaking.

The news of Adler's appointment did not escape the European Jewish press. The German Jewish weekly *Israelitische Wochenschrift* took note of his appointment.[92] One can only surmise the German Jewish reaction to the news, but whatever happiness the glad tidings produced may well have been mixed with some disillusionment. Geiger's dream of founding a Faculty of Judaica or, at the least, of having Jewish instructors teach Jüdische Wissenschaft within the context of a general university was slowly being realized, not in Germany as was once hoped, but in America.

At the outset, Adler enjoyed his tenure at Cornell. He especially appreciated the beautiful natural environment in which Cornell was situated.[93] He also enjoyed considerable popularity as a lecturer: "His classroom was at first crowded with students, professors, and townspeople."[94] His impact on some of his students can be seen from a letter of F. P. Smith, who wrote his teacher on April 1, 1875:

> While at Cornell, I attended all your lectures from the very first. The impartial manner in which you treated your subject made a deep impression upon my mind and the ideas you advanced opened up a new field of thought into which I never dreamed of entering. The idea of studying the history of the Jews as you would study the history of any other nation, of reading their works as you would Homer, Goethe, or Shakespeare, had never occurred to me. But after hearing you the scales fell from my eyes and now I am able to see somewhat. I have begun to lay aside those prejudices to which unreasoning orthodoxy gives rise and to look upon those grand old records of the Jews with some degree of independence.[95]

But the pleasantness of his tenure did not last long. As professor of Hebrew and Oriental literature, Adler lectured not on what some may have expected to hear, but rather on the subject of greatest import and attraction for him—the history and comparison of religions and their lessons for contemporary religion. While his lectures have not been preserved, evidence from other sources—his Inaugural Address and a course outline[96]—clearly indicate that he discussed the very same topics and issues at Cornell as at Lyric Hall and at the various other public lectures. Introducing Cornell and the residents of Ithaca to the modern European scholarship on religion, Adler became embroiled in a heated religious controversy not entirely of his own making.

When Adler returned to the United States in 1873, he discovered an America grappling with many of the identical issues which he had faced in Germany. In the 1870s science—particularly Darwinism and Spencerism—supplemented by the broad discipline of comparative religion, was undermining traditional beliefs and inducing a spirit of religious liberalism, freethought, skepticism, and even atheism.[97] The Bible—New Testament as well as Old Testament—was losing its hold over many Americans; in its stead "evolution" became the rallying point of modernity, and most denominations struggled to formulate some type of approach to the theory consistent with their doctrinal ideals.[98]

Understandably, the intellectual centers of America—the universities—became the focal point and breeding ground of religious tension; they presented the stage for the confrontation between European scholarship and American Christianity. The attempt to maintain and improve the quality of education required keeping pace with modern ideas, and that, in turn, necessitated the increased intensification or introduction of scientific courses (depending on the institution) and the scientific spirit of free inquiry. In most instances, this spirit clashed with the sectarian ideologies dominating the vast majority of American universities. Universities, therefore, confronted their theological sponsors with the challenge of coming to terms with modern learning. As a result, the ensuing two to three decades witnessed the demise of much authoritarian dogmatism and sectarian control in the universities, plus a revolutionary change in the educational curricula and format of American higher education.[99]

From its inception in 1868, Cornell University lay mired in the center of religious controversy. It was one of the first universities founded as a nonsectarian institution and supported by state funds. Its founders, Ezra Cornell and Andrew White, had concentrated the school's educational program in science and only to a somewhat lesser extent in liberal arts. The educational and "nonreligious" direction of the school actuated an ongoing feud between the university and the conservative religious residents and militant churches of upstate New York. The latter feared that the religious liberalism fostered by Cornell would uproot the Christian faith; they took every opportunity to taunt Ezra Cornell, Andrew White, and the institution. For their part, Ezra Cornell and White tried to keep peace with their neighbors by attempting to establish a fragile equilibrium characterizing the school as a "nonsectarian Christian" institution.[100]

Adler stepped into an already volatile situation. Nevertheless, while other prominent visiting professors at Cornell had aroused anger and had been "declared dangerous"—men such as James Russell Lowell, Jean Louis Agassiz, Goldwin Smith, Bayard Taylor, Edward Augustus Freeman, and James Anthony Froude[101]—his scholarly analysis of religion and its diverse positive forms brought the festering religious antagonism to a head; his lectures were perceived as an outright attack against Christianity. In reality, his classes demonstrated the intellectual incoherency of maintaining a platform of "nonsectarian Christianity" since "nonsectarian" scholarship in religion implicitly disputed Christian premises. But Adler's intellectual rigor comforted neither Cornell's Board of Trustees nor the local residents: the board found its delicate balance upset; the residents felt their religion threatened. Trapped in the center of the debate, he was viewed as the primary cause of the latest anti-Cornell outcry.

Letters of Acting President Russel to Andrew White testify to the existence and nature of the antipathy toward Adler, an antipathy shared by Ithaca townspeople, their churchmen, and even some Cornell faculty, and arising in the very first month of his tenure. Some people objected to some of the ideas in his lectures. His description of the Immaculate Conception of the Buddha and of the Buddha as a Savior of Man outraged their Christian sensibilities,[102] as did his citing of Lubbock's contention that "God is not universal in the race but comes with civilization."[103] Adler conveyed his regrets to Russel on his depiction of the Buddha, but the damage had already been done.[104] He himself later noted "the adverse turn at Cornell" after this lecture.[105] In addition, his private Saturday class on David F. Strauss upset even the liberal Russel, who acknowledged Adler's right "to read anything he thinks profitable to the students," yet insisted "that we have no more right to teach antichristian than we have to teach Christian doctrine."[106] Finally, Russel commented that some people were annoyed with Adler's Buddha lecture, having been misled by the announcement that he would speak on Oriental history and literature only to discover him lecturing on religion: "The idea has been expressed that there was something indecent in publishing one title and lecturing on something else."[107]

This discrepancy between the Cornell community's expectations of what Adler would teach and what he actually did teach is alluded to on a more general plane by his former student Andrew B. Humphrey. Humphrey (Cornell, 1875) suggests that Adler was hired by White to introduce the Jewish religion to Cornell's growing number of journalism students, "who sought the broadest culture they could get."[108] Humphrey's analysis of White's motives for hiring Adler, however, is less significant as an objective historical explanation than as a subjective understanding of Adler's purpose at Cornell; for his appraisal reflects that of a larger group of people who understood Alder to be representative of American Jewry and Judaism. According to Humphrey, he was "announced as the son of the distinguished Rabbi Adler of New York and as 'a strict adherent to the Jewish faith.' " But as Humphrey notes, "Dr. Adler did not represent the orthodox Jewish faith and was manly enough not to conceal it." He cites an editorial of the *Cornell Review,* June 1874, which concluded:

> We have no objection whatever to the establishment of a course of lectures in the university, however rankly it may savor of rationalism, provided it is so declared and understood in advance.
>
> In the case of the lectures now under discussion, it is an undeniable

fact that this so called course of lectures upon Hebrew and Oriental Literature has been painfully calculated to develop in young minds, at least, strongly rationalistic views.

The deeply rooted antagonism to Adler found a variety of expressions. He was accused of cultivating an undefined "tendency," a "tendency" of which Russel remarked in Adler's defense, "in vain I ask 'tendency' of what?"[109] While Adler's opponents may not have been able to adumbrate "the tendency," their intuitive sense of its existence was historically justified; perceptions of "the tendency" were indicative of the growing American religious turmoil at that time.

Russel also referred to traits in Adler's personality that provoked furious opposition to him. He described him as "earnest," "bold," "speculative," but "unnecessarily reckless" and lacking in tact, as reflected in the Buddha incident.[110] Apparently concurring with White's estimation of Adler, Russel also observed,

> you [White] hit the trouble exactly. A. is very able, but he is conceited and he thinks it very noble to assume the role of advocate. . . . He wins many friends but makes some enemies. He is attractive by his courage and his clearness and impressiveness, but he expresses his opinions of those whom he considers his inferiors in a way that irritates them. . . . I am afraid that he mistakes opposition for progress and that he counts his gains by the number of his opponents. In fact, he is young, and a young Jew and very able.[111]

This was not the only time Adler was called conceited; in later years, even members of the Ethical Society found him haughty and somewhat imperious.

Adler's Jewish origin could only have inflamed the passions of the local populace. After having checked Cornell for its suitability for his son, E. D. Morris, brother of Cornell's Professor John Morris, wrote to President White objecting to Adler's presence on the staff. He felt that Adler was undermining the Christian nature of the school. He had attended one of his lectures and found it offering the "cheapest sort of infidelity. . . . Cornell cannot afford to have such a teacher on its faculty. . . . I do not know whether this young *Rabbi* [emphasized by Morris] is with you still."[112]

The very appointment of Felix Adler, a Jew, ignited discontent in some Christian quarters. The *Jewish Messenger* noted that the *Christian Statesmen,* "the organ of the Constitution tinkers, is horrified at the appointment of Dr. Felix Adler as a Cornell professor and thinks that Christianity is imperiled in consequence."[113] In response, and probably to show the

Jewish community that not all Christians opposed the appointment, the *Jewish Messenger* reprinted the following from the May 8 issue of the *Christian Union:*

> What harm can come to Christian students from receiving instruction in Hebrew history and literature from a thoroughly educated, nobleminded Hebrew? Other things being equal, is not a Hebrew, of all others, best qualified to give such instruction? What could be better calculated to awaken a suspicion that Christianity is pitiably weak than the fears for its safety which so many of its misguided champions exhibit?[114]

The existence of such a debate even before the delivery of his controversial lectures suggests that Adler's Jewish origin was a significant factor contributing to the animosity which he experienced after his appointment.

Russel's evaluation of the situation at Cornell one month following the appointment is rather apt: "On the whole I find a very pretty mess in the teakettle."[115] The townspeople were stirred up;[116] the *Ithaca Democrat* was fulminating against Adler;[117] Rev. Charles M. Tyler, the pastor of Ithaca's Congregational Church, was so disturbed that he refused to attend Adler's subsequent lectures;[118] Professor Waterman T. Hewett of Cornell thought he was "undermining our faith;"[119] and Cornell's register, W. D. Wilson, recommended to White that Adler not be permitted to deliver his Inaugural Address at the university commencement exercises, for in the face of the opposition to him and a declining enrollment at the university, he deemed it very "unwise."[120]

The situation at Cornell did not improve. For the duration of his three-year tenure, Adler was subjected to unceasing personal abuse from his conservative Christian opponents. When his contract expired in 1876, it was not renewed. He left Cornell, abruptly terminating a university-teaching career which did not resume until his appointment as professor of political and social ethics at Columbia University in 1902.

A controversy later arose as to the circumstances of Adler's departure from Cornell. Had the University refused to renew his contract, or had he left of his own accord?[121] Upon his death in April 1933, spokesmen for Cornell defended the university against the charge appearing in obituary columns that Adler "had been banished from Cornell University in 1876 for his radical ideas."[122] They insisted that he had left of his own volition with the best wishes of the entire Cornell community. "Dr. Adler . . . left Ithaca, followed only by the regrets of the University community that he could not become permanently identified with the institution for which he had done so much;"[123] and, "when Dr. Adler left the University he had the good will of all who knew him."[124]

The evidence does not support these claims but rather conclusively refutes them. In a letter written to Adler on March 12, 1877, William Russel apologized for having remained silent about his "chances of returning here."[125] Adler had previously expressed interest, either in oral or written communication, in retaining his position at Cornell. Aware of the trustees' opposition to rehiring him, Russel had refrained from discussing the issue with Adler earlier. But now, in this rather self-consciously defensive letter, Russel lamented his lack of power in the decision-making process. "Had I the power," he asserted, "I would make such an engagement, for I believe that your lectures here did nothing but good. . . . But I have no power in the matter and have no right to speak for those who do." This disclaimer did not deter Russel from somewhat feebly justifying his not taking up Adler's case before those very same people who did have such power on the grounds of his concern for the best interests of the school. "My charge is this University," he professed. "Besides my children I have no other interest. . . . Am I justified in seeking a conflict in which we may receive a disgrace which may last beyond the lives of all those who now control our decisions? True wisdom, it seems to me, forbids my bringing on a contest where victory would not be of greatest importance but where defeat would be of lasting injury." An administrative pragmatist, Russel knew that he could not overcome the trustees' antagonism to Adler and felt that any such attempt could have irreparably compromised the university's "usefulness." And despite his avowal to the contrary, it is not at all certain that Russel himself really wanted Adler to return.

Russel and the Cornell trustees were thrust into a rather delicate situation. Joseph Seligman had sent Russel a letter notifying him of his continued willingness to fund a grant renewing Adler's contract. Russel laid the letter before the Executive Committee of Cornell's Board of Trustees on May 3, 1877. The decision to reject Seligman's overture was a foregone conclusion. Adler was simply not wanted at Cornell. Men such as Henry Sage, the treasurer of the institution and a member of Tyler's Congregational Church, had found his religious views and the vehement popular reactions against them detrimental to the best interests of the university. The committee searched for a principle which would enable it simultaneously to reject Seligman's offer, thus excluding Adler from Cornell, and to dissipate religious tension in the community while preserving in a face-saving manner Cornell's reputation for academic freedom.

Russel's letter to Seligman on May 5, 1877 reveals the principle which was adopted.[126] While thanking Seligman for "his interest in the University" and appreciative of his liberality "in sentiment and in purse," Russel informed him that

> the Executive Committee of our Board of Trustees . . . object to having professors nominated to them from the outside. Views, often independent of talents and singleness of purpose on the part of the candidate, influence appointments and of such considerations none but those concerned in the management of educational institutions can judge. The Executive Committee, therefore, will not again accept any propositions for endowments where the choice of the incumbent is not left without restriction to the Trustees.

Russel personally concurred with the principle although he expressed regret at "its application to Dr. Adler." Objectively and in the long run, the principle enunciated was farsighted and made sound administrative sense; but the background from which it emerged and the time at which it was first invoked leave no doubt against whom it was specifically directed.

In an open letter addressed to the alumni and undergraduates of Cornell on May 4, 1877,[127] President White reaffirmed Cornell's commitment to academic freedom and its status as a nonsectarian institution. He also praised Adler and attempted to explain the reason for his departure. He lauded Adler's "devotion to study and . . . faithfulness to his convictions." He repudiated descriptions of Adler as an atheist or godless, observing that as a "graduate of one of the most renowned Christian colleges, [he] had been blessed with all the safeguards against error which an institution noted for its orthodoxy could throw around him." Adler had received the "highest commendations of his character and scholarship from Christian divines and professors," White informed the Cornell community and the public. He also reminded them that Adler had not proselytized students and that no student had been required to attend his elective courses. White created the impression that Adler's faculty position was entirely consistent with the character of the school and that Adler was, therefore, not coerced to leave because of Christian Church pressure on Cornell's trustees. Rather, he asserted, the trustees "prefer an incumbent who can reside steadily at the University and who can give his whole attention to it."

This explanation notwithstanding, White still fostered the misleading impression that Adler had left of his own accord, with the mutual understanding of the Board of Trustees, to devote "himself to a new work in our great metropolis [New York] which will doubtless require all his energies." This impression was totally false. Alder sought the reappointment and was hurt and disappointed when it was denied. In his "First

Anniversary Address" to the Society of Ethical Culture, less than two weeks after White's open letter, he recounted the abusive intolerance to which he had been subjected at Cornell. He underscored that Ezra Cornell's aim in founding the institution had been to create a university patterned after the University of Berlin; unfortunately, religious opposition militated against the full realization of this project and also forced his departure.

Adler himself never explained the full circumstances of his departure, and speculation as to whether it was freely chosen or a forced resignation continued through the summer in the *Daily Graphic*.[128] On a few occasions, the paper reported that Adler had been requested to withdraw his candidacy and that his refusal led to a formal non-reappointment.[129] While this account cannot be corroborated, it certainly appears plausible. The paper also insisted that Adler had been compelled to leave Cornell because of church pressure on its trustees.[130] Finally, it asserted that Adler declined to reveal the facts publicly because, despite the shabby treatment which he had received, he still considered Cornell to be the most liberal university in the country and did not seek to prejudice it.[131]

In a later letter to William Russel, Adler bemoaned what he conceived to be the trend of President White to "establish the Christian character of his university. It seems to me that when he used the word Christian he means thereby 'moral in the best sense.' But it is precisely this identification of the highest morality with so distinctly a sectarian system as the Christian that is particularly grating to the sensibilities of those who are not Christians and who do not desire to be classed as such."[132] Obviously, Adler still cared for the institution. And this concern for Cornell and all American universities found expression in his repeated regrets at the sectarian, intolerant spirit dominating American universities, especially when compared to their German counterparts.[133]

Adler's stormy tenure at Cornell foreshadowed the religious outburst which erupted in the Jewish community following the creation of the Ethical Culture Society. Only at this later date, in 1877, did the Jewish community realize the extent of the religious change which he had undergone. His tenure at Cornell also underlined one of the more curious ironies of American Jewish history: this man, who was only the second Jewish professor of Hebrew ever appointed to an American university, was actually passing out of his Jewishness (or had already done so) during his appointment;[134] and in fact this same professor was probably the first—and paradigmatic—American Jew to leave his socio-religious fellowship on strictly intellectual grounds. The irony, however, became apparent to American Jewry only one or two years following the termination of his Cornell professorship, and it was not much appreciated.

Adler's lectures at Cornell were not the sole matters of his concern during 1873–76. A number of times he wrote to his fellow Cornell professor James Morgan Hart of his preoccupation with "outside matters."[135] He busied himself with private study, preparation for guest lectures, and the writing of scholarly articles. In 1875 he attempted to advance scholarship in the field of his own greatest interest—comparative religion—by trying to establish a Journal of the Comparative Science of Religion. He sought to enlist the support of some of the world's most renowned men in the field: James Martineau, T. K. Cheyne, T. W. Rhys Davids, A. H. Sayce, and E. B. Tylor. While generally positively inclined toward the idea, these men pointed to the editorial, intellectual, and financial problems intrinsically involved in the endeavor. An enthusiastic Adler dropped the idea.[136]

In this period he also intimately acquainted himself with the stream of American Transcendentalism and the contemporary trend of American Free Religion. He personally met with some of the foremost intellectual and liberal religionists in the country: Ralph Waldo Emerson, Samuel Johnson, John Fiske, George Peabody, Wendell Phillips, O. B. Frothingham, and President Eliot of Harvard, among others.[137] He assiduously studied the writings of Theodore Parker and Emerson, which profoundly colored his religious and intellectual thinking. Emerson's sayings and essays, in particular, found repeated expression in numerous addresses of Adler throughout his lifetime.[138] Emerson's stress on individualism and self-reliance, on the spiritual appreciation of nature, and on the sense of the exalted significance of the present surfaced constantly in Adler's early writings. Emerson confirmed for him, and expounded in rather varied and eloquent fashion, the crucial lesson which Adler had already learned from the Prophets, from Kant, and from the awareness of his personal ability to actualize his desire to lead a spiritually elevated life—"the Higher Life is possible to man as a matter of experience."[139]

Consistent with his temperament and concerns, Adler's scholarly research was not divorced from his practical desire to implement a humanitarian religion. He still yearned to apply Lange's lessons to the American industrial-labor scene. His limited teaching term at Cornell permitted his return to Europe in the summer of 1875. In Germany he met with Pastor Gustav Werner, who was a pioneer in labor industrial-educational cooperation. He was very impressed with the agricultural and factory cooperatives which Werner had established in Reutlingen and Schwarzwald, South Germany, and with his religious ideology, which emphasized the love and deeds of Johannine Christianity rather than the prevailing faith and creed of Pauline Christianity.[140] One year later he visited the "Industrial Works Association" in Vermont. The association was a cooperative labor venture which organized all facets of life on a cooperative basis: work, recreation and culture, and education. From the association and a Mr. Ellis, its superintendent, Adler "received much valuable information, which [he] sincerely hope[d] may prove serviceable hereafter."[141] The association probably represented to Adler an American realization of Lange's notions of labor cooperation, and some of the early projects of the Ethical Culture Society mirror aspects of its activities.

In sum, following his return from Germany in 1873, Adler set about orienting himself to American religious life. Having spurned the Jewish ministry and having left Cornell, he was in need of a calling which would fulfill his yearning to apply practically an ethical religion founded on principles consistent with the modern scholarly and secular temper.

During 1873–76, his cognizance of the universality of his religion and religious demands crystallized and became sharply focused, especially as his acquaintanceship with non-Jewish thinkers of like mind grew. As a further step following his rejection of American Reform Judaism, Adler's increasing disenchantment with, and sense of alienation from, the American Jewish community during these three years is understandable. American Jewry possessed no intellectual figures of the stature of Emerson, T. W. Higginson, Samuel Johnson, Minot Savage, and O. B. Frothingham, men more in tune with his own religious-intellectual predilections and for whom he felt a strong spiritual affinity.

Certainly the American Jewish community was totally unprepared for the events of the next two to three years, at which time it branded Adler a heretic, traitor, and apostate Jew. American Jewry had completely misread its most prominent public son. It still considered him a Jew, putting forward "advanced religious views" perhaps,[142] young and inexperienced perhaps,[143] but a Jew nonetheless.[144] In fact, in July 1874, Adler was actually requested to officiate as rabbi at a Cleveland temple during the forthcoming High Holy Day services, a request which he did not fulfill.[145] American Jewry did not recognize the breach in his commitment to the Jewish socio-religious fellowship until the breach assumed a new institutionalized form. And when it finally realized that it had lost its most promising representative, its anger was not to be assuaged. Adler succeeded in cracking the broad consensus in American Jewry, and for this reason he came to be perceived as a dangerous threat to the seemingly stable nature of the American Jewish community.

Chapter IV

Creating a New Movement

The Founding of the New York Society for Ethical Culture

In a public lecture on Monday evening, May 15, 1876, Felix Adler and a few of his close friends introduced the idea of a Sunday lecture movement to be inaugurated in the fall. This lecture movement subsequently developed into the New York Society for Ethical Culture. The establishment of the society was fortuitous for Adler because it enabled him to satisfy both his spiritual goals and his material needs. The society furnished the necessary social group to implement his religio-ethical ideals; it also offered a job and professional calling for him as its leader, a position which he held, and in later years shared, until his death in 1933.

According to Adler, the man ultimately most responsible for the creation of the society was Julius Rosenbaum. Enthralled with Adler's Temple Sermon in 1873, Rosenbaum insisted that the "plan of the new religious organization" sketched by him in the sermon "should be put into operation . . . ; [he] would not let go [that] idea."[1] While Adler was at Cornell in the spring of 1876, Rosenbaum acted as the prime agent organizing the movement. He arranged the May 15 lecture, coordinated the raising of paid subscriptions to the lecture, and raised the greatest number of subscriptions himself.[2] He also was a constant source of personal encouragement. As opposition to the idea of a Sunday lecture series sponsored by Jews mounted, Rosenbaum assured Adler of the potential success of the movement, repeatedly encouraged him, and expressed the "hope that your courage and faith may not fail you in spite of any disappointments or obstacles that may present themselves and meet us on our way."[3]

While Rosenbaum's letters reflect his desire to establish a broad platform for Adler's ethical message, they also reveal the indefinite conception of the nature of the Sunday lecture movement in the mind of one of its major proponents. Rosenbaum regarded the "progressive movement" as an "experiment [which] can only be properly judged and its results estimated after a fair trial of six or twelve months."[4] He himself could not really have anticipated the character of the movement, for he wrote to Adler on May 5, 1876 that "the substance of our future plans and intentions . . . [is] left entirely to your discretion and judgment." Nevertheless, Rosenbaum, Adler, and a few of their intimate associates—Edward Lauterbach, Solomon Moses, Henry Friedman, and

Albert Levi—having amassed a paid subscription of one hundred members, convened a public meeting on May 15, 1876 at Standard Hall to announce the organization of a Sunday lecture movement.[5]

The audience was primarily Jewish, young, and for the most part—though not exclusively—consisted of members of Temple Emanu-El.[6] The Adler family, including Samuel, who had been "regularly posted" on the progress of the movement by Rosenbaum, attended as well.[7] Adler addressed the audience and outlined his understanding of the goals of the Sunday lecture movement. In light of the prevailing materialism and hollowness of life, in light of the grave doubts cast upon the faith of untold thousands, he proclaimed, "there is a great and crying evil in society. It is the want of purpose."[8] Man's inherent sense of right and wrong, grounded in his moral conscience, was losing its sway, Adler contended, and to achieve the needed individual and societal moral elevation, he proposed the formation of an association open to all which would set aside one day for weekly reunion to seek tranquility. The actual day selected, Adler asserted, was intrinsically irrelevant, but since American society had already chosen Sunday, for convenience's sake that day would be selected by the association. The Sunday meetings would feature no ceremonies, but simply a lecture and organ music to "elevate the heart." The lectures would attempt to trace the "history of human aspiration," he concluded, and to "set forth a standard of duty for today."

Adler explicitly renounced any desire to clash with existing religious denominations and sects by underscoring the exclusion of prayer and every form of ritual from the Sunday meetings. "Thus shall we avoid even the appearance of interfering with those to whom prayer and ritual, as a mode of expressing religious sentiment are dear." His exclusion of prayers and rituals reflected not only good diplomatic sense, but also his personal ideological position. He reiterated that the association wished to be a fellowship standing above all religious strife, a "common ground" where both worshipper and infidel could meet. "Diversity in the creed, unanimity in the deed. This is that practical religion from which none dissents," he declared. This universal fellowship dedicated to "the unselfish service of the common weal" really represented the means by which he could fulfill the goals he had already advanced in the Temple Sermon and hinted at in the Lyric Hall series.

In proposing a "practical religion" about which all could agree, Adler sought to avoid a confrontation with existing religions over his message; and, in fact, few people at the time regarded his message as a threat to Judaism and its institutions. Still, his lecture on the goals of the movement embodied a tacit denunciation of all positive religions. Underlying his suggestion to organize a fellowship to implement "practical religion" was the belief that positive religions were avoiding their own responsibilities in the "practical" sphere. Much to the chagrin of both Jews and Christians, he soon made explicit this implicit religious critique.

Adler's address excited many of the Jews in attendance, and the subscription list for future Sunday addresses in the fall steadily grew in number. By May 27 Rosenbaum's list totaled 132 names,[9] and by the autumn 252 people had contributed between ten and fifty dollars each to defray lecture expenses and had signed their names to the following declaration:

> We, the undersigned, agree to cooperate in a movement about to be initiated for the purpose of enabling Professor Felix Adler to deliver lectures on Sunday mornings during and after October next. The same to be accompanied by suitable music.[10]

The first Sunday lecture in the fall took place on October 15, 1876. Adler lectured every Sunday thereafter during the fall and spring, and he attracted an increasing following. In the course of the winter lectures, however, Adler ignored his previous renunciation of clashes with the positive religions. His lectures now incited the Jewish community, in particular, which began to view his lecture movement as a competing religious organization.

The leaders of the lecture movement decided to consolidate, and during the winter of 1876 agreed to form a more permanent religious association based on the lecture platform. On February 21, 1877, the New York Society for Ethical Culture was incorporated, declaring its fundamental object to be

> the mutual improvement in religious knowledge and the furtherance of religious opinion which shall be in part accomplished by a system of weekly lectures, in which the principles of ethics shall be developed, propagated, and advanced among adults, and in part by the establishment of a school or schools wherein a course of moral instruction shall be supplied for the young.[11]

A Board of Trustees was selected consisting of fifteen men: Joseph Seligman, Albert A. Levi, Henry Friedman, Edward Lauterbach, William Byfield, Joseph Seidenberg, Max Aberheim, Max Landman, Emil Salinger, Meyer Jonasson, Jacob Stettheimer, Jr., Samuel V. Speyer, Samuel A. Solomons, Julius Rosenbaum, and Marcus Goldman. Seligman was selected as the first president of the society. Adler was elected as lecturer, but he was also an ex-officio member of the board. He charted the direction of the organization, and as Radest correctly noted, "It was . . . Dr. Adler's society—and its members wanted it that way."[12]

The origin of the name "Ethical Culture" is somewhat shrouded in mystery. At the time of the society's creation, Adler does not appear to have publicly explicated what he meant by the phrase or the reasons for its selection. In later addresses, however, he reflected upon the term, and these reflections plus earlier clues shed some light on the issue. In his address "What Has Religion Done for Civilization?" November 14, 1897, Adler stressed the need for man to advance morally through the cultivation of his ethical capabilities. He acknowledged that however "curious" and "inadequate" the words "ethical culture" were— "I have wished a thousand times that we had some other words that would answer the purpose"—they still best reflected the "need of getting to work thoroughly and cultivating ourselves as you would cultivate the hard ground—rake it up and make it fruitful and do not spare the sharp spade in digging."[13]

In the 1870s, it seems that he envisioned the goal of one's ethical cultivation to be the harmonious development of man seeking perfection, much in the same sense as, and perhaps even identical to, Arnold's notion of "sweetness and light";[14] for in his address "The Ethics of Luxury," January 6, 1878, Adler appears to have subordinated morality to aesthetics. In citing the ends of humanity as the true, the good, the beautiful, love, and knowledge—that is, the "culture of the head and the heart"—he proclaimed ethical cultivation as the "instrument to bring this [the realization of these aesthetic ends] about, this longed for change."[15] He even suggested further that mankind needed more perfect models of humanity. If necessary, therefore, nine hundred and ninety people should work harder—some even in poverty if no alternative existed—so that ten more intellectually and aesthetically endowed people could be unburdened from their work and be free to think great thoughts, to live for art and music, and "to be guardians of what Arnold calls 'sweetness and light.' "[16]

But Adler's ethical philosophy developed over the years, and he came to identify moral advancement with the cultivation of one's singular innate qualities, imputing "worth" to an individual to the extent to which he perfected these qualities. He dismissed Arnold's cultural goal of the harmonious perfection of all things, and visualized the goal of Ethical Culture as the cultivation of one's characteristic quality, that is, the cultivation of one's own consciousness of "worth."[17] The phrase "Ethical Culture" still implied the cultivation of one's "ethical" behavior, but both the goal and the focus of "ethical" behavior had become modified.

Why did Adler choose the phrase "Ethical Culture" rather than, say, "Ethical Religion"? In the 1870s he seems to have regarded the meaning of the two terms to be identical; only later did he distinguish ethical *religion* from ethical *culture* with precise clarity.[18] Perhaps he revealed the primary reason for his preference for the one phrase over the other in a later address, "Huxley's Attitude Toward Religion," January 22, 1901. Adler unequivocally asserted in that lecture that he had wanted to attract as many people as possible "united in the passion for the Good" without having to wrangle over religion.[19] He had sought to establish as broad a base as possible for the society, and he feared that some liberals, freethinkers, agnostics, and atheists—wanting nothing to do with *religion*—might well have been repelled by an organization identified with and designated by that word. In a letter to Adler, April 29, 1876, in fact, Rosenbaum referred to the demand of some freethinkers—whether Jewish or not is not made clear—that his lectures be devoid of *religious* content.[20]

In retrospect, Adler's selection of the term *culture* was judicious. In the 1870s the broad term *culture* seems to have captured the imagination of much of the Western world, popularized in the main by Arnold's essays and subsequent book, *Culture and Anarchy.* Unlike the organized religions, "culture" appeared to many people to be in consonance with the temper of the times; many recognized the attainment of "culture" as a value replacing the religio-theological ideals of traditional religions, and the term *culture* acquired socio-religious status. One finds the *Jewish Messenger* analyzing Jewish spiritual, intellectual, and emotional accomplishments in terms of "cultural" achievements.[21] The liberal O. B. Frothingham went even further, proclaiming church-going as "a means of culture; its function is that of art; it belongs to those agencies by which men and women are refined in sentiment and desire."[22] In the world of religious scholarship "culture" had become an index by which to evaluate the relative degrees of sophistication of primitive and more "refined" religions. In sum, the term *culture* was quite fashionable, and Adler's selection of the word was in all probability prompted by the contemporary preoccupation with it.[23]

The reaction of the American Jewish community to the declaration of intent on May 15, 1876 to institute a Sunday lecture movement differed markedly from its later reaction to the lectures in the winter-spring of 1876–77. In the wake of the May address, the Jewish community only debated the nature of the lecture movement. In the winter-spring of 1876–77, however, the community had already begun to denounce Adler as a traitorous Jew. The divergent reactions resulted from the discrepancy between his May 15 promise not to interfere with the ritual sentiments of individuals and his severe criticism of accepted Jewish rituals and beliefs in subsequent lectures. The Jewish press generally understood Adler's May 15 address to claim nonintervention with the synagogues and temples of New York, and they reported this understanding to their Jewish readers.[24]

The fundamental Jewish reaction to the May address, as reflected in the Jewish press and in Rosenbaum's letters, revolved around one critical question: Was Adler initiating a *religious service* on Sundays? Except for one reference to his "practical religion," Adler himself did not refer to the Sunday lecture movement as a religious association, and he specifically ruled out prayer and religious rituals at the meetings, although not music. Nevertheless, indicative of the centrality of the sermon-address and organ music in Reform Jewish services,[25] some Jews interpreted the Sunday lecture movement to be a competing religious service threatening the integrity of the Jewish Sabbath. Rosenbaum's letters to Adler clearly suggest that the primary cause of opposition to the intended Sunday lecture movement was the *day* chosen. Rosenbaum wrote that Jews deem Sunday the Christian Sabbath and feel that Jews should not assemble "for the worthy purposes which we have in view." He added that even people who never attended the temple on Saturday would not attend their Sunday lectures.[26]

Through the spring and summer of 1876, the Jewish press abounded with discussions of the religious implications of the Sunday lecture movement. On June 9, 1876, the *Independent Hebrew* referred to it as a "Sunday Prayer Movement." One week later the paper cited an interview with a man connected with the movement who claimed that "prayers can always be said. If prevented on Saturday from saying them why not offer them on Sunday?" The reports in the *Jewish Messenger,* in particular, reflected the ambivalence of the Jewish community on the nature of the new movement. On the one hand, in reviewing the May lecture, the paper's reporter announced on May 19, 1876 that the Sunday lectures would be "devoid of religious references or bias" and were to be "wholly educational and practical." The reporter concluded that "provided the members do not swerve from it [the scope of the organization outlined above] in any respect, we can conceive no harm to be done by its establishment." In the same issue, however, under the heading "Some New Reformers," the *Jewish Messenger* editorialized against the possible change of the Sabbath to Sunday. Further, on June 2, 1876, a correspondent to the paper—"Ish Yehudi"—whom Rosenbaum identified as "young Isaacs" (son of the paper's editor)[27]—called Adler a "juvenile leader" and declared that the "institution of Sunday services among Israelites is a concession to Christianity." Yet two weeks later the *Jewish Messenger* reported that "the truth is that Dr. Felix Adler does not desire to institute so-called Sunday services."[28] It also printed letters from two correspondents, "Common Sense" and Alphonse A. Jacobi, who insisted that Adler did not intend to transfer the Jewish Sabbath to Sunday and that he was not endangering Judaism.[29]

Besides the Sunday issue, objections were raised about Adler's competence as a leader,[30] and it was suggested that self-employment might be his motive for organizing the association.[31] Still, the basic debate on the movement focused on the lecture day chosen—Sunday; no other aspect of his proposal received significant attention. A seemingly trivial issue side-tracked consideration of the underlying rationale for the lecture movement as outlined by Adler on May 15, 1876.

In reality, however, the Sunday services issue at this juncture in the evolution of American Judaism was by no means trivial; on the contrary, it was a crucial topic of concern. The contentiousness surrounding the institution of Sunday services in American Reform temples reflected both the direct impact of economics on Judaism and the subsequent American Jewish groping to define the essential character of the Jewish religion in the new socio-economic framework of American life. The debate over Adler's intentions was only part of a much wider debate in the American Jewish community, and it reveals a vitally significant chapter in American Jewish history.

By the 1870s, the Sunday service had become an important issue in Reform circles. The first attempt to institute Sunday services at an American temple in addition to Saturday services occurred in 1854 at the Har Sinai Temple in Baltimore; the services were discontinued after six months. Rabbi Samuel Hirsch introduced Sunday services in 1870 at the Kehillat Israel, Philadelphia, but they too were unsuccessful and were suspended shortly thereafter. Kaufmann Kohler initiated the first successful continuing Sunday service in 1874 at the Sinai Congregation, Chicago, to supplement his Saturday services. Upon his return from the Hochschule, Emil Hirsch followed Kohler's lead and was equally successful at the Har Sinai Temple in Baltimore in 1877. New York's Temple Emanu-El witnessed growing agitation during the 1870s for some type of Sunday service featuring a rabbinic sermon. Committees were appointed in 1874 and 1876 "to seek the advisability of instituting English sermons on Sunday."[32] In May 1879 Emanu-El members voted in favor of a Sunday address, 53–43; no action was taken, however, due to the close vote.[33]

In each case, the services were instituted or attempted because of the declining synagogue attendance on Saturdays resulting primarily from the Jewish preoccupation with business pursuits on the Sabbath. Through the decades from the 1850s on, the Jewish press constantly lamented Jewish religious laxity in general and the lack of Sabbath synagogue attendance in particular.[34] In his article of public repentance, Solomon Schindler perhaps best summarized the woeful synagogue-attendance situation. He recalled that upon his arrival at Boston's Temple Israel in 1874, he was faced with, and was expected to solve, one fundamental problem: filling the empty synagogue. He asserted that people were perfectly willing to pay for the construction and lavish decoration of the synagogue, as well as the salaries of its rabbi and its officers; they themselves, however, would not attend.[35] A Rosenbaum letter to Adler noted the identical phenomenon arising among prominent Emanu-El members such as Hallgarten and others.[36]

To combat this lack of attendance, Reform rabbis and their temples tried either to make the Saturday services themselves more attractive or to provide an alternate time for synagogue services featuring a rabbinical sermon. The prayer services were shortened, *piyutim* were dropped, German and Hebrew were increasingly replaced by English as the predominant language of prayer, family pews were adopted, and organs and choirs became standard. None of these innovations, however, really slowed the progressive decline in Saturday synagogue attendance.

On October 19, 1866, Rabbi Isaac M. Wise inaugurated late Friday night services centered around a sermon in his Cincinnati congregation. His action was emulated by New York's Temple Emanu-El and others. But Friday night services did not solve the problem, for they too suffered from a dearth of participants. Emanu-El, for instance, dropped these services in the 1870s.[37] During the 1870s, the Jewish press periodically suggested holding services featuring a sermon on late Saturday afternoons, a time considered more convenient for synagogue attendance by Jews working on the Sabbath.[38] The press cited the precedent of the 4:00 P.M. Saturday services including sermons at the Grand Temple in Paris,[39] but the proposal fell on deaf ears and was not implemented.

While only two synagogues embarked on Sunday services in the 1870s, and others, like Emanu-El, debated the merit of such action, individual Jews took matters into their own hands. Some New York Jews found an outlet for their spiritual needs at the Sunday lectures of O. B. Frothingham.[40] A fair number of these Jews, no doubt, were motivated by the desire to assimilate into a broader, universal American religious fellowship; others, however, sincerely sought spiritual guidance.

The felt need of Jews for spiritual guidance found its way into the correspondence section of the *Jewish Messenger*. On May 18, 1876, correspondent "H.L." expressed disappointment at Adler's May 15 proposals. He had expected the new association to offer Sunday services for those Jews not able to go to temple on Saturday.

I thought surely that some scheme would be devised to have Jewish lectures delivered every Sunday morning for the benefit of Jews, so that it would not be necessary for the hundreds who can not avoid breaking the Sabbath to listen to Frothingham, Hall, Hepworth and Taylor, in case they wished any religious instruction.

Instead, Adler proposed what "H.L." conceived to be a "series of moral and ethical addresses" which did not fulfill his spiritual needs.

A few months later, correspondent "Joseph" earnestly asked "whether there is any objection to the Jewish congregations holding services on some other day for the benefit of clerks and merchants who are compelled to labor on Saturday?"[41] He added that he had attended one of Adler's lectures and "could not understand his language or his drift. . . . I see that some arrangement is necessary, however, for we all need Sabbath instruction. What can be done?" The *Jewish Messenger* responded to this plea by advocating Saturday afternoon services with "an earnest address by the preacher, or some other competent speaker." No one took up the paper's call. As a result of Jewish preoccupation with business interests on Saturday, the Sunday service loomed large as the logical alternative for those Jews unable to attend the synagogue on Saturday; the agitation of American Jewry for Sunday services seems quite understandable.

No less understandable, however, was the opposition to the idea of Sunday services. Maintaining the integrity of the Jewish Sabbath was, of course, the immediate concern. The traditional *Jewish Messenger,* in particular, condemned the idea of Sunday services and upheld the significance of Saturday as the Jewish Sabbath.[42] The paper was not alone. Isaac M. Wise, David Einhorn, Samuel Adler, Gustav Gottheil, and most of those within the broad consensus of classical Reform Judaism supported Saturday as the Jewish Sabbath and objected to Sunday services. In Germany Holdheim's Berlin congregation stood alone in sponsoring Sunday services; neither the practical innovation nor its underlying ideology and rationale were accepted into the mainstream of German Reform Judaism. In America, in the 1870s, the only prominent Reform leaders who favored Sunday services were Kaufmann Kohler, Samuel Hirsch and his son Emil Hirsch, and Moritz Ellinger.[43]

The grave concern for the integrity of the Jewish Sabbath reflected the American Jewish response to a crucial problem of even greater import than the intrinsic value of salvaging the day itself: defining the parameters of both Judaism and Jewish identity in America. While German Jews were establishing their institutional, social, educational, and religious roots in America during the 1860s and 1870s, the impact of American socio-economic factors on them and their felt need for speedy acculturation hastened their process of reforming Judaism. American Reform Judaism thus evolved far more radically than its antecedent German form. Religious rituals, in particular, were excised with abandon, contrasting sharply with the very conservative implementation of reforms in Germany. The radical departures of American reformers shocked both Reformers and traditionalists who were accustomed to the religious modus vivendi achieved in Germany by 1848. Many American Jews displayed genuine alarm that Judaism would vanish by virtue of the radical drift of American Reform Judaism.

This apprehension was indicative of the need felt in many Jewish quarters for a new consensus in America, uniting both traditionalist and Reformer, to define "what is Judaism" and "who is a Jew." Theologically, at the very least, traditionalists and reformers were united in their affirmation of Jewish monotheism. In the face of massive Reform excisions of Jewish rituals, however, a ritual was needed to which one could point as representative of the particular character of the Jewish religion: the Sabbath became that ritual. Traditionalists and most Reformers during the 1870s consistently fell back upon the Sabbath as a symbolic hallmark determining the special nature of the Jewish religion. Allegiance to the Jewish Sabbath in principle—not necessarily its scrupulous observance—specified one's membership in the American Jewish consensus.

Commenting on Kohler's institution of a supplemental Sunday service for the convenience of those of his members who were prevented by "commercial competition" from attending on the Jewish Sabbath, Dr. Sonneschein of St. Louis, a Reform rabbi, asked: "What right has such a congregation to remain a distinctly Jewish one? Why not drop the Jewish denomination entirely?"[44] Sonneschein was particularly incensed at the motive for change—"convenience." He asserted that reforms based on convenience rather than on sacrifice "lead to deformation rather reformation. Take 'convenience' as the sole motive power of any religious reform, and there is no doubt whatsoever that such a reform will show itself a weakening instead of a strengthening act. And yet all the champions of the Sunday service insist mainly upon this very treacherous ground of 'convenience.' "[45]

The traditionalist *Jewish Messenger* echoed Sonneschein's sentiments. Referring to those seeking Sunday services, the paper declared on June 2, 1876:

> We behold the departure from all that is sacred by those who are dissatisfied with all that requires some self-denial. They would at one fell swoop destroy everything which bears the stamp of antiquity. . . . The extent of their belief is "deism." . . . The holy Sabbath is by them to be superseded by a Sunday's instrumental music and oratorical display.

On more than one occasion the *Jewish Messenger* reiterated that one cannot preserve Judaism without the traditional Sabbath.[46] And a correspondent to the paper, "Common Sense," underscored Sonneschein's challenge to Kohler and the movement for Sunday religious services. He noted that the Jewish Sabbath is the one truly uniting force of Jews the world over:

we "keep one day sacred in common with our brethren scattered all over the world." He concluded that the Jewish Sabbath was "one of the very few remaining dividing lines between the ultra-Reform Jew and the gentile brethren."[47]

From this perspective one can better appreciate the ambivalent reaction of the American Jewish community to Adler's May 15 address. Since commitment to the Jewish Sabbath symbolized one's positive identification with the Jewish community, Adler's proposal for Sunday lectures understandably precipitated widespread speculation as to the religious significance of the Sunday lecture movement.

One can also better understand why correspondent "Ish Yehudi" so vehemently rebuked Adler's Sunday proposal. He felt that a Sunday lecture service sponsored by a Jew was inimical and antithetical to Judaism, and he accused Adler of splitting the American Jewish community. The correspondent averred that the "institution of Sunday services among Israelites is a concession to Christianity. And such a concession is a secession from Judaism on the part of the participants in such Sunday services."[48] He asserted that Judaism had never split into sects, that the talmudic saying *"Yisrael af al pi shechata yisrael hu"* (a Jew who sins retains his status as a Jew) applied even to the ultra-Reformers. Orthodox Jews may consider them sinners, but they are still Jewish brothers. But "not so would be the case with a professional concession to Christianity with public and professional denial of the sacredness of the Sabbath. This would create a sect of Jews which the largest majority of coreligionists would not recognize as their brethren in faith." "Ish Yehudi" even went so far as to suggest that Jews wanting to hear Sunday lectures should attend Frothingham's addresses at Masonic Hall.

To be consistent, "Ish Yehudi" would have had to view Kohler and Emil Hirsch together with Adler as potential founders of a new sect rather than merely ultra-Reform Jews. We do not know his opinion. As the years passed and Sunday services gradually gained greater acceptance in American Reform Judaism, Kohler and Hirsch were continually recognized as Jews, ultra-Reformers to be sure, but Jews nonetheless; Felix Adler was not.

The Sunday Addresses: 1876–1879

In retrospect "Ish Yehudi" was right in fearing that Adler's association would foment a split in the ranks of American Jewry, but he was right for the wrong reasons. The reasons became apparent only in later months. In the course of his Sunday addresses over the following three to four years, Adler presented a forceful critique of the underlying theological and intellectual assumptions of Reform Judaism, punctuated by a sweeping rejection of all the still-cherished ritual practices of classical Reform. For the first time he publicly applied the conclusions of modern scholarship to Judaism.

In earlier speeches, he had critically appraised other religions alone, not Judaism. At worst, when aspects of Judaism were criticized, such as its creeds, the references were indirect, oblique suggestions set in the context of other religions. This public critical historicization of Judaism was the only new twist prominent in his early lectures (1876–79) following the formal inauguration of Sunday addresses on October 15, 1876. All the principal themes of his Sunday addresses—defining religion in terms of ethical behavior leading to social action, preaching the need for social justice and social improvement for the laboring class, forwarding Kant's objective of doing one's duty according to the dictates of one's conscience—all these ideas had already been advanced or hinted at in previous years.

In essence, Adler's views on religion were not actually more radical than those which he expressed between 1873 and 1876, but his application of religious criticism to Judaism was perceived by the Jewish community as a fundamentally radical, unacceptable departure from Judaism. By the spring of 1877, most of the established Jewish community, as represented by its press and most of its rabbis, ruled him out of Judaism. Furthermore, since Jewish Reformers defined Jewish socio-communal affiliation in terms of attachment to the Jewish religion, Adler was, in effect, dismissed from the Jewish socio-religious fellowship as well. For his part, Adler never contested his ostracization from the formal Jewish community, for it corresponded to his personal break with his Jewish religious and social identity. Through his universalist religious ideology and his new universal socio-religious fellowship, he sought to transcend both the particularist Jewish religion and the Jewish religious community.

In the course of his addresses over the next few years, Adler rejected the idea of the divine selection of the Jews.[49] Having already repudiated both theism and deism as historical anachronisms, Felix publicly affirmed that no personal, Providential deity could have "selected" the Jews, or anyone else for that matter. He maintained that the Prophets spoke to humanity in general, and not to the Jews alone,[50] so that Jews could not justifiably assert their being endowed with a unique ethical mission. He further contended that the "chosenness" of a group was an evolving historical idea whose claim of authenticity by each group was to be judged strictly by the contemporary relevance of the religious message which the group bore.[51] In December 1878, therefore, he had no compunction in portraying the proponents of Ethical Culture as the new "chosen people."[52] Claims of "chosenness" by new religious groups, such as those of the early Christians, generally signal religious schism, and Adler's claim appears to have followed the pattern.

In the first winter-spring series of Sunday lectures, 1876–77, Adler defined his position against dogmatic religion and sketched the general outlines of his new ideal.[53] In so doing, he shocked the Jewish establishment by publicly controverting traditional Jewish theological axioms, such as the existence of Providence, revelation, miracles and the supernatural suspension of nature, immortality, and the divinity of the Old Testament.[54]

His attack on Jewish rituals was equally provocative. He infuriated the Jewish community by depicting the rite of circumcision as a variant of the human sacrifices brought by ancient Near Eastern peoples (including the Israelites) in which mutilation and dismemberment were designed to prove that the person thus mutilated belong to God and lived by His grace. Adler pointed to an analogous custom practiced among young Indian braves, who cut off the joints of their fingers to conciliate the gods, and he concluded:

> The so-called rite of the covenant which is kept to this day by the Jews owes its origin to this, notwithstanding the many modern and ingenious explanations given of it. Taken as a religious usage it is simply barbarous in itself and utterly barbarous and contemptible in its origin. It is one of those superstitions which disgrace the very name of religion and if all those who practice it but knew its origin, it surely would not continue.[55]

He also pointed to the ridiculous inconsistency of Reform Jewish merchants who upheld the principle of the sacredness of the Sabbath and professed the need for its observance while they themselves worked on Saturday. Of this practice, he queried: "By whom should the Sabbath be observed? By women—is this conforming to the needs of the present?"[56] His later assertion of the "Chaldee" origin of the Sabbath, although admitting its prophetic transformation from a day of gloom to a day of moral refreshment, only added insult to injury.[57]

In the 1877–78 Sunday lecture series, Adler gradually broke his silence on the question of his belief or nonbelief in a God. While he had already been branded alternatively as a deist, an agnostic, and an atheist by the Jewish and non-Jewish press in 1877, some people were still uncertain as to his opinions on the existence of a deity in the universe. In his lecture "Conscience" in 1886, he confirmed that "concerning the belief in God, we have hitherto had little to say. . . . To us it seemed far more important to rouse men's minds with words that ought to be like blows upon the torpid soul to an appreciation of the practical moral needs of the day rather than to spin the gossamer threads of an abstruse and subtle philosophy which few men's minds are fine enough to grasp."[58] He did not propound a religious metaphysic at this time, as he did in the twentieth century, to replace the ones which he had rejected; nonetheless, toward the end of 1877 and particularly in 1878, he had begun to clarify his position on God. By the end of 1878 the differences of opinion on Adler's beliefs had been resolved; the Jewish press featured no further controversies in its pages; everyone knew what he believed, or at the very least what he did not believe.

In November 1877, Adler publicly pronounced God to be but the incarnation of supreme moral worth. "God" is but a moral power in the world making for righteousness.[59] The personification of this moral power, however, does not exist in reality, Adler affirmed. God is a person just as Liberty is a person, but he is neither man nor woman.[60] As Adler later observed, there is no good Being, only a good principle.[61] But by his own standards of religion, Adler strenuously denied being an atheist, and he turned the charge against the proponents of the traditional religions.

> If it be atheism to deny the existence of their man-god, of the idol which they have set unto themselves above the clouds and which verily they slander, they blaspheme, calling that highest—then we are atheists. But then all the best that have ever lived, are atheists with ourselves. But if there be another standard and a higher standard whereby to measure religious truth—if God and good, and good and God be one, if there is no God save as he dawns upon us in the increasing good—then we do retort with tenfold justice that charge of atheism upon the lying priests and cry aloud to the people against the atheism of their churches and their synagogues.[62]

In his Chicago address of March 26, 1878, Adler made it clear that he was not a traditional theist. He designated the conception of a Providential God rewarding virtue and punishing evil as "immoral," for the atrocious societal conditions proved otherwise.

> . . .That an omnipotent and omniscient being having in His hands the happiness of His creatures, having the wisdom to foresee how they would be tempted, having the power so to purify their virtue that they could not fall, should have left all these things undone, should have prepared a Hell for them from the beginning, should have consigned them to seventy years of miserable existence on earth in order to rack them with unspeakable agonies in endless eons of time, what human ingenuity had ever rivaled such cruelty? What Nero, what Torquemada

had been guilty of such malevolence! What fiend so fiendish as such a God![63]

Upset by the continuous charges of atheism leveled against him, particularly because of the "waste [of] energies on matters of creed," Adler lashed back at his detractors in an address on April 6, 1879 entitled "Atheism." He proclaimed:

> Long enough now have we kept silence; long enough have we allowed the charge of Atheism to be brought against us with indifference because we believed it to be dictated by personal motives. But there comes a time for breaking silence. . . . I say, then, that the charge of Atheism as directed against this society is false.

He concluded with a stirring testament of his own faith.

> The people want a confession of faith, I am told. Hear, then, mine—a simple one. I believe in the supreme excellence of righteousness; I believe that the law of righteousness will triumph in the universe over all evil; I believe that in the law of righteousness is the sanctification of human life, and I believe that in furthering that law I also am hallowed in the service of the unknown God.

Adler's criticism of Jewish theological beliefs and ritual practices aroused a storm of protest from the established Jewish community. Perhaps nothing so outraged them as his prediction that the Jewish people was destined to die. He asserted that history teaches that "races like individuals must perish, [that] there is no race, however gifted, however favored, that can hope to escape this ban of law, that there is a limit fixed for the life of each, a limit which it shall not and cannot transcend."[64] The Jews have been preserved until now because of their religion, which urged moderation in all indulgences, the sanctity of home life, the value of knowledge, and a spirit of religious independence which offered the self-conscious awareness of divine selection. But in this same lecture, he claimed that

> the perpetuity of the Jewish race depends upon the perpetuity of the Jewish religion. . . . So long as there shall be a reason of existence for Judaism, so long the individual Jews will keep apart and will do well to do so. So long as Judaism remains the living protest it is against Trinitarianism, so long its individual members do well to preserve its exclusiveness. But more and more as Trinitarianism crumbles away— and it is crumbling away fast, faster than many believe—when this

process is accomplished and the more it is accomplished the more will also the individual members of the Jewish race look about them and perceive that there is as great and perhaps greater liberty in religion beyond the pale of their race and will lose their peculiar idiosyncrasies, and their distinctiveness will fade. And eventually, the Jewish race will die.

This lecture was widely covered by the general press of New York. Both the *New York World*[65] and the *New York Herald*[66] published lengthy accounts of the address, with the *Herald* sarcastically asking: "If the Professor would be good enough to fix the time [of the death of the Jews] he might possibly place the Hebrews under something of an obligation." To the Jewish community, Adler's prognosis only confirmed the extent of his treachery to the Jewish cause. Already in the spring of 1877 he had been declared outside the pale of the Jewish socio-religious fellowship.[67] In effect, in this one lecture he underlined his fundamental conclusion on Judaism and the Jewish people at this time: the continued existence of the Jewish religion and the Jewish people is neither necessary nor meaningful; both the religion and its proponents will ultimately disappear.

The response was immediate: Rabbi Henry S. Jacobs of the 34th Street Synagouge, Rabbi Dr. Huebsch of the Lexington Avenue Temple, and Rabbi Frederick de Sola Mendes of the 44th Street Synagogue all wrote to the *New York Herald* affirming the viability, vitality, and promising future of both Judaism and the Jews.[68] The *Jewish Messenger* joined the chorus: the Jews had long withstood problems of faith and intermarriage, and both they and their religion will assuredly continue to prosper.[69]

In criticizing Jewish beliefs and rituals which he himself had once accepted—even holding some up to ridicule—Adler exhibited the youthful ardor of a self-assured idealist impatient with traditional, unscientific religious orthodoxy. The tone of his early lectures betrays a flavor of self-righteousness not atypical of one totally convinced of the rightness of his cause and dedicated to its acceptance by others. From a letter written to his close friend and associate Albert Levi on June 8, 1878, it is evident that Adler perceived himself to be a "religious emancipator" who "can be a help in breaking" new religious ground.

Of his assault on religious ideas and rituals, he asserted in December 1878:

It is necessary this destructive work. It is necessary to assail the towering superstitions of the day, painfully necessary, not only because they are absurd, but because they are immoral, because they tend to degrade mankind and to brutalize him.[70]

Particular dogmas, such as immortality, were most often assailed because he felt that they misled man into thinking that virtue is always rewarded. Not so, he declared: life is a constant struggle in which the good is not always nor even often rewarded. The new religion must teach man to do the good for its own sake and inspire and uplift him for the continuous struggle for its realization.[71]

Adler broke his promise of May 15, 1876 not to interfere with the ritual sentiments of adherents of positive religions. Once he realized that the new lecture association could indeed become that religious fellowship for which he had yearned, he made explicit all the provocative ideas on religion—including those on Judaism—that had been in the back of his mind since his student years in Germany. In May he proceeded cautiously so as not to incite too many people; as it was, he still precipitated considerable debate about his motives. But once the lecture movement gained support and momentum, caution became less necessary.

Actually, Adler must have realized that the confrontation between Ethical Culture and Judaism was inevitable from the first. Wanting to inculcate his followers with a practical, ethical religious ideology free from dogmatic considerations, and to wean people away from dogmas and creeds, he felt compelled to attack these ideas at their very core. The New York Society for Ethical Culture consisted mainly of Jews; to wean them away from their dogmatic beliefs, he perforce had to criticize Judaism.

And yet, despite his sharp public rejection of long-held Jewish theological beliefs and religious practices, Adler was not motivated by the vindictive or vengeful motives so typical of Jewish apostates throughout the generations. On the contrary, his lectures during 1876–79—and indeed all his later addresses—displayed a sound appreciation for the positive contributions of Judaism and the Jews. He did not rail against his ancestral religion. As a historian of religions, aware of the evolution of ideas, religions, and peoples, he lauded the good elements of the past and understood the historical development of the bad. With historical perspective, he recognized that to curse the past history of man would have been sheer folly, and he extended this historical orientation to his esteem for Judaism.

Adler may well represent a new paradigm of Jewish apostasy in modern history: the intellectual Jew passing out of the socio-religious group on intellectual grounds and without malice. Morris Raphael Cohen, his student at Columbia for a time, is an example of this prototype (in the years before his reaffirmation of his Jewish communal ties in 1933).[72] In fact, whether *apostasy* is an appropriate term to describe Adler's departure from the Jewish fellowship is debatable, for he conceived of himself and his society as evolutionary products of the glorious prophetic tradition.

In his address "Races and Religions," December 18, 1878, Adler denied that "we are guilty of irreverence at all toward the past. We are not destroying but fulfilling the Law and the Prophets." He declared that the Prophets taught him to love humanity, to pursue justice, and "to feel an unconquerable trust in the right, that it will triumph. . . . It is the Prophets themselves who are responsible for us; it is the Prophets themselves who have said: the outcome of religion must be social amelioration."

Feeling inexorably drawn to the mission of doing the "good" for all of humanity, Adler accepted no smaller sphere of action than a universal religious fellowship transcending all specific religious groups and ideologies. He beseeched Jews, though still revering their past, to follow his lead and to come to terms with the spirit and requirements of the new age.

> The Jew by birth who is filled with filial reverence for his ancestry but who now reads in the light of the new age and by the torch of science the message of the ideal,—he knows that the ideal can tolerate no distinctions of creed or sect but that it must embrace all who love the good.

Again, he attributed to the Prophets the keynote of his religious mission, but insisted that their message could not be, and was never intended to be, restricted to any one race. "The Prophets have said the task and mission of religion is to do good in the largest sense," Adler proclaimed. "But in this task, how can we limit ourselves to any people, in this mission, how can we restrict ourselves to any chosen race," he asked. "Are not all who are adopted summoned? Are not all who have the will and the heart in this work brothers and sisters?"[73] Perhaps these thoughts best illustrate Adler's commitment to religious universalism in the 1870s and best reveal his stark repudiation of Reform Judaism's teleological commitment to universalism only in the undefined future. Gottheil's understanding of the religious orientation reflected in the Temple Sermon of 1873 had been vindicated. Now, by the end of 1878, most everyone realized that Felix Adler stood outside the framework of Judaism and the American Jewish community.

Composition of the New York Society

During the first three to four years of the New York Society for Ethical Culture, Adler attracted huge throngs of people to his addresses. He was clearly fulfilling the social, intellectual, and spiritual needs of large numbers of New York Jews discontented with the current state of Judaism and religion. The vast majority of the audience was Jewish, although some non-Jews did attend. Letters to Adler from a Christian, Rebecca F. Coleman, and from a certain N. S. Gadbe, professing neither Judaism nor

Christianity, are indicative of his following among non-Jews.[74] Coleman praised Adler's *Creed and Deed* for having helped her to "shake off the old shackles of Catholicism in order to grasp for myself and little ones the right of free thought. . . . I thank you sincerely for your good influence." Gadbe, having attended a Sunday lecture, expressed the need to demonstrate "my high appreciation of your efforts and of its effect upon my mind." Few non-Jews, however, joined the society. Jews constituted the fundamental element of the New York Society for Ethical Culture in both attendance and membership.

A good deal of debate arose in the newspapers in regard to the Jewishness of Adler and his society: were they representative of Jews and Judaism or not? The *New York World* and apparently the *New York Sun* reported that they were;[75] the *Daily Graphic* and the *Jewish Messenger* tried to refute these allegations.[76] It is evident, however,that in the first few years of its existence, the society and its Sunday lectures drew an audience of Jews fairly representative of the broad spectrum of Jewish religious and communal affiliation. Harry Marks and Julian Werner, both journalists, recorded that some of the "worthiest members of the community" attended the addresses and were Adler's followers, "some of them high in the councils of the synagogue and directing its religious welfare and overseeing the functions of its ministers."[77] While it is true that most Jews still desirous of retaining their identity as Jews either dropped their membership or stopped going to the lectures after 1879–80, the situation was different in 1876–79. Not everyone attending the Sunday lectures sought to leave Judaism.

Basically, most of the Jews who attended were attracted to Adler's lectures and to the goals of his society because they were dissatisfied with the character of Jewish religious life. Some may have originally attended his addresses simply for Adler's unmatched oratorical eloquence and inspirational tone; still, dissatisfaction with Judaism and contemporary religion in general fanned their interest in him. As Marks noted, there was an "almost universal religious lethargy [among] the people,"[78] and Adler's intellectual ability, oratorical skill, and prophetic moral idealism aroused the slumbering religious consciousness of the Jewish community.

Discontent with the Jewish religion assumed essentially two shapes: displeasure with some or all Jewish ritual observances and "secondary" forms, such as rabbinic homiletics; and unhappiness with the intellectual, moral, and social response of the Jewish religion to contemporary conditions.

One cannot overestimate the significance of Adler's lecturing on Sunday. That alone guaranteed a large Jewish audience. The Sabbath was the primary ritual annoyance to many Jews because it conflicted with their economic interests. And as synagogue attendance on the Sabbath progressively declined in the 1870s, some Jews—their number cannot be determined—attended Frothingham's Sunday lectures.[79] But when Adler initiated his own Sunday addresses, these Jews, along with others who could not or would not attend the temples on Saturdays, streamed into Standard Hall to hear the discourses of a fellow Jew.

The large Jewish audiences on Sundays were also symptomatic of a more deep-seated problem for Judaism: many Jews had begun to resent their own religion, which denounced their Saturday business pursuits and pronounced them sinners. They sought to reconcile the contradiction between Jewish ritual demands and their own behavior. They were thus drawn to Adler; his lectures seemed to offer a religious alternative more amenable to their economic and psychological needs. Adler also solved a serious problem for Jews as parents. One can well understand "the declaration of one of the leaders of the Ethical Culture Society that he no longer wants his children to be taught that Sabbath breaking is a sin and that therefore their father is a rogue."[80] A *Jewish Messenger* report two years later echoed almost the identical thought: "Why do you belong to the Society of Ethical Culture? 'Simply because I will not have my children censure me for working on Saturday' was the strange reply."[81] The reply was not strange at all.

While the Sabbath constituted the most serious ritual problem for Jews, the state of the pulpit sermon—an intrinsic part and central focus of the synagogue service—was the cause of much additional dissatisfaction. The contemporary form and content of the vernacular sermon—regarded by Orthodox German Jews as a radical innovation and precipitating a religious furor in the German Jewish community in the early nineteenth century—were now considered outmoded. Many Jews, and particularly the younger ones, sought sermons of greater relevance to them, sermons that would discuss subjects of value and interest to Americans, and which were "not wasted on fanciful Talmudic speculations, or profoundly ingenious and entirely useless biblical researches."[82] Therein lay the reason for much of the Jewish attraction to Frothingham's addresses.[83] As Marks observed in his attack against the rabbis, "I do most emphatically complain of frittering away valuable time in discussions of purely literary, trivial or abstruse subjects, when there are terribly important questions at issue, questions actually involving the preservation of Judaism on this continent."[84]

The letter of correspondent "Sylvia," published in the *Jewish Messenger* on March 28, 1877, perhaps best underlined New York Jewry's considerable discontent with the extant pulpit sermon.

Would it be very wrong for our Jewish preachers to take a hint from the ethical professor, and discourse occasionally on themes not directly connected with the weekly *Parashah*. I have no personal objections to Bible texts, and feel sure that there is enough mental food in the old Book to last our pulpit until the millennium; but we must popularize the pulpit just as Mr. Thomas is compelled, despite his strenuous protests, to diversify his concerts. I think that once a month we might have our rabbi's idea of morality, contradistinguished from doctrinal religion, of ethics in fact, and leave *Moses, Jezebel*, and *Job* for other days. We are an enquiring age—we look for variety, *and if any of us drop in on Sunday's at Mr. Frothingham's or Dr. Adler's, it is not because we have abjured Judaism, but because we like to be instructed on subjects with which we sympathize.* We prefer to listen to all sermons on Saturdays; but if our rabbis decline to leave the beaten track and cull flowers for us in the open fields, do not blame us for figuring among the Sunday audiences. Besides, many of us young ladies are not long from school—a foreign accent, and occasional breaches of grammar, grate upon our ears, and not all the Saturday preachers are perfect orators. I like Vienna coffee, and if I cannot get it at my favorite old restaurant after repeated requests, I must perforce cross the street and patronize the new cafe.[85]

Adler's oratorical eloquence and the timely subjects of his addresses, therefore, were significant causes of attraction for New York Jewry. And as "Sylvia" pointed out, her attendance at Sunday lectures—like that of others—did not reflect abjuration of Judaism, but rather her desire to be instructed "on subjects with which we can sympathize." Her request for "our rabbi's idea of morality, contradistinguished from doctrinal religion" perhaps also suggested the crying need for a systematic exposition of Jewish ethics and its applicability to society at a time when discussion of morality and ethical concerns was in the air. Moritz Lazarus's *The Ethics of Judaism* and Simon Bernfeld's *Foundations of Jewish Ethics* appeared only years later. Adler was promulgating ethical ideals at the present time, and his refreshing moral idealism appears to have deeply impressed a large segment of the Jewish population.

One final example of the type of Jewish discontent with ritual demands concerns the marriage in 1870 of Edward Lauterbach, an early stalwart of the Ethical Culture Movement. Lauterbach, a specialist in railway law and a former director of the Hebrew Benevolent Society and Orphan Asylum, requested Rabbi David Einhorn to perform his marriage ceremony. Einhorn refused because the bride-to-be, a Miss Friedman, was the offspring of a mixed marriage in which the mother was a Christian who had never been formally converted. The girl was requested to undergo conversion, but both she and Lauterbach objected to the ritual process. Einhorn, long-standing foe of intermarriage, resolutely refused to participate. After "quite a stir" in New York, the Emanu-El board granted

permission to its English preacher, Rev. Gutheim, to perform the ceremonies, but only with his "inserting in the ceremony a confession of Miss
Friedman to continue to live as a daughter of Israel."[86]

This is a relatively minor incident, perhaps, but very telling nonetheless. Having rejected the conversion ritual as an identifying factor in
defining one as a Jew, Lauterbach gradually took a rather jaundiced view
of all rituals reflecting Jewish ethnic-religious exclusiveness, which culminated in his rejection of the very idea of Jewish exclusiveness. In the 1870s
he found Adler's ideas on Jewish rituals and Jewish exclusiveness in
consonance with his own, and for a time he became Adler's ardent
supporter. Lauterbach's attitude and its genesis no doubt typified that of a
growing number of Jews who abandoned ritual practices and who found
support for their actions in Adler's Sunday teachings.

In general, American Jewish laxity and abandonment of ritual
practices—or as Harry Marks commented, "the disregard of the spirit and
letter of Judaism"—in some degree resulted from the inherent instability
of Reform Judaism. German Reform leaders could not, and therefore did
not, promulgate a set of guidelines to establish the limits of religious
change. American Reformers fared no better. Jews simply relinquished
religious rituals which were felt to prevent their successful integration
into American society. Rabbinic leadership was weak; rabbis knew neither
what to do nor how to judge which reforms were legitimate and which
were not; no ostensible rules of procedure existed. More often than not,
they simply followed the desire of their congregants. Some Jews no longer
found meaning in any ritual practices; no congregation or rabbi, however,
was willing to go that far. Ethical Culture did, and in this sense it furnished
the logical end for the unchecked anti-ritual drift of many American Jews.
To many Jews, Ethical Culture represented liberation from all ritual
forms, and this perception motivated both their Sunday attendance and
their membership in the society.

Besides, and in many cases in addition to, their unhappiness with Jewish
rituals, some Jews were dissatisfied with the intellectual, moral, and social
response of Judaism to modernity. Adler attracted skeptics, "rationalists,"
"indifferentists," and "come-outers," Jews exhibiting varying degrees of
understanding of the problems of contemporary religion who "ceased to
hold the faith in which they were educated."[87] As a letter of the society's
trustees to the *New York World* indicates, some members of the audience on
Sundays "ceased to attach weight to religious dogmas" and were "chiefly
interested in hearing the history of their origin and influence."[88]

Whether one abjured Judaism or not, however, an essential factor of
Adler's attraction was his ethical concern. As the trustees noted, "the
Sunday morning discourses are designed to give full scope for an impar-
tial discussion of the great problems of life . . .; their ultimate purpose is to

bring out in clear relief the holiness of the law of duty as the one indubitable certainty." One need but read letters and autobiographies of some of the society's members to discover ethical idealism as the motive for their having joined the Ethical Culture Society.

Julius Rosenbaum, in a letter to Adler, June 4, 1876, affirmed that Judaism and its leaders were not meeting their ethical obligations. He encouraged him to "strike hard and vigorous blows at a system of morality whose interpreters under the cloak of religious inspiration desecrate the most sacred obligations of humanity."[89]

Henry Morgenthau recorded his fascination and total absorption with business, "but though business conquer pleasure, it could not conquer idealism; and idealism . . . asserted itself during business hours, and again and again demanded opportunities to exercise itself."[90] He then recalled how Adler had rescued his idealism from "complete annihilation" as a result of his preoccupation with business. Morgenthau participated in a number of Adler's social programs: he was a director of the United Relief Fund, a member of the team experimenting with model tenements on Cherry Street, and a sponsor of the first Ethical Culture School. Morgenthau was also a member of Adler's "Union for Higher Life," a very small group of selected people initiated at Cornell and devoted to moral purity, celibacy in bachelorhood, and simplicity in dress and manners. He recalled with fondness the group's adoption and support of eight children who were either orphans or whose parents could not care for them properly.[91]

Samuel Gompers, the celebrated labor leader, testified that his attraction to Adler and the society was based on feelings of moral idealism.

> As my own mind instinctively rebelled against the restraints of the Orthodox, I joined this little group afterwards known as the Ethical Culture Society. . . . We were trying to work out ethical standards that would have meaning in the affairs of everyday life—that was what appealed to me. I failed to see how men who claimed to believe in conventional religious standards—whether Christian or Jewish—could profit through the misery of human beings. The Ethical Society did not ignore ethics of industrial relations and became a power for good in the struggle to eliminate the tenement house cigar manufacturing system.[92]

Gregory Weinstein, a Russian Jew and later a prominent publicist, teacher, and civic worker on New York's Lower East Side, recalled that Sunday mornings he attended Adler's addresses. Adler's lack of dogmatic concern and his faith in man's inner consciousness of moral law appealed to him, as did his denunciation of socio-economic wrongs and his constructive remedial proposals. Weinstein's impression aptly described Adler's practical social activities: "He was a forerunner and pioneer in all movements for practical social betterment."[93] That image drew Weinstein and many other Jews to him.

Joseph Seligman, who has been characterized as a free-thinker in his last years,[94] and of whom it was said that "he followed his own intellectual bent,"[95] may not have joined Ethical Culture for Adler's moral idealism as much as for his "American substitute for old-world Judaism."[96] Nevertheless, he too was stirred by Adler's ethical passion. In a letter to his wife, January 6, 1877, he wrote: "I cannot let the holy Sabbath [Sunday] pass without fulfilling my holy and pleasant duty of writing to you my dear. . . . This morning I went dutifully to Dr. Adler's lecture where, as usual, I received much moral stimulus."[97]

Young Jewish men and women, in particular, found Adler's idealism appealing. Their attraction to him once again illustrated the sociological phenomenon of second- and third-generation offspring of immigrants who had comfortably established themselves, rebelling against parental values, in this case against Reform Judaism. These young Jews were unhappy with the materialism of their middle-class families and sought an idealistic alternative; Adler and his society provided it.

Not all the Jews who were originally attracted to Adler remained with him and his society. As his complete departure from Judaism became fully apparent in the late 1870s, many Jews chose to reaffirm their Jewish identity and religion and left Adler's movement. Some, like Harry Marks, realizing that Adler not only rejected rituals but really did not believe in a traditional theistic God, left the society on intellectual-religious grounds. Other Jews departed because of their heightened sense of Jewishness resulting from the anti-Semitic outbursts in Rumania and Russia. Indeed, in 1879 Adler felt compelled to admonish his listeners: "We do not believe, as some timid souls do, that now is the time to withdraw within the old lines [Judaism]—that we must seek shelter because a storm is coming. We will seek shelter, but in the new house which we have built [Ethical Culture] . . . upon the rock of right principles."[98]

Even Edward Lauterbach, vice-president of the society, one of Adler's staunchest supporters, and one of the two official witnesses at Adler's wedding in 1880, withdrew from the society in 1882. With the resurgence of anti-Semitism and pogroms and the arrival of impoverished Russian Jewish immigrants, Lauterbach advocated that the society devote its time and money first to these Jews and only secondly to others. Every race or sect tends to take care of its own, he contended, and since the society's Jewish membership totaled, at the least, four hundred out of some five hundred members, he felt that urgent Jewish requirements took precedence over the society's other areas of concern. "If we Jews do not look out for our fellow Jews, who will?" Lauterbach queried, echoing Hillel's classic rabbinic expression. "Let us take heed, therefore, and not in the name of liberalism—a mistaken sentimentalism—abandon those whom we owe loyalty and fealty, and who, if forsaken by us, would be entirely forgotten," he declared. "Let us devote our attention—after our families—first, to our own people: then to the world at large." But according to Lauterbach, Adler "insisted that in its management and in its charity the society should be strictly non-sectarian. . . . Upon this rock the Professor and I split."[99]

Most of the Jews who remained, however, broke with Judaism and the Jewish community permanently. The New York Society for Ethical Culture became a new socio-religious fellowship, whose membership, in the main, comprised individuals of "Jewish racial and ethnic origin." That was the way Adler and most of his followers conceived of their Jewishness. They did not revile their Jewish roots; their Jewish origin, however, neither related to their religious, institutional, and communal affiliations nor colored their day-to-day lifestyle and behavior. They did not conceive of their Jewish origins as a meaningful mode of identification, and to all intents and purposes, they no longer considered themselves to be Jews.

The phenomenal growth of the Ethical Culture Society in the first few years of its existence constitutes a trenchant indictment of the state of American Reform Judaism at that time. Theoretically, a movement dedicated to the practical goals of social justice could have arisen within the confines of Reform Judaism on a broad Jewish religious consensus centered on monotheism. The success of Emil Hirsch in the late 1880s and 1890s and the general social-reform trend in Reform Judaism in the twentieth century would seem to confirm this contention. By no means had all the Jews attending Adler's Sunday lectures at the outset discarded belief in monotheism. However, with the exception of Hirsch in later years, no rabbis possessing Adler's idealism, inspirational tone, social conscience, and creative social ideas emerged in the last quarter of the nineteenth century.

Historically, perhaps it is too much to have expected American Reformers to anticipate the Protestant Social Gospel. Like their Protestant counterparts, they too were preserving middle-class interests. Nevertheless, Adler anticipated the Social Gospel and based his social concern on the Prophets; perceptive and sensitive Reform rabbis springing from the same prophetic tradition conceivably could have done so as well. At any rate, it is to Adler's great credit that he was the first and, for some time, the only leader of Jewish origin to engage actively in social reform and the social reconstruction of society.

Was the desire for assimilation the underlying rationale behind all the other motives for Jews joining the society and remaining as members over the years? Some Jews certainly thought so. Waldo Frank, a contemporary author, philosopher, and publicist, found the main adherents of Ethical Culture to be "prosperous Jews" who looked to Adler to prepare them "for the life of respectable material dominion which America afforded."[100] Frank's description was part of an overall polemic against Adler's rationalism following his own mystical reconversion to Judaism and, therefore, cannot be taken at face value. The contemporary account of James Waterman Wise, son of Stephen S. Wise, however, cannot be so readily dismissed. A friend of Adler's, greatly influenced by him, and an astute observer of the American Jewish religious scene, Wise wrote in 1928: "What for Felix Adler was ethical emancipation became for his followers a racial exodus; his ascent of the spirit degenerated in them into an escape, a flight from Jewish life."[101] Simenhoff's more recent observation seems to echo that of Wise: "Jews in comfortable circumstances, seeking a comfortable assimilation, could find in the Society for Ethical Culture an escape without a flight. Here they felt at home among the same species as themselves. The small Gentile membership and the larger proportion of Gentile leaders made the society sufficiently cosmopolitan. Their children could mix, intermarry and glide more gently into the dominant majority."[102]

Adler, on the other hand, repeatedly disclaimed assimilation as the factor motivating the society's creation and promoting Jewish membership. Rather, he posited genuine idealism as the underlying motivation for Jews supporting the creation of a universal ethical-religious movement.

> The motive of those who with me formed the first Ethical Society was not . . . a desire to disguise their face, but the passionate desire to get rid of dead things—ceremonies and observances which had become obsolete, the fervent desire to reach out towards a new spiritual ideal, to progress beyond the bounds of traditional Jewish faith, and to join hands with those who were equally desirous of passing beyond the traditional Christian creed. It was a noble and not an ignoble motive that prompted them.[103]

Referring to two Jewish members of his movement, Solomon Rothfield and Martin Fechheimer, Adler commented: "Their attitude was not the same as that of Jews who were ashamed to be Jews. They felt the need of breathing fresher air, of a larger life, and hence of ministering to human need wherever it occurred."[104]

Who is right, Adler or Wise and Simenhoff? On a simple, factual, descriptive basis, the Jewish adherents of Ethical Culture—including

Adler—were obviously assimilated Jews. They appropriated the social-religious guise of a majority culture (European and American) and dropped their own religious forms, beliefs, and behavior patterns. While Reform Jews were also assimilating—dropping rituals such as the Saturday Sabbath, Kashrut, and others smacking of Jewish particularism—the Jewish members of Ethical Culture took the process to its logical conclusion and departed from the Jewish community.

When dealing with assimilation as a possible motive for the departure of Ethical Culture Jews from Judaism, however, one must distinguish between simple *assimilation* and *universalization* or *utopianism*. Assimilation implies the desire of a Jew to depart from the Jewish community and, to a greater or lesser degree, to be absorbed by another reference group. It implies a "running toward" something *already* possessed by Gentiles (or other absorbent media) and one's ambition to join them in some way. Thus, to the extent that Ethical Culture Jews sought to "escape" from Judaism in order to be more properly identified as Americans or to smooth out social differences between Christians and Jews, the desire for *assimilation* properly describes the phenomenon of their membership in the Ethical Culture Society. But if one leaves Judaism to "run toward" something *not yet* possessed by Gentiles, some neutral aim or ideal which transcends both Christianity and Judaism, then the word *assimilation* is inappropriate; the more accurate term depicting this process is *universalization* or *utopianism*.

The Ethical Culture Society no doubt contained Jews motivated to leave Judaism for each of the two reasons. But in determining the motive for the departure of any given individual, one is often thrust into a thoroughly gray area of investigation. One requires an intimate psychological, intellectual, and social portrait of each person in order to gauge the reasons for his having left the Jewish religion and the Jewish group.

Adler's motive in leaving Judaism, however, is rather clear. His very call for a universal socio-religious fellowship was not motivated by a desire for social assimilation, but from a sincere ideological conviction reflecting a new intellectual-religious departure transcending both Christianity and Judaism. He and probably some of his more intimate followers were not assimilationists, but rather universalists or utopians. Therefore, while the "move beyond particularism," to borrow Michael Meyer's phrase, was the ideological goal of the movement, social assimilation in the typical sense of the term was not the motive of all of the society's Jewish members; it was certainly not Adler's motive.

Chapter V
Reaction and Controversy

Jewish Press Response to the Sunday Addresses

Adler's early addresses (1876–78) and the fact that he was attracting large numbers of Jews to his Sunday lectures stirred a major storm in American Jewish religious life. The Jewish press of the period offers particularly revealing accounts of both the unfolding controversy surrounding Adler and the implicit diverse perceptions of what constituted one's Jewish identity in American Judaism.

In the first winter-spring series of Sunday addresses in 1876–77, Adler denied the divinity of the Old Testament, Jewish chosenness, and the relevance of Jewish rituals. As reflected in the Jewish press, the more traditional Jews (even within Reform ranks), feeling that Adler had betrayed the fundamental tenets of Judaism, dismissed him from the Jewish consensus. Other more liberal Jews, however, either saw no reason to question Adler's Jewishness or reserved judgment on his Jewish affiliation, since Adler had not taken a clear, formal, and public position in regard to his belief in monotheism. Only in the winter-spring of 1877–78 did he explicitly repudiate all forms of theism and deism in his addresses. Having thus denied monotheism, Adler was thereafter identified as a Jew by almost no one in the Jewish community; there seemed to be no possible basis for including him in the Jewish socio-religious fellowship.

A broad overview of the Jewish press reaction to Adler's Sunday lectures will provide a useful introductory perspective. The Jewish press almost never debated with Adler the fundamental intellectual issues underlying his opinions, that is, the ideas of modern science, history, philosophy, and comparative religion which had such a momentous impact on religion and on Judaism. The papers were clearly aware of some of the problems, having broached such issues as the potential conflict between science and religion in the past.[1] Yet when the papers opposed Adler's ideas, they reacted to his radical conclusions rather than to the intellectual premises on which they were based; they seemed either unwilling or unable to tackle the root problem—the synthesis of contemporary Judaism with modern scholarship. A singular exception is found in an editorial of the *American Israelite* from January 5, 1877 entitled "Manufacturing a New Religion," which challenged Adler's reliance on Kant's categorical imperative to underpin his principle of the "sacredness of duty." The paper contended that only God's existence and man's belief in Him justified morality absolutely and the "sacredness of duty."

Sometimes the Jewish papers acknowledged and even echoed aspects of Adler's critique of contemporary Jewish religious life, such as the paucity of competent rabbinic leaders and the inconsistencies between the beliefs and actions of Jews resulting in empty synagogues.[2] Like the rabbis, however, the press adopted a meliorative approach which treated the effects rather than the causes. Making the services more attractive, for example, was among the solutions advanced to increase synagogue attendance. But the underlying social and intellectual discontent of many Jews with the entire Jewish religious experience was not probed. While the need for more intensive Jewish education was put forward by the traditionalist *Jewish Messenger,*[3] the idea that rabbis should candidly discuss modern intellectual problems with the growing number of Jewish skeptics and religious "indifferentists" was not. This cry was uttered by correspondents to the press, men and women suffering from religious tensions, but rarely by the Jewish papers themselves.[4]

The Jewish press reaction ran consistent with each individual paper's religious ideology. The traditional Isaacs and his *Jewish Messenger* became enraged at issues hardly of consequence to the leftist Reformer Ellinger and his *Jewish Times.* While the *Jewish Messenger* strongly disapproved of Adler's historicization of the Old Testament in the winter of 1876,[5] the *Jewish Times* remained unconcerned, for in Ellinger's words, "nobody insists upon the strict historical truth of the Biblical narrative and other dogmas."[6] And yet the *Jewish Messenger* heartily endorsed Adler's critique of Reform Judaism long after it had dismissed him from the Jewish fellowship.[7] By the spring of 1877, all three major Jewish papers, the *Jewish Messenger,* the *Jewish Times,* and the *American Israelite,* concurred that Adler had ceased to be an identifiable Jew.[8]

The three newspapers covered the Sunday lectures fairly closely from October 1876 through the spring of 1877. Following that period, Adler received only sporadic attention from the *Jewish Messenger* and even less from the *American Israelite.* Except for its long review of Adler's "Reformed Judaism,"[9] the *Jewish Messenger* offered no major reviews of the lectures; rather, it periodically defended Jewish beliefs and rituals perceived to be under attack. From its reports the reader would not know that Adler was drawing overflow crowds.

The *Jewish Times* was not concerned with Adler's attacks on traditional Jewish beliefs, Ellinger having already proclaimed the nonexistence of dogmas in Judaism.[10] In the fall of 1877, the paper began to publish large abstracts of Adler's lectures, possibly because the paper's new editor, Harry H. Marks, still considered him a Jew. But in the spring of 1878, as Adler's views on God became more explicit, Harry H. Marks—one-time follower of Adler—grew disenchanted with him.[11] Marks subjected Adler's ideas to critical scrutiny and chose to reprint without comment his previously published adolescent works, "The Christmas Tree,"[12] "Friday Evening,"[13] and "Elegy on the Death of Moses Mendelssohn."[14] Adler's adolescent attachment to Judaism and its rituals was exposed to the public. Whether Marks sought to embarrass him or to dramatize his religious transformation is not clear. In response to an inquiry as to the real identity of the author of the works, Marks did provide a possible rationale for his action.

> We would, nay, we will inform an anxious community. The articles referred to were written by the same Felix Adler who is now lecturer of the Society of Ethical Culture; they were written some eight years ago [note—at least ten] but, in our opinion, they are fully equal, if not, indeed, superior, to anything he has written since.[15]

The response of the *American Israelite* was closer to that of the *Jewish Messenger* than to that of the *(Reformer and) Jewish Times*.[16] Like the *Jewish Messenger* it defended the integrity of the Torah, Sabbath, circumcision, and the Day of Atonement.[17] Following the spring of 1877, the paper abruptly ceased to review Adler's lectures. Isaac M. Wise, its editor, was unalterably opposed to Adler, and he had probably decided not to grant him an additional platform from which to propagate his heretical ideas. Curiously, however, both New York correspondents for the *Israelite*, Phil Point and his successor in 1877, Julian Werner, at first resolutely rejected Adler's religious drift, yet in the end grew to appreciate him. As late as May 10, 1878, on the occasion of the establishment of a Workingman's Lyceum, Werner termed Adler "a man of whom we Americans in general and we Jews in particular ought to be proud."[18]

The negative reaction to Adler's Sunday addresses developed in intensity over the winter-spring of 1876–77. Recalling his May 15 proposals, the Jewish newspapers discovered no cause for alarm at the outset of the lecture series. The three papers reviewed his inaugural Sunday address of October 15, 1876—the *Jewish Times* with no comment,[19] and the *American Israelite* with favor.[20] The *Jewish Messenger* recorded its first impression in the following terms:

> Dr. Adler's addresses are apt to be characterized by practical passages and scholarly recollection; they are not, however, designed to reach the masses, nor do we imagine that they will be so surprisingly novel as to warrant any apprehension that they will interfere with existing institutions.[21]

In November the *Jewish Times* registered the first critical appraisal of Adler's views on religion.[22] While the *Jewish Messenger* reprinted his laudatory essay on "Jewish Literature" from *Johnson's New Universal Cyclopedia,*[23] the *Jewish Times* exhibited a more perspicacious understanding of his intellectual direction. Praising Adler's scholarship and eloquence, the paper pronounced the attempt by a *Jewish* congregation to hold Sunday services a failure. "The attempt fails because it will have no impact on Jewish religious thought, being itself devoid of all *religion*."[24] Ellinger perceived that Adler had argued against the fundamental axiom of positive religion—faith in a creator and ruler of the universe, and since he regarded this axiom as both self-evident and the only fundamental ingredient of Judaism,[25] he could not consider Adler's Sunday lecture movement as either religious or Jewish. He did not yet formally charge Adler with abandoning Judaism, although the implication seems to have been there; in fact, he credited Adler with honesty and courage of conviction. It was not his fault "if people still labor under misapprehensions." Ellinger maintained that Adler was opposed to all the shackles of positive religions, which by extension applied to Judaism as well.

Ellinger demonstrated the only real understanding among the Jewish news editors of the dire need for modern religious instruction by Jewish ministers. He called not only for Sunday lectures, which he claimed to have done for years, but for a Sunday service with the "addition of lectures on religious subjects" to replace the traditional homiletical format. Failing the institution of such lectures, Ellinger predicted,

> we will have a crop of Jewish liberals that will smile at such antiquated notions as Jewish mission, will laugh at your superstition of a revelation, will shrug their shoulders at your notion of immortality of the spirit, and will pity you for still cherishing a belief in a living God. . . . [They] will advise you to close your synagogues and dispose of your temples, abjure the old faith and bow before the high priest of modern times, the evolutionist and the nihilist. . . . Leaders of Congregations! Your orthodoxy furnishes the fuel that feeds the new light.[26]

Ellinger accurately prophesied the future direction of many Jews, and in this image accurately portrayed Adler's own liberal posture. But even he failed to grasp the potential of Adler's universalizing ethical religion. Evolutionism and nihilism were not the only modern alternatives to positive religion; Ethical Culture was an additional option.

In December 1876, Adler really came under fire for the first time. He had inaugurated a three-lecture series on the Bible in the course of which he denied the divine inspiration of the text and the authenticity of its Mosaic origins.[27] The lectures provoked the traditionalist *Jewish Messenger,* which depicted him as an unoriginal critic presumptuous enough to play on the ignorance of his listeners and to "lead them astray by sophistry." The paper predicted that Adler's movement "will burn itself out unless fuel be added to the fire by excited bystanders."[28]

Adler's ideas profoundly disturbed the editors of the *New York World* as well, for the paper devoted considerable space to a vigorous rebuke of him.[29] The paper felt that Adler was assailing both Christianity and Judaism and proclaimed that "a more continent skeptic has not been seen since the late Thomas Paine." Calling him "trite and unoriginal," the *New York World* reproached him for upsetting the faith of many without replacing it with anything: "When he is prepared to affirm something, the public may have an interest in hearing him. His public negations are simply silly and indecent performances." Like Ellinger, the *New York World*'s editors could not fathom a religion without a personal God; unlike Ellinger, they still insisted on the sacredness of Scripture.

Phil Point of the *American Israelite*, obviously deeply stirred, cited major portions of the *New York World*'s rebuke in his own report to the *American Israelite*.[30] He commented that "theological Jews have turned on Dr. Felix Adler. Dr. Gottheil whose congregation is likely to be affected by the new movement has on several occasions referred to it. Dr. Einhorn alluded to the subject in his usual ingenious manner in his Thanksgiving sermon."

Ellinger, in his *Jewish Times*, also cited selections from the *New York World*, but he was less upset by Adler's attack on the Bible than he was mystified about the reasons for his critique.[31] Since to Ellinger Judaism had no dogmas and "nobody believes now or claims to believe in the biblical word of God, inspired or literal," he asserted that Adler seemed to have established straw men only to demolish them: "The professor puts up [dogmas] as targets only to destroy them."

In response to the *New York World*'s assault, the trustees of the lecture movement wrote a letter to the editor expressing regret at the attack. The trustees insisted that the lectures did not intend to undermine the beliefs of the faithful but rather were meant to provide direction for "those who have actually ceased to hold the faith in which they were educated, and who right or wrong will not return to it." These people, the trustees claimed, did not want to drift aimlessly, but wanted to "be secured by argument and appeal to the anchorage of moral principle."

> The audience of Professor Adler's lectures has practically ceased to attach weight to religious dogmas, as such, being chiefly interested in hearing the history of their origin and influence, while those who are still deeply involved with the necessity of doctrinal belief rarely come, if at all; for them the lectures were certainly not intended.[32]

The trustees' declaration was the first public renunciation of Jewish dogmas by people associated with the movement, and it was so perceived by others. The letter evoked a number of responses. The *New York World* logically queried that if the lectures were intended for those who had spurned creeds and dogmas, then why was Adler spending so much time debunking precisely those creeds and dogmas? That was beating a dead horse.[33] But the more significant responses illustrated the uncertainty in the Jewish community as to exactly what Adler's movement represented. Ellinger inquired as to where and to what the trustees were drifting. Certainly not to Judaism, Christianity, or even deism; rather to "Adlerism," he declared. In perplexity and with acerbic sarcasm, he queried: "Or is it a movement, really intended for the glory of Standard Hall, with the prospective exclamation 'Standard Hall is great and Adler is its prophet!' Is it this and nothing more? Or what is it?"[34] Ellinger sensed a new departure; he sensed that Adler was attempting to create an innovative fellowship different even from Frothingham's Sunday lectures. But neither he nor anyone else had yet conceptualized Adler's "spiritual" direction. Had Ellinger at the least equated Adler with Frothingham, he would not have been so surprised at his ideas; but he equated neither the two men nor their beliefs.

While the trustees' letter itself was clear and unambiguous, it nevertheless served to confuse some Jews as to the true nature of the society's membership and of its final religious direction. Thus, in a letter to the *New York World*, December 14, 1876, correspondent "Honesty" cited his great difficulty in reconciling the trustees' conception of the goals of the society with that previously enunciated by Adler. The trustees' description of the type of individual the society wished to attract—one no longer adhering to traditional religious faith—implied a clear departure from Adler's initial renunciation of interference with any individual's cherished doctrinal beliefs and ritual practices.

> The letter of the trustees published in Friday's *World* informs the public that the lectures are designed for those only "who have actually ceased to hold the faith in which they were educated, and who, right or wrong, will not return to it." This is news indeed, and we wonder whether the intention of the moving spirits of the association was clearly stated to the gentlemen who were asked for their subscription to its funds. Certain it is that nothing of the kind was said by Dr. Adler or any one of his supporters at the preliminary meeting last spring [May 15, 1876]. To that meeting the rabbis of the various congregations were invited. These surely, could not have been supposed to have lost the faith in which they were educated and who, "right or wrong, would never return to it."

Moreover, despite the trustees' claim that the lectures were not intended for those "involved with the necessity of doctrinal belief," "Honesty" found that the Jews who subscribed to the society still participated fully and quite actively in Jewish congregational life. Indeed, he demanded an explanation for this very puzzling and inconsistent situation, which saw ostensibly faithful adherents of Judaism remaining affiliated with a movement which, according to the trustees, was not intended for them.

> We are further puzzled by the fact that none of the subscribers to the society who were members of congregations before the starting of the movement have cancelled their membership; they and their families join in the public worship as they were wont to do; children attend the Sunday-schools just as regularly as ever and will in due time receive the rite of confirmation in the identical faith which the parents are supposed to have lost forever. The ethical problem to be solved, then, is this: Either many of the subscribers are lamentably inconsistent and trifle with the most solemn concerns of man, or they were kept in the dark as to the ultimate design of the promoters of the lectures, and were thus induced to lend countenance and support to objects which, if honestly declared, they would have at once repudiated. . . . We find it extremely hard to reconcile the statements in the letter explanatory with the actions of both trustees and lecturer.

The correspondent concluded by asking "in the name of common honesty . . . for a plain answer to a plain question: Were the subscribers to the fund made aware of the scope of the lectures as at present avowed? Perhaps the subscribers themselves will favor us with a reply, set our doubts at rest, and indicate their own conduct."[35]

"Honesty" received no reply. Few Jews attending the Sunday lectures were prepared to reconcile the inconsistencies to which "Honesty" pointed. Some probably found no inconsistencies, first because the movement was very young and no official statements by the lecturer had been outlined concerning the society's relation to Judaism, and second, because they were unconcerned with Adler's ideology and came simply for the pleasure of hearing an excellent speaker. Still, by underscoring Adler's breaking of his May 15 promise not to interfere with existing rituals, "Honesty" highlighted the fundamental uncertainty of the established Jewish community as to Adler's intent and final direction.

The controversy over Adler continued. On January 5, 1877, the *Jewish Messenger* printed a correspondence from A. J. Cortis, who rebutted Adler's contention that the Bible illustrated the existence of human sacrifices among the Hebrews. On the same day the *American Israelite* responded to the trustees' letter in the *New York World*, portraying these men as "commercial gentlemen" whose new religion will be a "negotiable, gilt-edged . . . religion, when in proper trim endorsed by men of wealth and commercial reputation." The paper advised the trustees to stick to their own business and not to try to create a new religion, sarcastically remarking, "you have no experience in that branch of business and the article will find no market, it being overstocked already." Later that January, the non-Jewish *Daily Graphic* printed the first formal statement recognizing Adler's departure from Judaism. In response to the *New York Sun,* which had deemed Adler representative of New York Jewry, the *Daily Graphic* acknowledged his rabbinic family background but emphasized that "he will hardly be recognized as a Jew in creed by either the orthodox or 'reformed' members of the body. In fact, he is so heterodox in his views that his disciples consider him far in advance of even O. B. Frothingham. . . . Dr. Adler preaches what is known in Germany as 'Humanism' and however just and liberal his views in regard to Christ may be, he is hardly in a position to speak for the Jews of this city as a sect."[36]

In February 1877 Adler was dismissed as a Jew by both the *Jewish Messenger* and the *Jewish Times.* On January 28, 1877, he had commenced a four-lecture series on the origin of the Hebrew religion. The third lecture, February 11, 1877, contained his reference to circumcision as a barbarous rite, and this brought the simmering tension to an explosive head. The *Jewish Messenger* was incensed, both by Adler's remarks and the loud applause which they received from the Jewish listeners and by the dangerous impression which he was creating among non-Jews. It cited the *New York World*'s reaction that "the fact that such a tirade from him was received by a representative Israelitish audience, with apparent approbation and unquestionable applause, certainly indicates a hitherto unsuspected progress of ultra and revolutionary ideas among those who are known as the 'Reformed' Israelites."[37] Fearing this negative impression of the Jews as a group, the *Jewish Messenger* reassured the *New York World* and its readers that Adler's audience was not representative of New York Jews, but rather consisted of those who "disclaim being Jews—except accidentally." The paper no doubt included Adler in this category. On the front page it leveled a blistering attack against him for "tearing down the fabric of the religion in which he was reared, and casting ridicule upon doctrines and forms. . . . He advertises himself as the great reformer of all creeds, a radical of the deepest dye, a defamer of revelation, a bitter reviler of his brethren, an enemy to all recognized faiths." The *Jewish Messenger* challenged the rabbis to break their silence and to prevent the destruction of Judaism. They must initiate a movement, it claimed, "by way of strengthening the rank and file of American Israelites in their faith and conviction that the history of Judaism is not a lie." The type of "movement," however, was not specified. Finally, the paper suggested that Adler could not tolerate indifference; consequently, the strongest weapon against him was simply for those who believe in the Bible and Judaism not to attend his addresses.[38]

The *Jewish Times* disagreed with the *Jewish Messenger*'s call for a rabbinic crusade against Adler, for it had written him off as a Jew. It contended that Adler did not promulgate his doctrines as a Jew and that his "opinions are of no greater consequence to the Jewish religion than those of Schuneman-Pott [an organizer of the Freie Deutsche Gemeinde, then residing in America] or Professor Haeckel. Professor Adler does not claim to be a Jew religiously," the paper affirmed on February 23, 1877, "as he repudiates all religious belief and leaves it optional to members of his congregation whether to believe in a personal God or not."

On March 2, 1877, the *American Israelite* printed an account of the controversy written by Julian Werner, its New York correspondent. Werner suggested three ways in which to nullify Adler's effect: keeping silent, making the services more attractive, holding services on Saturday afternoons.

From the reactions of the newspapers, one receives a glimpse of the agitation which erupted in many quarters of the American Jewish community. A felt need to respond to Adler and to diminish his influence found expression in a variety of proposals, none of which was really instituted. The rabbis, by and large, also remained silent, and Jews who ostensibly still identified as Jews continued to attend the lectures. Saturday afternoon services were not implemented. The Jewish community was at a loss over what to do. Indeed, the Jewish papers were so caught up in determining a proper approach to Adler that they neglected to announce the formation of the Ethical Culture Society in February 1877, either by conscious design or because the formal organization of the association was of secondary import at the time. It was left to the *New York Daily Graphic* to report the event and to publish the bylaws of the new organization.[39]

In March the *Jewish Messenger* continued its assault on Adler, calling him a blasphemer and reminding him of the mishnaic law that "he who violates the covenant of Abraham has no share in the world to come."[40] "Ish Yehudi," who had assailed Adler following his May address, now accused him of plagiarizing his ideas on circumcision from Voltaire.[41] He then took an approach which became more pronounced as time progressed—comparing Adler unfavorably to Frothingham.

The difference between Mr. Frothingham's aesthetical and really noble idealism and young Adler's coarser and mean attacks on established ethics and principles is precisely the difference between liberalism and libertinism, transcendentalism and Voltaireism.[42]

"Ish Yehudi" concluded with an attack on the members of the society: "Why quote history to a society of 'Dollar Aristocrats' who have no mind for reason, no respect for either the past or the future?"

In April the *American Israelite* joined the *Jewish Messenger,* the *Jewish Times,* and the *Daily Graphic*[43] in declaring Adler a defector from Judaism.

> He can do away with the *Thorah, Sabbath* and *Milah, Yom Kippur,* etc. and make a new sect and call that a new ideal or a new phantasmagoria; but they must not claim to be Jews. A Jew is one who believes in one God and one Thorah; rejecting the latter and doubting the existence of the former is the plainest case of apostasy, much worse than embracing Christianity, Islam, or any form of Heathenism.[44]

By the spring of 1877, therefore, all three major Jewish newspapers had dismissed Adler from the Jewish socio-religious fellowship; one may assume that the Jewish communal and religious establishment had done so as well.

But not everyone concurred with Adler's ostracization from the Jewish fold. Some confusion still arose because he had not yet publicly repudiated the belief in God; only toward the end of 1877 did he express his views on this subject more explicitly.[45] Consequently, a very revealing cycle of correspondence appeared in the *Reformer and Jewish Times* in the spring of 1877 debating Adler's status as a Jew.

Harry Hananel Marks (1855–1916) was the son of England's leading Reform rabbi, David W. Marks. He had arrived in America in the mid-1870s and was employed at different times by the *New York World* and the *Daily Morning News.* Marks became one of Adler's leading proponents in the public debate during the spring of 1877. He defended Adler against the "unjust and absurd persecution . . . by the daily and religious press of the city."[46] Having attended his lectures, Marks asserted that Adler disclaimed "any desire to meddle with dogmas, except in so far as they affect the correct solution of ethical problems. . . . I am satisfied that he made this disclaimer in perfect good faith." Marks pointed out, rather justly, that "no attempt has been made to controvert Professor Adler's opinions. They have been met only by coarse and personal attacks." Declaring that Adler's opinions were "no more radical than those of Mr. Frothingham, [but] they are infinitely more practical," he concluded:

> As for the effect upon Judaism of Professor Adler's preaching, I do not believe that a religion which for centuries withstood the combined attacks of church and State, of argument, persuasion, force and perse-

cution, is likely to be materially injured now by the teachings of one man or class of men. If this were a conflict between Adler and Judaism, which it certainly is not, I should have confidence enough to back Judaism without fear of the result and without recourse to bar-room rhetoric or "billings-gate" invective.

One year later Marks made good his promise to take the side of Judaism. As Adler clarified his views on the existence of God toward the end of 1877, Marks gradually realized the extent of his theological radicalism. He could no longer identify with Adler's point of view; he left the society, and as editor of the *Reformer and Jewish Times* did not refrain from criticizing his former leader.[47] At this earlier point, however, his contention of the lack of conflict between Adler and Judaism could only have reflected his personal belief in Judaism's freedom from dogmas and creeds, and unlike Ellinger, the twenty-one-year-old Marks had not yet discerned Adler's lack of faith in the existence of a creator.

Correspondent "Ben Brith" vigorously took issue with Marks.[48] Scoffing at the latter's youthful age, he pointed to the irreconcilable confrontation between Adler and Judaism. To Marks's assertion that Adler did not "meddle with dogmas," this correspondent countered that Adler did nothing else. He mocked Marks's view that Adler was not attacking Judaism: "Even God has been pushed out of sight and elbowed from the platform of Standard Hall." To Marks's claim that Ethical Culture would not harm Judaism, "Ben Brith" contended that if that were true, then the movement would fail because Adler's goal was to uproot positive religions. He called Adler an "Apostle of Atheism," and concluded, "What will the Society for Ethical Culture do with a member that has no faith in the new faith? If Marks is right, Alder is wrong; if Adler is right, Marks is wrong."

Marks disputed the charges of "Ben Brith" one week later.[49] He rejected his opponent's designation of Adler as "an apostle of atheism" as a "silly libel." If Adler—for the sake of argument—were an atheist, he asked, then what were all his supporters?

Are not the Temple Emanu-El people and some Forty-fourth Street synagogue people [Shaarey Tefillah] who attend these lectures atheists too? . . . If so, why aren't they excommunicated? Why do Temple ministers still draw pay from these atheists? . . . But "Ben Brith" knows and everybody knows that the members of Dr. Adler's society have not severed their connection with the synagogue; they and their families join in public worship as frequently as they ever did; they still contribute to the support of our charities and continue to be officers of our temples. Strange atheists these!

Underlying the disagreement between Marks and "Ben Brith" were their divergent perceptions of the extent of Adler's theological radicalism. In this sense, "Ben Brith" was the more astute interpreter of Adler's critique of religion and theology. But Marks's description above reflected more accurately the still unsettled position of New York Jewry in relation to Ethical Culture. In point of fact, the Jews attending Adler's lectures in the first two to three years were representative of much of the city's Jewish population, most particularly the predominant Reform element; they were representative of many of New York's Jews despite the *Jewish Messenger*'s protestations to the contrary. Not every listener was a freethinking agnostic or atheist. "Respectable" Jews still attended the Sunday addresses because not everyone dealt with ethical and cultural matters on an intellectual-ideological plane. Jews could still affiliate with the Jewish community and simultaneously enjoy the eloquent moral exhortations and youthful idealism of Felix Adler on Sunday.

Marks's defense of Adler elicited two letters to the *Reformer and Jewish Times*, one indicative of the uncertainty among some New York Jews as to Adler's religious status, the other typifying the animosity against Adler felt by other Jews. In a letter to the editor, "Onyx" wrote:

> The vigorous reply of Mr. Harry Marks to the letter of "Ben Brith" as to Dr. Felix Adler and the belief of his society, suggests that it would be well for Dr. Adler himself to come out and plainly and honestly tell what his opinion is. . . . What is he, fish, flesh, or fowl; Jew, Atheist, or Deist?[50]

Judah Sequor, on the other hand, announced that he knew what Adler was—a denier of both deity and religion.

> The teachings at Standard Hall are not of science, they are a rehash of the most vulgar outcroppings of Voltaireism; they lead to moral corruption and mental debauch. It is for the destruction of mental leprosy that the attendants at Standard Hall are preparing themselves.[51]

From later Jewish newspaper reports in 1878–79 on Adler's Sunday addresses, it is clear that the Jewish press assented to Sequor's perception. The *Jewish Messenger,* in particular, took pains to snipe at Adler or his members whenever the opportunity presented itself. On June 22, 1877, the paper almost gloatingly noted what it considered to be the divine retribution meted out to three members of the society who had abandoned Judaism: Rosenblatt and Frankenheimer, though qualified, were not admitted to the bar because of their Jewish origins, and Joseph Seligman had been refused lodging at Saratoga's Grand Union Hotel. In December the paper termed Adler's flowery, rhapsodic oratorical style the "dishwater of gush,"[52] and one week later, in its review of his first collection of addresses, *Creed and Deed,* it reiterated that "Adler distinctly resigned from Judaism."[53]

A number of factors explain the vehemence of the press attack against Adler. The American Jewish community was still relatively young and developing. Despite the differences between traditionalists and Reformers, and internal squabbles among the Reformers themselves, there were indications of a trend toward the unification of American Jewry through the vehicle of such organizations as the Board of Jewish Delegates and the Union of American Hebrew Congregations. But in assailing basic Jewish doctrines, and what is worse, doing so in public, Adler was perceived to be undermining Judaism and disrupting the fragile Jewish religious and communal consensus that was emerging. Terrified Jewish communal leaders, cognizant of the continuing overflow crowds attending Adler's addresses while synagogue pews remained largely empty on Saturdays, justifiably felt Adler to pose an ominous threat both to the cohesiveness of American Jewry and the future of American Judaism. To them the threat was immediate and very real, and without extending the analogy too far, one may assume that a good number of American Jews underwent a shock experience similar or even identical to that experienced by European Orthodox Jews upon the rise of Reform Judaism.

Then, too, the very deep seated antagonism to Adler stemmed from resentment of the perceived arrogance of a young "fledgling" "censuring and chastizing" the community.[54] Adler's vision of social reconstruction included creating better living conditions, providing health and educational services for the children of the working poor *before* they became sick and *before* they grew to realize their ignorance.[55] And with the society's institution of a Workingman's Lyceum, Free Kindergarten, Visiting District Nurses, and support of tenement reform in the late 1870s and early 1880s, he was able to implement many of his socio-religious goals. But in March 1877, at which time the ideals had only been spoken about and not acted upon, "Ben Brith" denounced his audacity, and that of his society, in censuring the Jewish community.

> What have they done . . . what excellent works achieved, what sacrifices made for the "neglected classes," what great truths revealed? Have they raised Jews and Judaism from the ghetto in which we found it? Have they reared temples and our charities? Do they spend their days and nights caring for the poor? Do they go from hovel to hovel to search out and relieve the sufferers? Have they provided instruction for the poor? . . . It is the chickens now who have not yet lived long enough to be able

to say whether a corn is a corn, who lead the mother-hen and scold her soundly if she attempts to call back the wayward.[56]

To a large extent "Ben Brith" was justified in his accusation. American Jews, after all, had established charitable, educational, and communal organizations; they had created institutions for the general welfare of American Jewry, and the Society for Ethical Culture had done nothing yet to match these achivements. But Adler was lecturing on the *social recon-struction* of society based on the uprooting of the woeful living and working conditions of American labor, and it was on this issue that "Ben Brith" and most others missed the point. Adler sought the social recon-struction of society as an *ideological goal* aimed at fulfilling the social justice for which he understood the Prophets to clamor. Despite its implementa-tion of the Jewish tradition of "charity," the American Jewish community, like its American Protestant counterpart, had not yet committed itself to this new ideology.

Adler was bitterly resented also because the Jewish community dreaded the impression he was creating among non-Jews. Radical religious views, whatever their source, were still frowned upon by the vast majority of American citizens. The last thing the sensitive American Jewish immi-grant community wanted was for Adler to be regarded as representative of both Judaism and the Jews. And, indeed this was the impression which a few New York newspapers reported.[57] American Jews had toiled diligently to establish their reputation in America as reliable, "God-fearing" people; they had to overcome anew whatever socio-religious stereotypes and stigmas native Americans imputed to them. Adler's radical views threathened to cause their newfound status in gentile eyes to come crashing down, and so they felt compelled to repudiate him in the harshest terms. Repeated references are found in the Jewish press dis-claiming Adler as both a representative Jew and a product of Judaism. The *Jewish Messenger* reassured the *New York World* and its readers that Adler did not represent American Jewry.[58] Judah Sequor lamented that Harry Marks "has given occasion to moral and religious people of other persuasions and denominations to believe that the sensuality and infide-lity taught at Standard Hall is an unavoidable and natural consequence of Jewish education. It is distressing to read in the daily press," he continued, "that the attendance is in largest number of the Jewish persuasion, since the Jew has no adequate means by which the Jew can separate himself from the hybrids of Jewish parentage, who will persist in calling them-selves Jews, whilst repudiating and renouncing every obligation which the religion of their fathers' requires to constitute them moral and cultured Israelites."[59]

"Ben Brith" best underscored the apprehension and problematic position of American Jews in regard to Adler. In responding to Marks that the Jews, not Adler, had shown the greatest forbearance by refraining from attacking him to date, he noted:

> Great as their [American Jews] indignation is, their self-respect imposes upon them a dignified reserve; they said: if some audacious youth shrink not from making us again a "hissing and by-word" in the eyes of the Gentiles, after we have barely succeeded in silencing their gibes—we shall not add to our disgrace by our own clamor.[60]

While "Ben Brith" was wrong about the "dignified reserve" of American Jews—the Jewish press had denounced Adler already in February 1877 and continued thereafter—he nevertheless accurately mirrored their horror and consternation at being disgraced in the eyes of the Gentiles.

Prior to his own repudiation of Adler, Harry Marks charged that the personal attacks against Adler by some of the non-Jewish press stemmed not so much from opposition to his liberal views as from the simple fact of his being Jewish.[61] Marks asserted that Adler's teachings were no more radical than those of Frothingham, yet he alone was characterized by the non-Jewish press as "a youthful notoriety seeker mounting the rostrum in a swaggering, blatant manner," "a wanton disturber of the public peace," and a "literary upstart." Adler alone was accused "of telling falsehoods," "repeating lies"; his utterances were described as "more incoherent than those of a lunatic," and he was accused of "having something wrong with his brain."[62] In some measure Marks's contention was no doubt accurate, for the American press was not necessarily free from the polite anti-Jewish social prejudice then prevalent in American society. All the more reason, however, for American Jews to put their best foot forward and not to "rock the boat," precisely what Adler was judged to be doing. Adler and the reaction to him highlighted the latent insecurity of American Jews resting beneath their veil of unbounded optimism in the land of freedom.

Other factors also inspired the vehement reaction against Adler in the Jewish press. Jews felt betrayed because their most prominent son seemed to have turned against them. Having hailed him as a potential leader of American Jewry, having proclaimed his appointment to Cornell as an excellent omen for the future of American Jewry, the *Jewish Messenger,* in particular, was outraged at being deceived. Its fulminations against Adler reflected this feeling.

Jews also felt jealously resentful because most had to acknowledge—however grudgingly—Adler's enormous intellectual talents. Few young American Jews were of equal caliber, Kaufmann Kohler and Emil Hirsch being the outstanding exceptions. In its October 1877 review of Adler's essay "Reformed Judaism," the *Jewish Messenger,* which had vilified him for months, wrote: "We look forward hopefully to the time when Professor Adler himself will be so inspired by the Jewish tone of his own essay that he will abandon without a sigh, the platform for the pulpit, and devote the rare powers which he possesses for the amelioration and development of his race."[63] The paper, having found in the first part of Adler's article "no scoffing, no ridicule, no tendency to be pedantic or gushing, but . . . a great deal of enthusiasm for Judaism," would eagerly have reclaimed him for the Jews and for Judaism, fully cognizant of his "rare powers." One can almost sense Isaacs, the editor, sighing, "If only he had remained a Jew. . . ." But such was not the case.

Finally, the Jewish press was frustrated. Very often, the editors found themselves concurring—consciously or unconsciously—with Adler's critique of the Jewish religious situation in America, yet their own solutions seemed to be of no avail. Consequently, they vented their deep frustration on Adler, whom they regarded to be—if not the source of the problems—at the very least responsible for exacerbating them beyond endurable limits.

Rabbinic Attitudes and Controversy

American rabbis, on the whole, remained surprisingly silent on Adler and his ideas. With the exception of Kaufmann Kohler, the rabbis did not publicly repudiate Felix Adler in the early years of the Ethical Culture Society. At various times, the Jewish press reported the rabbis to have taken up the issue of Ethical Culture: Gottheil and Einhorn "alluded to the topic";[64] Einhorn's Thanksgiving sermon of 1877 illustrated the need for the concept of God to substantiate ethics.[65] In his *American Israelite* of March 2, 1877, Rabbi Isaac M. Wise expressed joy at Adler's having selected "Society for Ethical Culture" as the name for his organization. To Wise, this name represented Adler's explicit declaration of his departure from Judaism, and Wise now felt less concerned about Adler misleading other Jews. Wise himself neither debated the issues with Adler nor polemicized against him. Apparently the rabbis—particularly New York's Reform ministers—sought to avoid a direct public confrontation with him.

The Jewish press often referred to the relative rabbinic silence on Adler and sometimes even admonished the rabbis for it. The European *Is-raelitische Wochenschrift*, in reviewing the North American Jewish religious scene, noted that "among the clerics only a few voices were heard."[66] In the wake of the uproar on circumcision, the *Jewish Messenger* queried, "do the ministers and officers of our congregations feel that the moment has arrived for ending the silence with which they have hitherto met these efforts of Dr. Adler and his followers to destroy Judaism. . . ?"[67] Harry

Marks observed, "what have the ministers done to counteract its [Adlerism's] effects? Some of them have preached all around it in terms of denunciation, others of them have simply ignored or just skipped about it, tapping it here and there and jumping back as though they were afraid it will explode and hurt them. Outspoken denunciation I have heard none."[68]

Marks suggested that congregations and ministers "have launched their anathemas against the Ethical Culture Society . . . in private," and once again his observation proved correct. In a private interview with Julian Werner, Gustav Gottheil reportedly commented that "the alarming prevalence of skepticism was solely caused by that wicked man, Professor Adler, who ought to be denounced in and out of season."[69] At a private membership meeting on May 6, 1877, Einhorn's Beth El members unanimously adopted a resolution tendered by Mr. G. N. Herman proposing that in light of the Ethical Culture lectures, which "aim not only to destroy the foundations of Jewish religious teaching but also aim to mislead the listeners in their beliefs, the community should therefore decide that the board of directors with the agreement of Reverend Dr. Einhorn take the appropriate steps to contain such misleading teachings."[70] The resolution, however, engendered no practical results. Neither Gottheil, Einhorn, nor their respective temples took positive steps to oppose Adler.

Moreover, on the occasion when some rabbis did publicly differ with Adler, as Adolph Huebsch, Henry S. Jacobs, and Frederick de Sola Méndes did in the "Judaism is dying" controversy in December 1878, they did not attack him or his movement, but only adduced evidence to illustrate the excellent prospects of American Judaism.[71] Huebsch was the sole Reformer to respond openly; Gottheil and Einhorn did not publicly voice their opinions. Further, his response was extremely mild. He remarked that in his opinion Adler "will be a good Jewish preacher yet; he is making wonderful progress; he is a young man yet and occasionally gives vent to juvenile expressions."

Undoubtedly, local Reform rabbis were opposed both to Adler and to his ideas, as evidenced by Gottheil's caustic reference to him as "that wicked man." It is curious, therefore, that they seemed to shun a public "locking of horns" with him. Adler was attracting their members to his lectures and was perceived to be undermining Judaism: why did they not lash out at him in public? Why the public reserve? Reports in the Jewish press offer at least one motive for the taciturn rabbinic reaction. The rabbis may have made a tactical judgment not to engage in polemics with him in order to check the further dissemination of his ideas. Both the *Jewish Messenger* and the *American Israelite* suggested at different times that public silence would nullify his effect.[72] The *Israelitische Wochenschrift* added that the rabbis "felt they shouldn't disparage him" so "that Adler shouldn't inflate himself as a martyr of his advanced wisdom."[73] Perhaps they also concurred with "Ben Brith" that "we [should] not add to our own disgrace by our own clamor."[74] While these tactical considerations may explain the initial rabbinic silence, they do not, however, furnish a rationale for the continued rabbinic silence in the face of the rapidly growing attendance of Jews at the society's Sunday lectures, especially since for some Jews these lectures competed with rather than simply complemented Saturday synagogue services.

Marks probably supplied the basic answer to the question. Reform ministers such as Gottheil, Einhorn, and Huebsch felt constrained in attacking Adler because their own members attended his lectures, members who did not sever their connections with their Reform temples.[75] As the *Daily Graphic* noted, "it is indeed quite remarkable that so many of the young members of the old Jewish families crowd to hear him that his hall is overflowing every Sunday."[76] But members of the older Jewish generations attended as well. Some of the most prominent families of Emanu-El subscribed to Adler's lectures in 1876–77 (although the presidium of the temple, led by Lewis May, did not). And as Marks pointed out, the ministers felt that they "cannot afford to offend members of the congregations."[77] Moreover, the rabbis' salaries were underwritten by some of the very people attending Adler's Sunday addresses. The rabbis were, therefore, compelled to tread the delicate path between their internal frustration and anger at Adler on the one hand and judicious intra-synagogue politics on the other.

The rabbis may also have refrained from publicly repudiating Adler for fear of having to engage in public debate with him over the intellectual challenges confronting Judaism, particularly those of Bible criticism. American rabbis were not as well trained in Bible criticism as Adler, and, for the most part, were quite unprepared to refute intelligently his critical religious views. Among American rabbinic leaders, only Kohler and Emil Hirsch could match Adler's knowledge of modern religious scholarship. Kohler openly polemicized against him; Hirsch, Adler's friend and fellow student at Geiger's Hochschule, refrained from criticizing his ideas since he himself agreed with most of them. The other established rabbis, however—Reformers and traditionalists alike—were simply not equipped with the most recent modern scholarship in religion; most masked their intellectual deficiencies with public silence in regard to Adler.

In criticizing the impoverished intellectual level of the clergy in general and in assaulting their legitimacy as religious leaders, Adler no doubt had the rabbis in mind as well when he wrote:

We have now a set of religious tramps in our pulpits, such as we have never seen before—a set of religious tramps, I say, beggarly spirited men, who feed on the offal of knowledge, men who seek with threats and idle words and fears, to draw the chilling tribute from the weakness of women and the ignorance of men. And those able theologians such as did exist find no successors in our day, or find successors whom they must blush to own.[78]

Adler's charge was confirmed and elaborated upon by members of the Jewish community as well as the Jewish press. Marks complained that "too many ministers content themselves with a mere perfunctory performance of their official duties."[79] They blame the extant evils of Jewish religious life on the "radicals" (cf. Gottheil's declaration to Werner, above), but Marks asserted that the ministers' own incompetence was responsible for the "radicalism." They did not know what they wanted in religion: "Congregations go from moderate reform to radicalism, from radicalism to Heaven knows what'ism, and then—the minister pleads 'Radicalism' did it." Correspondent "Veritas" in the *Daily Graphic* echoed Marks's view: "Reform ministers either do not know what they believe or they have not the courage to tell."[80] The views of both men underlined the unpreparedness of the American rabbinate to synthesize the modern social-intellectual conditions with Judaism. The *Jewish Messenger* described the situation best when it affirmed the dire lack of leadership in American Judaism in both Orthodox and Reform ranks. There was no good prospect ahead, the paper declared, "until experienced men and not platform preachers, take the ship in charge, until men with practical foresight, learning and God's inspiration about them, until men with ability to conceive and courage to execute, despite the howling of a timid crew, until men of character shall stand at the wheel and guide us clear of rocks and mist. A great deal of ballast and a great many preachers will have to be thrown overboard."[81]

The one major exception to the relative rabbinic silence on Adler is found in the reaction of Kaufmann Kohler, rabbi of Chicago's Sinai Congregation. Kohler was the sole rabbi to publicly contend with Adler and his views in the early years of the Ethical Culture Society. A series of events in March 1878 touched off a major confrontation between Kohler and Adler's supporters and resulted in Kohler's repudiation of Adler in full view of the general and Jewish public. The *Chicago Daily Tribune* was used by both sides to express their respective points of view, and the American Jewish press as well as the *Index*, a paper devoted to "free religion," reprinted long excerpts of the reported dispute.

Among the leading Reform theologians of the day, Kohler was perhaps the most intellectually able. He subscribed to the classical Reform theology: ethical monotheism, Jewish mission, and the ultimate emergence of religious universalism. Like Adler, he was not timid; he had the courage to maintain his beliefs in the face of any opposition, and he too possessed the requisite scholarship to support his ideology. He was well versed in modern religious thought, including Bible criticism, but his affirmation of classical Reform theology, which paralleled that of Geiger, had not been shaken. Kohler avowed theism and perceived Adler to be an atheist bent on destroying Judaism. Consequently, when he believed that Adler was about to be invited to speak at his own synagogue, he vehemently protested, precipitating yet another religious controversy involving Felix Adler.

On March 20, 1878, a committee of the Sinai Literary Association invited Adler to deliver an address during his forthcoming stay in Chicago. Founded on May 9, 1877, the Sinai Literary Association was a social-cultural organization which held its functions at the Sinai Congregation. While not an arm of the synagogue, it was, nevertheless, identified with the temple. Felix Adler accepted the invitation, but Kohler refused permission for the lecture to take place at his synagogue.[82] Because the association was identified with the temple, the emerging conflict between it and Kohler assumed the guise of a synagogue-rabbi dispute, which contributed to fanning the interest of Jews across the nation.

On March 21, 1878, the *Chicago Daily Tribune* printed a report by Julius Rosenthal of the Sinai Literary Association announcing that Adler would speak on March 26 at Standard Hall. The paper also printed the full text of Kohler's protest against the association's initially contemplated decision to hold the lecture in his synagogue, as well as the association's retort. In his protest, Kohler asserted: "Of what benefit to a society of Jewish young people the lecture of a man who has deserted the Jewish flag, and openly professes his disbelief in God and immortality, I really fail to see, unless the eradication of the Jewish faith is the object contemplated. . . . I shall not allow my temple to be disgraced by a lecture to be delivered within its walls by one who blasphemes God and Judaism."[83] The association defended Adler and denied that he had "deserted the Jewish flag" or that he had "blasphemed against God and Judaism." It added that Rabbis Felsenthal and Liebman Adler of Chicago both "had spoken of Dr. Adler in the highest terms" and that while admittedly Adler "did not build strictly on theological ideas, while Kohler did, . . . the Association should not lose the opportunity to hear so distinguished and able a man, notwithstanding Dr. Kohler's emphatic protest."[84]

Kohler's rejoinder to the association appeared in the *Chicago Daily Tribune* the next day, March 22. He protested

against the insinuation . . . that my friends and colleagues of this city approve the teachings of Dr. Felix Adler. . . . No rabbi, in or outside of America, dares consider himself a Jewish minister while approving the ideas and expressions with which the Standard Hall lecturer in New York most irreverently and insultingly assailed the Jewish religion, and which are now in a milder form, set forth in his words *Creed and Deed*. There is, without reserve, the belief in God and immortality discarded and the "Eagle of Liberty" (suggesting no doubt Professor Felix Adler himself) proclaimed as the moral governor of human society *in place of the great King of the world*.[85]

Kohler also denied Adler's originality and claimed that his ideas were appropriated from Lubbock and Tylor. He asserted that Adler "would hardly have created such a sensation in Jewish circles were he not the son of the venerable Dr. S. Adler and the pupil of Dr. Geiger, misleading thereby, and by fine oratory, many an advocate of Jewish reform." Finally, Kohler accused Adler of the most serious offense: the rejection of theism. Adler, Kohler proclaimed, "declares this divine ideal of perfection and fountainhead of inspiration to be a mere dream." Kohler's perception of Adler's renunciation of theism lay at the root of the controversy.

Julius Rosenthal, responsible for having arranged Adler's lecture, responded on behalf of the association in the next issue of the *Chicago Daily Tribune*, March 23. He denied having had any intention to use Kohler's temple, asserting that Standard Hall had been rented without any attempt to find another place. He disclaimed having insinuated that Felsenthal and L. Adler "approve of the teachings of Adler" but reiterated his earlier comments, in the *Chicago Daily Tribune* on March 21, that "they had spoken of Adler in the highest terms." He averred that Kohler had purposely misrepresented his statement to suit his own aims. Furthermore, Rosenthal reminded Kohler that he—Kohler—had been accused of controverting Judaism no less than Felix Adler. "If Dr. Kohler charges that Dr. F. Adler most irreverently and insultingly assailed the Jewish religion, I wish to remind Dr. Kohler that the same charge is made against him with equal strength and justice by more conservative laymen and clergymen."

Adler delivered the address entitled "The Advance of Liberalism in America" at Standard Hall on March 26. The *Chicago Daily Tribune* devoted much space to the speech on the following day, highlighting its major ideas. Five hundred people attended and heard Adler outline the basic goals of Ethical Culture as well as deny the charges of plagiarism and atheism against him. He expressed pain that the charges came from "a gentlemen for whom he has the highest respect." As for the existence of deity and immortality of the soul, he suggested that as aspects of positive religion they deserved the respect of Ethical Culture. The society did not blaspheme or irreverently regard them. Nevertheless, he undercut the reality of these doctrines.

> The teachings of religion, even the most fundamental, were true in the sense of ideals only; and by ideals they meant something which was not fact,—something that was related to fact as poetry was related to history, having a truth of its own indeed, but a truth of higher order. Religion had bright visions, high assurances, but it could never establish its teachings in the light of facts,—so establish them in our minds as the facts of science were established.[86]

Adler rejected the "immoral conception of the Deity" which taught that God rewarded all virtue. Experience, he argued, clearly proved the contrary. Instead of the traditional concept of God, he advanced the moral ideology of liberalism, which instructed man to be good not because of the promise of immortality but for the sake of good alone.

Adler's speech elicited an immediate response from Kohler, published in the *Chicago Daily Tribune* on March 31.[87] Kohler again accused Adler of unoriginality, plagiarism, and blasphemy. He asserted that his idea that "human salvation does not depend upon human creeds but on a virtuous life is not new ethico-cultural but an old Jewish doctrine by Antigonos of Sochoh in the second century before the Christian era in his saying, 'Be not like slaves who merely serve their master for the sake of recompense.' " Kohler also charged Adler with borrowing his "hobby theory" of the origin of monotheism stemming from the deep affection of the Jews for their family from Otto Caspari's *Urgeschichte der Menschheit*, volume II, page 467. He accused him of attempting to replace the rule of God on earth with "human arbitrariness," concluding that "Felix Adler or any other man is to rule instead of an absolutely holy and divine will." And he repeated his earlier denunciation of Adler as a blasphemer: "I am very sorry to state that in this very lecture the professor in calling the God worshipped by Jews and Christians a 'fetish,' corroborated anew my charge of blasphemy brought against him." Finally, Kohler reaffirmed the fundamental theological view of all Reformers, that conscience was an insufficient ground on which to base morality: " 'The rock of human conscience' is not firm enough to build society upon it, unless it is, as religion shows it to be, founded upon a divine will re-echoed in the heart of man."

The matter did not end there. Kohler's charge of plagiarism induced some Jews to try to verify the accusation; no one could. In a letter to the editor of the *Chicago Daily Tribune* published April 2, 1878, Oscar Jacobsohn claimed that he had "compared and critically studied what Caspari says, and has done the same with Adler's writings, and [is] utterly unable to find anything sustaining Dr. Kohler's charge." Jacobsohn expressed his confidence in and respect for Kohler but suggested that a mistake must have been made: "Will Dr. Kohler, whom I assure of my highest personal regards, please rise and explain?"

Julius Rosenthal also sought corroboration or refutation of Kohler's charge. He wrote Bernhard Felsenthal soliciting his opinion on the matter, and on April 2, 1878, Felsenthal replied:

In compliance with your request, I have carefully read and re-read in the two volumes of Caspari's *Urgeschichte der Menschheit* not only page 467, but also the preceding and following pages, and as you have asked me to give you the result of my examination, I cannot but state that in my opinion not the least mention is there made of prophetic monotheism, or of any other kind of monotheism, or of the source of monotheism, or of any connection between family-affection and monotheism, and so forth. It is utterly inconceivable to me how it could have been asserted that on said place (p. 467, Volume II) the theory be set forth that "the deep affection of the Jews for the members of their family was the source of prophetic monotheism" [Kohler's assertion of March 31].[88]

Felsenthal had second thoughts about getting involved in a controversy with his rabbinic colleague, so he impressed upon Rosenthal, in a letter of April 3 headlined "Confidential," not to publicize his opinion.

You probably received my lines dated from yesterday. I now request that you not make public use of them. You will understand that it must be unpleasant for me to be pulled into the controversy. If you wanted to point out the complete truth to the world on this point, you could do it better by challenging Herr Dr. K. [Kohler] to find men to confirm his contention and that you would give $100 to charity if these men declare that they found in Caspari's book Vol. II, p. 467, discussion of the origin of monotheism. I hope I'm surely not exposed to a misinterpretation of the above-mentioned request.[89]

Felsenthal and Oscar Jacobsohn were both correct, for Caspari does not at all mention the origin of monotheism.[90] How Kohler could have made such a mistake is not clear, unless he purposely made the charge of plagiarism only for polemical reasons, not expecting anyone to check. That, however, is unlikely, and the issue remains to be resolved.

Adler himself was apparently prepared to write the Chicago paper in his own defense but decided against it. An undated, unsigned, and unfinished manuscript has been preserved which begins "To the Editor of the Chicago Tribune" and reads:

My attention has been directed to an article headed "Alleged Plagiarism" published in your issue of April 2 [Jacobsohn's letter]. Now which is the particular portion of Dr. Adler's book that tends toward indicating plagiarism from Caspari! . . . Will Dr. Kohler please rise and explain? . . . Dr. Kohler publicly charged me with plagiarizing from Otto Caspari's work on the primitive history of Mankind. Can you imagine the utter surprise with which on turning to the passage in question I found that it offers not even an apology for Dr. Kohler's very decided and deliberate assertion. . . . I have submitted the passage quoted to several men of sound judgment and high repute and they concur with me. . . . In this whole unfortunate matter I cannot but deplore that over-great zeal for his cause should have misled an excellent man into so wrong [a] position. His attack saddened me compared with the kind treatment received at the hands of other clergymen both of the Christian and Jewish faith.[91]

The upshot of the affair was that in April 1878, the Sinai Literary Association expressed its regrets to Kohler if he had been offended, that not having been the intention of the society. The society further informed him that it had enlarged upon its original objective of studying Jewish history and literature to include all aspects of culture. The society now characterized itself as nonsectarian, yet thanked Kohler for his own lectures in the past and expressed the hope that he would address it in the future.[92]

The controversy was followed closely by the American Jewish community, and all three major Jewish newsweeklies covered the dispute. The support and praise Kohler received from the Jewish press is perhaps best illustrated by Harry Marks's comments in the *Reformer and Jewish Times* on March 29, 1878:

It is not a common thing to find a minister with the courage of his opinions. Our clergymen are often over-timid, and trot all around a danger instead of grappling with it boldly as Dr. Kohler has done. We believe he is the only Jewish minister who has come out over his own name and charged Professor Adler with being a "Blasphemer of God and Judaism." There is no denying that Dr. Kohler has acted the part of a man who has the courage to think for himself, and the courage to speak his thoughts when the occasion requires. In this respect, we think he may serve as an example to some of his brother ministers here and elsewhere.

The non-Jewish *Index,* on the other hand, edited by the radical liberal Francis E. Abbot, referred to Adler's "encountering heated denunciations from bigoted Jews, who can neither understand nor tolerate the advanced position he has taken with reference to Judaism; and even 'Reform Jews' shrink away from his side."[93] In retort to the *Reformer and Jewish Times*'s praise of Kohler's courage and honesty, the *Index* wrote:

> This may be conceded, as one conceded courage and honesty to the Grand Inquisitor Torquemada, who used to burn Jews for the crime of Judaism; but one may well wonder that such flaming intolerance should call forth no word of rebuke from a Jewish "reformer."

Actually, Abbot's "wonder" stemmed from his misconception of Adler's relation to Reform Judaism. Adler's views on theology necessarily clashed with Reform Judaism. Kohler was not "intolerant," but rather, in reaffirming theism, was acting as a vocal defender of the Jewish faith. Even Rosenthal's reminder to Kohler that he too had been severely criticized for his religious views was not entirely in place; while Kohler did depart radically from the traditional ritual observance of the Sabbath by holding supplementary services on Sunday, he, nevertheless, drew the line at changing fundamental Reform theology. To him, Judaism without theism was not Judaism; an attack against theism was an attack against Judaism.[94] Kohler's perception of Adler as an atheist whose opinions threathened to lead Jews astray justified his assault.

In this sense, Adler was wrong when he noted of Kohler's attack on him: "It was sad on its own account that one so liberal should be so bitter in his denunciations of another whose only difference is that his liberalism is called by another name."[95] Kohler was not simply a "liberal" of "another name": he was a liberal still rooted to a particular creedal view antithetical to Adler's entire conception of religious reality. Intellectual harmonization of the two views was impossible, and Kohler was the sole Reform minister to publicly proclaim this fact. The *Reformer and Jewish Times*, therefore, was more accurate in its evaluation of the polemic when it wrote:

> From Dr. Kohler's point of view of Professor Adler's opinions and teachings he was certainly justified in refusing to allow him to lecture in the temple. Most assuredly, one who "blasphemes God and Judaism" has no business in a Jewish house of worship; and no doubt, Dr. Kohler is satisfied that Professor Adler does blaspheme God and Judaism. Dr. Kohler deserves great credit, at least, for the bold stand he has taken in the matter, and for the promptness with which he has asserted what he considered his rights and performed what he deemed his duty.[96]

A number of factors help explain why Kohler reacted so vigorously in public while his Reform colleagues remained silent. By profession Kohler was a theologian and by temperament a fighter.[97] In the face of a crucial threat to his theological beliefs, this combination proved explosive. In addition, as a respected modern scholar of religion, he did not fear a public confrontation with Adler; he could hold his own. Then, too, Kohler's circumstances in Chicago differed from those of his New York colleagues. His temple members did not simultaneously belong to both the Ethical Culture Society and his synagogue; his salary was not paid by members with dual loyalties and commitments, and he did not have to worry about offending his own congregants (although one gets the impression that nobody could have intimidated him under any circumstances). Finally, Kohler's security in his temple was enhanced by his own religious progressiveness. Having introduced Sunday services, he had responded to the socio-economic-spiritual needs of his congregants. He was not susceptible to the charges of rabbinic timidity and myopia so prevalent in the Jewish press. Indeed, he himself was often accused of being overly progressive in regard to his Sabbath innovation. No doubt some, if not all, of these factors contributed to his outspoken condemnation of Adler.

In the wake of Kohler's charges and the public furor which they caused in the American Jewish community, Samuel Adler defended his son in his response to a letter from his close friend, Felsenthal.[98] Expressing his "gratitude for your [Felsenthal's] words of esteem and friendship as well as your appreciation of my son," Adler continued:

And yet it is difficult for me to answer your letter fully for I do not feel strong enough to discuss the subject. In fact I try not to feel harshly against those who have joined in branding a pure and idealistic soul as godless and immoral because it does not agree with their own ideas. It is quite natural that they should attempt to make me too a target for their arrows. I am to be forced to exert my fatherly authority in order to silence my son. Honest fanaticism is blind, but hypocritical fanaticism aims to obstruct and confuse people's vision. They do not understand nor wish to recognize that in the face of a search for truth a father's authority is at an end. Even if I had such authority I should consider it a sin to exercise it. I am convinced that the aim and purpose of my son's work is a deeply sacred and religious one, that the attribution of Atheism and Materialism and other impure motives are purely malicious slanders. If his convictions in some respects are not the same as mine, they are entitled to as much consideration as my own. For this reason I allow all these near and contemptible criticisms to pass over me and endeavor to support them with as much patience and resignation as my sense of duty and devotion to God allow me to do.

This letter testifies to Samuel's enormous love for his son, his abiding respect for Felix's intellectual integrity, and his total commitment to free religious inquiry. It also testifies to the unbridled hostility of much of the Jewish communal leadership which confronted Felix Adler at that time.

The warm and friendly reaction of Rabbi Bernhard Felsenthal to Felix Adler represented a singular exception to the general hostility erupting in the Jewish community and simmering in rabbinic quarters. Felsenthal respected and admired young Adler; he assented to his basic religious ideal of fostering social justice and ethical behavior. He believed that Adler and his society could still remain within Judaism despite Adler's religious ideology, and he attempted to convince Adler to identify himself and his society within the broad framework of the Jewish consensus. No doubt Felsenthal's interest in having him retain his Jewish identification reflected his long-standing intimate friendship both with Samuel and Felix Adler, evidenced in his extensive correspondence with them.[99] But perhaps more significantly, Felsenthal's concern over Adler's Jewishness may suggest his having held a broader conception of the religious nature of the Jewish consensus than hitherto advanced by Reform Jews.[100]

In his letter to Adler, January 25, 1878, Felsenthal lauded "the excellent lectures which you published in *Creed and Deed*," which appeared in late 1877, and noted:

My favorable bias for you, dear sir, and for your endeavor, was not shaken through your book, on the contrary, it was heightened. Your lectures are full of light and clarity, full of warmth and full of enthusiasm for everything beautiful and good, and you prove from this that your noble soul is completely filled with these thoughts, and that you contribute with all your might to realize the ideals of humanity which you carry in your mind.[101]

But Felsenthal expressed concern over the means by which Adler was trying to realize his religious goals.

The only thing that I'm afraid of is that the means which you employ should not prove effective. It has already been tried several times on the basis of mere Deism or Humanism to achieve a new community. All attempts have been unsuccessful, of all drastic strivings, nothing has come of them.

He, therefore, offered Adler an alternative.

And why shouldn't you try to realize this new life ideal on a Jewish basis?

Ah, you say, even if I'm not pushed in the direction of dogmatic company, it is required of me to confine myself to a Race, to be within my Race. But I don't care to recognize any Race division anymore in the society which I wish to construct, at least not among those who live comfortably together.

But who forces you then, basically, to cling to the Race if you are of the opinion that religion and ethics should be denationalized?[102] If you and the esteemed Society declare that your association is a Jewish association then I don't know how any zealot could push you out of Judaism. In a "Jewish" association, you could in the end declare the same things which you declare in your non-denominational Society, stand on the same principle in your Jewish association which you now profess, teach the same fundamental ideal which you now so spiritedly proclaim, then you could still find many non-Jewish groups who share your opinions. As you once so courageously declared in your lectures dear Dr., that you don't insist on circumcision, then you could do what you think is expedient in your Society when you accept new members. So I at least don't comprehend why your association cannot have the byword Jewish attached. A name does much for the cause.[103]

Felsenthal seems to have contended that the Ethical Culture Society could be a Jewish society if only Adler would so designate it. According to him, Adler's commitment to religious universalism and to a de-nationalized, nondenominational religion free of racial restrictions did not preclude his inclusion and that of his society within the Jewish consensus. But what would have defined the society as Jewish—simply an expression of intent by Adler that "his association is a Jewish association"? If, as Felsenthal suggested, race and nationality did not define one's identity as a Jew, then what would? Ideas? If so, which of Adler's ideas would have qualified him for membership in Judaism? Aware that Adler had rejected the belief in monotheism, which heretofore had constituted the fundamental basis of the Reform Jew's Jewish identity, Felsenthal, in his letter, did not seem to provide the reason for his considering Adler still to be a Jew.

Almost a year later, in a letter to Adler on December 13, 1878, Felsenthal again broached the idea of his remaining within Judaism. He lamented the "blind fanaticism and vulgarity, crudity and thoughtlessness which ganged up on you, dear Doctor, the brave religious teacher. . . . In fact dear friend, such grievous occurrences strengthen my conviction that often more true piety and sincere religiosity is found more in the world of 'Atheists' than we find among those who continuously have *heichal hashem, heichal hashem* ['The temple of the Lord, the temple of the Lord'] on their lips and who constantly exude piety."[104] But Felsenthal went on:

Don't believe that I completely agree with your effectiveness. I told you this before, orally and in writing, and I have to maintain my previous statements. I do not oppose the content of your teachings—specifically, a religion of the deed but not the creed—*in which also my religious teachings can be found, with the exception of the indisputable acknowledgment to a higher world-ruling being;* not with the content of your teachings do I quarrel but with the form in which you present them to the world. *In my judgment, you should proclaim your teachings as teachings of Judaism and proclaim them under that name. You should give to the existing life-powerful, newly rejuvenated Jewish organism a great, meaningful, far-reaching effectiveness and not to restrict yourself overnight to form a new free society.* [105]

Since Felsenthal acknowledged Adler's lack of belief in theism while still portraying his religious orientation as Jewish, it would appear that at this time he did not hold the theological espousal of monotheism to be the sine qua non criterion of membership in the Jewish consensus. If tenable, this highly suggestive conclusion reflects a significant departure on Felsenthal's part from previous Reform Jewish ideology.

What, then, defined the Jewish consensus in Felsenthal's opinion? Certainly Jewish religious considerations rather than national or racial ones.[106] In suggesting to Adler that he proclaim his "teachings" as Judaism, in asserting that his own religious teachings also upheld the primacy of the deed over the creed, in apparently minimizing the significance of the theological divergence between them, Felsenthal may well have conceived the humanitarian religion of Kantian-prophetic ethics and of social reform which Adler was preaching to be the new Judaism of the modern era. If so, then social action and proper moral behavior—not theological beliefs—indicated one's affiliation with Judaism; by these standards Felsenthal could still welcome Adler into the broad frame of Judaism.[107] In fact, Felsenthal's conception of Judaism as interpreted here seems very reminiscent of that which Adler himself presented in his Temple Sermon in 1873.

In January 1879 Felsenthal published his four articles in the *Jewish Advance,* apparently again bidding Adler and his society to identify themselves as Jewish. But in a letter of March 16, 1880, Adler—with regret—unequivocally informed Felsenthal that he could not abide by this wish. He apologized that it had taken him over a year to respond to the articles, but he just could not bring himself to clearly affirm his departure from Judaism to his esteemed friend for fear of hurting him.

I only wish to say that despite the bad appearance, I hold the same high esteemed and grateful conviction for you as before. Your articles in the

Jewish Advance touched and moved me deeply. I recognized from it rightfully your mild, far from dogmatic temperament, and the noble way of thinking towards others that hold different beliefs which distinguishes you. If I remained silent, when you might have expected to hear an immediate word of explanation as to how your ideas affected me in every possible way, the reason for this was—if I may express myself freely?—just this, that I deep down felt, that in your expectations, now and never can I express that I in fact stand on a completely different ground concerning Missuri [*Mesurei?*] Israel and it was and remained for me until now impossible to tell you this. It seemed to me as if I would grieve you with such a definite declaration. . . . It must appear ungrateful as it is now impossible otherwise for me to persist in my once-grasped fundamental idea.[108]

Adler wanted to be certain of retaining Felsenthal's friendship in light of his pronouncement, and so continued:

Now months have passed since those remarks appeared in the *Jewish Advance* and I blame myself for letting myself be restrained by various considerations instead of insuring myself in the meantime of the continuance of your friendly sentiment. You yourself have pledged this [friendly sentiment] to me for the future, in beautiful words, *even if an uneliminatable difference of opinion should separate us.* It would do me extraordinarily good if I would have the certainty through a few words from you that I am not deluded or misled in my hopes.[109]

A letter of Adler to Felsenthal dated May 15, 1881 suggests that Felsenthal, in fact, did respond to his request, although the response unfortunately has not been preserved;[110] and Adler continued to enjoy Felsenthal's warm friendship over the years.

The "uneliminatable difference" to which Adler alluded in his March 1880 letter most probably referred to Adler's own belief that monotheism was the intrinsic and necessary ingredient of Judaism. According to Adler, specific theological ideas prescribed the bounds of the Jewish religion and therefore—to him—the nature of the Jewish consensus. To him, there existed a substratum in Judaism that remains unchangeable: the "spirit of the Bible." This spirit is "expressed in two fundamental propositions: the existence of one God, the Author and Governor of the Universe, and the Messianic mission of the people of Israel."[111] Having discarded monotheism as well as the concept of Jewish mission, Adler found no intellectual reasons to justify Felsenthal's proposals that he remain an identifying Jew. His sincere universalist orientation dismissed the underlying implications of Felsenthal's call to him, which implicitly labeled humanitarianism as Judaism. The Prophets spoke to all, Adler declared, not simply to a chosen race.[112] In the early twentieth century, however, the emergence of Rabbi Stephen S. Wise and his Free Synagogue seemed to fulfill Felsenthal's apparent goal of creating a humanitarian society dedicated to social justice within the ranks of Judaism.

Neither heated controversy, public polemics, nor warm friendship deterred Adler from attempting to fulfill his life's mission. He himself recalled that his gradual separation from Judaism during the 1870s left him a different person traveling through "a new country."[113] His loyalties and energies were rerouted and dedicated to the furtherance of the Society for Ethical Culture in New York and the Ethical Culture Movement in America and abroad.

Adler's Ethical Culture Society was indeed "a new country"; it represented a novel feature in modern Jewish history. Modern Jewish history is marked by the Jew's attempt to redefine himself as a Jew and to cope with his religion and identity in the modern world. Broadly speaking, three distinct categories have appeared—the secular Jew, the denominational Jew, and the nationalist Jew. Adler's conceptual formulation and concrete founding of the Society for Ethical Culture created the possibility of the emergence of a fourth type of Jew: one who retained the memory of his historical ethnic-racial origin, but who felt no need either to promote or renounce his Jewishness. This Jew identified himself neither with any form of denominational Judaism nor with any secular or nationalist alternative, but rather associated himself with a universal religious fellowship. Ethical Culture permitted the simultaneous shedding of Jewish particularism with the retention of religiously motivated action, all without the conversion which would have been necessary in Europe. This phenomenon—as an achieved aim—was new to modern Jewish history.

As the years passed, however, few Jewish members of the society continued to regard Ethical Culture as a *religious* movement, but rather they conceived of it as an ethical movement for the social amelioration of society. The "religiousness" of the movement was defined by Adler's ideology, which matured and became more sophisticated over the years; but few members kept pace with his intellectual elaborations. And as time went by, one witnessed a gradual intellectual separation and ultimate estrangement between the leader and his own society.

Adler recognized this fact, but reaffirmed his contention that room existed for everybody under the roof of Ethical Culture. Indeed, he said, "the ethical movement is religious to those who are religiously-minded and to those who interpret its work religiously, and it is simply ethical to those who are ethically minded."[114]   Nevertheless, cognizant of the deep gulf separating him from his members, he held private Sunday meetings for a select group of people more attuned to his way of thinking. He found the highest and noblest interpersonal relations only within this elite central core of the society, a group whose intellectual proclivities and abilities matched his own.[115] While the *possibility* of a universal *religious* fellowship had been created, in the long run the society as a whole, for the vast majority of its members, was an ethical—not a religious—fellowship.

Adler's intention to create a platform for the discussion of ethical-religious problems and to practically implement social justice had been largely fulfilled by the Ethical Culture Society. He himself, however, passed beyond this apostolic, "prophetic" stage. From the mid-1880s on, his booming proclamations of the sublimity of the moral law and his call for the institutionalization of prophetic ethics mellowed. By his own admission, his marriage in 1880 to Helen Goldmark, daughter of forty-eighter Joseph Goldmark, stimulated his intellectual maturity, for it "deeply impressed on my attention the idea of complementary as against uniform relation."[116] Adler's outlook on ethics evolved beyond Kant's uniform ethical ideal and demanded a differentiated ethical ideal recognizing the individual needs of each person. He found it in his concept of individual "worth."[117]

Further, as other groups and movements, such as the Protestant Social Gospel, Christian Scientists, Reform Judaism, and Socialists, incorporated platforms of social action through the years, Adler was constantly forced to outline the continued uniqueness and relevance of Ethical Culture. Repeatedly, he addressed his old and new members in the 1890s and in the twentieth century on the topic entitled "What Do We Mean By Ethical Culture" and the like. The need to distinguish the uniqueness of Ethical Culture helped him to refine his religious-ethical ideology. He defined the bounds between ethics and religion more clearly, and even couched his own religious ideas in traditional metaphysical language, such as "Godhead" and "leap [of faith] in the dark." He continued to seek a viable ideology to discover the meaning of life in the face of increasing human suffering, and he conceived of this quest as ethical *religion*.

Most of his membership, however, did not follow him in this pursuit. They remained at his initial stage of prophetic idealism and adhered to the aim of trying to live moral lives while contributing to the social welfare of mankind. Brought up in the age of logical positivism and pragmatism, the children of the original members, in particular, manifested little sympathy for or understanding of Adler's religious pursuit couched in the language of philosophical idealism. Then, too, by the turn of the twentieth century, the practical, nonintellectualized social work of John L. Elliott, Adler's associate leader in the New York Society, contrasted sharply with Adler's penchant for abstract metaphysical speculation and presented a much more understandable and personally compelling form of leadership than Adler's.

By the end of World War I, Adler's thinking could no longer be taken to reflect accurately the Ethical Culture Society's spiritual and intellectual direction. Adler's growing sense of isolation from the membership was a source of deep frustration to him, and in 1930 he expressed his conscious awareness of being dated and alienated from his own society. In an atuobiographical note under the byline "Psychological Analysis," he reflected: "Eye opening. The world has changed. Instead of being in the van of reform, I discover that I am rated as backward. . . . The world wants none of your wisdom."[118]

To an extent, in addition to his intellectualist orientation, Adler's own personality had contributed to his isolation. Wherever he served in a professional capacity, be it in public or even within the New York society's institutional life, he exuded an air of formality, propriety, and a dignified bearing which commanded respect but which also projected an image of stiffness and stuffiness, aloofness and austerity, that annoyed some and even instilled fear in others.[119] His intellectual elitism—a trait held since adolescence—his increasing authoritarianism and attitude of noblesse oblige, ultimately upset the Ethical Culture leadership itself.[120] Ironically, yet almost predictably, the man who had fought countless battles against dogmas and doctrines through most of his adult life persisted in dogmatically upholding the truths and visions at which he had finally arrived.

One wonders how much more successful the New York society might have been, how much more receptive even to Adler's ideology, had the other side of his personality been more openly displayed. To his family and intimate acquaintances, Adler revealed an aspect of himself radically different from the more well-known "forbidding" image which he cast in public. In private, he was totally informal, at ease, boisterous, and even jocular; he was a teaser, a lover of word games—especially puns, however bad—and an impish prankster. His hundreds of letters to his wife—some easily classifiable as love letters—exhibit the feelings of a tender, even passionate husband and an extremely affectionate father. It was probably unfortunate for the Ethical Movement as a whole that these more endearing, "humanizing" traits of Adler did not surface in public more often.

Be that as it may, one cannot help but marvel at the deep irony of Adler's work: a man who from the 1870s on had sought the most universal of religious principles, the most inclusive of associations, the most modern of intellectual methods, the most practical-ethical of purposes—he became the patron of a rather narrow circle of the enlightened at the fringe not only of American Judaism but of American (and Western) life generally. The man who in the 1870s and 1880s had been in the vanguard of social and religious reform, who had first introduced American Jews to the idea of progress and evolution in religion, who had announced Ethical Culture's supersedure of all religions as a matter of historical evolution, had now been deemed outmoded and left behind. In a very real sense, Felix Adler's devout belief in social and religious progress in history had been vindicated, and he had now become its victim.

In less than ten years Felix Adler had undergone a dramatic and radical religious transformation. Just as Samuel Adler had felt spiritually liberated by traveling along the path from the Orthodoxy of his father, Sirig, to Reform Judaism, so too his son Felix felt liberated by departing from Samuel's Reform Judaism and continuing the religious journey to Ethical Culture. Unlike Samuel Adler's religious odyssey, however, that of his son led him outside the pale both of Judaism and the Jewish community; in the 1870s, Felix Adler came to regard Judaism as a sophisticated religion of the past, but as an outmoded vestige in the present.

Chapter VI

Adler and the Jewish World
After 1880

Attitude to Judaism and the Jewish Community

Despite having broken with Judaism and the Jewish community in the 1870s, Felix Adler maintained a lifelong scholarly interest in the evolution of the Jewish religion and in Jewish history and historical personalities. His voluminous library contained some of the most prominent contemporary works of Christian scholars in the field of Jewish religion, including George F. Moore's *Judaism,* Julius Wellhausen's *History of Israel,* Johannes Pedersen's *Israel: Its Life and Culture,* W. Robertson Smith's *Religion of the Semites,* and Emil Schürer's *The Jewish People in the Time of Jesus,* to list but a few. Adler's archival remains are replete with short essays or brief sketches in note form which comment on these and other works on religion and ancient Near Eastern history.[1] His library also contained some of the latest research by Jewish scholars, including Simon Dubnow's *History of the Jews in Russia and Poland,* Moritz Lazarus' *Ethics of Judaism,* and Louis Ginzberg's *Legends of the Jews.* He wrote brief critical notes on these books too, as well as on such figures as Philo, Jehuda Halevi, Maimonides, Bahya ibn Pakuda, and Moses Mendelssohn.

From the 1880s on, Adler's point of view in discussing Judaism shifted significantly. Unlike his addresses on Judaism in the 1870s, in which he tried to demonstrate the historical contingency of Jewish rituals and beliefs in order to undermine their authority, Adler's main interest in his lectures on Judaism in subsequent years centered on the analysis of the merits and shortcomings of Judaism as a system of ethics. This new orientation corresponded to a general development in his thinking beginning in the early 1880s. Announcing his intention, in 1881, to undertake a comprehensive study of the entire history of ethical thought in order to propound an ethical theory applicable to the modern age and an ethical ideal appealing to modern man,[2] Adler became engrossed in the study of the Prophets and those sections of the Old Testament dealing with ethical behavior and moral injunctions. He now critically evaluated the Jewish ethical tradition, as seen in the few speeches on specifically Jewish topics which he delivered to the society from the 1880s on, as well as in numerous notelike portraits of individual Prophets.[3]

Adler's intensive study of ethical thought over the years led him to view the Jewish religion as but the first of three great ethical movements of mankind, followed in turn by Christianity and Ethical Culture.[4] He concluded that the Prophets had revolutionized the notion of religion in the ancient world by introducing ethics in religion; and that "the religious development of the human race took a new turn in their sublime predications."[5] Nevertheless, already in 1885, Adler declared that the Old Testament—specifically the prophetic literature—reflected but an incomplete stage of ethical truth, since he had come to regard the ethical content of both Judaism and Christianity to be just as historically contingent as religious rituals and theological creeds.[6] To Adler, the claim of ethical finality by each religion was logically untenable, for the historicization of ethics implied for him the relativization of all ethical systems.

Adler adumbrated this logical idea in historical terms. Emerging from particular historical settings, the ethical teachings of Judaism and Christianity were inextricably bound to basically anachronous religious ideas and methods. In addition, the intrinsic nature of the ethical approach of each religion was critically colored by the historical setting in which it first appeared. Consequently, the radically distinct historical setting of the modern world required an ethical vision which neither Judaism nor Christianity could supply, and the Jewish religion was not a sufficient ethical ground for contemporary needs.

In his final conception of the Jewish religion, Adler distinguished between the "religion of Israel" and "Judaism." The latter comprised the Jewish religion of the last two thousand years of Jewish history; the former, the Jewish religion of the first one thousand years.[7] "Judaism" focused primarily on the "sacred law" and "intellectualism," not on ethical development. It added nothing to Jewish ethical thought. The desire for and emphasis on ethical living, however, constituted the fundamental leitmotif of the "religion of Israel." This religion emerged from the two quintessential concerns of the Jewish people: the striving for moral perfection born from the Jews' experience of injustice, suffering, and anguish in a morally disjointed world; and the intense patriotism of the Jews for the nation of Israel and the Jewish commonwealth. The "religion of Israel" evolved from the Jews' reaction "against palpable wrong, against acts of oppression, and [from] the feeling that these acts of oppression would spoil the idolized commonwealth."[8]

These historical experiences engendered the two theological ideas central to the Jewish religion throughout history: monotheism and the divine election of the Jewish people to spread ethical monotheism.

Now the steps that led to monotheism, explain monotheism, are very clear. The Jews said, wrong at present is triumphing over good. That cannot be . . . right must triumph over wrong. Then there must be a power in the world that makes it triumph, and that led him [the Jew] to the idea that his ancient God who had been very much like the heathen God, must be conceived of henceforth as the power that makes right triumph over wrong. . . . [Hebrew monotheism] was the offspring of a certain kind of anguish, the woe felt over the approaching disintegration of the chrysolite Jerusalem, and the cause to which that contributed the injustice.[9]

As for the notion of Jewish mission, Adler affirmed that

the faith of Israel was the faith in Israel, the faith in Israel as the Messianic people. . . . The best men of Israel felt a heavy obligation of being exemplary in the moral life, of being the moral commonwealth, the pure and translucent chrysolite, the light of which shall shine out over the whole earth, so others might come and copy its conduct.[10]

Prophetic ethics were, therefore, inextricably interwoven with and circumscribed by the ideas of monotheism and ethical mission. According to Adler, to be meaningful, the ethics of the Prophets presupposed the existence of a "supernatural power that interferes, intervenes from above," a "righteous judge [who] must deal righteously, and [who] must be exalted above Nature, [who] must be the Eternal nature that inhabiteth Eternity, [who] must be God of the heavens and of the Earth . . . in order that he may use nature to accomplish his moral purpose."[11] Moreover, according to Adler, prophetic ethics were necessarily grounded in the notion of Jewish mission as well, for the Prophets conceived of the Jews as necessary agents of God, as "the teachers of mankind in respect to the spiritual interpretation of morality."[12] Without the Jews' conception of themselves as divine agents, they would not have believed that the ultimate moral regeneration of mankind could be fulfilled. The idea of the mission of the Jewish people, Adler contended, was the inherent Jewish ethical method for the realization of the ethical ideal.

But, to Adler, precisely because of the historical fusion of prophetic ethics with religio-theological ideals, the ethical outlook of the Jewish religion could not meet contemporary needs: the two cardinal concepts underpinning the Jewish ethical system—monotheism and Jewish mission—were controverted by modern scientific thinking.[13] The limitations of the Jewish religious conceptions severely restricted both the scope and the validity of the traditional Jewish ethical teachings as crystallized by the Prophets.

Asserting that the ethical orientation of the Prophets (and of all religions for that matter) was colored by the historical setting from which it emerged, Adler perceived in the "religion of Israel" the dominant motif that "wickedness is to be conquered by the extermination of the wicked. That is not the best view."[14] According to him, this rigorous demand for justice was rooted in the Jewish desire to create an ideal commonwealth, and displayed little regard for the plight of consistent sinners.[15] He cited a number of prophetic declarations that the end of the wickedness is to be realized by "putting an end to the wicked," and he deemed this attitude ethically deficient: "The wicked should be regenerated, not destroyed."[16] For him, the prophetic emphasis on the justice idea was inadequate to serve the purpose of social reconstruction.[17] The justice idea of the Prophets "is sound as far as it goes, but it does not go far enough."

> It is negative, rather than positive; it is based on the idea of non-violation. What we require today is a positive conception, and this implies a positive definition of that holy thing in man that is to be treated as inviolable [his personality]. To the mind of the prophets, justice meant chiefly resistance to oppression, since oppression is the most palpable exemplification of the forbidden violation. The prophets in their outlook on the external relations of their people stood for the weak, the oppressed, against the strong, the oppressor. They stood for their own weak little nation, the Belgium of those days, against the two over-mighty empires, Egypt and Assyria, that bordered it on either side. In the internal affairs of Israel, they espoused the cause of the weak against the rich and strong. . . . Ever and ever again, the same note resounds, the same intense, passionately indignant feeling against violation in the form of oppression. But this aspect of justice, as I have said, is the negative aspect—inestimably important, but insufficient. Where oppression does not occur, have the claims of justice ceased? Is there not something even greater than mere non-infringement, greater than mercifulness or kindness, which in justice we owe to the personality of our fellows, namely, to aid in the development of their personality? Righteousness, yes, by all means,—but does the righteousness of the prophets of Israel exhaust or begin to exhaust the context of the vast idea?[18]

Adler responded in the negative; indeed, he lauded Jesus for having considerably advanced the ethical thought of the Prophets.[19]

Over the last thirty to forty years of his life, Adler witnessed American Reform Jews attempting to repristinate Judaism by defining contemporary Judaism solely in terms of the prophetic ethics of centuries ago. Geiger's theory of the final goal of Judaism anticipated this attempt, but it was left for the more radical American Reform Jews to practically implement his theory by dropping an ever increasing number of Jewish rituals and traditional theological concepts developed since the prophetic era.

Many liberal Christians and Social Gospelers engaged in a similar repristination process by returning to the ethical teachings and example of a
humanized Jesus for ethical guidance. But Adler looked askance at all
such attempts and regarded them as intellectually indefensible.

According to Adler, Judaism, along with the more advanced religions
of the past, contained "a fund of truth . . . [which] should be rescued out
of the wreck."[20] Yet it was impossible to return to the Hebrew religion of
the past; it was impossible to separate "the dross from the gold, the error
from the truth, explicating what is implicit in that truth and adapting it to
the needs and conditions of the modern age."[21] It was impossible because
the Jewish and Christian religions were both determinate entities, incapable of adaptation and of claiming finality.

> It [any religion such as Judaism and Christianity] is a closed circle of
> thoughts and beliefs. It is capable of a certain degree of change but not
> of indefinite change. The limits of change are determined by its leading
> conceptions—the monotheist idea in the one case, and the centrality of
> the figure of Jesus in the other. Abandon these and the boundaries by
> which the religion is circumscribed are passed.[22]

Since organized religions are defined and characterized by their fundamental ideas, the Reform attempt to repristinate Judaism in its original
prophetic form was—for Adler—doomed to failure because the Prophets'
ethical orientation was intrinsically united to monotheism, and
monotheism was unacceptable to modern man. No repristination of
Judaism could ever reconcile the Jewish religion with modernity.

While Adler left Judaism, unable to accept it as an ethico-religious
system, he continued to harbor deep feelings of respect and appreciation
for his former religion. And he was not averse to expressing his warm
sentiments in public. "It is very important to know of Judaism," he
maintained,

> because the religion of the Jew and the religion of Israel is one of the
> great events in the world's history. . . . We [of the Ethical Movement]
> stand for something new and distinctive, but we cannot stand for that
> distinctive and new thing rightly without understanding our relation to
> the Jewish and the Christian religion. The Jewish and the Christian
> religions are the two great ethical movements of the past, and the
> Ethical Movement of today can only define itself if it understands its
> relation to those two great ethical movements.[23]

But Adler's esteem for Judaism was rooted in more than a historical
admiration for the Jewish religion. His regard for Judaism sprang from a

sense of deep personal reverence for it. In his Sunday address "The Essentials of Christianity," delivered one week following his lecture on "The Essentials of Judaism," Adler declared:

> I have dealt reverently with the religion of Israel, that was natural. There was a feeling of filial piety there. I am like one who has gone out of his father's house and built him[self] a new home. I am a religious emigrant who has left the old country in religion, and gone to a new continent, and thinks lovingly of the old mother-land.[24]

Adler's loving thoughts of the "old motherland" readily manifested themselves in brief notelike reviews of books which he felt disregarded or slandered the value of the ethical religion of Israel. In an archival note on Eduard Meyer's chapter on the Jews in the third volume of his *History of Greece and Persia,* Adler assailed the scholar's bias against Jews. He sharply criticized what he considered to be Meyer's unfavorable contrast of Jewish with Greek ethics. He rebuked Meyer's emphasis on the legalistic aspect of the religion of Israel and his conception of the Prophets as exceptions to the Jewish religion who antedated the true spirit of the Jewish people. To Adler, the Prophets were not antecedents of the true Jewish spirit, but rather represented its most outstanding products.[25] He similarly lashed out against Werner Sombart for having failed to appreciate the Jewish prophetic tradition in his book *The Jew and Modern Capitalism.*[26]

On more than one occasion Adler also stressed the need for each human being to familiarize himself with his religious and racial origin. For Jews, that implied the study and appreciation of their Jewish roots. As he wrote, "I am certainly American in sentiment, in allegiance, in aspiration. But nonetheless, I have taken some pains to know—I wish my children to know—something of the race from which they have sprung."[27]

Adler elaborated on this thought at greater length in "The Essentials of Judaism." In this address he outlined three ways in which people departed from their religious traditions. Some, like Thomas Paine, left with hatred for the old religion.

> He foams at the mouth when he speaks of the old faith of his fathers, he hates it like a man hates his enemy. . . . All Radicals feel that way, the old religions did them harm, injured them, it shore them of the joy of life, it repressed their natural instincts, what-not; they have the bitterness and the rancor that one feels toward a foe.[28]

Others departed with disenchantment.

This is due to the fact that religion consists of symbols, and the value of a symbol depends on the association connected with it. When the associations disappear, the symbol seems ludicrous, and one is even disturbed at oneself that one should have ever been enchanted by something so worthless, because the associations have gone.[29]

The attitude of those who have lost the association is one of "surprised disillusionment and lack of understanding." This is particularly true of Jews, more so than of individuals of Christian origin, for understandable historical reasons. Jews deliberately seek to remain ignorant of their past, Adler averred, because their history reminds them of their former status as a social, political, and religious minority, and of the continual persecutions to which they were subject. With Jewish emancipation in the last century, there is

> nothing they desire less to remember than the exclusive position which they were once compelled to occupy. So they are rather incurious, they do not want to know about Ghetto days, they do not wish to have the musty odor of the Ghetto life in their nostrils. It is to be a clean sweep and a new deal. There is much to be said for that point of view, but it is not very wise, it is not the best, it is not the finest point of view.[30]

Adler suggested a third way in which one may leave his religion and religious fellowship, an alternative which best portrayed his own departure from the Jewish socio-religious consensus.

> The finest point of view [when leaving one's tradition] is to keep in touch with one's racial past, to keep in touch with the roots out of which one sprang, because always the sap of life comes out of those roots; it is a part of self-respect not to cut off one's memory, not to wish to bury the past out of sight—a part of self-respect, and it is part of the best kind of spiritual development to know the fountain out of which one has been drawn, to know the past.[31]

Adler's thought reflected a "common-sense" psychological and historical approach to Judaism. Not displaying the traditional vindictiveness of Jewish apostates, Adler did not revile his Jewish origins and racial roots, but acknowledged their impact on him. He appreciated the positive contributions of his religious tradition and, with historical perspective, understood what he felt to be its shortcomings for the present day.

Adler's sense of reverence for the Jewish past and his warm recollections of his religious tradition did not, however, induce a commitment on his part—either practical or ideological—to the preservation of Judaism and the Jewish people. In discussing intermarriage between members of different faiths, he remarked:

It is not the perpetuation of anything that matters. No race, no people, is immortal, or can claim any permanence. A race grows, it reaches maturity, it passes, it leaves its records behind; as the Hellenic race, in its art, in its poetry, in its science; as the Hebrew race in its scriptures. The old order passes, the new is dawning. . . . If you find congeniality among those of your own stock, it is well. If you find it among those of a different stock, it is well. Spiritual congeniality alone matters.[32]

Adler's own children apparently followed his advice. The three of five children that married—Waldo, Lawrence, and Ruth—all selected non-Jewish spouses.

Nor did Adler's regard for his Jewish origin militate against his adoption of festivals generally associated with Christianity both in his institutional and private life. Christmas and Easter were occasions for Adler to deliver major addresses to the Society for Ethical Culture on the contemporary symbolic meaning of those festivals for the modern age. His own family held Christmas parties featuring a Christmas tree and an exchange of gifts; the hope for a "Merry Christmas" often ended many of his letters to his family.[33] Adler's observance of Christmas festivities alerts us to the deep irony of his passionate youthful outburst against Jews bringing Christmas trees into their homes; Christmas was the one ritual custom identified with a theistic religion which he celebrated.

To be sure, Adler did not adopt the Christian meaning of the day but found the origins of Christmas in the pagan festivities celebrating the appearance of longer days following the winter solstice. Still, "there is something of salvation to be hoped for," he wrote, "not from the one child, but from the elect among the many that come into the world. . . . [Thus] we retain . . . the pleasant custom of giving gifts to one another, stressing the feeling of natural kindness."[34]

While the meaning of Christmas for Adler was universalized in accordance with his ethical ideology and removed from the doctrinal background of Christianity, one may still find his embrace of the outer trappings of this festival somewhat inconsistent with his universalist orientation. Adler's acceptance of the visible symbols of this holiday, however, is understandable. He consistently proclaimed the human need for symbolic festivals, and the dominant symbols of society were most suitable for adoption. Acting on the basis of such pragmatic considerations, moreover, made good sense from both a personal and an institutional point of view: it helped Adler to fulfill his wish of assimilating his family and the society into the broader community following his break from Judaism.

Adler's final conception of his relation to his Jewish past may be succinctly stated in one sentence: he seems to have proudly identified himself as a man of Jewish ethnic-racial origin who had left his religion and socio-religious fellowship. As he wrote to his wife on August 31, 1896, "respect and tenderness for the past of the race of which I come is very strong within me." But simply to label him a Jew following the 1870s is both not meaningful and a serious misnomer. Applied to him, the term *Jew* only points to his ethnic origin, not to the new religious and moral identity which he adopted following his break. Adler conceived of himself as an American national whose religion was Ethical Culture.

And yet, despite his own self-conception, over the years others either could not or would not understand his personal transition. Some Gentiles and Jews felt that his racial origin stamped him with a Jewish identity for all time. Thus, when the prominent Jewish leader of the American Federation of Labor, Samuel Gompers, died, leaving a request for a Jewish funeral, the Gentile leaders of the federation suggested that "Rabbi" Felix Adler be one of the officiating ministers.[35] In 1906, on the occasion of the anniversary of 250 years of Jewish settlement in the United States (1655–1905), the American Jewish Historical Society published addresses delivered at Carnegie Hall the previous Thanksgiving, as well as newspaper editorials and communications, in honor of the American Jewish milestone. A selection from the *New York Evening Post* entitled "Jewish Idealism" was among the newspaper articles published. After first listing the achievements of Jews in family life, institutional creativity, and charitable affairs, it cited the special contributions to morality of two Jews—Felix Adler and Oscar Straus, noted Jewish diplomat, jurist, and public servant—in the same breath. Apparently, the paper's editors still characterized Adler as a Jew.[36]

In 1908 Adler's Jewishness was the subject of a good deal of international discussion. J. W. Burgess, Adler's colleague at Columbia, had strongly endorsed him before Columbia's trustees for a position which he himself once held, Theodore Roosevelt Exchange Professor at the University of Berlin. The trustees then proposed Adler to Roosevelt, who accepted their proposal and appointed Adler to the prestigious one-year post in 1908. A good deal of debate arose as to the acceptability of a "Jew" to the Prussian government, but despite the initial controversy, Adler was deemed acceptable, and he fulfilled the appointment in 1908–9.[37]

The *American Jewish Chronicle* probably best reflected the Jewish image which Adler and his society projected to some. As late as 1918, it wrote:

The Ethical Culture Society in the city of New York, with its branches outside of this city, is considered by Jew and Gentile alike as a purely Jewish society, notwithstanding that many Gentiles may be members of it. . . . Educated Gentiles, who are not well versed in the secrets of the American synagogue, also considered Dr. Felix Adler as a sort of rabbi and the Ethical Culture Society as a branch of the American synagogue.[38]

His personal socio-religious transcendence of his Jewish identity notwithstanding, Felix Adler was still perceived as a Jew by a segment of the American population.

While the relationship between Felix Adler and the American Jewish community in the late 1870s was surrounded by controversy and polemics, from the 1880s on the nature of the interaction between Adler and the Jewish community changed significantly. To all intents and purposes, Jewish communal and press concern with and debate over Adler's religion terminated by the end of the 1870s. Except for Gustav Gottheil's public refutation of Adler's suggestion that in light of the Pittsburgh Rabbinical Platform (1885) Reform Jews join Unitarianism, religious polemics between Adler and Jewish communal and spiritual leaders ceased.[39] On May 24, 1918, the *American Jewish Chronicle* did publish a vitriolic critique of Adler's book *An Ethical Philosophy of Life* because of the nature of its evaluation of prophetic ethics, but this type of attack was the exception rather than the rule.

The Jewish community's shock at Adler's departure from its ranks had worn off. By the end of the 1870s American Jews more fully grasped his religious orientation, and they "cut their losses" so to speak. They seem to have realized that little could be gained by continued disputations.

More significantly, historical circumstances may have been most responsible for American Jewry's declining interest in Adler's religious departure. The waves of Eastern European Jewish immigration to America from the 1880s on dramatically altered the locus of American Jewish communal activity. During the 1870s American Jewish leaders were still very preoccupied with founding Jewish institutions and creating a viable Judaism in America. Adler's defection and its institutional outcome struck a hammerblow at the heart of American Jewish communal and religious life. Understandably, polemics seemed to be not only in order, but necessary at the time. From the 1880s on, however, American Jews, predominantly German in origin, were confronted with the crucial problem of assimilating the thousands upon thousands of East European Jews into American life, Jews whose culture, religion, and values were totally alien to them. In the face of this socio-religious challenge, American Jewish leaders did not consider a continuation of religious polemics with Adler to be either meaningful or relevant.

Furthermore, from the 1880s until the early decades of the twentieth century, the New York Society for Ethical Culture stopped expanding. Its membership figures did not climb, rarely approaching seven hundred, and the original influx of Jewish members in the late 1870s abated. Consequently, Adler and his Society were no longer regarded as serious threats to Judaism in America, and debating Adler seemed to serve no purpose. The society was conceived of as a marginal group of former Jews which did not warrant communal apprehension. By 1918 many Jews concurred with the *American Jewish Chronicle*'s estimation of Ethical Culture as but a "small sect together with tens of thousands of other sects."

This lack of attraction of Ethical Culture for most American Jews may also be attributed to external historical circumstances. Adler himself suggested that the reemergence of virulent religiously motivated anti-Jewish activities in Russia and the Balkans and the appearance of political-racial anti-Semitism in Germany in the late 1870s were, in a large part, responsible for Jews turning back to their Jewish socio-religious fellowship rather than transcending their racial-religious roots by joining Ethical Culture.[40] These trends continued, and over the years Adler reiterated his observation in subsequent addresses implicitly linking Ethical Culture's failure to win the support of American Jews to the reappearance of widespread anti-Jewish feelings.[41]

In the twentieth century the Jewish Reform Movement's increasing sensitivity to the need for social action, and the inception of Stephen Wise's Free Synagogue, enabling modern idealistic Jews to fulfill their social reform aspirations within the bounds of Judaism, also helped to curtail Jewish interest in Ethical Culture.

While the Jewish community more or less ignored Adler's religious ideology from the 1880s on, it took note with increasing favor of his efforts and those of his society on behalf of social reform benefiting Jews and non-Jews alike. Edward Lauterbach correctly underscored the non-sectarian direction of the Ethical Culture Society's social-action program upon his departure from its ranks; he also correctly asserted that the society, despite its preponderance of Jewish members, did not regard aid to impoverished Eastern European immigrant Jews as a first priority. Institutions established by the society—the Kindergarten, Workingman's School, and District Nursing Department—though serving the poor and the sick of every creed and color, catered primarily to Catholics and Protestants. Yet growing numbers of New York Jews, particularly the newly arriving Eastern Europeans, came to benefit directly from the activities of Adler and members of his society, and prominent Jews such as Edwin Seligman and Jacob H. Schiff joined in their work.

Immigrant Jews were major beneficiaries of Adler's quest for decent housing for the poor. Acutely aware since his youth of the horribly substandard living conditions of New York's poor, Adler in the 1880s stood in the vanguard of those advocating housing reforms. His open criticism of the unsanitary conditions under which laborers had to live led to the formation of the Sanitary Commission of the 10th Ward of New York (Lower East Side) in 1885. Among the accomplishments of this committee was the creation of a cheap but clean lodging house for poor immigrants, who at the time were primarily Jewish.[42]

Adler also initiated a campaign against tenement house evils in 1882, resulting in the formation of the Committee of Fifteen, presided over by William H. Baldwin, president of the Long Island Railroad, which fully studied and publicized the outrageous conditions in New York's Lower East Side dwellings. In 1884 a Tenement House Commission was appointed by the governor of New York. As a member of the commission, Adler proposed the establishment of a private corporation, subsidized in part by the government, to initiate slum clearance and create model tenement buildings. By 1887 the first such homes, on Cherry Street in Lower Manhattan, were ready for occupancy.[43] Again, Jewish immigrants were the beneficiaries of Adler's social initiative, although George M. Price, the Russian-born Jewish superintendent of the Cherry Street project, complained that only 40 percent of the apartments were opened to Jews in order to curry favor with the non-Jewish sponsors of the plan. Price, however, admitted that Adler's successor as director of the project, Copeland Kelly, restricted Jewish admission even more by filling the homes with a preponderance of his Irish countrymen.[44]

Adler's genuine sympathy for humanity and his striving for reforms in housing and politics[45] brought him recognition and much praise in the 1880s from Jewish circles. In an editorial in the *American Israelite*, July 7, 1882, Jacob Voorsanger, though declaring Adler's teachings a failure, observed that "as a philanthropist, Dr. Felix Adler is deserving of the love and admiration of mankind." Adler also gained the respect of some who had been his foremost religious antagonists in previous years. During the Pittsburgh Rabbinical Conference of 1885, Kaufmann Kohler lauded his social activity, remarking that "it must be stated to the credit of the Ethical Culture Society at New York . . . [that] a great deal of good is accomplished by the continued efforts of its membership."[46] Even the *Jewish Messenger,* Adler's vociferous critic in the late 1870s, acknowledged his positive contribution to Jewish social welfare.

> Stimulated by the ready cooperation of Professor Adler who in his capacity as one of the State Commissioners to report on the condition of New York's tenements, was brought face to face with the unsavory character of a section largely occupied by Israelites, a number of gentlemen have organized a Montefiore Society for Tenement House Reform, whose object shall primarily be the improvement of the Jewish tenement house population, and the erection of healthier and more commodious dwellings.[47]

Adler's consistent accent on and personal implementation of social action as part of his religious ideology found an outlet in the institutional framework of Reform Judaism as well. Myer Stern's speech to an Emanu-El congregational meeting on May 16, 1883, insisting that the scope and meaning of synagogue religious activity be broadened, doubtless reflected the critical impact of Adler's ideology on the Jewish religious establishment.

The time has gone by when in the eyes of an enlightened community the functions of a religious congregation can be deemed limited to celebrating Divine service in its house of worship and imparting dogmatic instruction to its own members and their children. The ideal church, temple, or synagogue of today is a place where men and women are to meet together, not merely for the culture of their religious sentiments (using that expression in its narrowest signification), but also for the furtherance of all measures of a philanthropic character. Prayers and praises to the Almighty in a public assemblage are but means to an end. Preaching and music stimulate the emotion, but unless the emotions are utilized for good purposes, and some practical end, there is simply a waste of vital force. . . . It is not enough that the members of our Congregation as individuals are charitable. The Congregation itself as an organized body must engage in the humanitarian work, so that the community can see plainly the good effects of the religious exercises.[48]

Adler's socio-religious teachings may also have influenced the acceptance of Emil Hirsch's social-justice plank as the eighth and concluding paragraph of the Reform rabbis' Pittsburgh Platform of 1885. The paragraph reads:

In full accordance with the spirit of Mosaic legislation which strives to regulate the relation between rich and poor, we deem it our duty to participate in the great task of modern times, to solve on the basis of justice and righteousness the problems presented by contrasts and evils of the present organization of society.

Hirsch, contemporary and friend of Adler, was stirred by the same passion for social justice as he was; the text of the paragraph reflects his genuine commitment rather than simple imitation of Adler.[49] Nevertheless, while the paragraph's incorporation into the platform was insisted upon by Hirsch, the actions of Felix Adler, plus those of the emerging Social Gospelers, such as Washington Gladden, Josiah Strong, and R.

Heber Newton, and the great labor unrest in the 1880s created the necessary atmosphere for its ratification by the rabbinic assembly.

The pledge to implement social justice in a platform outlining the fundamental ideology of Reform Judaism represented the first formal recognition by Reform rabbis of the intrinsic religious nature of social action. Adler's pioneer teachings were thus confirmed by the Jewish Reform establishment in 1885. With the exception of Emil Hirsch's activities in Chicago, however, Reform and other Jews, by and large, did not engage in practical social action as a function of religious ideology until the twentieth century.

In addition to spearheading reforms in the socio-political arena, Adler and his society also became engaged in attempting to relieve the burden of Americanization confronting European immigrants, including Eastern European Jews. Adler, in fact, seems to have evinced a long-standing particular interest in the welfare of Russian Jews, both those remaining in Russia and those arriving in the United States. To be sure, the plight of the Russian Jews was not a priority, nor did it occupy much of his time or energy when compared to the efforts he expended on multifarious projects of national and international scope.[50] And yet, curiously and paradoxically, this German-born Jew, who had left the Jewish community, manifested a concern—even an affectionate concern—for Russian Jews both in word and in deed.

Adler's diaries of the late 1890s and the first decade of the twentieth century, containing his thoughts on events of the day, people he had met, books he had read, and the progress of Ethical Culture, show no interest in any Jewish questions whatsoever save one: the condition of the Russian Jews. He noted the terrible environment of young Russian Jewish girls living in New York's tenements (February 6, 1900); on two occasions he recorded the occurrence of pogroms and massacres of Jews in Russia (January 2, 1906; November 21 [year not dated]); he jotted down the responses of two different Russian government officials to his questions on the circumstances of Jews in Russia (June 3, 1905; October 14, 1907). And in a later address, "Zionism and Its Ideal" (November 7, 1915), he publicly deplored the Jews' fate in Russia in the strongest terms, although he rejected Zionism as an impractical solution to their problem.

A partial explanation of Adler's affinity for the Russian Jews may lie in a remark once made to me by the late Professor Friess. According to him, Adler was deeply impressed by the high caliber of intellectual life maintained by some immigrant Jews in spite of their impoverished Lower East Side existence. Friess related that Adler was amazed and extremely pleased to discover among these Jews individuals pursuing the study of

Spinoza. Indeed, Adler candidly confessed his admiration for the strong intellectual bent of Russian Jews in one of his Sunday addresses.[51] But perhaps Adler not only respected their intellectualism, but also saw in them—though they clung to their Jewishness—a partial concretization of his ideal vision of a spiritually, culturally, and morally elevated working class capable of transcending the outrageous physical environment in which it was forced to live. It is not too surprising, then, to find Adler personally involved in projects to help in the Americanization of Russian Jews and also keeping himself informed of the various settlement-house activities on the Lower East Side of New York in which some members of the Society for Ethical Culture were participating.

In 1882 Adler received permission from the vice-president of the Hebrew Free School Association in New York to use some of its classroom space at night to teach the English language to Russian Jews. He provided the funds for instructor and materials, and classes had already begun when some members of the Association board—objecting to the class because of Adler's sponsorship—took up the issue at the next board meeting. At that meeting, the majority of the board voted to rescind permission for the class. The Hebrew Free School provided free instruction in Judaism to Jewish children, and most of its board members declined to associate the institution with someone whom they perceived to be defiling the very religion they were trying to teach. The class was abruptly canceled two weeks after it had begun, precipitating a heated exchange of letters in the *Jewish Messenger* between M. S. Fechheimer of the Ethical Culture Society, who denounced the action, and Jacob H. Schiff, who, though personally favoring Adler's cause, attempted to justify the board's decision.[52]

In fostering the Americanization of immigrant Russian Jews, Adler did not wish the process to be achieved at the expense of their obliterating their past "race history and race consciousness." His personal and scholarly respect for Judaism and its ethical teachings led him to hope that the Russian immigrants would continue to take pride in the past accomplishments of the Jews and develop a feeling of "race pride in the contributions of what is best in the Jewish race making it all culminate in American citizenship."[53] Thus, to heighten awareness of the majesty of prophetic ethics among immigrant Jews, who he feared might come either to repress their Jewish past totally or to neglect the ethical aspect of Judaism in favor of the ritual dimension, Adler contributed "several hundred dollars" to a learned Jewish scholar named Dobsevage "to preach in Yiddish on 'The Ethics of Judaism' among the downtown Jews."[54] And when sent a copy of Rabbi Jacob Joseph's inaugural sermon as chief rabbi of New York's Orthodox Jews in the summer of 1888, a sermon which highlighted the ethical mission of the rabbi's future activity, Adler heartily endorsed the moral tone of the address.

> I have read the address with interest and profound satisfaction. If such is to be the tenor of the new rabbi's teachings, we must all, no matter what our opinions, welcome his advent to this country and congratulate the congregations over which he presides upon the choice they have made. Rabbi Joseph has struck the keynote of true religion, and the standard of piety which he describes is one by which we must all abide.[55]

Rabbi Joseph's affirmation that his "principal effort shall be to gain recognition and to attract the adherence of others to laws of grace and truth by virtue . . . of our moral living and our deeds of liberality and kindness" was a sentiment which Adler could readily applaud.[56]

Adler also highly commended the work of other Jews trying to "elevate" Eastern European Jewry. He praised Moses Montefiore's humanitarian "single-hearted fidelity to elevating his Jewish brothers."[57] In Adler's view, Montefiore demonstrated to the world that one can be an Orthodox Jew of the "old-fashioned type" and yet have "fine values." "With his religious convictions we have little sympathy," wrote Adler, "but because they were his convictions, we entertain for them perfect respect."[58]

Adler did not personally take part in the settlement-house endeavors which, from the 1880s on, played such a large role in helping Eastern European Jews acculturate in America. His aristocratic, elitist, and somewhat authoritarian personality did not easily lend itself to the type of social work in which people like Lillian Wald and his own associate, John L. Elliott, excelled. Nonetheless, he kept abreast of the problems and achievements of the settlement houses.

For a time, between 1899 and 1913, the New York Society for Ethical Culture was the "silent" patron, in terms of financial and personnel support, of the East Side Ethical Club on Madison Avenue (founded 1898); on an institutional basis, at least, it became very much related to downtown immigrant Jews. The uptown society did not "appear publicly as a patron" for fear of provoking the disapproval of the downtown population, which might have resented uptown influence and interference.[59] The society also probably wished to avoid the image of being labeled "gentlemen reformers," a not unrealistic possibility, given the nature of its predominantly upper-middle-class membership.[60]

The leader of the downtown club was Henry Moskowitz, a second-generation American Jew of Rumanian descent. Moskowitz went through the ranks of the University Settlement, attended college, and undertook graduate study sponsored by Adler and the New York society.[61] From

1899 to 1914, he served as assistant and later associate leader of the New York Society while simultaneously organizing functions at the East Side Ethical Club.

The downtown club held classes for adults and children in ethics, comparative religion, philosophy, and the arts, and by 1911 had attracted over five hundred members, a large portion of whom were Jewish. But while these Jewish immigrants were attracted to the club's wide variety of social-cultural activities, they showed no interest in the Ethical Movement and its ideology. Consequently, many members of the uptown society, more interested in the furtherance of the Ethical Culture Movement, ceased to support the downtown club. The dream of merging the East Side Ethical Club with its uptown patron had to be abandoned, and the organic connection between the two formally and symbolically ended in 1913, when the name of the East Side Ethical Club was changed to Madison House.

Thus, while Adler's Ethical Culture Society contributed to the social and cultural betterment of some Eastern European Jews, Adler's own interpretation of the religious and spiritual meaning of Ethical Culture had a negligible impact on them. Jews in the East Side Club were not interested in it. The Brooklyn Ethical Culture Society, led by a Jew of Eastern European origins, Henry Neumann, fared no better in attracting immigrant Jews to its cause.[62] By and large, immigrant East European Jews were either socialists, secularists, or traditionally pious. Adler's eclectic, nontheistic religion of social reform held no ideological appeal to any of these three subgroups. Perhaps the Christian origin of all of Adler's early associates—Stanton Coit, William M. Salter, S. Burns Weston, Walter L. Sheldon, Percival Chubb, John L. Elliott, David S. Muzzey— may also have deterred Jewish membership.[63] But then Jews such as Moskowitz and Neumann also made no appreciable headway in fostering the ideals of Ethical Culture among Eastern European Jews.

That Ethical Culture did not attract the overwhelming majority of American Jews of Eastern European origin between 1880 and 1920 assured it of a totally marginal status, if even that, in Jewish communal life. With Reform Jews beginning to engage in social-reform projects, there was no longer an identifiable subgroup within American Jewry that found Ethical Culture to be either meaningful or especially attractive.

Except for his ongoing interest in settlement-house activities, Felix Adler appears divorced from American Jewish communal affairs from the 1890s on. Over the years he retained his personal friendships with such Reform leaders as Rabbis Felsenthal, Emil Hirsch, Samuel Sale,[64] Abraham Cronbach,[65] and Stephen Wise,[66] and with Jewish lay leaders such as Jacob H. Schiff.[67] He did not inject himself into the local issues of

American Jewish life. On the two major international Jewish issues of the day—anti-Semitism and Zionism—however, he was quite outspoken.

Anti-Semitism and Zionism

From the late 1870s on, two international issues dominated Jewish attention across the world: the intensification of religious persecution of the Jews in Eastern Europe with the simultaneous rise of political economic, and racial anti-Semitism in Germany and France; and the Jewish reassertion of a national identity ultimately leading to a Jewish national movement. Historically, the two trends were intimately linked. The anti-Jewish outbursts and prevalent anti-Semitism posed an ominously incisive question to the Jews: how could they best live as Jews in the modern world? Pragmatically, large numbers of East European Jews responded by emigrating to America. Some Jews, however, sought a more compelling ideological solution to the problem and consciously reevaluated their assumptions for Jewish existence. These Jews found an alternate answer to the question: a meaningful and fruitful Jewish existence for them depended on the revival of the Jewish national identity and Jewish national life. Particularly to the modern, educated, and more assimilated Jews, Jewish nationalism furnished the only viable rationale for continued Jewish existence in the modern world.

As the East European immigrants streamed into America from the 1880s to the early 1920s, American Jews were personally exposed to the consequences of anti-Semitism; they had to assist its victims in settling down. As a result of the reemergence of persecution and their personal exposure to its effects, many American Jews turned inward to reacquaint themselves with their socio-religious identity, and many lessened their drive for social assimilation. Because of the persistence of anti-Semitism, even Reform rabbis such as Bernhard Felsenthal and Gustav Gottheil (and his son Richard) reevaluated their positions on Jewish existence, ultimately forsaking explicit Reform ideology by joining the Zionist cause in the 1890s.

Felix Adler was very much aware of both anti-Semitism and the proposed Zionist solution. He delivered a number of lectures on anti-Semitism from 1879 to 1922 and on Zionism during World War I. He vehemently denounced the various forms of religious and political persecution of the Jews. Indeed, next to his critical evaluation of Judaism's ethical system, anti-Semitism is the primary topic of his addresses on Jewish issues in later years. Adler's "filial piety" for his religious and racial origins no doubt provoked his interest in, and colored his reaction to, the serious problem. But in addition, his preoccupation with anti-Semitism was also motivated by his desire to discourage Jews from withdrawing into their old religious lines in light of the persecutions. He rejected Zionism both as a solution to anti-Semitism and as a national movement on its own merit. Both his attitude to Jewish existence in light of anti-Semitism and his opposition to Zionism reflected his ideological conclusion that there existed no rationale for continued separate Jewish existence in the modern age.

Adler delivered eight addresses on anti-Semitism and its broad human implications from 1879 to 1922: "The Recent Persecution of the Jews," December 28, 1879; "The Anti-Jewish Agitation in Germany," December 19, 1880; "Larger Tolerance," December 26, 1880; "The Anti-Semitic Movement in Germany," April 9, 1893; "The Anti-Semitic Prejudice and Its Evil Consequences," December 12, 1897; "Lessons of the Dreyfus Case," October 29, 1899; "The Revival of Anti-Semitism," December 5, 1920; and, "The Persistence of Race Prejudice," October 12, 1922.[68]

Three common themes and attitudes appear in the addresses: Adler's unalterable antipathy to all forms of anti-Jewish demonstrations and ideas; his constant regret at the Jews' return to Judaism or to a national identity in light of anti-Semitism;[69] and his firm belief that, ultimately, the only manner in which Jews can transcend anti-Semitism is for them to leave Judaism and the Jewish fellowship and join a universal religious fellowship, Ethical Culture in particular.

The clearest expression of this last idea is found in one of his final addresses on the anti-Semitism issue, but it is implicit in all the previous lectures.[70] Adler did not conceive of this proposal as a means of escape or assimilation for the sake of easing the Jewish socio-political burden; rather, he perceived it as a natural outgrowth of his universalist religious ideology. Nevertheless, on one level, one may view Adler's suggestion as a secularized or liberal religious translation of medieval Christianity's justification of persecution of the Jews: anti-Jewish activities would cease when the Jews converted. To be sure, Adler's conclusion differed radically in both tone and content from that of the Christian, and one must not stretch the analogy too far; moreover, he consistently and unhesitatingly denounced the persecution of the Jews. Unlike medieval Christian leaders, Adler did not have the power to cause the fulfillment of his own prophecy, nor would he have exercised it if he had. Nonetheless, the formal logic of his position seems identical to that of medieval Christian ideology: anti-Jewish acts would terminate when Jews stopped being Jews.

Adler's earliest addresses on anti-Semitism were marked by a sincere optimistic conviction of the ultimate eradication of anti-Jewish hatred. His 1879 address, "The Recent Persecution of the Jews," occasioned by the renewed religious persecution of Jews in Eastern Europe, betrays his early, almost heady liberal ardor and his unquestioning faith in the inevitable progressive direction of religion in the world. He announced that he did not approach the subject of persecution from a spirit of partisanship for the Jews, although he admired many of their qualities; rather, he perceived the recent persecutions as a "general sign of the times," intimately related to the broader, more significant issue of religious progress.[71]

Adler distinguished three types of anti-Jewish passion, each of which he considered to be but a historical phase of the one phenomenon of "Jew-hatred" and corresponded to a particular stage of religious progress in the world. The first type and historical stage of anti-Jewishness was motivated by *religious* enmity; the second stemmed from *political-economic* considerations; and the third arose from *social* prejudice.

According to Adler, the worst and most primitive form of anti-Jewishness was that motivated by religious hatred, and for that reason it was understandably located among the "semi-barbarous," "uncivilized" countries of Russia and the Balkan states (Serbia, Bulgaria, Rumania). But as the spirit of religion progressed, marked by the decline of sectarianism and advances in culture and civilization, religiously motivated persecutions of Jews gradually disappeared. Consequently, the political anti-Semitism of Germany, for example, represented to Adler a historical manifestation of religious progress from the Russian religious persecution of the Jews, for it originated from secular political-economic passions. One may legitimately hope, Adler asserted, that with a change of political status and material well-being, Germans would repudiate their hatred of the Jews and would realize their own disgrace. At all costs, the secularization of anti-Jewishness reflected world religious progress.[72]

The third phase of Jew-hatred, the social prejudice found in America, though painful, is a "cheering sign," for it is "the last attenuation of the old hate which in the days of yore flared out in fires of inquisition."[73] In this sense, the American social bias against the Jews represented a decisive improvement over the German brand of political anti-Semitism, and a further indication of the religious (moral) advance in the world. Adler's deep appreciation and esteem for the American tradition of liberty came to the fore. He considered Germany—despite its intellectual preeminence—to be deficient politically; the idea of freedom had not yet taken root.[74]

Adler concluded that religious persecution was worst where ignorance reigned; but where religious ideas of liberty, equality, and morality took hold, anti-Jewish feelings were dissipated. For him, "the path of progress, the path of religious emancipation, is the only real path of safety."[75] He proclaimed the need to make the ignorant less so, to "do actual good for people," to "gain their confidence by sincere efforts," and to "elevate their minds and improve their *material* lot."[76] These deeds would help to destroy religious persecution.

But what specifically must the Jews do? Adler proposed that Jews "fight against the narrowing restrictions of the creeds" and not "withdraw within the old lines."[77] Adler's correlation of the waning of religious persecution with world religious progress—highlighted by the removal of all creeds—implied to him that the Jews should emancipate themselves from their religion and identity in order to overcome anti-Jewish sentiments.

In December 1880, on the occasion of a petition presented to Bismarck to severely curtail Jewish legal and political rights in the German Reich, Adler again took up the issue of anti-Jewish demonstrations, except this time in relation to German racism, not Eastern European religious persecution.[78] Confronted with the phenomenon of racial anti-Semitism, Adler, in his address, betrayed as much emotion as critical analysis. He regarded racial anti-Semitism to have originated from base political considerations. In his view, the German Conservative party sought to discredit the Liberal party among the voters by exciting the slumbering prejudices of the country against Jews and then characterizing the Liberal party as a "Jewish" party. Because this racial animosity was rooted in political concerns and was employed as but a means to gain political ends, Adler judged it to be "artificial in its origin."[79] Nevertheless, he warned that men deficient in moral culture were now fanning the flames of racial enmity among the masses with potentially destructive results; racial anti-Semitism, he cautioned, should not be taken lightly. Adler railed against the celebrated historian Heinrich von Treitschke and especially against his own former philosophy teacher Eugen Dühring for their vile racial prejudice and moral backwardness. He castigated their indiscriminate attribution of unattractive racial qualities existing in a few individuals to every Jewish person, utterly denying the validity of such generalizations.[80] He saw in Dühring's book *The Jewish Question* the real source for the anti-Jewish proposals contained in the petition to Bismarck.

Still, Adler concluded his first address, "The Anti-Jewish Agitation in Germany," by expressing confidence that the agitation would fade once political and material conditions improved. In the meantime, he trusted that the Germans would recognize the importance of harmony between diverse groups of people. He believed, naively, that Jews and Christians would soon meet in mutual understanding "until at last the time shall come for all, as it has already come today for the more advanced, when Christians and Jews will be separated no longer, but will be content to be *men*, and will be united in holy and lasting union by working jointly in mankind's common cause."[81]

Adler developed the theme that the deficiency of moral culture causes the spread of racial anti-Semitism in his address "Larger Tolerance" one week later. In this address, he imputed this deficiency to the Aryan race as a whole, not simply to individuals like Dühring and his followers. Contending that all races featured both cultural excellences and deficiencies, Adler limned the Aryan race as the "classical" race of science, philosophy, art—of intellectual culture; he protrayed the Semites as the "classical" race of religion—of moral culture. Both races and their most outstanding representatives—Germans and Jews—complemented and needed each other, but in the contemporary world a sharp "artificial contrast has been set up" between them, thus further precipitating widespread racial anti-Semitism. But, Adler declared, "the two races are born to be friendly, are designed by nature to work in common toward the same good and it is due to lacking culture if they still stand apart today."[82] Because Adler felt that this racial hatred stemmed from cultural differences and deficiencies which could be modified as cultural advances continued, he held out hope for its ultimate eradication.

> Culture is the main desideratum of both sides. . . . The more intellectual culture is spread, the more does it tend to wipe out the fortuitous criterions, the false standards which still play so great a part in the world. And the more moral qualities are spread, the more men of all creeds, of all parties, of all classes, work in common for practical good and noble purposes, the more will they become one and united, through the sacred efficacy of those grand common aims which they follow. And so it is in intellectual-culture, in moral culture that we shall find the solution of this race question, as of every other social and moral question that troubles mankind.[83]

Yet while Adler attempted to explain the emergence of German racial anti-Semitism, even proposing a solution to the problem in general outline, he does not seem to have indicated the place of this phenomenon within his own historical scheme of religious progress. If, as he argued, secular forms of anti-Semitism signified an advance over religious intolerance and persecution, was racism to be regarded as "progressive"? This conclusion hardly seems likely. But if Adler recognized the need to harmonize the appearance of secular, racial anti-Semitism with his own theory on religious progress, he did not attempt such a reconciliation in his lectures.

Certainly Adler, like everyone else, did not envision a secularized form of anti-Semitism leading to racially dictated mass murder. Indeed, already by 1920 his youthful optimism, which anticipated the ongoing decline of virulent expressions of anti-Semitism, had all but vanished, rendering obsolete his earlier historical periodization of the phenomenon. And with the rise of Hitler, he openly declared that the German anti-Semitism of the previous decades had constituted a "relapse to a stage of subcivilization."

Adler's solution in 1880 to the racial prejudice of the Germans was expressed in his call for the reunification of disparate religious and racial groups. Again, in "Larger Tolerance," Adler appears to have regarded the termination of Jewish particularism as the means for ending the hatred of the Jews; he seems to have implied that, in order to extirpate racial anti-Semitism, Jews should not only transcend their religious traditions but also should not restrict themselves within their racial line.[84]

Adler discussed the anti-Semitic movement in Germany again in 1893, but unfortunately his address has not been preserved. In 1897, in an address entitled "The Anti-Semitic Prejudice and Its Evil Consequences," he reiterated his belief that the persecutions of the Jews in Russia did not exemplify an instance of modern anti-Semitism, but a "fainter echo of medieval passions and ideas."[85] He expressed the conviction that with religious progress they too would disappear in the course of time. Simultaneously, Adler sincerely regretted what he considered to be a singularly unfortunate consequence of Jewish persecution, "the return of the Jews to separatism."[86] He no doubt referred to the First Zionist Congress, held in Basle in 1897, as well as to the general trend of Jewish reidentification with Judaism.

By 1920, in the aftermath of World War I, Adler's earlier liberal optimism for the imminent disappearnace of hatred of the Jews appears to have faded. He retained his faith in the progress of religious morality in the world, but he acknowledged that such progress would require much time.

> The world is not so far along as over-sanguine optimists [including himself] had supposed. The lightning instinct is still as active as ever. The exploitation of the weak by the strong has hardly become more merciful. . . .[87]
> In its progress toward the far-off moral ideal . . . the human race is still in the early stages. . . . The objects of prejudice will not be able, in a generation or two, to wear off the stigma. The world was not made for man to be at ease in.[88]

Adler raised the question as to why anti-Jewishness still persisted as strongly as ever. He was particularly distressed at the world's reception of the spurious *Protocols of the Elders of Zion,* and he defended the Jews against its vicious slanders. He responded with a newly added psychological interpretation of the phenomenon of anti-Jewishness (anti-Semitism) extending beyond his cultural-historical analysis. He now regarded racial antipathy to be not simply a deficiency of moral culture, but rather a crude "primeval instinct."[89] He now viewed anti-Semitism not simply as a phase corresponding to a stage in the historical evolution of religion, but as a "primitive tendency" grounded in the human psychological need for a scapegoat.[90]

"And how should the [anti-Jewish] prejudice be met?"[91] Adler explicitly asked the question implicit in all his previous addresses on the issue. And he provided substantially the same answer in unmistakable terms: the Jew ought to transcend his Jewishness—as should the non-Jew transcend his religious fellowship—and join the universal religious fellowship of Ethical Culture.

> Let not the Jewish question loom so large in your mind as to obscure the world questions. . . . There is need, as everyone who has fathomed the malady of our day realizes, of a new moral ideal to guide mankind in its task of reconstruction, a new plan according to which to reshape the relations of men and of peoples. And to this ideal each stock, each race, can contribute. There is not, there cannot be, a monopoly of spiritual truth and insight. The pride of synagogue and church in this respect at last must be laid aside. There are chosen spirits, spiritually minded personalities in every people, and these must co-operate in religion. . . . To Jew or Gentile I speak and say: Let us join together in the endeavor to create the most wonderful thing to which the human mind can give birth, the holy vision—holier than any that the past has known—that shall guide mankind through its sorrows and its labors towards the better time to come. This is the sense and purpose of our Ethical Movement. And in this among ourselves and those whom we can reach, will be finally transcended the thing that is called anti-Semitism.[92]

In 1925 Adler admitted that the Jewish race would perpetuate itself long into the future, although not forever. "Its race consciousness is so tenacious, and its birthrate so high, that its discontinuance is not to be expected. But . . . I see no reason why any race should claim earthly immortality. . . . Everlastingness is not to be met in the realm of space and time."[93] This new approach reversed his earlier prophecies of 1878[94] and 1915[95] in which he had predicted the not too distant end of the Jewish race. He resigned himself to the fact that "at certain times when anti-Semitism is afoot, and spits its venom in actual persecution or ugly discriminations, there is sure to be a swing back to the old lines."[96] He understood this attitude; it was "perfectly natural," although to him "not the finest attitude to take."[97] Adler remained true to his fundamental conviction that the finest attitude for the Jew to take was to "go out into life, walk on the great thoroughfare, mingle with thy fellows. . . . Prejudice cannot be argued down, it must be lived down."[98] Anti-Semitism, therefore, did not lead Adler back into the Jewish fold as it did so many others; he steadfastly maintained his universalist religious ideology.

Adler died in April of 1933, just as Hitler came to power. He repudiated the early anti-Jewish outbreaks of the Hitler regime in February–March 1933 in the strongest terms. Unable to attend the Madison Square Garden rally on March 27, 1933 to protest these anti-Jewish riots, because of the cancer which was shortly to claim his life, Adler was asked to send a message. Read by John Elliott, the message expressed Adler's joy that American diplomats and consular representatives had apparently received explicit assurances from the German government that "outrages on Jews in Germany have virtually ceased." Adler continued:

> At the same time the real evil is anti-Semitism, a poisonous plant of which the recent excesses are but the baneful fruit. Anti-Semitism has been egregiously fostered in Germany, especially during the last few decades. It is a monstrous thing, a relapse to a stage of subcivilization which one had believed that mankind had advanced beyond. But Germany is not the only country in which anti-Semitism is poisoning the minds of people; and if this present meeting, representing thousands of men and women of good will, will rebuke and repudiate anti-Semitism as such, it will render a service far exceeding the present emergency.[99]

According to Elliott, the message was well received and elicited loud applause. Still, in his letter to his daughters, Adler expressed grave concern over the extremely alarming situation, "especially as the Nazis have now taken up their dastardly work in Vienna."

How would Adler have viewed the issue of continued Jewish existence in light of the Nazi atrocities and the Holocaust which followed? One can only conjecture, of course, but it seems apparent that his views on Jewish existence would not have changed. His opposition to Zionism and Jewish national life was irrevocable, as was his estimation of the ethical shortcomings of the Jewish religion. By rejecting Jewish religious and national options, Adler could not have subscribed to continued separate Jewish existence, for he had rejected the basic categories of meaningful Jewish identification. The break which Adler made with Judaism, with the premises upon which it was based, under no circumstances could have permitted his return to the Jewish fold on intellectually consistent grounds. And without such consistency, Adler would not have returned. As he wrote in 1918, "one cannot take the position that the Ethical Culture societies have taken, and at the same time go back to Jewishness."[100]

Besides anti-Semitism, the other Jewish issue of international prominence during the last half of Adler's life was Zionism. Adler recalled that his first contact with Zionism came from his exposure, in the early 1880s, to the intense national fervor of the Eastern European Jewish immigrants living on New York's Lower East Side, which introduced him to a nationalist option for Jewish living.[101] Adler did not become a Jewish nationalist, but many others around him did. "At or about 1881," he remembered, "that lovely American poetess, Emma Lazarus, first struck the strings of the Jewish lyre. She had been indifferent. She had held aloof. Her subjects were in another field. Suddenly, she became an intense Zionist."[102] Retrospectively, Adler realized that the pogroms of the 1880s and the emigration of East European Jews had changed Emma Lazarus, just as they had changed so many leaders of the Zionist movement who "up to a certain time of their life, did not care a fig for anything Jewish."[103]

Over the years Adler followed the course of Zionism as it materialized from an idealistic dream to a concrete national movement. He almost could not help but note its development, since some of his closest Jewish friends, such as Rabbis Felsenthal and Stephen S. Wise, had become active leaders of American Zionism. Moreover, by 1910 his own brother-in-law, Louis Brandeis, had become an outspoken advocate of the Zionist cause.[104]

Judging from his addresses on Zionism and from the large number of unpublished notes on the topic in the Adler archives, Adler seems to have been rather agitated by the issues of Zionism from about 1915 on. At that time the Zionist movement appeared to be making giant political strides, which ultimately culminated in the Balfour Declaration and the British Mandate permitting Jewish settlement in the National Home of Palestine. Having witnessed these events and the concretization of significant Zionist goals, Adler was quite disturbed. To him Zionism represented Jewish withdrawal into Jewish particularism, which he deeply regretted, and which directly opposed his mature religious outlook. "Zionism itself is a present day instance of the segregating tendency,"[105] he noted. He understood Zionism, by implication, to challenge both the validity of the choice of Jews to join Ethical Culture and the legitimacy of the decision of many Jews to remain non-Zionists.

> Zionism hits the Jew as a member of the race, and asks him to turn away from these new departures, and, as it puts it rather boldly, to resort to Jewishness. So that Zionism in a way questions the right of persons of Jewish birth to be Ethical Culturists. And that challenge of course [is] interesting to me. I do not say that this is openly so stated, but to my mind, it is implied.[106]

Adler also interpreted Zionism to represent a challenge to Americans of Jewish blood because it declared that "we are remiss unless we join the Zionist standard."[107] He felt it necessary, therefore, to publicly express his position on the issue, and he outlined his views on Zionism in two public addresses, "Zionism and Its Ideal," November 7, 1915, and "Nationalism and Zionism," December 8, 1918, as well as in later unpublished notes. An inner unity and coherence exists in Adler's views on Zionism, and one can definitely speak of his undifferentiated approach to the Jewish national movement.

Adler respected Zionism as an idealistic movement but differed radically from its ideals. As he wrote,

> I love the Zionists because of their idealism and not because of their ideals. . . .[108]
>
> Zionism is an idealisitic movement. It sees things not in the matter of fact way. . . . It is for this reason that I have natural sympathy with such a movement. . . .[109]
>
> I have never indulged in carping, cavilling criticism [of Zionism]. I have never attempted to minimize the fine strain of enthusiasm which they display.[110]

Nevertheless, he deemed the Zionist ideal "delusive"[111] and asserted that his "divergence from it . . . is radical."[112]

Zionism appealed to Adler insofar as it had changed the lives of its many adherents. "It has given to lives that were empty a noble content. It has taken people who were drifting at sea and selfish, and has made them feel for the first time the over-arching, overawing presence of collective powers and forces." He admired the colonization aspect of Zionism, for "any movement that offers a home, that gives promise of offering a home to the homeless is mightily appealing." He was also touched by the Zionist stimulation of the interest of Jews in their own little-studied history. "I am therefore in sympathy with the movement insofar as it calls attention to this vast tract of human experience [Jewish history], those human documents that have not yet been deciphered."[113]

Yet despite these praiseworthy Zionist achievements, Adler firmly opposed the Zionist movement because its essential ideal was to create a Jewish national state: "Zionism is a movement for the restoration of a national state. My sympathy is with it so far as it attempts to offer a home. I am not in sympathy with the effort to reestablish a nation, a nationalist state."[114] And he propounded a number of reasons to elaborate on and justify his opposition. In his opinion the Jews were not a nation, and the attempt to fashion them into a nation-state he thought both idealistic folly and a practical impossibility. Then, too, the supposed derivative benefits of Jewish nationalism, such as the resuscitation of Jewish spiritual genius in Palestine, he felt unrealizable. Further, Palestine for him not only was not a Jewish land by any moral or historical right, but also was presently occupied by other religions and national groups. And finally, he made clear that Zionism as a segregating tendency contradicted his final religio-ethical vision of human and societal relationships and also undermined his conception of the Jewish role in creating the desired "spiritual" democracy in America.

Following World War I, the world was beset with the contentious problem of displaced European nationalities demanding national self-determination, particularly in the Balkans. In "National Self-Determination and Its Limits," Adler addressed himself to the issue and attempted to formulate an ethical approach to the problem. In doing so, he emphatically endorsed nationalism, but a nationalism limited by ethical considerations.

> The self-determination of nations is a natural presumption. The burden of proof is on the side of those who would prescribe limits to it. . . . [But] the right of any population is limited by the interests of mankind. And by the interests of mankind, I mean the interests of the moral advancement of mankind.[115]

He vigorously advocated nationalism and not cosmopolitanism because he held that "the fulfillment of nearer duties is a condition of one's ability to fulfill wider duties" and believed in accepting "the obligations to my [American] people . . . as the prior condition to attaining the grade of world citizenship."[116] Moreover, he supported nationalism because

> the spiritual nature of man can only reveal itself in the rich variety of the gifts of the different members of the human species, and because each people is the custodian of the peculiar gifts or talent with which it is endowed, or which may be latent in it, not only for its own good, but for the good of mankind. Those peoples who are striving to find themselves in national self-expression, whose natures and whose spiritual voices have been stifled, whose potential contributions have been ruthlessly denied the opportunity of manifesting themselves, they too shall be invited to come into the light. This, as I see it, is the ethical basis for a purged, ennobled nationalism.[117]

And for this reason Adler wholeheartedly endorsed the national demands of the Poles.

What legitimated a nation's claim to be recognized as a nation? Certainly the existence of a common language, history, law, and art were vital factors. But for Adler "the determining consideration is national self-consciousness itself—the indescribable, unanalyzable almost instinctive feeling of a folk that they are *one*, that they belong together, that they have a common gift, a common character to express."[118]

Judging from these criteria, Adler seems to have offered a compelling argument in favor of *Jewish* nationalism, for the Jews appear to have possessed most of the requisites for admission into national existence. Adler was fully aware of this implication, for in his address "Nationalism and Zionism" two weeks later, he asked: does not "the logical outcome of my last Sunday address two weeks ago . . . point straight in the direction of Zionism?"[119]

Adler unequivocally responded in the negative; the Jews have not been and are not now a nation, but a religious community "hanging together by religious threads."[120] The Jews are not a nation because "a nation for one thing must have land. A migrating nation is an absurdity."[121] Moreover, a nation must be homogeneous and the Jews are not. Indeed, "among all the Western nations among whom they have lived," Adler averred, "Jews are distinguished by the fact that they invariably exhibit the characteristics of the people among whom they live—to an extent even more marked than those peoples themselves." Disraeli is the ideal Conservative Englishman, because "Jew that he was, he out-Englished the English in his character, in his traits."[122] The same was true of Henri Bergson in France, Heinrich Heine in Germany, and Georg Brandes in Scandinavia.

Further, Adler asserted, the soul of a people is expressed in its literature. "Jews do not possess their own literature; and yet, they occupy the highest rank in the literature of the world. This situation arises because the Jews have the capacity of expressing the soul of the Western nations." And as for Hebrew being the Jews' national language, he felt that Western Jews did not, and probably could not, accept it as such, despite its being the language of prayer to many.[123] Each Jew—French, English, German, Danish—was for him a distinct type with distinctive habits of mind. For each of them to have adopted Hebrew as a national language would have entailed a revolutionary change in mode of thinking which would only have "straitjacketed" their minds.

To the claim that Zionism reflected a unified Jewish national self-consciousness, Adler pointed to the fragmentation of world Jewry, including the internal divisions within Zionist ranks, to discount it. Zionism "is not a unanimous Jewish people's movement. A large fraction are opposed to it."[124] No consensus existed even within the Zionist movement, he argued, and he cited the distinctive ideologies of the Palestine-oriented nationalists, the territorialists, the freethinkers, the Orthodox Jews, and the democratic socialists to prove his contention. As to a Jewish national consciousness, therefore, Adler concluded that "the Jews are individualists—always have been."[125]

For all these reasons, Adler denied the existence of a Jewish nation and rejected Jewish nationalism as neither a viable nor a morally legitimate national movement. And contrary to Zionist arguments, he maintained that Jews were under no moral obligation to join the Jewish nationalist cause. With this assertion he responded to the Zionist contention that Jews by birth were bound to belong to the Jewish national movement.[126] Not so, Adler declared, for while one may be ethically obligated to belong to the nation into which he was born *if the nation already existed,* one was not obligated *to try to constitute* a hitherto nonexistent nation. To Adler, that, in effect, represented the Zionist ideal, and he believed it to be ideologically inconsistent with the Jewish past and practically untenable in the present.

Without doubt the Reform Jewish ideological opposition to Jewish national existence, first implanted in Adler by his father, Samuel, in large measure underlay his own denial of Jewish nationalism. Felix Adler had accepted this view of the religious and non-national character of the Jews as an adolescent in the 1860s, when Zionism was not yet a living option for world Jewry. As he matured, and even following his break with Judaism, he still regarded Jewish existence to be contingent on the affirmation of basic religious ideas. In this sense, his conception of Judaism and his opposition to Zionism shared marked ideological similarities with the views of such Reform rabbis as Kohler, Emil Hirsch, and Henry Berkowitz, and such Jewish laymen as Henry Morgenthau.[127]

Not only did Adler regard the notion of Jewish nationalism to be ideologically untenable, but also he deemed it extremely and even ridiculously impractical. He understood Zionism to be a direct product of anti-Semitism.[128] He asserted that Herzl and his colleagues accepted the anti-Semitic definition of Jews as foreigners,[129] and this led them to conclude that only a Jewish national state could successfully counter the nationalism of other countries, which inevitably engendered anti-Semitism. "The idea was that anti-Semitism was incurable so long as the Jewish people were scattered as individuals and as communities. There must be a national country in order to impose respect upon the enemy, the foe."[130]

But, Adler queried, Palestine at best could accommodate one-fifth of the number of persecuted Jews in places such as Russia and Poland; how would a Jewish state practically aid the other four-fifths? For example, how was a "petty Jewish state of two million" going to affect the situation of a Jewish soldier in the Czar's army who had lost an arm for his country and returned home only to find his family evicted due to anti-Semitism?[131] Moreover, would the prestige of the Jewish state affect the autocracy of Russia when its ambassadors came to Jerusalem? The Russians did not even respect American ambassadors, let alone Russo-American treaties. "Get down to business—look at the facts," he declared. "How does Zionism affect the situation of those people who need most to be helped?"[132]

Adler himself offered no immediate practical solution for the plight of

Russian Jews. While he noted that "my heart bleeds for the Jews of Russia today,"[133] he proclaimed that

> the only light I can see in this blackness is revolution in Russia, which I hope and trust need not be a bloody one, a change from autocratic to liberal government. I think that the fate of the Jews in Russia is bound up with the fate of their country. Their emancipation will come with the emancipation of their fellow citizens, and not with the erection of a little state in Palestine. . . . The fate of the Jews in Russia depends upon the progress of liberalism.[134]

Theoretically, Adler probably would not have been averse to sending Russian Jews to Palestine as a haven of refuge rather than as a Jewish state. After all, he professed sympathy with Palestine as a *home* (not a *national* home, however) for the Jews. While he never elaborated on this issue, it nevertheless appears that he considered this type of transfer of Jews to be impossible. In reference to the one and a half million homeless Jews wandering about in Poland after World War I, Adler remarked that one could not bring them to Palestine. "It takes a good many transports to carry a million people. And you cannot carry these one and a half million as you would soldiers. You cannot settle them, colonize them. I do not see that this is an expedient. I am so much preoccupied by the real situation, the existing situation, that I cannot see how the remedy fits the disease."[135]

Other severe practical impediments which, Adler felt, prevented the fulfillment of the Zionist goal were the multifarious forces and vested interests controlling Palestine at the time. He reminded Jews that Palestine lay in the grip of Turkish, Greek Orthodox, and other churches, as well as in the hands of Arab residents. It would be sheer folly to assume, he asserted, that the residents and rulers of Palestine would allow the creation of a Jewish state. Even more hopeless was the faith that the various churches would permit a Jewish state to be founded in the land of Christ.[136] Balfour may have approved, but Adler quickly noted that Balfour was a skeptic, as evidenced by his *Foundations of Belief.*[137] And further, he argued, the serious internal dissension among the Zionists themselves precluded the successful organization of a Jewish state. Therefore, "it is very doubtful to my mind if the great orthodox powers were to relinquish their grip on Palestine and one or two million Jews were collected there, whether the national state would long last."[138]

Ideologically ill-conceived and practically unsound, Herzl's political Zionism was found wanting; for Adler, a Jewish state could not be the antidote to anti-Semitism and would not solve the "Jewish question." But some Zionists justified the need for a Jewish state by affirming that the return of the Jews to their historic national home would resuscitate the genius of the Jews, long hampered by artificial constraints. For them, "Palestine is to be the vessel of the Holy Grail so to speak," Adler suggested.[139] But he rejected this Zionist proposal for a "spiritual center"; while he did not actually use the phrase of Achad Haam, the idea of a "spiritual center" seems to be what he attacked.

Adler rejected this Zionist argument for four reasons. First, he maintained that Jewish history proves that the Jewish genius "has never been at its best when they [the Jews] were segregated. . . . Jewish genius, Jewish mentality has done its best at the contact points with alien minds."[140] Moreover, "the best that the Jews have contributed to the world's literature and science has been contributed at these contact points where their minds struck sparks with the mind of other peoples by whom they were challenged, with whom they were in close contact, in close touch."[141] And he cited the achievements of outstanding Jews and Jewish life in Babylonia (Second Isaiah), Alexandria (Philo), Moslem Spain, Holland (Spinoza), and the efflorescence of Jewish scholars and scientists in Italy, France, and Germany to substantiate his claim.[142] Historically, Adler demonstrated that Palestine had not been the center of Jewish creativity.

Second, Adler disagreed with the Zionist position which affirmed the necessity of Palestine for Jews to absorb themselves in Jewish culture. He doubted that the study of Judaism and Jewish history would "flourish better in Palestine than elsewhere. I do not deny that the enthusaism of those who return to Palestine is one fact to be counted with, but it does not seem to me an essential factor."[143] He recounted his own experience that "propinquity to sacred soil has not had the effect upon me that perhaps in my romantic youth I expected."[144] Thus he found that his pilgrimages to the homes of Goethe and Shakespeare did not bring him closer to their spirits than when he read their works in New York's Adirondack Mountains. "And so I do not believe that it is necessary to be in the Holy Land in order to fathom these waters, in order to be profoundly interested in this great tract of human experience that is called the history of the Jews. It is a spur to some; it is not essential."[145]

Third, Adler insisted that the singular genius of the Jewish people manifested itself in religion. "Their gift has been religious";[146] "whatever else they have accomplished in science and art is relatively a byproduct of their proclivity to see things *sub-specie aeternitatis.*"[147] But the most exalted expression of their religious genius has been prophetic ethics, and these ethical conceptions did not suffice for the modern world. Consequently, he asked:

> Then for the development of a religion do you want to go back to Palestine as Jews? Do you want to go back in order to have the prophetic religion? I challenge that position absolutely. I do not believe that the

ethics of the prophets is the last word. It is the dawn and not the perfect day, and it is bound up with ideas [monotheism and Jewish mission] that hamper the more perfect [ethical] development.[148]

Since, according to Adler, the genius of the Jews found its supreme expression in a *dated* prophetic morality, the argument favoring a Jewish state for the purpose of reviving the Jewish spiritual genius lost its force. Referring to spiritual Zionism, he concluded, "Zionism, as I see it, is a logical conclusion from the undertaking to repristinate the prophetic ideal."[149] And for that precise reason, he viewed the Zionist ideal of creating a center for the development of the Jewish spiritual genius, and for the realization of the prophetic ideal of an exemplary righteous commonwealth consisting of Jews, as both historically unjustified and anachronous.

Finally, Adler contended that not only was the Jewish religio-ethical genius dated, but that the Jews lacked the specific genius necessary for the establishment and administration of a national state: political genius. He claimed that the Jews had never manifested a political aptitude; they had never distinguished themselves in a political capacity "because they seem to lack the art of compromise. They are very uncompromising in their opinions."[150] Consequently, he could not imagine how a Jewish state comprising six hundred thousand Arabs, Greek Orthodox, Russian Orthodox, Roman Catholic, and Protestant Christians and Orthodox and secular Jews could possibly function. "Unless the art of compromise should be developed," he declared, "I am afraid that the Jewish state would only repeat the history of the old Jewish state."[151] And Adler felt that, in fact, Jews inherently could not develop this political trait on any significant scale because of "the sharp, intellectual Jewish mind, and the individuality of the Jews."[152] "I cannot conceive," he concluded, "how all these various elements could be harmonized so as to cooperate."[153] In proposing that the administration of a Jewish state required a political capacity which Jews did not possess, Adler underlined his belief that the idea of a Jewish national state based on the revival of a Jewish genius was utterly without foundation.

Other factors came into play in Adler's general opposition to a Jewish state in Palestine. He thought the Jews to possess no intrinsic legal, historical, or moral right to the land. Ironically, he adopted Orthodox Judaism's position that the Jewish title to Palestine rested solely on God's promise to Abraham that his children would inherit the land: but "if this title is questioned, what remains?"[154] Adler, like many others who did not accept the divinity of the Bible, disputed this title on historical grounds. Historically, no such promise was granted; furthermore, the Jews were neither the original owners nor the first residents of Palestine, and therefore it could not be conceived solely as the Jewish homeland. Palestine was the homeland of the Hittites and Canaanites centuries before Hebrew raiders entered and dispossessed them of their lands.[155] The Jews themselves later lost the land—"and they have lost it for two thousand years nearly";[156] in what sense, then, Adler asked, could Palestine be considered the Jewish homeland?

Also, since Palestine was not a vacant land—six hundred thousand Arabs lived there—it could not support everybody, Adler argued.[157] And he further asked, "When has a people the right to return to a land which it once occupied, especially if the return implies the ousting of the present population? Is there not a statute of limitations?"[158] Moreover, even if the Jews did not dismiss the native Arabs from the Jewish state in Palestine, they would govern the state as a minority ruling the Arab majority, since it would take a long time before they constituted a majority in the land. This situation of minority rule, however, contradicted the basic tenets of democratic government.[159] Adler was, therefore, quite dismayed by the Balfour Declaration calling for a National Home for the Jews. To him, Jewish National Home as applied to Palestine was a radical contradiction in terms. A nation is a political organization, and a national home is the home of a nation; but how could the promise of a Jewish national home be redeemed, Adler questioned, if the Palestinian government was to be shared between two races without the Jews being preponderant? And if the Jews were to be preponderant, the basic principle of democracy would be violated, since the political power of the Jewish minority would be disproportionate to its numerical strength.[160]

Adler's opposition to Zionism on all these grounds—that the Jews did not constitute a nation, that Palestine was not needed for the revival of the Jewish genius, and that the Zionist ideal would necessarily violate the political rights of the native Arabs—was not overly original. One finds similar ideas in the works of other prominent American anti-Zionists, such as Kohler, Emil Hirsch, Morris R. Cohen,[161] and Henry Morgenthau, as well as in the formal positions of Reform Jewish institutions, such as the Central Conference of American Rabbis and Hebrew Union College,[162] and the anti-Zionist petition of Rabbi Henry Berkowitz and Morris Jastrow to Woodrow Wilson in 1919.[163] But in objecting to Zionism as a segregating tendency antithetical to his own ethical-religious vision of the future and as a movement undermining Jewish spiritual creativity in America, Adler added a distinctly personal flavor to his dispute with Zionism.

A description of Adler's final ethical-religious vision of the future lies beyond the scope of this study. Suffice it to say that from the 1890s on, Adler's primary ethical preoccupation shifted from concern for *social* reform in society to the problem of *internal* reform of the individual by which process an ethical society could be created. Adler focused on the centrality of the inviolate human personality and affirmed that each human being contains a unique personality with irreplaceable qualities which constitute his "worth." According to Adler, this "worth" represents "an indelible trace of divinity . . . a latent preciousness in him [man] which the world cannot afford to go without."[164] In the process of interacting with their fellow human beings, people bring out the latent "worth" of others while simultaneously enhancing their own. This mutual "interlacing of lives" represents the dynamic spiritual principle necessary for realizing the ethical end of life, the creation of an ethical society.[165] As Adler wrote, "we are socially-minded in religion. We realize that if we are to get nearer to moral perfection, it must be in a society that is striving, and by the cooperation of a society in which each member contributes his own undifferentiated share."[166]

Adler posited a social model couched in theological terms for his new socio-religious conception to replace the former individualized model of perfection, God; he termed his model *Godhead*. The Godhead was the model of a perfect modern society and state to which each society should aspire. It was a plural model because, in Adler's view, perfection could not be an attribute of any one individual or society but only of the totality of "divine" human personalities acting in concert with each other. The Godhead, therefore, was a model "of infinite being as constituted by an infinity of beings, each of whom is indispensable to the whole, like the members of an organism, and the unity of which consists in the perfect interplay and interaction of the parts."[167]

A corollary of this conception, which Adler himself seems to have recognized, is that the degree of perfection of any society is in some sense proportionate to the number of individual members which it could sustain; for the intrinsic and necessary differentiated "worth" of each human being contributes to the society's diversity, thereby increasing its potential for perfection. Consequently, movements such as Zionism, which segregated a small number of individuals to isolated areas of the world, were antithetical to Adler's religious conception. Indeed, the very conceptual notion of separatism contravened his religious ideal, which could be best realized precisely when large numbers of individuals with their unique qualities interacted with each other. And Zionism was particularly unacceptable because Palestine's limited natural environment and resources could not sustain the diverse, fully differentiated societal life which was essential for an ethical society.

The little patch of land on the East shore of the Mediterranean is not suited [to materialize the religious ideal]. . . .[168]

Palestine is unfavorable to the existence of a diversified Common-wealth. There is little waterpower, no deposits of coal and iron, no basis for any considerable development of industry.[169]

While Palestine was not suited to foster Adler's model of a modern, technological religious society, America was.

The environment needed for the development of which we have the grand conception is open spaces, vast horizons, a land in which the forces to be harmonized are huge, in which the energies are un-exhausted. The cradle of the new religion will not be a state near the shores of the Dead Sea below Jerusalem. It will be set upon a continent on which mighty oceans break on either shore.[170]

And here we come to the final reason for Adler's basic rejection of Zionism: his utter commitment to America as his national home and as the prototype of his spiritual ideal of democracy.

Adler asserted that the creation of a Jewish state would impose a problem of dual national loyalty on all of world Jewry. "To belong to two nations is impossible. Citizenship is indivisible; the allegiance must be perfect."[171] True, one can have divided loyalties. "You can be loyal to your family, your college, your club, your professional colleagues, your voca-tion, and you can also be loyal to your nation. . . . But it is forgotten that these loyalties to family and college are included within the citizenship, within the national loyalty."[172] Adler's choice of examples—extremely similar to those used by Brandeis in his 1915 speech to Reform Jews entitled "The Jewish Problem and How to Solve It"[173]—indicates that he was responding directly to Brandeis' repudiation of a dual-loyalty prob-lem for American Jews. Adler rhetorically asked whether one can be loyal to two nations, "to your nation, the nation in which you live, and to another nation,"[174] and unequivocally declared this to be impossible. And he for one proclaimed his fealty to America: "For my part I am not and never can be a Zionist. I am a lover not of Zion, but of America. I am not a Palestinian. I am an American. I do not wish to bring fresh garlands to ancient sanctuaries, but to crown with unwithering honor the beauteous head of ideal America."[175]

Adler rejected Brandeis' formula that an American Jew who is a Zionist will be a better American. He understood Brandeis to suggest that because "Zion is to be a model state based on the democratic principle . . . the American Jew who helps that will be in line with the finest ideals of democracy, and will therefore be a better citizen of this country."[176] But to Adler the democracy of the Prophets differed radically from American democracy: their democracy was theocratic and "consistent with the privileged, elect position of the Hebrew people";[177] American democracy was neither theocratic nor consistent with any idea of an elect people. The Brandeis formula, to Adler at least, was therefore invalid.

Adler attributed to American democracy the potential to serve as more than just an intermediary for securing "the lesser things—security of life, security of property, opportunity for material independence—things very well in their way."[178] He conceived of American democracy in a spiritual sense because it could reflect the highest societal expression of his idea of the Godhead. To Adler, in fact, America was endowed with a spiritual mission to become a democratic spiritual ideal, exemplifying spiritual democracy before the world. Thus, his ties to America go beyond the expression of mere national loyalty avowed by such anti-Zionist American Jews as Morgenthau. Adler's deep-seated commitment to America was rooted in a devout emotional and ideological affirmation of America's spiritual role in the world which precluded any attachment to another nation.

Hence, one can better understand Adler's great sense of loss that American Jews were contributing their moral idealism to the cause of creating a Jewish state rather than to the furtherance of the "ideal America." And he blamed the Zionists for siphoning off this idealism.

> My chief reason for feeling a certain soreness about the Zionist movement is that it is taking these fine young people from the task which belongs to them here, the Americans of Jewish birth. . . .[179]
> For the Zionist himself . . . I have only cherished feelings of respect, and in some cases, where I am bound by personalities, feelings of deep, deep affection. But there is one grievance which I cannot deny: I am jealous for America's sake just of that idealism, just of that fine enthusiasm of my Zionist friends—that it should be deflected toward a Homeland thousands of miles away—which is no Homeland—a little patch on the shore of the Mediterranean—when the Homeland is here. For if the American Jew has anything remaining in him of that ethical power that once flamed up in the prophets of Israel, here it should be expended, in order to give a spiritual interpretation to democracy, which is basely interpreted; in order to lift democracy out of the dust with which it is covered, and place it on a high hill among the divine things that have been revealed to the mind and heart of man.[180]

Perhaps nothing portrays Adler's deep emotional relationship to America more poignantly than his brief commentary on the Psalmist's query, "I lift mine eyes to the hills, whence cometh my help." Adler asked: "To which hills? I fix my gaze steadfastly on the glimmering of a fresh morning that shines over the Alleghenies and the Rockies, not on the evening glow, however tenderly beautiful, that broods and lingers over the Jerusalem hills."[181]

Adler formulated his basic ideas on Zionism in his two addresses of 1915 and 1918. But the Adler archives contain numerous unpublished notes on the subject. Although undated, most of them seem to have been written following the creation of the British Mandate, for they contain Adler's ruminations on the fait accompli of continued Jewish colonization of Palestine. In the main he concerned himself with the political injustice which he felt was meted out to the native Arab residents,[182] and with what he regarded as the spiritually unsatisfying nature of the Jewish colonization efforts. Adler appears to have said "I told you so" to the spiritual Zionists, for he did not see any hint of the genius of the Jews unfolding in Palestine. While disapproving of spiritual Zionism's repristination of Judaism, he would have liked to have seen some "spiritual" direction in Zionist undertakings, even if only reminiscent of the prophetic ideals he had deemed outmoded. But he could find no such orientation. Jews were creating socialist colonies, a university, and were succeeding at technical undertakings such as irrigation, sanitation, and the exploitation of the Dead Sea; but "there is no glint of any new development of the prophetic or spiritual genius of the Jews."[183] And he concluded that Zionist Jews would have to choose whether these colonies would stand on an *exemplary* or a *secular* plane; if the former, they would have to develop a morality beyond the prophetic type; if the latter, their ideal was at variance with the intent of all of ancient Scripture and the meaning of Jewish history.[184]

This last idea underscores both the motive force and the basic shortcoming of Adler's approach to Zionism. He approached the issue of Jewish national existence with a preconceived ideological definition of the Jews as a religious group bearing particular religious-ethical ideals which happen to be dated. To Adler, a Jew was a Jew only by virtue of his affirmation of monotheism and the Jewish mission. Adler's definition of Jewish existence only in terms of religion was born from his interpretation of Scripture and Jewish history, and from his early Reform Jewish education. And while he adduced practical reasons to support his contention that the Jews could not be considered a nation, the heart of his position lay in his fundamental assumption. In Adler's view, the Jews had not been a nation in the past, and therefore it would be ideologically inconsistent with the meaning of Jewish existence and history for them to constitute themselves as a nation in the present.

Zionists, however, dismissed Adler's assumption. They interpreted Scripture and Jewish history in their own way, perceiving a Jewish national identity underlying Jewish religious life throughout the ages. Horace Kallen considered the Jewish religion subordinate to Jewish nationality;[185] Mordecai Kaplan defined Jewish existence in religio-national terms.[186] Regardless of the specific conceptions at the bottom of the various Zionist ideologies, however, the focus of the Zionists' dispute with Adler's ideas centered on their antithetical assumptions on the nature of Jewish existence.

On Continued Jewish Existence

Given Adler's rejection of Zionism and Jewish national identity, his declaration of the inadequacy of prophetic Judaism, and his suggestion that Jews transcend their Jewishness to overcome anti-Semitism, it is clear that he conceived of no ideological rationale for the continued separate existence of the Jews; he found neither meaning nor purpose in Jewish religious and ethnic separatism. Preferably, he felt that Jews should transcend their Jewish racial and religious identity and merge with their fellow citizens in the nations in which they live. And even if individual Jews had not yet passed out of their Jewishness, in 1915, at least, Adler deemed this merger to be historically inevitable. He predicted that Jews would ultimately recognize that the insufficiency of the Jewish religion disqualified it as a raison d'être for Jewish existence; and once anti-Semitism disappeared—as he then still believed it would—Jews would understand that Zionism signified but race-consciousness without religion that was kept alive by anti-Jewish persecutions. At that time, Jews would reject Jewish nationalism as well.[187] While Adler's certainty of the disappearance of the Jews waned by 1925, he maintained his position on the needlessness of continued Jewish existence.

In dismissing the need for Jewish existence, however, Adler seems to have been troubled by two questions which frequently recur in his undated notes: since the Jews possessed a peculiar religious genius—"moral insight conditioned by blood"[188]—"on the principle of the conservation of resources, why should not the human race be interested in preserving the Jewish tree?"[189] Should not the Jewish group be preserved for the sake of potentially new expressions of its genius?[190] Then too, did the Jews have any further contribution to make to contemporary civilization?

"New original contributions are not to be expected from the Hebrew group," Adler proclaimed, "since its chief characteristic is its compact, molecular coherence."[191] It was diversity that was needed in the modern world. Moreover, "there is no such thing as a genius for religion in general. . . . [Jews possess] a genius for a particular kind of religion—a very excellent kind . . . a kind of religion that has left its deposit, and is to be subsumed in any later form, but not a final and all-around religion."[192] According to Adler, the new religious morality required differentiation, diversity, and "the genius of no one people is competent to produce that ideal religion towards which the history of the religious movements of the various peoples of the earth may be made to tend."[193] Consequently, having long since fulfilled their religious genius by introducing prophetic ethics to the world, the Jews *as a group* were judged by Adler to have no further contributions to make; the world need not be interested in the perpetuation of the Jewish race.

While the Jewish race as a whole could not be expected to contribute anything new, Jewish individuals still could. Possessed of the racially transmitted Jewish ethical genius, individuals could "tread the path of religious novelty."[194] How? Not by segregating themselves within Jewish lines, Adler insisted, but rather by breaking the constraints of the Jewish community and joining with others in a racial union in America to develop the new moral ideal. And to him this idea of racial union represented an ethical point of view fundamentally distinct from ordinary assimilation. The assimilationists, in his view, were either agnostics or individualists who left everyone free to choose his affiliations at his own pleasure. They did not concern themselves with the moral goal of each man contributing his racial endowment to humanity. The ethical point of view, however, regarded this task to be every person's responsibility; consequently the moral duty of the Jews was to express "the religious gift of their race by going beyond their race."[195] To Adler, the new religious ideal must come from a racial union. "The ethical ideal of humanity and segregation on racial lines seem to be mutually contradictory. . . . religious fellowship combined with racial segregation is impossible."[196]

And when the Jew finally does merge his racial stock with others,

> there will shoot up here and there and everywhere, new testimony, new productions, flowing from the effects of the union of Jewish mentality with alien minds, the crossing of races, the crossing of mentality. There is still in store for humanity riches of which we have as yet no conception. If the Jewish race dies, before it dies, it may have some of its most notable contributions still to make because of the crossing of races as the condition of its highest fulguration.[197]

By itself, the Jewish religious genius transmitted along racial lines was, for Adler, without value in contemporary life; merged in racial union with other races, it would contribute substantially to the spiritual ideal.

Adler, then, presented an ideology for Jewish existence steeped in paradox: Jews fulfill their spiritual and racial potential as Jews only when they *leave* their religious and racial points of origin, that is, when they cease to be Jews. And yet the paradox is not as novel as may appear at first glance; in effect, it is but a religious analogue to classical Reform Judaism's own vision of the messianic goal which awaited the Jews' merger with the nations of the world at the end of days, at some point in the undefined future. Adler, of course, regarded the dissolution of Jewish separatism as a religious ideal to be actualized in the immediate present.

Despite his ideology, Adler did not hate or polemicize against Jews who did not subscribe to his ideas. His genuine appreciation of human personality and freedom, his deep affection for his Jewish past, and his sincere friendship with Jews such as Stephen Wise and Emil Hirsch precluded his reaching such sentiments. He approached the whole matter of Jewish existence with the sense of patient, historical understanding so typical of his mode of thinking. At various times during his life, he expressed certainty, to a greater or lesser extent, of the imminent historical end of the Jews. But besides acting on his own in creating and leading his Ethical Society and trying to convince others by dint of rational argument, he allowed history to pursue its own course.

As for himself, he wrote,

> whether the historical prospect be as I have traced it or not . . . so far as I am concerned, in departing from these race limitations I have had no choice. There are those who still bear me a grudge because after forty years they think of me as a leader lost to their cause, as a deserter if not a renegade. But Oh Friends! I have had no choice, I have desired to express religious truth sincerely, that is in me. I felt that in order to do so, I should try to preserve what is essentially best in the Hebrew tradition, but not preserve what is deciduous and obsolete; and also what is best in the Christian tradition. For my eyes had opened to see, as most of my fellows of old did not see that there is truth in Christianity as well as in the Hebrew scriptures which we must preserve. And so, because those who have been educated in a certain tradition best understand that tradition and can preserve what is best in it, therefore, I felt that we must try and establish a movement in which Jew and Gentile, those who had the Hebrew and those who had the Christian teaching can come together, in which there shall be a crossing of race mentalities.[198]

This description also represented Adler's mature understanding of the purpose of the Ethical Culture Movement. The idea of racial union reflected a significant development from the Ethical Society's original design of social reform; and Adler identified himself with a new religious model, Paul, or Saul of Tarsus.

> Though he was a Hebrew of the Hebrews, [Paul] felt that he must win a situation in which he could include a common bond Jew and Gentile, bond and free. So I felt that we must include in a new Convenant not yet

existent, as they are included in our Ethical Societies . . . those of the tradition of the Hebrew prophets, and those of the Christian tradition united in one Covenant . . . facing and fronting the future and reaching out to a truth that is beyond and transcends both the Hebrew and the Christian tradition. . . .[199]
Paul felt that [the Hebrew heritage] was too narrow, and that he must go out and unite men of every stock in order to found a new religious fellowship, on a new basis. The solution which he found is not one which we can accept, but the problem of Paul is the problem that faced me fifty years ago, and that faces us all—the problem of how to unite with men and women of every stock and every heritage, in order to found a new and wider spiritual fellowship.[200]

And so, Adler's break with Judaism reached its final expression. From his initial discontent with the Jewish religion and his break from the Jewish socio-religious consensus in the late 1870s, Adler ultimately was led to devise an ideology calling for the end of the Jewish ethnic and religious heritage, an end to Jewish existence. True, already in 1878 Adler had suggested that one need not restrict oneself to a particular race.[201] Indeed, in that year Adler remarked that "questions of race, distinctions of birth are accidental and can have no meaning for us on the platform whereon we stand."[202] Even then Adler assented to the idea of intermarriage between two persons united by a broad spiritual outlook and unfettered by any particularist theological creed.[203] But it seems that only following his encounter with Jewish nationalism and Zionism did Adler explicitly insist, *as a matter of religio-ethical ideological policy,* that Jews remove themselves from the Jewish racial community.

Vilified by Jews and non-Jews alike in the 1870s for his radical religious and social ideas, in the end Adler had earned the respect of much of New York's population. In an editorial two days following his death, the *New York Times* wrote that "he brought so much good to the community. . . . He was indeed like a tree planted by the rivers of water whose leaves did not wither with the years. . . . And wherever he passed was holy ground in his definition of it, as 'the place where men meet to seek the highest.' "[204] In a letter to Adler's widow on January 6, 1934, President Franklin D. Roosevelt, apologizing for his tardy expression of condolence, mourned the "passing of a profound philosopher, a cultural leader of spiritual force, a philanthropist and a beloved citizen."[205] Prominent Christian clergymen such as Bishop William T. Manning and Dr. Harry E. Fosdick also paid tribute to Adler's noble idealism.[206] Even some Jews mourned his passing with a feeling perhaps best reflected in the statement by Temple Emanu-El's Rabbi Samuel Schulman:

It is with shock and sincere regret that I hear of the death of Felix Adler, the great ethical leader and one of the greatest quickening spirits for the ethical life in the world. He has stood out as an apostle to mankind of pure idealism. Though profoundly differing from him in my religious outlook, I have always revered him as a master. The synagogue, the expression of Israel's soul has always keenly felt the loss of its sons. We still sing in our temple the confirmation hymn which he wrote, and as I said in a letter congratulating him on his 80th birthday, our love for him made us sometimes even impatient.[207]

Adler had long since departed from the Jewish socio-religious fellow-ship, but his ethical idealism had left an indelible impression on at least some members of the Jewish community, Stephen S. Wise in particular. Wise's wife, Louise Waterman, along with her family, had been an ardent member of the New York Society for Ethical Culture prior to her marriage, and she was responsible for her husband's initial acquaintance with Adler. As late as March 1933, she wrote to Adler professing her continuing admiration for him and related that his place in her life "has never changed despite the years that have passed and the fact that we do not meet."[208] But Stephen Wise came to appreciate Adler on his own; and notwithstanding his differing with Adler in formal religious affiliation, he called Adler "the one prophetic Jewish voice in the life of the city."[209]

In his eulogy of Adler at the service held at the Society for Ethical Culture, Wise revealed for the first time that "one generation ago . . . I turned to him [Adler] for guidance, for spiritual guidance and for moral help." The "uncompromising veracity of his soul, more than all other help that could come to me, strengthened my resolve to be true to truth as he, in a larger way and in a greater arena, had been utterly true to truth."[210] Just as Adler's commitment to truth as he understood it had taken him out of the Jewish world, so too Wise's recognition of the unyielding truth of his total commitment to the Jewish people led him to devote himself with even greater fervor to its cause. Wise, therefore, patterned himself somewhat after Adler, but made the people Israel the focal point of his concern. In a letter to his wife in 1900, he wrote:

What Felix Adler is and might have been in larger measure—you would have and will help me to be—the ethical leader of a church. You would not have me faithless to Israel—you love me too much—you would have Israel like myself—faithful to the best and the highest.[211]

Intensely loyal to the Jewish people, Wise was determined to "interpret the message of social justice of Ethical Culture to itself and to my people."[212] He wanted to illustrate that "Judaism as truly as the Ethical Society posits the moral life as the supreme thing."[213]

At the founding of the Free Synagogue in 1907, Jacob Schiff remarked that "it should be possible to accomplish within Judaism what the Ethical Culture Movement has done without the ranks from which it sprung."[214] In 1878 Rabbi Bernhard Felsenthal had urged Adler to declare his social-justice society a Jewish association, despite Adler's theological views, in order to give "newly rejuvenated life to the Jewish organism." Because he identified Judaism with specific anachronous theological ideas, Adler could not oblige. But with the creation of Wise's Free Synagogue Movement in 1907, Jacob Schiff perceived the fulfillment of Felsenthal's vision; to him, and probably to other New York Jews, Stephen Wise represented a truly "Jewish" Felix Adler.

Adler had no less of an impact on other prominent Reform Jews, some of whom remained within the mainstream institutional and/or theological frame of Reform Judaism, and others who passed out of either one or both. Included in this group was Stephen Wise's own son, James Waterman Wise, who as a youth was sent to the Ethical Culture School. James Wise did not complete his rabbinical studies at the Jewish Institute of Religion and was "unable personally to share and therefore to teach the theological conceptions of Judaism."[215] One need but read his *Liberalizing Liberal Judaism* to discover some of Adler's essential ideas and attitudes interspersed throughout the book and sometimes formally referred to by Wise in his own critique of Reform Judaism.[216]

Before joining the faculty of Hebrew Union College in Cincinnati, Abraham Cronbach came under Adler's influence in New York. A humanist and universalist, his characterization of religion as reverence for the human personality, his passion for social justice, and his attempt to apply religious ethics to contemporary society all reflected the imprint of Adler's personal and intellectual stamp on him.[217] At Hebrew Union College, Cronbach was somewhat of a singular personality, known more for his personal idealism and active engagement in the causes of social justice than for his academic scholarship. He was also the only member of the faculty at the time who performed mixed marriages. Cronbach corresponded with Adler from Cincinnati, and on the occasion of the fiftieth anniversary of the Ethical Culture Society, he wrote Adler on May 15, 1926:

> Although the institution with which I am identified is not among those which are felicitating you and the movement which you lead upon the occasion of the golden jubilee, I cannot refrain from expressing my individual personal sentiment of admiration and good will. You and the cause which you head have reached deeply into my life. Who can tell

how many others have been influenced although not officially attached to your organization?[218]

More in the mainstream of Reform Judaism's institutional and theological life, Rabbi Samuel Schulman of Temple Emanu-El revealed Adler's impact on him in a letter to Adler on September 30, 1931 on the occasion of the latter's eightieth birthday. Schulman confessed that without Adler knowing it, the Ethical Culture leader had been a great influence in his life. He noted that while a young college student, he had been debating in his mind which career to pursue, the Jewish ministry or law, "for which I had a strong inclination." Rabbi Gustav Gottheil of Emanu-El urged him to prepare for the rabbinate, but young Schulman remained unconvinced. For two years, between 1883 and 1885, he regularly attended Adler's Ethical Culture lectures at Chickering Hall to hear his "eloquent ethically quickening and spiritually stirring addresses." He informed Adler that these addresses deeply impressed him and motivated him to "take up the kind of work you were doing. Your idealism quickened in me my aspiration. And so I decided to become a teacher in Israel. I have not regretted it."[219]

As in the case of Stephen Wise, Adler—the Jew who had left Judaism and the Jewish community, and who had rejected the rabbinate—helped to channel Schulman into a rabbinical career. In the case of Schulman, the historical ironies arising from the development of his professional career are compounded: unacceptable to Emanu-El as an associate rabbi in 1873, Felix Adler contributed to the molding of a rabbi congenial to the very congregation which had earlier rebuffed him; moreover, whereas the urgings of Rabbi Gustav Gottheil apparently had failed to decisively sway Schulman to enter the rabbinate, the exhortations and engaging personal idealism of Felix Adler, the man whom Gottheil had vehemently denounced, had succeeded.

Chapter VII
Adler's Significance for Jewish History

Adler's passing out of Judaism both reflected general Jewish trends in modern times and manifested particular religious proclivities unique to him. On the one hand, his departure from Judaism is representative of a fundamental motif in modern Jewish history: it typifies one Jewish response to modernity marked by grappling with the problematic status of Jewish particularism.[1] Having left Judaism for intellectual reasons, Adler's departure from the Jewish consensus can be compared with that of other modern Jewish intellectuals. Valuable insights into the nature of modern Judaism and Jewish identity might be gained by comparing Adler's break and its motivations with those of men such as Solomon Maimon, Heinrich Heine, the Jewish Saint Simonians, and the Jewish Freemasons, as well as by comparing the reasons for his attraction to Kant with those of other Jewish Kantians, such as Maimon, Markus Herz, Lazarus Bendavid, Solomon Steinheim, Hermann Cohen, and Leo Baeck, who were attracted to the categorical imperative because it offered a secularized form of the *mitzvah*.[2] Adler should be included in any attempted typology of the modern Jewish intellectual struggling with his religion and identity.

On the other hand, Adler's "move beyond particularism" is of consequence beyond the mere fact of its exemplifying general drifts in Jewish history. His break resulted in an institution and ideological conceptions new to modern Jewish history: a universal, nondenominational (religious) fellowship based on a novel, eclectic religio-ethical ideology; a religiously motivated ideology of universalism for contemporary times (distinct from Reform Judaism's universalist vision of the messianic era); and an unusual, if not new, model of apostasy proposing the simultaneous shedding of, yet deep-felt reverence for, the Jewish religion and ethnic-racial origin.

Adler's religious change and the Jewish reaction to it is of even greater import to American Jewish history because it exposed in bold relief the religious forces, tensions, and problems confronting American Jewry in a salient decade of its growth, the 1870s. The German Jewish immigrants in the previous two to three decades had begun to firmly establish themselves in the socio-economic framework of American society. They had concentrated on building Jewish social, cultural, charitable, religious, and educational institutions, so that the decade of the 1870s climaxed an aggressive period of material and communal expansion. Ostensibly the American Jewish community appeared vigorous and healthy, and its success at this time seemed to promise continued Jewish achievements in the future. And yet the external trappings of Jewish life betrayed a decaying internal spiritual life. Despite the founding of the Union of American Hebrew Congregations and the Hebrew Union College, Jewish spiritual and intellectual life in America had reached a low ebb in the 1870s; American Judaism, particularly the dominant Reform Judaism, was evolving as a haphazard, reflexive Jewish reaction to the exigencies of socio-economic considerations. Jewish rituals were altered or dropped at will for the sake of convenience; Jewish religious-intellectual life was confined to a few individual rabbis, and applied moral idealism was virtually nonexistent. Reform temples multiplied and increased in membership, but many American Jews were, nevertheless, alienated from their religious heritage. Synagogue membership often represented but a nominal form of Jewish identification; it certainly did not guarantee synagogue attendance, as many rabbis in the 1870s discovered much to their dismay.

Adler's activities and lectures in the 1870s did much to reveal the spiritually impoverished state of American Jewish religious life. He was both an ardent critic of extant conditions and a compelling force for religious change. He underlined the intellectual and religious incompetence of many Jewish ministers; he pointed to the inherent inconsistencies of Jews' religious behavior, such as their affirmation of the sanctity of the Sabbath while simultaneously working on Saturday; he illustrated the need to revamp the stylized pulpit sermon and make it more relevant for American Jews; and he demonstrated the urgency of confronting the modern intellectual challenges to religion, for some Jews were dispensing with religion altogether because of the impact of science. He also forced community members to take cognizance of the immediate requirement to strengthen Jewish education. "Mr. Adler's frankness has opened the eyes of those who participated in the *laissez-faire* policy of American Judaism," the *Jewish Messenger* observed on July 27, 1877. Now, the paper claimed, all recognized the need for a more intensive and meaningful Jewish education for children, and people would no longer remain content with the capricious alteration of Jewish liturgy.

In the 1870s Adler's Sunday lectures at the Ethical Culture Society provided either an alternate or a supplementary religious outlet both for Jews sincerely discontented with Judaism and those simply seeking a more convenient form of assimilation. At the very least, Adler's emphasis on social reform galvanized the latent moral idealism of young and old alike and instilled a greater sense of social responsibility among numerous American Jews.

Adler's success in the 1870s justifiably agitated the Jewish communal leadership because it threatened to fragment the Jewish community and to destroy the fragile religious-institutional consensus which was in the process of being established. The great appeal of his Sunday addresses, which attracted huge, predominantly Jewish crowds, contrasted sharply with the lack of enthusiasm for the Saturday services led by the rabbis. New York's rabbis often found themselves speaking to largely empty synagogue pews; even public lectures of rabbis such as de Sola Mendes, offering "cheap tickets," were poorly attended compared to the attendance at Adler's addresses.[3]

Adler's activities in the 1870s also had a significant and immediate impact on Reform Judaism. He split the ranks of New York's Reform Jews by drawing both his audience and his membership mainly from New York's Reform congregations, especially Emanu-El and Beth El; his society seemed to present the logical end for the anti-ritual drift so prevalent in Reform circles. Adler also forced more Reform Jews to consider seriously the implementation of Sunday services. The popularity of his Sunday lectures, together with the very real image of vacant synagogue pews, no doubt helped cause Emanu-El's board to vote in 1879, by a 53–43 margin, in favor of the motion to hold Sunday services, a motion twice defeated in earlier years and as late as 1876. One can well imagine the apprehension and consternation of some Reform Jews, who dreaded the collapse of the entire recently erected structure of American Reform institutions.

It is not surprising, therefore, that in reference to a proposed rabbinical synod in England, the English-born editor of the *Reformer and Jewish Times,* Harry H. Marks, expressed the wish in his paper on September 6, 1878 that the synod would improve the Jewish religious situation and learn from the Jewish Reform experience in America. He hoped that the synod would "preserve them [English Jews] against the ills of American Reform and its latest bantling, Ethical Culture."

Paradoxically, Adler's division of New York Reform Jewry helped, in some measure, to foster a national unity in the institutional life of American Reform Judaism that had long been absent. His success in New York, perceived as a clear threat to Reform as a whole, was one important factor which hastened the rapprochement between the Eastern and Western factions of American Reform Judaism. For years the two main protagonists, Isaac M. Wise and David Einhorn, had polemicized against each other's religious goals and ideological orientation. When Wise created the Union of American Hebrew Congregations in 1873, only midwestern and southern congregations affiliated; led by the example of Einhorn's Temple Beth El, eastern congregations refrained from joining. And yet, in April 1878, only a few weeks following the Kohler-Adler controversy, the Beth El congregation joined the Wise-inspired Union, signaling a reconciliation across long-standing personal animosities and doctrinal differences. Apparently, when danger lurked from without—in the person of Felix Adler—theological and sectional rivalries between East and West were put into abeyance in order to meet the challenge.[4] To be sure, other factors contributed to this development, such as the growing homogeneity of American Jewry, with the subsequent desire for unity among congregational lay leaders of the East despite their rabbis' personal designs, and the need for national support for the fledgling Hebrew Union College.[5] Still, Adler's role in this process cannot be underestimated.

The Reform Jewish establishment during the 1870s was, therefore, painfully aware of Felix Adler. Had not external factors, such as anti-Semitism and Eastern European immigration to America, deflected the course of American Jewish history and induced Jews to withdraw within their own religious lines, Adler's long-range impact on American Jews and Judaism might have been of far greater consequence. As it turned out, however, his appeal to Jews subsequently declined; save for his social reforms benefiting immigrant Jews in the 1880s, his influence and central position in American Jewish history proved transitory and was restricted primarily to the 1870s.

Besides his direct influence on American Reform Judaism, Adler's critique of it significantly aids our understanding of its ideological posture, all the more because his critique was not motivated by a Jewish nationalist orientation. Unlike the Zionists, who completely reversed the locus of Jewish identification by rejecting Reform's predication of Jewish existence on a religious mission, Adler did not dispute its religious premise by substituting a nationalist one in its stead. Rather, he challenged religious Judaism, and especially the Reform movement, from within the framework of its own religious ideals. Even following his own break from Reform, he accepted Reform Judaism as the final evolutionary outgrowth of the Jewish religion; he adopted its conception of the validity of Jewish existence predicated on a religious mission as an accurate reflection of Jewish historical self-consciousness; and he concurred with classical Reform's definition of Jews as a non-national racial group united by religion.[6] And yet his religious opposition to Reform was as serious a challenge to it as any put forth by the Zionists.

Adler's renunciation of the twin pillars of Reform theology—monotheism, and the divine election of the Jews to fulfill a religious mission—by itself did not represent as contentious an issue to Reform as did the implication of his overall critique, which underscored the conceptual inconsistency of American Reform's ideological rapprochement with modernity. He discerned this inconsistency in Reform Judaism's declaration of religious universality and in its approach to prophetic ethics and Bible criticism.

In the course of its evolution in Germany and America in the nineteenth century, Reform Judaism aligned itself with the progressive tendencies and beliefs of the modern world: liberalism, science, and evolution. Reformers stressed that Judaism, as they conceived it, was reconcilable with the most liberal phases of thought,[7] but in reality they walked an ideological tightrope. Because of their utter commitment to progress, they had to confront and make peace with the most recent liberal, universalist implications for religion being drawn from the scholarship of natural and biblical sciences; at the same time, they sought justification for the continued separate existence of the Jews.

From about the 1870s, American Reformers promulgated a formula which seemingly resolved the problem. They declared Reform Judaism to be free from dogmas and creeds and proclaimed it the one truly universal religion of humanity. This formula was repeated by Reformers into the twentieth century, and even a partial list of those employing it is extensive: Rev. H. M. Meyers,[8] Moritz Ellinger,[9] Rabbi I. S. Nathans,[10] Rabbi Guinzburg,[11] Rabbi Isaac M. Wise,[12] Rabbi Solomon Schindler,[13] Rabbi Kaufmann Kohler,[14] Rabbi Emil Hirsch,[15] Rabbi Emanuel Schreiber,[16] and Rabbi Samuel Sale.[17] The declaration of the creedlessness of Judaism was intended to stave off the challenges of both natural science and comparative religion; the affirmation of the universality of Judaism was intended both to harmonize Reform with the universalist temper of the age and to vindicate the Jewish raison d'être. It was argued that since Reform Judaism was the one true religion of humanity, representing the ideal of ethical monotheism toward which all mankind was striving, the bearers of this religion—the Jews—had both a right and a responsibility to exist as Jews. Together with the notion of a divinely ordained Jewish mission to disseminate the religious ideal, this belief appeared to have furnished a solid rationale for the continued separate existence of the Jewish religious group.

Yet this Reform response to the universalist drift of the modern age was rather problematic. Apart from the fact that Christians such as Minot Savage and James F. Clarke also had proclaimed the universality of their religion, the Reform formula contained an inner tension which many Reformers at that time either ignored or evaded, but which Adler consistently exposed: the implicit conceptual inconsistency between Reform Judaism's claim of religious universality and its concomitant affirmation of the divine election of the Jews.[18] Adler was not the only one sensitive to the problem. In avowing the universality and exemplary humanitarianism of Judaism, Reformers like Ellinger, Guinzberg, and Nathans, speaking at the conventions of the Free Religious Association, avoided all mention of the election of the Jews. The Pittsburgh Convention of 1885 itself reflected the tenuous balance struck between universalism and Jewish particularism. Unlike the fifth resolution of the Reform Philadelphia Conference of 1869, the Pittsburgh Platform omitted any mention of the divine election of the Jews; it did refer to a Jewish *mission* twice, but almost en passant and without alluding to its *divine* origin.[19] Moreover, it acknowledged the mission of Christianity and Islam "to aid in the spreading of monotheism and moral truth."[20] Apparently, many Reformers were still uncomfortable with the notion of divine election and an exclusive Jewish religious mission; they seemed to straddle a conceptual fence between their competing desires to be recognized as universalists and to retain their particularity at the same time.

Furthermore, the conceptual problem was exacerbated because the Reform idea of the universality and universalization of Judaism was, in fact, a teleological ideal of the future rather than an accurate portrait of contemporary reality. And since the Reformers jealously guarded their sectarian status, their very claim to being religious universalists at that time was questionable.[21] In reality, the Reformers were more intent on maintaining Jewish separatism than on fulfilling their own vision of religious universalism. They advanced no proposals as to the dynamics of eventually realizing their ideal of the religious future, and any recommendations that Reformers join with religiously like-minded Gentiles at the present time were rebuffed out of hand.

Thus, Adler's proposal, in the wake of the Pittsburgh Platform, that the Reformers begin to universalize their religious ideals by fusing with the Unitarians was quickly repudiated by Gustav Gottheil.[22] Adler contended that since the Reformers regarded themselves to be only a religious community (article V of the Pittsburgh Platform), and since religious communities were held together by common religious beliefs, "why then do not the Reformers labor to bring about a fusion between themselves and Unitarians? What possible reason is there why this step should not be taken—why this logical outcome of the principles of Reformed Judaism should not be clearly stated?"[23] Adler raised a potent logical question which, intellectually and historically, was not so far-fetched. No serious theological differences existed between the groups. In fact, the Reform Rabbi I. S. Nathans informed the Free Religious Association that "Judaism has always been a true vindication of pure, clear Unitarianism,"[24] and years later the distinguished orientalist and opponent of the Reformers Morris Jastrow declared that Unitarians were "manifestly closer to Reform Judaism than to any of the sects connected with Christianity."[25]

But Gottheil rejected Adler's proposal and announced:

If a rapprochement between the two [Judaism and Unitarianism] is at all possible—it must come from the other side, because the more powerful and the more popular [*sic*]. The daughter must seek reconciliation with the mother, not the reverse. What the Unitarian church found after long centuries of error and estrangement, the Jew has preserved intact from the beginning until now and he would only abase himself were he to go begging to church-doors for admission and recognition.[26]

Significantly, in his effort to substantiate Jewish particularism, Gottheil did not concentrate on the ideological distinctions between Reform Judaism and Unitarianism, although he briefly mentioned that in his view Unitarianism was still Christian; rather, Gottheil's main argument against the suggested fusion was that Judaism had a *prior claim* to the fundamental religious truth, and therefore it should not be the religion to initiate a merger. But such a position betrayed more of an *emotional attachment* to the Jewish past than an *intellectual commitment* to the practical realization of the Reform vision of the Jewish future.

Indeed, Gottheil's response illustrated that despite the ideological affirmation of universalism by Reform Jewish thinkers, most were deeply and emotionally rooted in their own religion. Except for the cases of Adler, Rabbi Charles Fleischer, and Rabbi Solomon Schindler (until he recanted), the implicit tension between universalism and particularism in the Reform ideology always led to the reaffirmation of separate Jewish existence by Reform leaders; any attempt to fulfill Reform's teleological vision in the present led the Reformer outside of the Jewish consensus.[27] In regard to this issue, Jastrow's observation that emotional-social rather than ideological factors cause modern people to remain within their native religious traditions seems particularly appropriate: "Tradition and custom, and the heritage of common experiences prompt people to hold together in their manner of worship long after the justification for such clannishness in religion has passed away."[28] Undoubtedly, external factors such as anti-Semitism were responsible for a good number of Reform Jews remaining in the Jewish fold, but this phenomenon only adds greater weight to the sociological approach in attempting to explain the continued adherence of individuals to their religious group.

Perhaps the crux of Reform's attempted rapprochement with modernity lay in the approach of its intellectual leaders to Bible scholarship and comparative religion. Bible criticism probably represented the most serious challenge to the integrity of any religious Judaism, for the historicization and relativization of the Old Testament text seemed to undermine the authority and contemporary relevance of Jewish values, traditions, rituals, and the very legitimacy of Jewish existence. But consistent with their wholehearted commitment to modern science and the reconciliation of science and religion, the Reformers tried to come to terms with this vital product of progressive scientific thinking. As early as

1869, Rabbi Max Lilienthal had posed the question as to whether Bible criticism should be taught in Jewish schools;[29] and in the decades following, Reform Judaism attempted to outline both a practical and an intellectual posture on the issue of Bible criticism.[30]

The Conservative Jewish scholar Solomon Schechter resolutely affirmed that "the Bible is our sole raison d'être."[31] While the Reformers may not have formulated this idea in such unqualified terms, the concerted scholarly efforts of men such as Kaufmann Kohler,[32] Emil Hirsch,[33] Samuel Sale,[34] and Julian Morgenstern[35] to preserve the Bible as the foundation of Jewish values and inspiration tend to reflect their agreement with Schechter. However, while Schechter adamantly rejected most higher Bible criticism—labeling it "Higher Anti-Semitism"—the more progressive Reformers enthusiastically embraced it.[36] Sale argued that Bible criticism "will only result in bringing out the imperishable worth of the Bible as a help toward 'the perfect ideal of religion' ";[37] Morgenstern contended that biblical science vindicated the "legitimacy and sanction of Reform Judaism";[38] and Kohler and Hirsch adopted similar views.

The conceptual problem confronting the Reformers, however, was how to preserve the "divinity" of a historically contingent biblical text. Essentially, American Reformers contributed no significant conceptual advances in their approach to the Bible; they all more or less adopted Geiger's solution of reinterpreting revelation, and they echoed his fundamental ideas: the Bible reflected an evolving literature of human composition and was not the product of a miraculous supernatural revelation; it was divinely inspired, however, because it portrayed the ongoing process of Jewish revelation, that is, the development of the Jews' unique spiritual insight into the moral nature of man.[39] The vanguard of American Reform scholars did not fear biblical criticism as a threat to Judaism; rather, these men treated it as a welcome investigative tool with which to uncover the historical evolution of the Jewish religion, which culminated, in their view, in prophetic ethics.

Because the Bible contained the prophetic teachings, Reformers regarded it to be of critical and *lasting* significance to the Jews. Like Geiger, American Reform thinkers arbitrarily distinguished between the eternal value of prophetic ethics and the temporal biblical record of creeds and rituals. As Plaut has remarked, "the Torah was approached with an eye for selectivity, while the Prophets were wholeheartedly embraced."[40] Over the years, classical Reformers presented Reform Judaism in the form of the prophetic ethical religion, and they depicted the Prophets as the bearers of the most sublime and final expression of religio-ethical ideas.[41] The prophetic ethical religion served as both a contemporary religious model for Reform Judaism and a source of validation for the continued relevance of the Hebrew Bible. Ultimately, the repristination of Judaism, to borrow Adler's term, constituted the Reformers' rapprochement with biblical science in the modern age.

But Adler discerned a fundamental logical contradiction between the Reformers' repristination of Judaism and their ideological allegiance to human progress and evolution; and again he pointed to the conceptual inconsistency in Reform's intellectual rapprochement with modern thought.[42] The Reformers had adopted the modern liberal view that man developed intellectually, culturally, religiously, and morally over generations; indeed, they too conceived of contemporary man as the highest stage of human evolution. But if so, Adler asked, how could Reform Jews claim finality for their religious and ethical conceptions? How could they—with intellectual consistency—advocate an ideology of progress while simultaneously reverting to the biblical ethical religion of the past? The notions of human progress and evolution logically implied that the prophetic ethical religion could not be the final religious ideal. Since ethical values reflected the moral state of man at any given time, they too must have evolved over time and in correspondence with man's own development. And just as biblical man did not represent the final evolutionary product of mankind—a fact repeatedly asserted by the Reformers—neither did his ethics. Consequently, the very attempt to return to the biblical text for complete spiritual guidance for the present implicitly contradicted the idea of human progress.[43]

Apparently very sensitive to this problem, Julian Morgenstern tried to parry the thrust of the question with an imaginative suggestion.

> The prophets were religious geniuses so immeasurably in advance of the standards and capabilities of their age and of succeeding ages that only today in an absolutely literal, and in no wise boastful sense, have we come, through Reform Judaism, to appreciate the full significance of their teachings and ideals. Only today have the prophets of Israel found true followers; only today can we speak truly of the religion of the prophets.[44]

In effect, Morgenstern attempted to resolve the problem by uprooting the Prophets from their historical context in a less-developed, earlier stage of mankind and directing their message to the modern age. He sought to preserve the notion of human evolution by implying that only now, in contemporary times, had man come to fully understand the prophetic teachings. But Morgenstern's creative explanation evaded the fundamental issue and did not resolve the inherent conceptual problem: how could one reconcile the appearance of men so utterly advanced for their times with the modern idea of progressive human evolution in history? The very exceptional status of the Prophets would appear to contradict that idea.

For Adler, Reform Judaism's logically inconsistent claims of religious universalism and the finality of prophetic ethics, as well as its untenable theological assumptions of monotheism and Jewish mission, were evidence of its conceptually inadequate rapprochement with the modern age; this seems to have been the underlying factor separating him from Reform Judaism. American Reformers endeavored to establish themselves within the intellectual framework of modern liberalism, but they could not fully succeed. Neither ideas of religious universalism and of the progressive evolution of man nor the conclusions of critical Bible scholarship could be intergrated completely into Reform Judaism without controverting their fundamental implications. Indeed, in a sense the logical implications of these distinctive ideas of the liberal age contained the seeds of Reform's ideological dissolution. Adler recognized this fact, and because he sought a totally consistent alliance with modern liberalism, he could not remain within the Jewish fold. Felix Adler was a Reform Jew who took the characteristic modern ideas of religious universalism and progressive human evolution to their logical conclusion; he was truer to the liberal ideology of the modern age than either the Reform Jewish leadership or most other religious liberals of the period.

Should Adler's break from Judaism be considered an inevitable product or extension of Reform Judaism? Some of Adler's contemporaries in the 1870s certainly thought so. In a polemical letter to the editor published in the *Daily Graphic*, April 7, 1877, "Veritas" condemned the Jewish Reformers, who, in his opinion, were destroying Judaism. He accused Reformers of "stand[ing] before the world in the attitude of men anxious to break away from the past, but lacking the courage to do so thoroughly. . . . Adlerism is a legitimate and natural consequence of so-called Reform Judaism." In its attack against Reform rabbis on September 14, 1877, the *Jewish Messenger* asserted that "genuine reform was possible without breaking down the barriers between Judaism and irreligion. The logical result of what the leaders did and left undone is the apparent growth of Adlerism." In his review of Adler's *Creed and Deed* for the *Daily Graphic*, "J.D.B." also conceived of Ethical Culture as the logical outgrowth of the disintegration of Judaism by Reform.[45]

But Adler's intellectual and social break with Judaism was only one solution among others. Most Reform Jews were not as perturbed by intellectual contradictions as he was. Adler represents a special instance. Given his exposure to the dire intellectual challenges confronting religion in the last third of the nineteenth century, given his totally intellectualistic orientation and commitment to basic modern ideas, and given his religious idealism and incontrovertible zeal for coherence between his beliefs and actions, one can discern the necessity of his break with Judaism. A constellation of external historical (intellectual) factors in concert with Adler's distinctive psychological temperament channeled his ideological direction and precipitated his departure from the Jewish consensus. The shortcomings of Reform Judaism did not cause his break; most of them were but symptoms of the impact of the same external factors that were operating directly on Adler.

Why with but few exceptions did Reform Jewish intellectual leaders not follow Adler and leave the Jewish fold? Adequate answers to this question cannot be forthcoming until Adler's reaction to modernity is thoroughly compared with those of individual Reformers; until then any response remains rather speculative. Still, it is not too implausible to suggest that many Reform thinkers, like Reform laymen, were irrevocably committed to the prepetuation of Jewish existence *regardless of intellectual problems*, be this commitment motivated by external factors, such as anti-Semitism, or by the intrinsic emotional and social attachment to their religious tradition which Jastrow had emphasized. Clearly, underlying the Jewish identity of Reform Zionists like Stephen Wise and the Gottheils lay an unequivocal dedication to the past and future of the Jewish people. The assurance of continued Jewish existence was more compelling to these Reformers than any ideological considerations; with Adler, precisely the reverse was true. This is not to say that these Reformers did not believe in the essential truth of their Reform theology; they definitely did, but ultimately the preservation of the Jews seems to have been their primary concern. In this regard, it is interesting to note that while Stephen Wise concurred with basic Reform theology, he eschewed theological discussions.[46] Unlike Emil Hirsch, who actively engaged in both the pursuit of social justice and religious-ideological discussions, Wise neglected the latter and participated in social reform and the Jewish national movement. As for Gustav Gottheil, the priority of his emotional dedication to Reform Judaism has already been noted.

Other Reformers, especially Kohler and Hirsch, were vitally concerned with ideological-theological problems, and they addressed themselves to these issues in lectures and published works.[47] These men reiterated classical Reform theology and believed in its fundamental truth. For that reason they did not withdraw from the Jewish consensus. But why were they satisfied with Reform's theology while Adler was not? Could it be that they did not perceive the conceptual contradiction in their loyalty to progress and simultaneous assertion of the finality of prophetic ethics? Or did they perceive the issue but deny its significance as a problem because of a prior (emotional) commitment to Judaism and Jewish existence? The answers to these questions are not at all clear.

On the surface at least, it appears that Emil Hirsch, for one, was sensitive to Adler's ideological problems with Judaism. Adler's classmate at the Hochschule, Hirsch was exposed to the same intellectual and social forces in Germany which had so changed Adler, and he too was influenced by them. Over the years Hirsch and Adler remained good friends, and Hirsch formulated an ethical religious ideology remarkably similar to that of Adler, save for his belief in monotheism and a Jewish mission.[48] And yet, according to Bernard Martin, Hirsch fluctuated in his theological views. He seems to have wrestled with the theological problem of the nature of God throughout his life. It is not surprising, therefore, that in thanking Adler for having sent him a copy of *An Ethical Philosophy of Life*, he reflected,

> I have leafed through the volume [and] I have found much to interest me and much which agrees with my own views. I believe the gulf between your position and mine is neither wide nor deep. *Sometime*[s] *I regret that I did not take the step which you have.* At other times I feel that you ought to have staid [*sic*] with us.[49]

Ostensibly, the gulf separating Adler and Hirsch appears to have been an ideological one. Acknowledging the good which that "great man" had wrought, Hirsch commented:

> We have found no cogent reason to abandon our fellowship within the historical synagogue on the plea that the ethical ambition is within the old lines—cramped, or obscured, or limited by certain creedal postulates. These postulates are involved in the very warp and woof of the ethical conception of the universe and human life.[50]

But again one may ask whether the underlying reasons for Hirsch's attachment to Judaism's "postulates" stemmed from total intellectual conviction or from an emotional need to find a rationale for the preservation of Reform Judaism. And again one must respond that the answer is not clear and that additional research is needed. One thing is certain, however. In contrast to those Reformers whose allegiance to Reform Judaism and Jewish existence may have been *ultimately* prompted by emotional, nonideological considerations, emotional loyalty could not keep Felix Adler within the Jewish consensus. Despite the anguish which his break from Judaism caused him—he himself described it on more than one occasion—Adler followed his intellectual predilections to their logical conclusions. Intellectually he found Judaism—even its Reform variety—wanting; he therefore left the Jewish religion and the Jewish community.

Felix Adler induced controversy and religious change in the Jewish community. His religious break and the Jewish reaction to it helped to expose the external and internal tensions which confronted the American Jewish community and its religion. His religio-ethical idealism energized many Jews lulled into religious slumber by economic prosperity. And he accomplished what no other Jew in modern history has done: the creation of an ongoing universal, social—and, for some, religious—fellowship.

Notes

CHAPTER I: GROWING UP AS A REFORM JEW

1. Details of Samuel Adler's family history and his years in Germany can be found in his autobiography, addressed to his children and written sometime between 1868 and 1874. The autobiography has been published in *Lives and Voices*, ed. Stanley F. Chyet (1972).

2. Some of the views on religious and ritual reforms which Adler advocated during the three rabbinical conferences are referred to by David Philipson in his *The Reform Movement in Judaism* (1931 ed.). See pp. 147, 150, 163, 167, 172, 197–211.

3. Chyet, p. 32.

4. Adler cited a number of instances of government interference in his religious activities and even in his prospective appointments to rabbinic positions. See Chyet, pp. 15–16, 22, 27–30.

5. *Ibid.*, pp. 9, 14, 18.

6. *Ibid.*, pp. 27, 30.

7. *Ibid.*, p. 31.

8. On this theme, see Leon A. Jick, *The Americanization of the Synagogue, 1820–1870* (1976).

9. See B. Korn, "The Temple Emanu-El Theological Seminary of New York," in *Essays in American Jewish History* (1958).

10. "Minute Book of the Temple Emanu-El Trustees," April 3, 1864. Hereafter cited as "Em. Min."

11. *Ibid.*, January 11, 1863.

12. Cf. Adler's own *A Guide to the Instruction in Israelitish Religion*, trans. M. Mayer (4th ed., 1868). Hereafter cited as *Guide*. The book attempts to provide a full elaboration of the purpose, role, and meaning of Judaism and Jewish existence. In its day it became a basic text in Jewish Sunday schools, part of its wide popularity arising from its noncatechismic form. Adler also revised and corrected Emanuel Hecht's *Biblical History for Israelitish Schools*, trans. M. Mayer (1860; 14th ed., 1874).

13. The various articles were later collected in Adler's *Kovets al Yad* (1886).

14. H. Zafren, "Samuel Adler: Respondent," in *Essays in Honor of Solomon B. Freehof*, ed. W. Jacob et al. (1964), pp. 311–15.

15. Jick, pp. 95, 174.

16. Eleanor Adler, chap. 2, p. 5. The material here referred to as "Eleanor Adler" comes from unpublished information in the archives of the Ethical Culture Society of New York collected by Felix Adler's eldest daughter, Eleanor Adler. Following Felix Adler's death in 1933, Eleanor Adler, assisted by her sister Margaret, attempted to write a biography of her father. She removed material from the archives, specifically numerous autobiographical notes and early diaries written by Adler. She compiled this information into a number of chapters. Unfortunately the biography was neither completed nor published, and many of the original manuscript notes on which the intended work was based have been misplaced. Some have recently appeared in the new material donated by Mrs. Ruth Adler Friess to Columbia University.

The chapters themselves are titled, but as a historical work they are deficient in organization and rigor, clearly indicative of their unfinished status. Some chapters simply reproduce letters between Felix and his family. Judging from the style and content of *extant* autobiographical notes (see n. 17), Eleanor Adler's material would appear to be either total or elaborated reproductions of the missing data. Some of her material, such as the letters between Felix and his family during his stays in Europe and at Cornell University, are certainly reproductions of primary material as well, for in all cases where her statements and accounts could be checked against outside material, Eleanor Adler's chapters proved to be fundamentally accurate. Whenever possible, in citing Eleanor Adler's material, I also cite corroborating evidence from other sources. Where this is not possible, I accept the accounts in her chapters if the probability of truth is high.

17. Eleanor Adler writes in chap. 2, p. 2: "The children felt a touch of greatness in his [Samuel's] nature and had a childish awe of his combined role of father and minister." In chap. 2, pp. 4–5, she records that Felix was particularly impressed with Sabbath and festival observances. Nevertheless, Felix himself recalled that his "home atmosphere was liberal. [There was] no compulsion in matters of religious observances." "Auto," "Talk to the Sunday Evening Clubs, Sunday March 17, 1912 on the Meaning of the Words Ethical Culture," p. 1 (see below in this note for an explanation of the "Auto" reference). Presumably, not all ritual practices were observed. No records exist which describe the precise degree of ritual observance in the Adler home. Samuel himself distinguished between Judaism's eternal essence and its time-bound ceremonial forms. "Religion must change her dress according to the times and the climate . . . and according to the dictates of advanced science, enlightened insight, more cultured taste, broadening conditions of life—in short, according to the needs of the world today" (*Predigt über das erste Buch Moses 44:20 gehalten in der Synagogue der Gemeinde Ansche Chesed* [New York, 1860], pp. 9–10). But his own practical course of action in light of this theory is nowhere described.

The reference "Auto," which hereafter appears throughout this study, requires explanation. Felix Adler possessed a strong intellectual sense which was not confined strictly to intellecutal pursuits. Apparently, he was keenly aware of the process of his growth and maturation, and sometime during his sixties and seventies, he recorded his thoughts and opinions about the various stages in his life in Autobiographical Notes. The notes are extensive, and yet, as mentioned, not all are available because of Eleanor Adler's activities.

Whether Felix intended to publish these notes is not known, although some published autobiographical material can be found in his *An Ethical Philosophy of Life* (1918). Some of the extant notes are sketchy and consist of simply one- or two-line statements one after the other. Other notes consist of more elaborate paragraphs and even small essays. The notes are usually 2–3 pages long, although one is 9 pages. Their subject matter varies greatly: from reflections on Felix's own past, his attitudes to religion, his family, and his experiences in Germany, to more intellectual topics such as a critique of Kant and Emerson. More often than not, the notes are undated and simply titled *Autobiographical Notes*. According to Professor Friess, they were invariably written in the second and third decades of the twentieth century. The notes come in no particular order and one is not related to another. Apparently, at various times, Felix simply recorded his thoughts of the moment, for the style and flavor of these autobiographical sketches indicate that they are of the type for which research would not have been done. Felix describes events, attitudes, and ideas from memory; and where his descriptions can be cross-referenced with other contemporary material, one finds his memory to be particularly strong and accurate.

The lack of any specific titles, dates, and order of these sketches makes reference to them in this work troublesome. In addition, most of them were obtained from the personal collection of the late Professor Friess. Since a personal system of classification would be essentially meaningless to the reader, I have adopted the following procedure for identifying the individual autobiographical sketches and notes: where specific dates and/or headings exist, I refer to them to identify the notes; where they do not, I cite the first line of the first page as a means of identification. References to all of these sketches are introduced by Felix, "Auto."

18. Samuel Adler was reputed to possess one of the largest personal libraries in New York at that time. He willed his collection of sixteen hundred bound volumes and three hundred pamphlets of Hebraica and Judaica to the Hebrew Union College of Cincinnati, where it has been housed since his death in 1891. This collection was the first major acquisition of the

college. Michael A. Meyer, "A Centennial History," in *Hebrew Union College–Jewish Institute of Religion at One Hundred Years,* ed. Samuel E. Karff (1976), p. 25.

On a later trip to Cincinnati, February 10–16, 1893, Felix Adler met with Drs. Philipson and Deutsch of Hebrew Union College and remarked in his diary: "It was strange to see my father's library in the new surroundings—the books that had made a part of our home in an institution! They are, however, well placed and will be of advantage, at least to a few."

19. Cf. Eleanor Adler, chap. 2, p. 8, where she writes: "He [Felix] had found little to inspire him in the teaching at college and *kept up his work with his father during all four years.*" Emphasis added. Felix, in "Auto" ("Akiba the martyr is condemned to death by Fire . . ."), wrote, "At about age 12, I was introduced to the study of my religion by beginning and reading through the Torah." As for talmudic studies, an intellectual digest which Felix kept while a late teenager is sprinkled with references to tractate *Berachot.*

This intellectual digest, or book of jottings, as it is hereafter referred to, is a small notebook of 112 pages which was discovered by this author in the archives of the New York Ethical Culture Society. It can be identified as definitely having been written by Felix: first, by comparing the handwriting with other manuscripts of Felix, and, second, by three differing signatures of Felix Adler on the inside cover. Apparently he was experimenting with his signature, much as any youth is wont to do.

Essentially, this notebook is a digest and potpourri of any and every subject which interested Felix at the time of its compilation. Sometimes Felix wrote paragraphs and small essays; other times he just noted fleeting references to source materials or expressions. There is no internal order to the book. References to science, literature, biographies of philosophers, religion, and Judaism are totally intermixed. No particular reference is dated so that one cannot determine the time intervals between notes. Much of the book refers to material in science and history which Felix learned at Columbia; some of the books he cited appear as readings for courses in the Columbia catalogues of his day. But about one-third of the book contains statements about religion and Judaism, often from Jewish source books like the Talmud, and from the later works of Jüdische Wissenschaft scholars such as Zunz, Graetz, and Geiger.

The book is undated and untitled, but internal evidence indicates that Felix compiled it during the course of his junior year at Columbia, 1868–69, when he was seventeen. The reason for this assumption is that the book's final 10–15 pages consist of a number of excerpts from Juvenal's *Satires,* Aeschylus' *Seven Against Thebes,* and Milton's *Paradise Lost.* All three works were part of the required curriculum of the *second* semester of the junior year at Columbia College according to Columbia's catalogue of 1868–69. Since Columbia allowed no electives, Felix, along with the rest of his classmates, studied these works during the spring of 1869. As for the beginning of the book, it was probably started during the *first* semester of the junior year, the fall of 1868. The opening pages of the book discuss magnetism and telescopes, and the book as a whole constantly refers to science, which Felix had only begun to study as a junior. A check with the Columbia catalogue of the junior year indicates that the whole class was introduced to science only in its junior level, and that the first courses taught were natural philosophy (physics) with Ogden Rood and mechanics with William Peck. Rood was a European-trained physicist whose specialty was optics and light; it is highly likely, therefore, that Felix's references to magnetism and the telescope and to other natural phenomena reflect his initial study of physics with Rood, which took place in the fall of 1868.

The book as a whole is an invaluable source for some of Felix's fundamental characteristics and attitudes, especially since it also reflects a change in Felix's religious beliefs in the course of his junior year.

The book of jottings is often sketchy and, despite Felix's usually felicitous use of the English language, passages are sometimes ungrammatical and punctuated incorrectly.

Sometimes MS words are illegible, and in such cases this is duly noted. I identify the book of jottings as "B. of J." in all subsequent references. The book is not paginated, so page references are my own and correspond to the book's pages, beginning with Felix's first written page as page 1.

20. References to all these works are found in the "B. of J." References to *HaMeassef* and *Bikkure Halttim* come from two of their poems, which Felix had translated and published in the *Jewish Times*. See his translation of Wessely's "Elegy on the Death of Moses Mendelssohn," from *HaMeassef*, Adar 1786, in *Jewish Times*, September 17, 1869, and his translation of M. Strelisker's "The Dreamer," from *Bikkure Halttim*, 1828, in *Jewish Times*, October 29, 1869.

21. Eleanor Adler, chap. 2, pp. 7–8.

22. On Isaac Adler, see *Jewish Encyclopedia* (1901 ed.), vol. 1.

23. Eleanor Adler, chap. 2, p. 2.

24. Chyet, p. 20.

25. See "Em. Min.," October 14, 1859; the procedure of collecting on Shemini Atseret was repeated in 1863—see "Em. Min." of September 27, 1863.

26. *Ibid.*, March 12, 1864.

27. Felix, "Auto.," "Biography—Principal Rubrics, Atlantic City, March 1930," p. 7.

28. *Ibid.*

29. *Ibid.*, p. 1.

30. Eleanor Adler, chap. 2, pp. 1–2.

31. *Ibid.*

32. Felix, "Auto.," *loc. cit.*, p. 1.

33. See Goethe's *Dichtung und Wahrheit*, trans. John Oxenford (1969), esp. pp. 7–8, 83–85, 99, 208.

34. Interview with Prof. Friess in his New York residence, June 27, 1973.

35. Eleanor Adler, chap. 2, p. 2.

36. "B. of J.," p. 72. Felix himself underlined *Parents* and *childhood,* perhaps to stress that his parents were the chief proponents of this folly of emulation during his childhood when he should have been allowed and encouraged to develop his individual personality.

37. The scrapbook, *Columbia University Annual Commencement 1870–1881*, features an article from the *Cap and Gown* in which an unnamed reporter cites the oldest graduate in the class of 1870 as twenty-eight, the youngest as seventeen, and the average age as twenty-one. Felix was eighteen at the time of his graduation in June 1870.

38. Columbia faculty related to the Episcopal Church included Henry Drisler (1818–1897), professor of Latin and Greek, John Howard van Amringe (1835–1915), professor of mathematics, Charles Short (1821–1886), professor of Latin, Francis Lieber (1800–1872), professor of economics and history. See *Dictionary of American Biography* on all of these men. All taught Felix at various times during his Columbia years.

39. George T. Strong, *The Diary of George Templeton Strong Post War Years 1865–1875*, ed. A. Nevins and M. A. Thomas (1952), p. 43.

40. Felix, "Auto.," "Biography, Atlantic City 1930," p. 1.

41. Felix, "Auto.," "For Biography," p. 1.

42. "Germany was our [himself and other Americans] teacher, our liberator. She breathed fresh life into *the dull stale atmosphere of our institutions of learning, with their compulsory chapel attendance, a graceless external conformity, and their philosophy lectures delivered by superannuated clergymen*. . . . It was in Germany, the land of political bondage, that intellectual liberty then grew apace and flourished." Speech of November 22, 1914, "False Ethics in the Discussion of the War," pp. 14–15, MS. Emphasis added.

43. See Herbert W. Schneider, *A History of American Philosophy* (1946), p. 453, n. 25.

44. Barnard's "Inaugural Address" in the *Proceedings at the Inauguration of Frederick A. P. Barnard, Oct. 3, 1864* (1865), p. 62.

45. See John Spencer Clark, *The Life and Letters of John Fiske* (1917), I, 237. Cf. Alexander von Humboldt, *Cosmos: A Sketch of a Physical Description of the Universe,* trans. E. C. Otto (1882).

46. "B. of J.," p. 10. This attitude may also have reflected Felix's understanding of Reform Judaism's intellectual character. It implies that only the educated can achieve spiritual perfection. Later, in an 1876 article on Reform Judaism, Felix criticized Reform's cerebral and intellectual nature. Cf. "Reform Judaism," in Appendix of his *Creed and Deed* (1876).

47. "B. of J.," pp. 21–22. See also, pp. 19, 23.

48. Felix, "Auto.," "On My Eightieth Birthday," p. 1. Also, "Auto.," "Character Traits of X."

49. Eleanor Adler, chap. 2, p. 4.

50. See *Jewish Times,* June 17, 1870.

51. "Em. Min.," May 16, 1870.

52. See R. Ernst, *Immigrant Life in New York City, 1825–1863* (1949), p. 173; Basil L. Lee, *Discontent in New York City, 1861–1865* (1943), p. 142; E. R. Ellis, *The Epic of New York City* (1966), p. 298.

53. Eleanor Adler, chap. 2, pp. 4–5.

54. Felix, "Auto.," "S. is a highly sensitive nature . . ." pp. 2–3.

55. Cf. "The Negro Problem in the United States," January 10, 1904; "The Negro Problem as a Test of the Supreme Moral Law," November 25, 1906; and "The Fiftieth Anniversary of the Emancipation Proclamation," January 5, 1913. All three addresses are found in typescript in the archives of the New York Society for Ethical Culture. By contemporary standards, Adler's views on Negroes would probably be regarded as conservative and reflecting a noblesse oblige attitude. However, because he consistently opposed slavery and reaffirmed the fundamental worth of Negroes as human beings, Adler's later views on Negroes were considered very liberal in his day.

56. Eleanor Adler, chap. 2, p. 5. Adler's eulogies were printed by the *Jewish Record,* April 21, 1865 and June 12, 1865, and the *Jewish Messenger,* June 9, 1865. See *Abraham Lincoln: Tribute of the Synagogue,* ed. Emanuel Hertz (1927), for a collection of rabbinic eulogies on Lincoln, including an edited version of one of Samuel's eulogies.

57. Eleanor Adler, chap. 2, p. 4.

58. See Lee, chap. 1, "New York Before Sumter."

59. See *New York Times,* September 25 and 28, 1869, for a description of the attempt by Jay Gould and James Fiske to corner the gold supply on Wall Street in September 1869. See *New York Herald,* December 8, 1869, for a description of the unprecedented corruption of Tammany Hall's Tweed ring during its tenure in municipal office, 1869–71.

60. *Jewish Times,* October 29, 1869. Translation of Mordecai Strelisker's poem in the *Bikkure Halttim* of 1828.

61. Felix, "Auto.," "My state of mind . . ." p. 2.

62. Felix, "Auto.," "I found myself attracted . . ." p. 1.

63. Felix's address on "Geiger," May 15, 1910, p. 21.

64. Felix, "Auto.," "Reflections," "I have lived my life in the presumption . . ." p. 2.

65. S. Adler, *Guide,* p. 10. See also Gershon Greenberg, "The Dimensions of Samuel Adler's Religious View of the World," *Hebrew Union College Annual* 46 (1975), which outlines Adler's views on God, history, Jews and Judaism, and their interrelation.

66. S. Adler, *Guide,* p. 10.

67. *Ibid.,* p. 64.

68. "B. of J.," p. 22

69. *Ibid.,* p. 20.

70. S. Adler, *Guide,* p. 64.

71. *Ibid.,* pp. 40, 42.

72. *Ibid.,* p. 64.

73. "B. of J.," p. 13.
74. *Ibid.*, p. 10.
75. *Ibid.*, p. 23.
76. S. Adler, *Guide*, p. 10.
77. *Ibid.*, p. 34.
78. "B. of J.," pp. 23–24. Felix's belief in Providence was apparently quite strong at this time for only a few pages later he writes a second time: "They say God is too great to regulate the petty concerns of everyday life. It is as if you would say the ocean is too great to fill the little bays and inlets that line the coasts of the mainland. Even because of its greatness does it fill them" ("B. of J.," p. 31). Both passages on Providence seem to have been written almost as a response to the writing(s) or oral opinion(s) of someone or some people. The phrases "It is sometimes contended" and "They say God is too great" undoubtedly refer to some source challenging Felix's belief in Providence. This source may have been scientists in general, one or more of his science teachers at Columbia, or perhaps his brother, Isaac, and his cousin Isidor Walz, who were enthusiastic advocates of science.

Both passages were written when Felix first was exposed to natural science at Columbia in the fall of 1868; he must also have been confronted with naturalistic conceptions of religion attempting to harmonize science and religion. In this reconciliation, the scientific view acknowledged God as the author of natural law and the universe but neglected His Providence. These two passages represent Felix's initial reaction to the scientific view and his defense of the threatened concept of Providence.

79. See Samuel's attack on Orthodox Judaism in "Predigtskizze aus einem Vortrag gehalten am 2 Mai, 1857," *Sinai* 2 (1857). Excerpts cited in Bernhard Cohn, "Early German Preaching in America," *Historia Judaica* 15 (October 1953): 96.

80. "B. of J.," pp. 9–10.
81. *Ibid.*, p. 41.
82. *Ibid.*, p. 11.
83. Cf. *Sinai* 1 (1856): 55.
84. S. Adler, *Guide*, p. 16.
85. Samuel, however, arbitrarily chose to follow the text of Exodus 20:11, which links Sabbath observance to creation, rather than the text of Deuteronomy 5:15, which links Sabbath observance to the memory of the Jews' redemption from slavery in Egypt.
86. The comparison between Israel and the dove occurs in numerous places in the Talmud. Cf. tractates *Shabat* 49a, 130a; *Gitin* 45a; *Sanhedrin* 95a; *Berachot* 53a. Felix is paraphrasing the *Berachot* passage. All except one of his talmudic citations in the book of jottings come from *Berachot* (the one exception comes from *Baba Batra*), suggesting that either this was the only tractate he studied with his father or that it was the tractate he studied in the year of the compilation of the jottings. Given Samuel's dedication to talmudic study, the latter idea is the more probable of the two.
87. S. Adler, *Guide* p. 42.
88. The parenthesis "(the reform view)" is Adler's. Reference is to tractate *Berachot* 28a.
89. The talmudic text cited by Felix serves as an excellent illustration of the different approaches of the Reformers and the Orthodox to Jewish law. The *Berachot* reference features a disagreement between R. Gamaliel and R. Joshua as to the permissibility of a certain Ammonite proselyte named Judah to enter the Israelite community. R. Gamaliel held that it was forbidden, R. Joshua held it was permitted. The Halacha was decided in favor of R. Joshua. To support his position, R. Gamaliel cited a verse from Deuteronomy 23 which states that Ammonites and Moabites are forbidden to enter the community of God, that is, Israel. R. Joshua countered that Ammonites no longer exist because Sennacherib, king of Assyria, had completely mixed up all the nations of the world. Therefore, this Judah should not be considered an Ammonite: they don't exist. From this talmudic text, no doubt

pointed out to him by Samuel, Felix deduced that because events witnessed the destruction of the Ammonites, the biblical precept of Deuteronomy 23 is not applicable, nor is it legally authoritative. An Orthodox reading of the Talmud, however, would not come to the same conclusion. Rather, it would deduce that the biblical law remains eternally valid. Historical changes do not affect the *eternal validity* of the law, but only the terms of its *applicability*. Consequently, should a *proven* Ammonite wish to enter the Jewish fold today, he would be refused entry; the classical Reformer would admit him.

90. Philipson, *Reform Movement*, p. 147.

91. S. Adler, *Kovets al Yad,* p. 76.

92. *Sinai* 1 (February 1856): 1–4.

93. S. Adler, *Kovets al Yad,* p. 80.

94. *Ibid.,* pp. 76, 79.

95. "B. of J.," p. 56. Source is *Berachot* 6b. The identification of these five *kolot*, voices or sounds, is disputed in the Talmud. R. Aha points to a passage in Jeremiah 33 in which the term *kol* appears five times in the context of "the happy sounds of a bride and groom"—*kol sason vekol simcha, kol chatan vekol kalah, kol haomrim hodu et hashem*—and therefore feels the participants at the marriage feast will be rewarded with great happiness. R. Joshua contends that the *kolot* refer to those heard at Mount Sinai (cf. Exodus 19), and in his interpretation, the talmudic passage implies that the participants' reward will be a greater knowledge of Torah.

96. "B. of J.," p. 37. *Berachot*, chap. 2.

97. *Ibid.,* p. 48. Reference is to *Berachot* 28b.

98. S. Adler, *Guide*, p. 12.

99. *Ibid.,* pp. 16, 66.

100. *Ibid.,* p. 68.

101. E. Hecht, *Biblical History*, p. 135.

102. F. Adler, "An Adress Delivered Before the Hebrew Orphan Asylum," December 11, 1869, MS, p. 7.

103. "B. of J.," p. 13.

104. *Ibid.,* p. 22.

105. F. Adler, "Address," December 11, 1869, p. 9.

106. "B. of J.," pp. 42–43.

107. S. Adler, *Guide*, p. 12.

108. "B. of J.," p. 36.

109. F. Adler, "Address," December 11, 1869, pp. 10–11.

110. Felix, "Auto.," "I found myself attracted . . . " p. 1.

111. Felix, "Auto.," "My state of mind as far as I can recall . . . " p. 1.

112. S. Adler, *Guide*, p. 64.

113. "The Christmas Tree," *Jewish Times*, December 31, 1869.

114. F. Adler, "An Address Delivered Before the Hebrew Orphan Asylum," November 20, 1869, MS, p. 4.

115. Is it mere coincidence that Felix concluded his book of jottings with a selection from Milton's *Paradise Lost* (Bk. VI, ll. 33–37) which reads:

> And for the testimony of truth hast borne
> Universal reproach, far, worse to bear
> Than Violence; for, this was all thy care
> To stand approved in sight of God, though worlds
> Judg'd thee perverse.

Milton here describes God commending Abdiel, his "Servant of God" (1. 29), for his fidelity. Abdiel was the one Seraph in heaven who refused Satan's call to revolt against God (cf. Bk.V, especially ll. 896 to the end). Could Felix have seen in Abdiel—who testified to the truth of God's omnipotence and presence in heaven—a symbolic model for the martyred Jewish people, a people which was also "judg'd perverse" by the world for bearing its "testimony of truth" that God exists and is one? Could not Felix—suffering from his separateness as a Jew at Columbia—have found in Milton's Abdiel a character with whom to personally empathize?

116. F. Adler, "Address," December 11, 1869, pp. 11–12. Interestingly, Felix rather freely translated the Shema in the following manner: "Hear O Israel, the Eternal is the One and Only God in Unity." The "Lord our God," the usual and literal translation of *Hashem Elokenu*, was replaced by a message of God's unity, clearly indicative of the absolute import of its message to Felix.

117. *Ibid.*, p. 17. That Felix's description of the martyred Jewish youth Castro-Tartas was a historical concretization and representation of his own feelings of martyrdom is a tantalizing suggestion which, unfortunately, must remain as speculation.

118. Emphasis added.

119. Eleanor Adler, chap. 2, p. 5.

120. Source for this talmudic discussion is *Berachot* 41a–b. Felix's use of the standard of *rimon* is puzzling. There is no talmudic standard of *rimon* in connection with Yom Kippur. The standard which describes "eating" is the eating of a *betsah*, the size of an egg. Also, *peras* refers to a substance equivalent to the size of 3–4 eggs consumed within a designated time limit, estimated by later halachic authorities to be approximately nine minutes. This standard applies to all forbidden foods, such as the prohibited leavened substances on Passover.

121. "B. of J.," p. 72.

122. See his address "The Day of Atonement Among the Jews," February 24, 1878, and "The Day of Atonement," March 3, 1878, both found in the Felix Adler Papers, Columbia University.

123. "The story of Lot and the Sodomites raised the unpleasant question: what is sodomy?—a question that stuck in the mind and was not answered. Only it was there—an unpleasant and obscene thing." Felix, "Auto.," "Akiba the martyr is condemned . . . " p. 1.

124. "A primitive ritual was left unexplained." *Ibid.*

125. "Why was it that his willingness to sacrifice his son was accounted to him for righteousness? The reverse should have been the case, his unwillingness to sacrifice his son, his recognition of the fact that human sacrifice could not be an expression of the divine will. As the story stands, he is praised for being willed to do what was morally horrible, and then because of his willingness, an animal is introduced as a substitute. Very queer ethical teaching for the young." *Ibid.*

126. "Think of a wife accused by her jealous husband of infidelity and subjected to this outrageous ordeal—holy water mixed with dust from the floor of the sanctuary. There was more dust than holy water in it. And the ashes of the red heifer as a means of purification." *Ibid.*, p. 2.

127. *Ibid.*, p. 1.

128. Felix, "Auto.," "My state of mind . . . " p. 1.

129. "B. of J.," pp. 72–73.

130. F. Adler, "Address," November 20, 1869, p. 6.

131. S. Adler, *Guide*, p. 30.

132. Felix, "Auto.," *loc. cit.*, p. 2.

133. F. Adler, *An Ethical Philosophy of Life* (1918), p. 21. Hereafter referred to as *Eth.P.L.*

134. Cf. S. Adler, *Guide*, pp. 22–28.

135. "B. of J.," p. 20.

136. *Ibid.*, p. 96. Cf. H. Graetz, *History of the Jews,* II (1895), p. 498. Interestingly, this translation by Felix—adding "alone"—of the Hebrew *tsadik be'emunato yichyeh* is Lutheran.

137. See, for example, Edward Hitchcock's *The Religion of Geology and Its Connected Science* (1854).

138. This course replaced McVickar's "Evidences on Christianity" when McVickar retired in 1864. The change in title is indicative of a new orientation.

139. Frederick A. P. Barnard, "Inaugural Discourse," *Proceedings at the Inauguration of Frederick A. P. Barnard as President of Columbia College October 3, 1864* (1865), p. 53.

140. *Ibid.*, p. 58.

141. *Ibid.*, p. 62.

142. *Ibid.*, p. 56.

143. *Ibid.*

144. The views of Barnard and the deists only agree partially because Barnard still asserted "that God works perpetually before us now" in continuing the harmony of the universe. But this reference is to God as constant keeper of order, law, and harmony in the universe, not to His Providence.

145. *New York Times*, September 15, 1869.

146. Alexander von Humboldt, *Cosmos*, I, p. 1.

147. "The geography of animal and vegetable organisms must limit itself to the consideration of germs already developed of their habitation and transplantation . . ." *Ibid.*, I, p. 360.

148. See Sidney Warren, *American Freethought 1860–1914* (1943), pp. 51–54.

149. Joseph L. Blau, *Men and Movements in American Philosophy* (1952), pp. 160–64.

150. In the junior year, he received a 27 out of 90 in Peck's first-semester mechanics course and an 18 out of 60 in Joy's second-semester chemistry course.

151. F. Adler, "Address," December 11, 1869, pp. 5–7.

152. *Jewish Times*, September 17, 1869.

CHAPTER II: RETURN TO GERMANY: 1870–1873

1. Eleanor Adler, chap. 3, pp. 1–4.

2. Felix, "Auto.," "I have lived my life . . . " p. 1.

3. Cf. "Reverence," typescript of an address before the Society of Ethical Culture, undated, Felix Adler Papers, housed in the Rare Book and Manuscript Library of the Columbia University Libraries. Hereafter, all references to material at Columbia are designated by Col. Material housed at the New York Society for Ethical Culture prior to September 1977 is designated by E.C.S. All lecture references are to *typescript* material unless otherwise indicated and refer to lectures given to the Ethical Culture Society.

4. Eleanor Adler, chap. 2, p. 7.

5. Eleanor Adler, chap. 3, p. 8. Refer also to Felix, "Auto.," "Reminiscences," "My grandmother . . . " pp. 1–4. Bancroft was very friendly to American students in Germany and assisted them in outlining their study programs as well as in extracurricular activities. Cf. J. W. Burgess, *Reminiscences of an American Scholar* (1934), pp. 84–86, 105. Bancroft obtained tickets for a number of American students. *Ibid.*, p. 96. He was particularly fond of Felix, whom he invited regularly to his Sunday evening receptions. In the fall of 1871, Bancroft requested that Felix become his private secretary, but Felix would not forsake his studies. Cf. Eleanor Adler, chap. 3, p. 8; see also the *Jewish Messenger*, September 29, 1871, which reported the minister's invitation and Felix's rejection of it.

6. Felix, "Auto.," *loc. cit.*, pp. 3–4.

7. Despite Felix's disclaimer, an apparently erroneous tradition seems to have arisen that Felix was sent to Germany financed by Emanu-El. Among those holding this view are: Philip Cowen, a contemporary of Felix's, in his *Memories of an American Jew* (1932), p. 394; Richard Gottheil, another contemporary, in his biography of his father, Gustav Gottheil, *The Life of*

Gustav Gottheil (1936), p. 40; Beryl H. Levy, S. V. "Felix Adler," *Universal Jewish Encyclopedia* (1939–43); Morris U. Schappes in his *Documentary History of the Jews in the United States, 1654–1875* (1950), p. 374, fn. 13; Harry Simenhoff, *Saga of American Jewry* (1959), p. 178.

That Felix's studies abroad were paid for by Emanu-El cannot be substantiated. Certainly nothing about Felix's having been sent and financed by Emanu-El is recorded in the "Minute Book of the Emanu-El Trustees." B. Korn, in his "The Temple Emanu-El Theological Seminary of New York City," p. 367, correctly points out, based on the Emanu-El minutes, that the board of trustees did not adopt the concept of financial maintenance of American students at European seminaries until July 6, 1871, and that Felix was not among the students sent.

It is conceivable that Emanu-El gave Samuel Adler money for his son's trip in the form of a grant, gift, or minister's raise. Felix would then have received temple money, all the time thinking it was his father's. This hypothesis, however, is unsupported by any evidence.

8. See letter of Samuel Adler to Felix, June 23, 1873 (E.C.S.).

9. Letter of Samuel and Henrietta Adler to Felix, Feburary 16, 1871 (E.C.S.). Cf. also Samuel's letter to Felix, September 16, 1872 (E.C.S.), and Eleanor Adler, chap. 3, p. 9. Felix's letters to his parents have not been preserved; only the letters from his parents to him remain.

10. Refer to C. F. Thwing, *The American and the German University* (1928). The author cites the views of a number of leading American professors on their very positive intellectual experiences in Germany. Cf. pp. 58–59, 63–64, 143–44. See, too, Burgess' most favorable evaluation of various German professors, pp. 99–100, 121, 125.

11. Cf. Felix's addresses "The Work of Liberalism," November 4, 1877, "14th Anniversary Discourse," May 14, 1890 (Col.), and "False Ethics in the Discussion of War," November 22, 1914 (Col.).

12. Dr. Adolphe de Castro, former American consul in Madrid, and a member of Steinschneider's private class along with Felix, wrote to Gideon Chagy, editor of the *Standard,* on December 17, 1948, that "Steinschneider favored him [Felix] because he was able to practice English which he made a valiant effort to master." Letter is found in E.C.S.

13. Felix, "Auto.," "Biography, Principal Rubrics," March 1930, p. 6.

14. "Summer Notes," 1923 (Col.).

15. "Post-Aristotelian Philosophy," undated (Col.).

16. Cf. his lecture "Geiger," May 15, 1910, p. 21 (Col.).

17. See Felix's notes on Steinthal, undated, in Col., entitled "Steinthal."

18. "Summer Notes," 1923 (Col.).

19. Undated, untitled note in Col.

20. He reflected on the "exceptional massive mental power and astonishing and extraordinary pride" of Cohen and suggested that "whomever [sic] lays stress on intellectualism as Cohen does cannot escape pride, cannot really regard human beings as ends per se, but will necessarily accept the gradations that exist among them, at least in his inward attitude." Cf. "Herman [sic] Cohen: Pamphlet on the Characteristic Peculiarity of the German People," undated (Col.).

21. "Memorandum," undated (Col.).

22. Letter of Samuel to Felix, December 1871 (E.C.S.).

23. Letter of Samuel to Felix, February 28, 1872 (E.C.S.).

24. Undated Memorandum in Col.

25. I am indebted to the late Professor H. Friess for this information. Geiger's gift to Felix is in the possession of the Friess family.

26. Letter of Geiger to B. Felsenthal in "Felsenthal Papers" housed in the American Jewish Historical Society, Waltham, Mass. This letter was published by G. Kisch in his

"Founders of 'Wissenschaft des Judentums' and America," in *Essays in American Jewish History* (1958).

27. Cf. Memorial lecture, "Geiger," December 5, 1874, and a second address, "Geiger," May 15, 1910, esp. pp. 21–23. Cf. also Felix's letter to Felsenthal, November 14, 1874, in which he lamented the loss of his teacher and friend and asks, "Ist einer da, der die Luecke, die er hinterlaesst, auszufuellen vermoechte?" This letter is part of the "Felsenthal Papers" and was published by Eric Hirshler in his *Jews from Germany in the United States* (1955), p. 173.

28. For example, see Felix's articles "Jews," "Judaism," and "Jewish Literature," in *Johnson's New Universal Cyclopedia* (1876–77); cf. the precis of his lecture "The Old Testament in Light of Biblical Criticism" before a meeting of the American Oriental Society in the *Proceedings of the American Oriental Society* (May 1874); and see his six lectures given at Lyric Hall from November 1873 to March 1874, esp. "The Fall of Jerusalem" and "Mohammed," MSS (E.C.S.).

29. Cf. Burgess, p. 105.

30. Letter of Samuel to Felix, May 13, 1873 (E.C.S.).

31. Letter of Samuel to Felix, June 23, 1873 (E.C.S.).

32. Cf. Felix, "Auto.," "Biography," March 1930, p. 1, and "Auto.," "My state of mind . . ." p. 1.

33. *Ibid.* The identity of the "Jewish theologians" is unclear. Felix could be referring to the Conservative Cassel and the Orthodox Lewy at the Hochschule, but this is only conjecture.

34. Felix, "Auto.," "My state of mind . . ." p. 1.

35. Felix, "Auto.," "Biography," March 1930, p. 1.

36. Eleanor Adler, chap. 3, p. 9.

37. *Ibid.*, pp. 13–15A. See letters of Frieda to Felix, November 26, 1871, June 1873, and August 1873 (E.C.S.).

38. Undated letter of Henrietta Adler to Felix, probably written in the spring of 1873 (E.C.S.).

39. Address "What Evidence Is There That Man Is More Than a Higher Animal?" November 26, 1922, p. 8 (E.C.S.). Cf. *Eth.P.L.*, p. 8, for a similar expression.

40. Cf. his two addresses on "Marriage and Divorce," 1905 (Col.). See also his note on "Kissing," undated (Col.).

41. Felix, "Auto.," "Experience," p. 2.

42. Koppel S. Pinson, *Modern Germany: Its History and Civilization* (1966), p. 220; Marshall Dill, Jr., *Germany: A Modern History* (1961), p. 160.

43. Felix, "Auto.," "Talk to Sunday Evening Club," March 17, 1912, p. 2.

44. Speech of Frothingham to the assembly of the Free Religious Association in New York, October 1873. Quoted by the *Israelite,* October 31, 1873.

45. *New York Times,* October 16, 1882.

46. Cf. Voltaire, *Essai sur les moeurs et l'esprit des nations* and Karl Löwith's essay on Voltaire in his *Meaning in History* (1962).

47. See E. B. Tylor, *Primitive Culture* (1871), and John Lubbock, *The Origin of Civilization* (1870). A good analysis of the significance of the works of these men for religion can be found in M. Jastrow, *The Study of Religion* (1901), and George W. Gilmore, S.V. "Comparative Religion," *New Schaff-Herzog Religious Encyclopedia* (1969).

48. Gilmore, p. 192.

49. Letter of Samuel Adler to Felix, March 14, 1872 (E.C.S.).

50. Felix, "Auto.," "Talk to the Sunday Evening Club," March 7, 1912, p. 2.

51. Cf. his lectures "The Bible," December 3, 1876; "Social Progress," January 11, 1880; and "The Need for a New Moral Movement in Religion," February 11, 1883. All in Col.

52. See MSS of his six Lyric Hall Lectures (E.C.S.).

53. See his essay "The Origin of Monotheism," based on lectures to the Society in the

winter of 1876, typescript in E.C.S., and published in the appendix of Adler's *Creed and Deed* (1877).

54. Sunday lecture "Moral Education," dated either 1880 or 1881 (Col.). Cf. also Adler's "14th Anniversary Address," May 1890, pp. 1–2 (Col.), for a similar description. Refer as well to his *Eth.P.L.*, p. 12.

55. "Geiger," December 5, 1874 (Col.).

56. See his "Anniversary Address" in May 1881 and May 1885 (Col.).

57. Cf. his articles in *Johnson's New Universal Cyclopedia* (1876–77) and his two Peabody Lectures in Baltimore, MSS, spring of 1876 (E.C.S.).

58. "Geiger," May 15, 1910, p. 21 (Col.).

59. "Geiger," December 5, 1874, p. 11. Cf. the newspaper coverage of the address, *Jewish Messenger,* December 25, 1874.

60. "Geiger," December 5, 1874, p. 6.

61. *Ibid.,* p. 14. Consult Geiger's *Judaism and Its History* (1911 ed.), pp. 37–38, 48, 92. See too Michael A. Meyer, "Universalism and Jewish Unity in the Thought of Abraham Geiger," in Jacob Katz, *The Role of Religion in Modern Jewish History* (1975), pp. 91–104.

62. "Geiger," December 5, 1874, p. 12.

63. *Ibid.,* p. 13. See also Max Wiener, *Abraham Geiger and Liberal Judaism* (1962), who suggests that Geiger was considered too conservative by segments of Berlin Jewry (p. 41). On the tension in Geiger's intellectual life created by his devotion to the scholarship of Judaism and his concern with community leadership and direction, see Michael A. Meyer, "Jewish Religious Reform and Wissenschaft des Judentums: The Positions of Zunz, Geiger and Frankel," *Yearbook of the Leo Baeck Institute* 16, (1971): 19–41.

64. "Geiger," 1874, p. 12.

65. *Ibid.,* p. 13.

66. "Geiger," May 14, 1910, pp. 16–23.

67. "Geiger" 1874, p. 13.

68. Meyer, "Universalism," p. 93.

69. *Ibid.,* p. 98.

70. This rejection of the universality of Judaism marked the only substantive difference between Adler's "Geiger" lectures of 1874 and 1910.

71. "Geiger," 1874, p. 14.

72. "Geiger," May 15, 1910, p. 14.

73. "Geiger," 1874, p. 14.

74. Refer to the "6th Anniversary Address," May 1882 (Col.), and his lectures on Judaism in the twentieth century.

75. "Geiger," 1910, pp. 20–21.

76. Max Wiener, "Abraham Geiger's Conception of the 'Science of Judaism,'" *Yivo Annual of Jewish Social Sciences* XI (1956–57): 153–54. This view comes from Geiger's "Allgemeine Einleitung in die Wissenschaft des Judentums," a series of lectures which Geiger delivered at the Hochschule in 1872–74, some of which Adler heard. Geiger asserted that Judaism is relevant to life because it focuses on a people with a language and a history of its own. Cf. *Ibid.,* p. 155.

77. Julian Morgenstern, "The Significance of the Bible for Reform Judaism in the Light of Modern Scientific Research," *Yearbook of the Central Conference of American Rabbis* 18 (1908): 219. Hereafter abbreviated *CCARY.*

78. Geiger, *Judaism and Its History,* p. 47.

79. *Ibid.,* pp. 47–48.

80. *Ibid.,* pp. 45–46. Geiger never clearly explained *why* the Jews were endowed with this special genius. Were they the possessors of an "inborn" moral talent, in consequence of which God chose them, or had they been endowed with religious genius as a result of His

selecting them? A tension exists here which Geiger's writings do not resolve. The same questions can be posed in reference to God's biblical command to Abraham to "get thee out of the land, etc." Was Abraham selected because of intrinsic merit, or did Abraham recognize his creator only after God chose him?

81. Cf. B. Kraut, "The Approach to Jewish Law of Buber and Rosenzweig," *Tradition* 12, nos. 3–4 (Winter–Spring 1972): esp. pp. 54–57.

82. Cf. John D. Haney, *Lessing's "Education of the Human Race"* (1908), and Henry E. Allison, *Lessing and the Enlightenment* (1966), esp. pp. 121–161.

83. The arbitrariness of deeming prophetic ethics "eternal" escaped Geiger and all the Reformers. As a religious axiom, however, this claim filled a vital Reform need.

84. See Acting President Russel's letter to President Andrew D. White of Cornell University, May 19, 1874, Cornell University Archives, MS, pp. 4–5. Cf. David F. Strauss, *The Old Faith and the New* (1873 ed.).

85. Felix, "Auto.," "Experience," p. 1.

86. Loose notes in Col. entitled "Steinthal," undated, pp. 1–2.

87. Steinthal, "An die Eltern," *Über Juden und Judentum* (1910), pp. 5–12. See, too, "Schämen wir uns," pp. 42–45.

88. "Judentum und Patriotismus," *ibid.*, pp. 67–71.

89. *Ibid.*

90. "Schämen wir uns," Cf. also "Bescheidenheit," in *Über Juden*, pp. 18–24. Reportedly Steinthal declared that "we are an association built upon common blood."

91. "Schämen wir uns."

92. "An die Eltern."

93. Cf. Steinthal's "The Legend of Samson" in I. Goldziher, *Mythology Among the Hebrews and Its Historical Development* (1967), pp. 420–32. Refer also to Adler's use of this idea in his "Inaugural Discourse" at Cornell, published in the *Ithaca Daily Journal*, June 30, 1874; and his second "Geiger" lecture, May 15, 1910, p. 2 of the postscript.

94. "Mythos und Religion," in Steinthal, *Zu Bibel und Religionsphilosophie* (1890–95), p. 142.

95. "The Legend of Samson," pp. 420, 430.

96. *Ibid.*, pp. 428–29.

97. *Ibid.*, p. 434.

98. See esp. the essays "Die Erzählkunst der Bibel" and "Glaube und Kritik."

99. "Glaube und Kritik," p. 9.

100. Cf. Adler's comments on this in "Steinthal," undated notes in Col., p. 1.

101. Steinthal was not alone among nineteenth-century intellectuals in his inability to relate his scholarship to his religion. John Lubbock, eminent evolutionary anthropologist, archaeologist, and zoologist, exhibited a personal pietism throughout his life capped by daily church attendance. J. M. Robertson, *A History of Freethought in the Nineteenth Century* (1929), p. 362.

102. "Schämen wir uns," p. 44.

103. *Ibid.*

104. Cf. Felix, "Auto.," "My state of mind . . ." p. 2; "Auto.," "On my Eighteenth Birthday," p. 2; "Auto.," "Before the Ethical Society was founded . . ." p. 1; "Auto.," "Notes from a Private Autobiography," pp. 1–2; *Eth.P.L.*, pp. 10–12. Cf. also letters of Samuel to Felix, September 16, 1872, November 21, 1872, and letters of Henrietta Adler, January 6, 1873, and Isidor Walz, April 27, 1872, May 1872 and November 22, 1872. All letters in E.C.S.

105. The most sophisticated expression of the final ethical views at which he arrived can be found in his *Eth.P.L.*, pp. 73–141.

106. Cf. Patrick Gardiner, "The German Idealists and Their Successors," in *Germany*, ed.

M. Pasley (1972), p. 377. Cf. also Theodore M. Greene's introductory essay in Kant's *Religion Within Limits of Reason Alone,* trans. Theodore M. Greene and Hoyt H. Hudson (1960), pp. ix–lxxviii.

107. See I. Kant, *Critique of Practical Reason,* trans. L. W. Beck (1949 ed.).

108. Cf. for example, Adler's "The Religion of Humanity," November 1, 1877, p. 1 (Col.), and "Atheism," April 6, 1879, pp. 5, 16–17 (Col.).

109. Felix, "Auto.," "Biography," March 1930, p. 6.

110. "Races and Religions," December 18, 1878, p. 10 (Col.). Cf. his appreciation of Isaiah as the greatest ethical teacher, "The Bible as a Means of Ethical Culture," December 10, 1877 (Col.).

111. Cf. his lectures "Races and Religions," December 18, 1878, p. 10, and "The Danger of Irreligion Among the Young," April 27, 1879 (Col.).

112. Kant, *Religion Within the Limits of Reason Alone,* p. 155. On Kant's feelings about Judaism and the Jews, cf. N. Rotenstreich, *The Recurring Pattern* (1964), pp. 23–47.

113. Felix, "Auto.," "My state of mind . . ." p. 2; also, *Eth.P.L.,* p. 10.

114. "Atheism," April 6, 1879, p. 16.

115. Whether Adler felt he was interpreting Kant in emphasizing the power of the moral law or was consciously venturing on his own is not clear. As an interpretation of Kant, this stress is probably incorrect.

116. See the "Conclusion" in Matthew Arnold's *Literature and Dogma* (1873). Also, Adler's "Religion of Humanity," "Atheism," and other lectures of this period in Col.

117. Cf., for example, M. J. Savage, *The Religion of Evolution* (1876), p. 64, and Andrew D. White, *A History of the Warfare of Science with Theology* (1896), p. xii.

118. David F. Strauss, *The Old Faith and the New;* cf. Herbert Spencer, *First Principles of a New System of Philosophy* (1864 ed.); John Fiske, *Outlines of Cosmic Philosophy* (1874); John Stuart Mill, *Three Essays on Religion* (1874).

119. Felix, "Auto.," "Burne Jones says . . ." pp. 1–2.

120. Felix, "Auto.," "Three attitudes may be compared . . ." p. 1. Refer also to *Eth.P.L.,* p. 12.

121. Pinson, p. 240.

122. *Eth.P.L.,* pp. 11–12.

123. *Ibid.*

124. Felix, "Auto.," "Talk to the Sunday Evening Club," March 1930, p. 1. Cf. also his addresses "Religion and Social Reform," February 19, 1878 (Col.), and "The One Thing Needful," December 30, 1877 (Col.).

125. "Races and Religions," December 18, 1878, p. 10.

126. "6th Anniversary Address," May 1882.

127. Kant, *Religion Within Limits,* p. 5.

128. *Ibid.,* pp. 79, 142.

129. On these questions, see, for example, the illuminating article by Theodore M. Greene, "The Historical Context and Religious Significance of Kant's *Religion,*" pp. ix–lxxviii, and the article by John M. Silber, "The Ethical Significance of Kant's *Religion,*" pp. lxxix–cxxxiv, in their translation of Kant's *Religion Within Limits.*

130. Letter of Isaac Adler to Felix, February 14, 1873 (Col.).

131. *Eth.P.L.,* pp. 11–12.

132. *Ibid.*

133. *Ibid.*

Chapter III: Setting the Scene: 1873–1876

1. "Em. Min.," October 6, 1873.
2. "The Judaism of the Future," typescript in E.C.S.
3. *Jewish Messenger*, October 17, 1873. This issue of the *Messenger* and the *Jewish Times*, October 17, 1873, both reprinted the sermon in its entirety. The *Messenger* supplemented the address with a brief reporter's account of the temple's atmosphere and the congregational reception of the sermon.
4. "The Judaism of the Future," p. 3.
5. *Ibid.*, pp. 3–4.
6. *Ibid.*, pp. 7–8.
7. *Ibid.*, p. 7.
8. *Ibid.*, p. 10.
9. *Ibid.*, p. 8.
10. *Ibid.*, p. 9.
11. *Ibid.*, p. 10.
12. Eleanor Adler, "The Temple Sermon," p. 2.
13. Cf. in particular, the *American Israelite*, February 4, 1876, which three years after the fact wrote en passant that Adler's sermon "so frightened the conservative members of that congregation by its radicalism that they were only too glad when Cornell University offered him a professorship." Myer Stern, secretary of Emanu-El at the time of the sermon, observed that "Dr. Adler's address awakened much criticism from the fact that the views he expounded were much broader than those that prevailed at the time, and it was noted that during the entire address he made no reference to God. He was severely criticized at the time, but his earnestness and elegance of diction attracted considerable attention and approval." *The Rise and Progress of Reform Judaism* (1895), p. 67. H. Radest, in his *Toward Common Ground* (1969), pp. 17–18, gives too one-sided an account of the criticism which the sermon provoked. Michael Meyer is somewhat more accurate when he "suspect[s] that Adler's words did not scandalize his Reform listeners as much as Radest believes." "Beyond Particularism: On Ethical Culture and the Reconstructionists," *Commentary* 51, no. 3 (March 1971): 72. Nevertheless, Meyer should not underestimate the alarm of some Emanu-El members.
14. Richard J. H. Gottheil, *The Life of Gustav Gottheil* (1936), p. 41. Cf. also the *Israelite*, January 1, 1875, for its account of the events of October 1873.
15. The temple had sought an English-speaking preacher of standing since the late 1850s. At various times it settled for humorist R. J. De Cordova and Reverend J. Gutheim of New Orleans. It even tried to engage Max Lilienthal of Cincinnati, but he declined the offer. See "Em. Min." from 1858 on. Gottheil was hired in the spring of 1873 and was eagerly awaited. See especially "Em. Min.," May 10 and September 1, 1873.
16. Eleanor Adler, chap. 3, pp. 2–3, and the *New York Times* obituary column on Felix Adler, April 26, 1933.
17. "When Are We Justified in Leaving Our Religious Fellowship?" March 18, 1886, p. 13. Adler often reminisced about his Temple Sermon. Cf. "Anniversary Address," May 14, 1890; "Thirtieth Anniversary Address," May 13, 1906; and *Eth.P.L.*, p. 26, in which he describes the debate within him as to whether he should remain a "teacher of religion within the Jewish fold," and his resolution that he could not teach ideas in which he no longer believed.
18. Gottheil, p. 4.
19. *Jewish Messenger*, October 17, 1873; *Herald*, October 12, 1873.
20. "Judaism of the Future," p. 2.
21. *Ibid.*, pp. 2–3.

22. Gottheil, p. 41. The original letter is lost, but Richard Gottheil asserted this to be the basic drift of his father's feelings.

23. "Judaism of the Future," pp. 6–7, 9.

24. *Ibid.,* p. 9.

25. Stern, p. 67.

26. Consult Henry May, *Protestant Churches and Industrial America* (1963 ed.); A. I. Abell, *The Urban Impact on American Protestantism 1865–1900* (1943); cf. also, L. Mervis, "The Social Justice Movement and the American Reform Rabbinate," *American Jewish Archives* 7, no. 2 (June 1955).

27. "Judaism of the Future," pp. 5–6.

28. *Ibid.,* p. 6.

29. Address of O. B. Frothingham, "The Religion of the Future," at the New York Convention of the Free Religious Association in late September 1873. Cited in the *Israelite,* October 24, 1873.

30. See his first Lyric Hall lecture, "The Fall of Jerusalem," November 24, 1873, MS (E.C.S.).

31. Gottheil, p. 40.

32. Minutes of Board of Trustees Meeting, New York Society of Ethical Culture, December 5, 1927, quoted by Radest, p. 27. Cf. also Adler's address "Ethical Religion and the Idea of God," November 13, 1921, p. 11 (E.C.S.).

33. *Eth.P.L.,* p. 14.

34. Eleanor Adler, chap. 5, p. 2. Apparently, Isaac's opposition to Felix was short-lived. He is listed among the contributors ($10) to the Sunday lectures series initiated by Felix in May 1876. Cf. MS (undated) of list of subscribers (E.C.S.).

35. Unpublished letters of Adler to Felsenthal, June 29, 1901, in "Felsenthal Collection." Cf. also his feelings toward his father expressed in letters to Felsenthal at the time of his father's death, June 10, 1891, and July 4, 1891. These last two letters are part of the "Felsenthal Collection" and were published by Kober in his "Jewish Religious and Cultural Life in America as Reflected in the Felsenthal Collection," *Publications of the American Jewish Historical Society* 45, no. 2 (1955): 106–7. Adler also expressed his close attachment to his father in "Ethical Religion and the Child," December 9, 1931, p. 6 (E.C.S.), and "Geiger," May 15, 1910 (Col.).

36. Other names which are clearly legible in the MS include: Dr. Julius Sachs, H. Oppenheimer, G. Davidson, M. Davidson, Julius J. Baur, A. Wolf, M. Goldman, Sam Schafer, Ephraim Jacob, Isaac Bernheimer, P. Pfeifer, Max L. Mayer, Lazarus Rosenfeld (the father of Felix's friend Edward, who died in Germany), S. Loeb, L. Riess, E. Nainburg, L. Herman, Julius Holzinger, Jacob Silberman, Isaac Rosenfeld, M. Rosenfeld, Louis Rosenfeld, Rudolph Wolff, Martin S. Fechheimer, M. Herzog, and R. Brickman. Thirteen names are illegible to this author, MS (E.C.S.).

37. Each MS can be found in the E.C.S. The expenses of advertising, printing, and hall rental were paid for by M. Bruhl, G. Rosenbaum, M. Goldman, Dr. J. Sachs, A. Wolf, J. Heller, S. Bass, and G. Rosenblatt. Cf. MS receipt dated April 9, 1874 for Lyric Hall Lecture expenses.

38. "Martyrs and Martyrdom," p. 2.

39. "The Triumph of Mohammed," p. 21; "The Fall of Jerusalem," p. 1.

40. "Brahma," p. 5; "Martyrs and Martyrdom," p. 13.

41. "Brahma," p. 1; "The Triumph of Mohammed," p. 3.

42. "Brahma," p. 3.

43. "The Fall of Jerusalem," p. 6; "Brahma," p. 12.

44. "A Sign of the Times," MS, p. 1; cf. also "The Fall of Jerusalem," MS, p. 1, for a similar self-portrayal. Also, refer to the *Jewish Messenger,* November 28, 1873.

45. "A Sign of the Times," p. 22.

46. "Martyrs," p. 13.

47. *Ibid.*, p. 2.

48. "Brahma," p. 8.

49. "Mohammed," pp. 21–25.

50. "A Sign of the Times," pp. 19–20.

51. "A Sign of the Times," p. 22. Emphasis added.

52. "Martyrs and Martyrdom," p. 15.

53. *Ibid.*, p. 8. Cf. also *Eth.P.L.*, p. 18, n. 3, for a very similar reflection. Adler here noted that no man makes such a sacrifice unless propelled by an "inward coercion" to do so.

54. "The Christmas Tree," *op. cit.*

55. "The Fall of Jerusalem," p. 9. See too, "Martyrs and Martyrdom," p. 8, for a very positive analysis of Jesus as a religious reformer.

56. "Martyrs and Martyrdom," p. 25.

57. See, for example, *Jewish Times*, November 28, 1873; *Jewish Times*, January 2, 1874; *Jewish Messenger*, March 6, 1874.

58. *Jewish Messenger*, January 23, 1874.

59. *Ibid.*, January 2, 1874.

60. *Ibid.*

61. See the *Jewish Times*, November 28, 1873, reporting on "The Fall of Jerusalem." Curiously, the paper did not report on the final lectures. Could this Reform paper have been informed of Adler's retort to Emanu-El's trustees about his unbelief in their God?

62. *Jewish Times*, October 17, 1873. Cf. also *Jewish Times*, December 22, 1876.

63. *Ibid.*

64. For example, *Jewish Messenger*, January 2, 1874, March 6, 1874, March 27, 1874.

65. *Ibid.*, November 28, 1873, commenting on Adler's "The Fall of Jerusalem."

66. *Ibid.*, January 23, 1874, commenting on "Martyrs and Martyrdom." Adler disturbed some other Jews by his lecture, for a correspondent to the *Jewish Messenger* rose to defend the integrity of Jewish martyrs such as R. Akiva, R. Ishmael bar Elisha, and the others listed in the Midrash of the Ten Martyrs. "These men were not political schemers, ambitious demagogues stirring up the people to revolt, but simple teachers of the law who strove to elevate the moral and religious tone of their nation. They refused to be silent at the Roman's haughty command, when God's voice bade them speak, and for their idealism and loyalty they suffered the martyr's death." *Ibid.*, February 13, 1874.

67. *Ibid.*, March 27, 1874.

68. *Ibid.*, January 2, 1874.

69. *Ibid.*, January 16, 1874.

70. *Ibid.*, March 27, 1874.

71. *American Israelite*, September 24, 1875.

72. See *Ibid.*, September 24, 1875 and October 6, 1876; *Jewish Messenger*, September 29, 1876.

73. Consult Benjamin Rabinowitz, "The Young Men's Hebrew Association (1874–1918)," *Publications of the American Jewish Historical Society* 37 (1949): 233.

74. See the report of Adler's lecture on "Buddha" to the Liberal Club in *Jewish Times*, September 11, 1874; see the text of his lecture "The Influence of the Physical Geography of Palestine on Hebrew Thought" to the American Geographical Society in three issues of the *Jewish Times:* June 4, 1875, June 11, 1875, June 18, 1875. A report on this address is found in the *Jewish Messenger*, May 28, 1875; cf. abstracts of Adler's address on the "Exegesis and Criticism of the Old Testament," in the *Proceedings of the American Oriental Society*, May 1874. An abstract of a subsequent lecture, "On the Talmud Considered in Its Relation to Early Christianity," is found in the *Proceedings*, October 1874.

75. Letter to Adler from F. A. P. Barnard, July 17, 1876, MS (Col.).

76. See *Johnson's New Universal Cyclopedia*, II, pp. 1407–21. Adler's essays offered almost

nothing novel in Judaica scholarship even by the standards of his day. All three reflect his borrowing from nineteenth-century German Jewish scholars. His historical survey of "Jewish Literature" from biblical to modern philosophical material is a laudatory, not particularly critical essay relying heavily on Steinschneider. The *Jewish Messenger* thought enough of this essay to publish it in its entirety on November 10 and 17, 1876. His "Jewish Sects" focused in the main on the Pharisees and Sadducees and was based totally on Geiger. His article on the "Jews" very sympathetically outlined the main events of Jewish history and adopted the historical biases, historical orientation of "Kultur- und Leidensgeschichte," and historical periodization of Graetz.

The only real point of historical interest in Adler's essays lies in the conclusion to the article on the "Jews" in which he alludes to his own religious goal. He describes modern Jews as "disposed to regard the achievement of higher conditions of human life [in modern times] as the fulfillment of Messianic prophecy and the furthering of this end in intimate union with their fellow men as the highest dictate of their union." That clearly was true for him, but whether he himself actually believed this description to be an accurate one for "modern Jews" in general remains uncertain.

77. Eleanor Adler, chap. 5, p. 3.

78. Who initiated the idea of hiring Adler—whether White, Seligman, or other friends of Adler—is not known. An exchange of letters between Seligman and White did take place. Professor Friess informed me that letter(s) from Seligman to White exist, but I have only seen one letter from White to Seligman. Cf. MS letter dated March 10, 1874 (E.C.S.).

79. The *Jewish Messenger,* April 17, 1874, happily reported this arrangement. The originator of the idea for Jewish financing of this position is also not clear. From White's letter to Seligman, it seems that White suggested the notion, being aware of Cornell's poor financial state. Yet Professor William C. Russel of Cornell, in a letter to White, referred to "Seligman's plan." Cf. letter of Russel to White, MS, March 19, 1874, housed in the archives of Cornell University. Hereafter all references to these archives are listed as C.U.

80. Letter of White to Adler, April 16, 1874 (E.C.S.).

81. Letter of White to Seligman, March 10, 1874.

82. Cornell was particularly strong in these areas. Consult Morris Bishop, *A History of Cornell* (1962), p. 165; also cf. *Cornell Alumni News,* May 18, 1933.

83. Letter of Russel to White, March, 19, 1874, MS (C.U.).

84. A former student of Adler's, Andrew B. Humphrey, expressed this view in the *Cornell Alumni News,* June 8, 1933, p. 393.

85. Cf. Letter of Russel to White, May 19, 1874, MS (C.U.).

86. Letter of White to Seligman.

87. Letter of Russel to White, March 19, 1874, MS (C.U.).

88. *Ibid.*

89. *Ibid.* Russel's reference to Jews "push[ing] on further and find[ing] what they want where the Cornell boys found their starting point" may suggest a missionary idea, but if so, the nature and goal of his missionary zeal are not clear. Evolutionary deism? Liberal Protestantism? All of this is rather speculative.

90. Letter of Joseph Seligman to Adler, May 6, 1874, MS (E.C.S.).

91. Letter of Geiger to Adler, May 27, 1874 (Col.).

92. *Israelitische Wochenschrift,* May 14, 1874, p. 162.

93. Letters of Adler to his sister Sarah, April 24, 1874, April 30, 1876 (E.C.S.).

94. Report by Andrew B. Humphrey, *Cornell Alumni News,* June 8, 1933.

95. Smith's statement indicates the extent to which Adler had assimilated Voltaire's philosophy of history. In his "Histoire," *Philosophical Dictionary,* Voltaire revolutionized the study of history by proclaiming: "We will speak of the Jews as we would speak of Scythians or Greeks." Cf. Löwith, p. 110. Letter from F. P. Smith to Adler, MS, April 1, 1875 (E.C.S.).

96. His Inaugural Address was delivered on June 29, 1874 over the opposition of Registrar W. D. Wilson. Cf. Wilson's letter to White, June 7, 1874, MS (C.U.). The address was delivered and published by the *Ithaca Daily Journal*, June 30, 1874, and July 24, 1874. The course outline is an undated MS in (E.C.S.).

97. The literature on this topic and its various component parts is enormous. See Sidney E. Ahlstrom, *A Religious History of the American People* (1972), esp. chap. 46, "The Golden Age of Liberal Theology."

98. See, for example, H. W. Schneider, "The Influence of Darwin and Spencer on American Philosophical Theology," *Journal of the History of Ideas* 6, no. 1 (January 1945).

99. Consult Allan Nevins, *The Emergence of Modern America, 1865–1878* (1928), "The Deepening of American Culture," pp. 264–89.

100. Bishop, p. 190.

101. Cf. White's open letter to the alumni and undergraduates of Cornell, in *Cornell Era*, May 4, 1877.

102. Letter of Russel to White, May 15, 1874, MS (C.U.).

103. Letter of Russel to White, May 19, 1874, MS (C.U.).

104. *Ibid.*

105. Felix, "Auto.," "Biography, Principal Rubrics, March 1930," p. 3.

106. Letter of Russel to White, May 18, 1874.

107. *Ibid.*

108. Article by Andrew B. Humphrey in *Cornell Alumni News*, June 8, 1933. Originally a letter to the *New York Times*, May 30, 1933.

109. Letter of Russel to White, May 19, 1874.

110. *Ibid.*

111. *Ibid.* Russel added a gratuitous statement reflecting his acceptance of the stereotyped image of Jewish aggressiveness: "Were he a Teuton he might correct his opinionativeness, but being a Jew he will be hard to change."

112. Letter of E. D. Morris to President White, November, 8, 1874, MS (C.U.).

113. *Jewish Messenger*, May 21, 1874.

114. *Ibid.*

115. Letter of Russel to White, May 19, 1874, MS (C.U.).

116. Letter of Russel to White, May 15, 1874, MS (C.U.).

117. *Cornell Alumni News*, May 18, 1933.

118. Letter of Russel to White, May 19, 1874.

119. Letter of Russel to White, May 15, 1874.

120. Letter of W. D. Wilson to White, June 7, 1874, MS (C.U.).

121. Cf. *Daily Graphic*, May 15, 1877, June 23, 1877, September 29, 1877.

122. *Cornell Alumni News*, May 18, 1933, June 8, 1933.

123. *Ibid.*, May 18, 1933.

124. *Ibid.*, June 8, 1933.

125. Letter in Col.

126. Letter in Col.

127. Found in the *Cornell Era*, May 4, 1877.

128. See his "First Anniversary Address," May 14, 1877 (Col.), and the *Daily Graphic* report of it, May 15, 1877.

129. *Daily Graphic*, May 15, 1877, June 23, 1877, and September 29, 1877.

130. *Ibid.*, June 23, 1877 and September 29, 1877.

131. *Ibid.*, September 29, 1877.

132. Letter of Adler to Russel, April 22, 1885, MS (C.U.).

133. Cf., for example, "The Work of Liberalism," November 4, 1877 (Col.); "Fourteenth Anniversary Discourse," May 14, 1890 (Col.); and, "False Ethics in the Discussion of the War," November 22, 1914 (Col.).

134. The first Jew to teach Hebrew at an American university was Isaac Nordheimer (1809–1842), who was appointed professor of Arabic and Oriental languages and was acting professor of Hebrew at New York University from 1835 to 1842. I am indebted to Professor Paul Ritterband for having alerted me to this fact.

135. Cf. letters of Adler to James Morgan Hart, May 10, 1875, April 17, 1876, MS (C.U.).

136. Cf. replies to Adler of N. Trubner, prospective publisher of the Journal, November 13, 1875; James Martineau, November 1, 1875; E. B. Tylor, November 11, 1875; A. H. Sayce, October 31, 1875; T. K. Cheyne, November 5, 1875; and T. W. Rhys Davids, November 5, 1875. All are MSS found in the E.C.S.

137. He referred to visits with these men in letters to his sister, Sarah, February 29, 1876, and to his sister-in-law, Frieda Adler, June 6, 1876 (E.C.S.).

138. On Parker, see Adler's "Theodore Parker," April 29, 1879 (Col.), especially pp. 2–3. On Emerson see his *Eth.P.L.,* pp. 27–30, and "Emerson," October 18, 1903 (Col.), especially p. 26. Adler regularly cited selections from Emerson's essays such as "Essay on Self-Reliance," "Essay on the Over-Soul," "Essay on Circles," "Essay on Worship," and "On the Method of Nature."

139. Emerson did not instigate Adler's early religious orientation but served to deepen it; his influence on Adler's early religious outlook must, therefore, not be overstated as is often the case. See, for example, Radest's *Toward Common Ground* and Rodwin's "Ethical Religion in America" (1952). Adler's new religion grew out of the contemporary scholarship in religion in Europe to which Emerson's outlook and mode of expression were congenially assimilated. As Adler matured, and as he developed, in the twentieth century, a metaphysical analogue to his new emphasis on the social interrelatedness of people, he found Emerson's stress on individualism and independence limiting and unacceptable. He cited the danger of Emerson's view giving a false sense of splendor to man and generating a spiritual aristocracy. See his "Diary," February 20, 1906, p. 37, and May 9, 1906, p. 101. See too *Eth.P.L.,* pp. 27–30.

140. Cf. Adler's undated four-page favorable description of Gustav Werner, entitled "Gustav Werner" (Col.).

141. Cf. letter of Adler to his sister, Sarah, June 7, 1876 (E.C.S.), in which he detailed some of the cooperative ventures of the association.

142. *Israelite,* March 20, 1874.

143. *Jewish Messenger,* January 23, 1874.

144. Only one Jewish public statement exists in this three-year period hinting at Adler's departure from Judaism. In relating the events of the Temple Sermon more than one year later, Phil Point, New York correspondent to the *Israelite,* wrote, "it would be difficult, I fancy, to find in any of his discourses anything which conclusively proves that he believes in the Jewish religion." *Israelite,* January 1, 1875.

145. Cf. letter of Sigmund Mann, president of Tifereth Israel Congregation, Cleveland, Ohio, July 31, 1874, MS (E.C.S.). Rev. Dr. Jacob Mayer had resigned the position, and the temple sought a replacement for the holidays. Unfortunately, Adler's reaction to this letter is not known, nor is his reply—if indeed he sent one—extant. Given his problems with his Jewishness, it is not at all surprising that he did not take the job.

CHAPTER IV: CREATING A NEW MOVEMENT

1. See Trustees Minutes of the New York Society for Ethical Culture, December 5, 1927 (E.C.S.), and quoted by Radest, p. 27.

2. Cf. Rosenbaum's letters to Adler: April 11, 1876; Arpil 23, 1876; April 29, 1876; May 5, 1876; May 27, 1876; June 4, 1876. All are MSS in E.C.S. Adler's correspondence with Rosenbaum unfortunately has not been preserved.

3. Rosenbaum letter, April 11, 1876; see also his letter of April 23, 1876.

4. Rosenbaum letter, April 11, 1876.

5. Cf. the copy of the call issued to the New York public, May 12, 1876, MS in E.C.S.

6. Consult the *Independent Hebrew*, May 19, 1876, and the *American Israelite*, May 19, 1876, for accounts of the lecture.

7. Rosenbaum letter to Adler, April 29, 1876, and Radest, p. 27.

8. Cf. typescript of May 15 lecture in E.C.S. All further citations in the text refer to this document.

9. Letter of Rosenbaum to Adler, May 27, 1876.

10. Typescript copy of undated declaration found in E.C.S.

11. Article III of the Certificate of Incorporation of the Society for Ethical Culture. This certificate, including the preamble and bylaws of the society, can be found in its entirety in the *Index,* April 4, 1878.

12. Radest, p. 29.

13. "What Has Religion Done for Civilization?" November 14, 1897, pp. 10–11 (Col.); also "Social Changes and Social Conservatism," December 29, 1878, p. 6 (Col.).

14. Cf. Matthew Arnold, *Culture and Anarchy* (1932).

15. "The Ethics of Luxury," January 6, 1878 (Col.).

16. Cf. "Social Changes and Social Conservatism," December 29, 1878, p. 6 (Col.).

17. Cf. "Ethics and Culture," January 9, 1888 (E.C.S.), and "Matthew Arnold's Philosophy of Life," November 12, 1905 (Col.). On Felix's concept of "worth," cf. R. S. Guttchen, "Felix Adler's Concept of Worth," *Journal of the History of Philosophy* 11, no. 2 (April 1973), also included in his book *Felix Adler* (1974).

18. Cf., for example, "The Cardinal Teachings of an Ethical Religion," November 5, 1899 (E.C.S.).

19. "Huxley's Attitude Toward Religion," January 22, 1901 (E.C.S.).

20. Rosenbaum letter to Adler, April 29, 1876.

21. *Jewish Messenger,* July 19, 1872.

22. Frothingham, "Why Go to Church?" (1874), in his *Knowledge and Faith* (1876), p. 5.

23. For an interpretation of Adler's late ideas on "culture" and their relevance for contemporary society, consult Radest's unpublished doctoral dissertation for Columbia University, "Toward a Philosophy of Culture" (1971); see, too, Robert S. Guttchen, *Felix Adler* (1974), esp. pp. 206–50.

24. *Independent Hebrew,* May 19, 1876; *American Israelite,* June 2, 1876.

25. Cf. Rosenbaum letter to Adler, April 11, 1876, in which he asked him if music was essential, probably in fear of creating the impression of a religious service.

26. Rosenbaum letter, April 29, 1876; also, refer to his letters of April 11, April 23, and May 5.

27. Rosenbaum letter to Adler, June 4, 1876.

28. *Jewish Messenger,* June 16, 1876.

29. *Ibid.,* June 9, 1876, June 16, 1876.

30. *Independent Hebrew,* June 16, 1876.

31. Cf. correspondent "H.L.," *Jewish Messenger,* May 19, 1876, and correspondent "Common Sense," *Ibid.,* June 9, 1876. Cf. Jacobi's refutation of this charge in the next issue, June 16, 1876.

32. "Em. Min.," May 1, 1876. Cf. *American Israelite,* May 19, 1876.

33. *Ibid.,* June 7, 1875, and Stern, p. 69.

34. See, for example, *Jewish Messenger,* January 14, 1859 and January 29, 1864; *American Israelite*, May 30, 1879. One of the more interesting contemporary newspaper accounts of the poor religious situation is provided by the *Jewish Messenger,* May 19, 1876, in which a Beth

El congregant, in response to the question whether his store was closed on Saturday, replied—"no, I'm a Protestant Jew."

35. Cf. Solomon Schindler's confession in the *Jewish Advocate,* March 31, 1911.

36. Rosenbaum letter to Adler, April 29, 1876.

37. "Em. Min.," December 18, 1875.

38. See *Jewish Messenger,* July 1876 and October 14, 1876.

39. The precedent was first cited by the *American Israelite,* March 2, 1877, and repeated later by the *Jewish Messenger,* May 23, 1879.

40. *American Israelite,* May 5, 1876.

41. *Jewish Messenger,* October 20, 1876.

42. *Ibid.,* June 2, 1876, September 5, 1879.

43. On Ellinger, see *Jewish Times,* November 3, 1876.

44. Sonneschein's reproach of Kohler appeared in an issue of the *Israelite* and was reprinted by the *Jewish Messenger,* April 17, 1874. I quote from the latter source.

45. *Ibid.* Interestingly enough, this same Sonneschein became more radical as time passed, allowing the "Lord's Supper" to take place in his synagogue, an act which so infuriated the *Jewish Messenger* that it preferred Adler's Ethical Culture Society to Sonneschein's religious attitude. See *Jewish Messenger,* January 24, 1879. Sonneschein's relations with Unitarianism and its ministers caused a furor in the 1880s. Cf. Kober's "Jewish Religious and Cultural Life in America as Reflected in the Felsenthal Collection," p. 97.

46. Cf. *Jewish Messenger,* May 19, 1876, for two separate articles dealing with the issue. Refer also to the issue of September 5, 1879.

47. *Ibid.,* June 9, 1876.

48. *Ibid.,* June 2, 1876.

49. "The Religion of Humanity," November 25, 1877 (Col.)

50. "Races and Religion," December 18, 1878 (Col.).

51. "The Chosen People," December 15, 1878 (Col.).

52. *Ibid.*; cf. also, "Sixth Anniversary Lecture," May 1882 (Col.).

53. "Second Anniversary Discourse," May 27, 1877 (Col.).

54. See his three lectures on "The Bible," December 3, 10, 17, 1876; later published in a slightly shorter version as "The Old Testament in Light of Biblical Criticism," in the Appendix of his *Creed and Deed.* See also, "The Bible as a Means of Ethical Culture," December 10, 1877. On immortality, see "Reward and Punishment as Affecting the Doctrine of Immortality," October 29, 1876; "Immortality," November 12, 19, 1876, and May 6, 1877. Cf. also "The Day of Atonement Among the Jews," February 24, 1878 (Col.).

55. "The Second Stage of Religion—the Religion of Force," February 11, 1877 (Col.).

56. "Liberal Judaism," April 8, 1877 (Col.).

57. "The Sabbath," undated (Col.), probably early 1880s.

58. "Conscience," 1886 (E.C.S.).

59. "The Religion of Humanity," November 11, 1877 (Col.).

60. "The True Conservatism," December 22, 1878 (Col.).

61. "Sixth Anniversary Address," May 1882 (Col.).

62. "Facts and Fancies in Religion," March 10, 1878 (Col.).

63. "The New Religion or the Advance of Liberalism," March 26, 1878, printed in the *Chicago Daily Tribune,* March 27, 1878.

64. "The Chosen People," December 15, 1878 (Col.).

65. *New York World,* December 16, 1878.

66. *New York Herald,* December 16, 1878.

67. Cf. *Jewish Messenger,* February 16, 1877; *Jewish Times,* February 23, 1877; *American Israelite,* April 20, 1877. The non-Jewish press concurred; refer to the *Daily Graphic,* January 22, 1877 and February 16, 1877.

68. *New York Herald,* December 18, 1878.

69. *Jewish Messenger*, December 20, 1878.

70. "The Chosen People," December 15, 1878 (Col.).

71. *Ibid.* See also his Chicago address quoted in the *Chicago Daily Tribune*, March 27, 1878.

72. Cf. Morris R. Cohen, *Faith of a Liberal* (1946); also refer to his *A Dreamer's Journey* (1949) and *Reflections of a Wandering Jew* (1950).

73. "Races and Religions," December 18, 1878 (Col.).

74. Cf. typescript of letter of Rebecca F. Coleman to Adler, September 3, 1878 (E.C.S.); cf. MS letter of N. S. Gadbe of Salt Lake City to Adler, January 16, 1881 (E.C.S.).

75. *New York World*, December 5, 1876; the *New York Sun* apparently made the same claim, because the *Daily Graphic* responded to it, January 22, 1877.

76. *Daily Graphic, loc. cit.; Jewish Messenger*, December 8, 1876.

77. Marks in *Reformer and Jewish Times*, March 9, 1877 and September 18, 1877; Werner in *American Israelite*, March 2, 1877.

78. *Reformer and Jewish Times*, September 28, 1877.

79. Cf. *American Israelite*, May 5, 1876, in which Phil Point suggested that one-tenth of Frothingham's audience was Jewish; yet William Russel, in his letter to President A. White, March 19, 1874, MS (C.U.), claimed that the Jews comprised one-half of the audience. Point, on the scene personally, is probably more accurate, but a precise figure is impossible to obtain.

80. *Jewish Messenger*, May 19, 1876.

81. *Ibid.*, December 20, 1878.

82. *American Israelite*, May 5, 1876.

83. *Ibid.*

84. *Reformer and Jewish Times*, September 28, 1877.

85. Emphasis added.

86. Cf. "Em. Min.," January 3, 1870, for an account of this episode.

87. *New York World*, December 8, 1876; *American Israelite*, October 27, 1876; *Daily Graphic*, January 22, 1877.

88. *New York World*, December 8, 1876.

89. Letter of Rosenbaum to Adler, June 4, 1876, MS (E.C.S.).

90. H. Morgenthau, *All in a Life Time* (1922), pp. 94–95.

91. *Ibid.*, pp. 96–97.

92. Samuel Gompers, *Seventy Years of Life and Labour* (1967), I, p. 433.

93. Gregory Weinstein, *The Ardent Eighties* (1928), p. 99.

94. Stephen Birmingham, *Our Crowd* (1967), p. 149.

95. George S. Hellman, "Joseph Seligman, American Jew," *Publications of the American Jewish Historical Society* 41, no. 1 (September, 1951): 33.

96. Birmingham, p. 124.

97. Cited in Hellman, p. 33. Note Seligman's reference to Sunday as the Holy Sabbath. Seligman was in the forefront of trying to institute Sunday services at Emanu-El in the 1870s, having served on the two committees in 1874 and 1876 looking into the matter. Cf. "Em. Min." Emanu-El's failure to implement Sunday services may have been the primary motive for his attraction to Adler.

98. See his address "The Recent Persecution of the Jews," December 28, 1879 (E.C.S.).

99. *New York Star*, June 4, 1882. See, too, Lauterbach's remarks in the *American Hebrew*, May 19, 1882, on the occasion of the laying of the cornerstone of the Home for the Aged and Infirm Hebrews, in which he stressed the need to take care of urgent Jewish needs.

While Lauterbach was clearly a strong supporter of Jewish causes, his departure from the society may also have been rooted in or hastened by more political and less idealistic motives. He contended to the *New York Star* reporter who interviewed him that as vice-president of the society he was next in line for the presidency, but that Adler felt the society would be better represented by "some one less closely affiliated with the religious body to which, by birth and original education, we both belong." A non-Jew was selected, and "upon this I withdrew." In light of his comment to the same reporter that he had departed over the principle of the nonsectarian nature of the society, one is left uncertain about his true motives. To be sure, Adler was not above playing politics with the presidency. A few years later, he chose Edwin Seligman over Alfred Wolff because the former needed the extra impetus to work for the society whereas Adler recognized that Wolff would be a dedicated worker regardless of title (Radest, *Toward Common Ground,* p. 135). Perhaps having been slighted aroused Lauterbach to champion the cause of Jewish immigrants and symbolically and publicly to affirm his Jewish attachments and ties.

Withdrawal into Jewish lines by Jewish members of the Ethical Culture Society because of identification with the plight of fellow Jews suffering from anti-Semitism recurred throughout the history of the Ethical Movement. In 1931, for example, prominent Jews in Pittsburgh, led by Professor Max Schoen of Carnegie Tech, organized an Ethical Society. With Hitler's rise in 1933, the group disintegrated. Radest, p. 236. In the New York Society, many Jews also began to feel guilty at this time over having cut their Jewish ties. *Ibid.,* p. 267.

100. Waldo Frank, *Our America* (1919), pp. 86–87.

101. James Waterman Wise, *Jews Are Like That* (1928), p. 136.

102. H. Simenhoff, *Saga of American Jewry* (1959), p. 183.

103. Undated "Note for the Sunday Address, an Address with an Autobiographical Background," Typescript, p. 10 (E.C.S.). Probably written in the 1920s.

104. Felix, "Auto.," "The Letter of Paul Schurz . . ." p. 2 (E.C.S.).

CHAPTER V: REACTION AND CONTROVERSY

1. Cf. *Jewish Messenger,* December 11, 1874 and July 14, 1872; see also *Jewish Times,* October 17, 1873 and January 23, 1874.

2. Refer to *Jewish Messenger,* December 28, 1877; *Jewish Times,* November 3, 1876; compare Adler's attack on the quality of the clergy, including the rabbis, in "Office of the Clergy," April 14, 1878 (Col.), with H. H. Marks's sharp criticism of the rabbis in *Reformer and Jewish Times,* September 28, 1877.

3. *Jewish Messenger,* July 27, 1877.

4. Phil Point, New York correspondent to the *American Israelite,* at least was aware of the problem and noted that Jewish skeptics and indifferentists, having no other place to go, attended Adler's lectures. *American Israelite,* October 27, 1876. The only instance of a paper calling for rabbinic lectures on religion in response to this problem is found in the *Jewish Times,* November 3, 1876.

5. Cf. *Jewish Messenger,* December 8, 1876.

6. Compare the *Jewish Messenger,* December 8, 1876, with the *Jewish Times,* December 22, 1876.

7. *Jewish Messenger,* October 12, 1877.

8. *Ibid.,* February 16, 1877; *Jewish Times,* February 23, 1877; *American Israelite,* April 20, 1877.

9. *Jewish Messenger,* October 12, 1877.

10. *Jewish Times,* December 22, 1876.

11. Cf. Marks's defense of Adler in *Jewish Times,* February 23, 1877 and March 9, 1877.

12. *Reformer and Jewish Times,* January 17, 1879.

13. *Ibid.,* January 24, 1879. I could not find Adler's essay in earlier issues of the *Jewish Times.* But in a later response to an inquiry Marks asserted that all three works were earlier products of Adler. The essay itself clearly proved this to be true, for in it he bemoaned Jewish disobedience of the Sabbath laws and called for Friday night services to mitigate the extent of Jewish unconcern with the Sabbath.

14. *Reformer and Jewish Times,* January 31, 1879.

15. *Ibid.,* February 28, 1879. Cf. Daniel de Leon's defense of Jews adopting the Christmas tree in *ibid.,* February 14, 1879.

16. The paper changed names March 1, 1877.

17. *American Israelite,* April 20, 1877.

18. *Ibid.,* May 10, 1878, and refer also to an earlier issue, March 15, 1878.

19. *Jewish Times,* October 20, 1876.

20. *American Israelite,* October 27, 1876.

21. *Jewish Messenger,* October 20, 1876.

22. *Jewish Times,* November 3, 1876.

23. *Jewish Messenger,* November 10, and 17, 1876.

24. *Jewish Times,* November 3, 1876.

25. *Ibid.,* December 22, 1876.

26. *Ibid.,* November 3, 1876.

27. Cf. "The Bible," December 3, 10, 17, 1876 (Col.).

28. *Jewish Messenger,* December 8, 1876.

29. *New York World,* December 5, 1876.

30. *American Israelite,* December 15, 1876.

31. *Jewish Times,* December 22, 1876.

32. *New York World,* December 8, 1876.

33. *Ibid.*

34. *Jewish Times,* December 22, 1876.

35. *New York World,* December 14, 1876. While no sources exist to prove that "Honesty" was Jewish and, therefore, expressing *Jewish* opinion, the nature of his concern and comments, his intimate familiarity with Adler's May 15, 1876 address and the practices of the Jewish community lend credence to the belief that he was indeed Jewish.

36. *Daily Graphic,* January 22, 1877.

37. *Jewish Messenger,* February 16, 1877, citing the *New York World,* December 12, 1877.

38. *Ibid.* Cf. letter of "M.L.G." castigating Adler for his views on circumcision, *American Israelite,* March 16, 1877. Adler, however, only anticipated views expressed later by Reform scholars. Cf. Kohler's reference to the rite as a "national remnant of savage African life," in "Proceedings of the Pittsburgh Rabbinical Conference," *CCARY,* 1923, p. 16; see too Morgenstern's reference to it as growing out of the "grossest forms of phallic worship," *ibid.,* 1908, p. 229.

39. *Daily Graphic,* February 16, 1877.

40. *Jewish Messenger,* March 2, 1877.

41. *Ibid.,* March 23, 1877. "Ish Yehudi" is incorrect. While Adler did appropriate Voltaire's approach of tracing the primitive non-Jewish origin of circumcision, his negative judgment on the rite extended beyond that of Voltaire. Voltaire did not call circumcision a barbaric rite. Cf. Voltaire's *Dictionnaire Philosophique,* "Circumcision" s.v. (1967 ed., pp. 138–42). If anything, Adler may have acquired this judgment from Geiger, who in a letter to Zunz, March 19, 1845, termed it a "barbarous bloody act." Cf. Philipson, p. 136.

42. See too *Reformer and Jewish Times,* March 2, 1877, for a similar comparison by correspondent "Ben Brith." If "Ish Yehudi" was in fact Isaacs' son, then one sees an interesting shift in outlook by the Isaacs family. In 1873, on the occasion of the Free Religious Association's September Convention, the *Jewish Messenger,* October 24, 1873, printed a very sarcastic editorial on Frothingham. Following Adler's arrival on the scene, it treated Frothingham with greater respect. Cf. the July 5, 1878 issue of the paper.

43. *Daily Graphic,* February 16, 1877.

44. *American Israelite,* April 20, 1877.

45. Cf. *Daily Graphic,* June 23, 1877, which correctly noted that while Adler's enemies deemed him an atheist, he himself never denied the existence of a God, but simply avoided all mention of Him.

46. *Jewish Times,* February 23, 1877.

47. He published extensive excerpts of the Kohler-Adler dispute in the Chicago press. See *Reformer and Jewish Times,* March 29, 1878 and October 25, 1878.

48. *Ibid.,* March 2, 1877.

49. *Ibid.,* March 9, 1877.

50. *Ibid.,* March 16, 1877.

51. *Ibid.,* March 23, 1877.

52. *Jewish Messenger,* December 28, 1877.

53. *Ibid.,* January 4, 1878.

54. Cf. "Ben Brith" in *Reformer and Jewish Times,* March 2, 1877.

55. Refer to "A Great Reformation," January 7, 1877 (Col.); "The New Ideal," January 21, 1877 (Col.); "Dreams and Ideals," March 25, 1877 (Col.); and especially the five-lecture series on "The Ethics of the Social Question," January 13–February 10, 1878 (Col.).

56. "Ben Brith," *op. cit.*

57. Cf. *New York World,* February 12, 1877; and the *Daily Graphic*'s response on January 22, 1877 to the *New York Sun,* which had reported Adler as a representative Jew.

58. *Jewish Messenger,* February 16, 1877.

59. Judah Sequor's letter to the *Reformer and Jewish Times,* March 23, 1877.

60. "Ben Brith," *op. cit.*

61. *Jewish Times,* February 23, 1877.

62. *Reformer and Jewish Times,* March 9, 1877.

63. *Jewish Messenger,* October 12, 1877. Adler's essay appeared in the September–October 1877 issue of the *North American Review.*

64. *American Israelite,* December 15, 1876.

65. *Jewish Messenger,* November 9, 1877.

66. *Israelitische Wochenschrift,* April 26, 1877. Among the few voices was that of Frederick de Sola Mendes, rabbi of the 44th Street Synagogue in New York. He criticized Adler's views in the *Jewish Record,* March 9, March 16, April 27 and May 4, 1877. Cf. Moshe Davis, *The Emergence of Conservative Judaism* (1963), p. 194. I was not able to uncover the original *Jewish Record* sources, but from Davis it appears that most of his criticisms were not direct attacks against Adler, but more traditional defenses of Jewish rituals and beliefs.

67. *Jewish Messenger,* February 16, 1877.

68. *Reformer and Jewish Times,* September 28, 1877.

69. *American Israelite,* May 15, 1878.

70. Beth El General Minutes, May 6, 1877. I am indebted to Hyman B. Grinstein, professor of Jewish history at Yeshiva University, for this source.

71. See the opinions of the three men on the prospects of Judaism, in the *New York Herald,* December 19, 1878.

72. *Jewish Messenger,* December 8, 1876; *American Israelite,* March 2, 1877.

73. *Israelitische Wochenschrift,* April 26, 1877.

74. *Reformer and Jewish Times,* March 2, 1877.

75. *Ibid.,* March 9, 1877.

76. *Daily Graphic,* April 7, 1877.

77. *Reformer and Jewish Times,* September 28, 1877.

78. "Office of the Clergy," April 14, 1878 (Col.).

79. *Reformer and Jewish Times,* September 28, 1877.

80. *Daily Graphic,* April 7, 1877.

81. *Jewish Messenger,* October 12, 1877.

82. Gunther Plaut, *The Growth of Reform Judaism* (1965), pp. 134–38.

83. *Chicago Daily Tribune,* March 21, 1878. Full text reprinted in Plaut, p. 135; *Reformer and Jewish Times,* March 29, 1878; and *Index,* May 16, 1878.

84. *Chicago Daily Tribune,* March 21, 1878. Plaut quotes this portion of the paper without identifying its source, giving the unfortunate impression that the description is his. Cf. Plaut, p. 135.

85. *Chicago Daily Tribune,* March 22, 1878. Emphasis is Kohler's.

86. *Ibid.,* March 27, 1878.

87. Reprinted in full in the *Jewish Messenger,* April 15, 1878.

88. Letter of Felsenthal to Julius Rosenthal, April 2, 1878, MS (E.C.S.).

89. Felsenthal letter to Rosenthal, April 3, 1878, MS (E.C.S.).

90. Cf. Otto Caspari, *Die Urgeschichte der Menschheit* (1873).

91. Undated, unsigned MS written sometime in early April 1878 (E.C.S.).

92. Plaut, pp. 137–38.

93. *Index,* April 11, 1878.

94. Kohler's line of thinking reflected the need of all Reformers for a theistic God idea. See Sonneschein's attack on Adler in 1887—"a religious movement without the God idea is sheer nonsense." Cited by Radest, *Toward Common Ground,* p. 54.

95. Undated, unsigned MS of Adler, April 1878.

96. *Reformer and Jewish Times,* March 29, 1878.

97. On Kohler's fighting temperament, consult chapter 2 of Michael A. Meyer, "A Centennial History," in *Hebrew Union College–Jewish Institute of Religion at One Hundred Years* (1976), esp. pp. 58–70.

98. Undated letter of Samuel Adler to B. Felsenthal, probably April or May 1878 (E.C.S.).

99. Cf. the "Felsenthal Papers," containing letters (many unpublished) between Felsenthal and the Adlers, and about forty letters between him and Samuel Adler over three decades (1850s–1880s) in Col. Cf. also Felsenthal's eulogy of Samuel Adler in the *New York Staatszeitung,* June 21, 1891.

100. Felsenthal wrote four articles on Adler and Ethical Culture in the *Jewish Advance,* II, 30–34, January 3–24, 1879. I am hampered in this discussion because, according to the *Union List of Serials in Libraries of the United States and Canada,* 3d ed., no institution has volume II of this paper. The *Index,* February 20, 1879, featured a small selection of Felsenthal's material, and Radest, in his *Toward Common Ground,* cited an even smaller extract taken from the *Index.* The two Felsenthal letters to Adler cited below do, to some extent, correspond to the drift of the available *Jewish Advance* material, but without all four articles it appears that a full knowledge of Felsenthal's opinions on Adler and his society will not be determinable.

101. Letter of Felsenthal to Adler, January 25, 1878, MS (E.C.S.).

102. This point is the basic idea cited from a Felsenthal article in the *Jewish Advance* by the *Index.*

103. Felsenthal considerably understated Adler's position on circumcision. He did not "not insist" on it, but categorically repudiated it as a barbaric, superstitious rite. Adler's reply to Felsenthal, if any, is not extant.

104. Letter of Felsenthal to Adler, December 13, 1878, MS (E.C.S.). The phrase *heichal hashem, heichal hashem* is taken from Jeremiah 7:4, where it appears three times consecutively, and according to one interpretation represents the people's response to the Prophet's admonition of them to amend their ways. By proclaiming the phrase, the people retort that their ways are indeed pious, that they are not guilty of sinning—the Temple is not and will not be destroyed. Another interpretation puts these words in the mouths of false prophets who deceive the people. The phrase, then, essentially symbolizes the false and deceiving proclamation of piety by the impious.

105. *Ibid.* Emphasis added. Adler's reply to Felsenthal, if any, is not extant.

106. Refer to the small section of his article in the *Jewish Advance* cited by the *Index.* Note that Felsenthal, like some other Reformers, changed his mind in the 1890s as a result of anti-Semitism, and became an ardent advocate of Jewish nationalism and Zionism.

107. If our analysis of Felsenthal's position is correct, then a severe problem arises which Reformers like Kohler and Emil Hirsch later appeared to face: what of the non-Jew who acts in the manner that Felsenthal prescribes—is he to be called a Jew? This issue seems to have disturbed Kohler and Hirsch, for they fall back on Jewish *race* as the criterion of defining who is a Jew. *Birth* defines membership in the Jewish religious group according to both.

108. Letter of Adler to Felsenthal, March 16, 1880, MS "Felsenthal Papers."

109. *Ibid.* Emphasis added.

110. Letter of Adler to Felsenthal, May 15, 1881, MS, "Felsenthal Papers."

111. Cf. his essay "On Reformed Judaism" in the Appendix of his *Creed and Deed* and published in full in the *American Israelite,* September 7, 1877. Adler maintained this view, which clothed basic Judaism in a nonchanging ideological garb, in later life.

112. Cf. especially "Races and Religion," December 18, 1878, p. 14 (Col.).

113. *Eth.P.L.,* p. 14.

114. "The Ethical Movement After Thirty-Four Years," May 8, 1910, p. 8 (E.C.S.).

115. Radest, *Toward Common Ground,* pp. 144–45, 199–200.

116. Felix, "Auto.," "Burne Jones says . . ." p. 2 (E.C.S.).

117. Cf. *Eth.P.L.,* chapters on Kant and on "worth." Also, "Auto.," "My state of mind . . ." p. 8 (E.C.S.), and "Auto.," "Talk to the Sunday Evening Club, 1912," p. 2 (E.C.S.). Refer also to Guttchen, *Felix Adler,* chap. 1.

118. Felix, "Auto.," "Biography, March 1930," p. 3 (E.C.S.).

119. See Eleanor Adler's "Reminiscences," undated (Col.), and Radest, *Toward Common Ground,* pp. 22–25, 106.

120. Refer to his letter to Percival Chubb on August 18, 1921 for his perception of the relationship between humility and noblesse oblige (Col.); also, Radest, *Toward Common Ground,* p, 235.

CHAPTER VI: ADLER AND THE JEWISH WORLD AFTER 1880

1. All these notes are found in the archives at Columbia.

2. "Fifth Anniversary Discourse," May 1881 (Col.).

3. Cf. Adler's Sunday addresses: "The Value of the Old Testament from the Human Point of View," 1888; "Moses and the Prophets," November 26, 1893; "The Idea of God and of Futurity as Conceived by the Prophets of Israel," December 3, 1893; "The Ten Commandments," April 21, 1895. All found in E.C.S. Refer, too, to the numerous notes on the Prophets in Col., undated, but all written post-1880. Some of the titles are "The Radicalism of Isaiah," "Hosea: Elements of Love," "Jeremiah," "Abraham's Sacrifice," "The Prophet Amos," to list but a few. Cf. also the only two addresses on the Jewish religion that he delivered in the twentieth century, "The Essentials of Judaism," November 2, 1913 (E.C.S.), and "The Difference Between Ethical Culture and Left-Wing Judaism," November 9, 1925 (E.C.S.). Refer also to the chapter "Hebrew Religion" in his *Eth.P.L.*

4. "The Essentials of Judaism," p. 6.

5. *Eth.P.L.,* p. 16; cf. also "What Is Religion?" November 21, 1897, p. 11 (E.C.S.).

6. "Ninth Anniversary Address," May 10, 1885, p. 5 (Col.).

7. Cf. "The Essentials of Judaism," pp. 9–20, for the following analysis.

8. *Ibid.,* p. 19.

9. *Ibid.,* p. 20.

10. *Ibid.,* p. 22. See also *Eth.P.L.,* p. 19.

11. "The Essentials of Judaism," p. 20.

12. *Eth.P.L.,* p. 19.

13. *Ibid.,* pp. 19–23.

14. "The Essentials of Judaism," p. 21.

15. "The Difference Between the Ethical Movement and Left-Wing Judaism," November 9, 1925 (E.C.S.), p. 7.

16. *Ibid.*, p. 22.

17. *Eth.P.L.*, p. 22.

18. *Ibid.*, pp. 22–23.

19. *Ibid.*, pp. 32–40. Cf. too, "The Difference Between the Ethical Movement and Left-Wing Judaism," p. 7.

20. *Eth.P.L.*, p. 15.

21. *Ibid.*, p. 17.

22. *Ibid.*

23. "The Essentials of Judaism," p. 4.

24. *Ibid.*, p. 2.

25. Undated, untitled typescript review note of Meyer's book (Col.).

26. Undated, untitled typescript review note of Sombart's book (Col.).

27. "The Anti-Semitic Prejudices and Its Evil Consequences," December 12, 1897, p. 19 (E.C.S.).

28. "The Essentials of Judaism," p. 1.

29. *Ibid.*, p. 2.

30. *Ibid.*, p. 3.

31. *Ibid.*, p. 4. Cf. also, "Zionism and Its Ideal," November 7, 1915, p. 13.

32. "Is Agreement in Religion Essential in Marriage?" December 15, 1919, p. 13 (E.C.S.). Cf. also "The Difference Between the Ethical Movement and Left-Wing Judaism," November 19, 1925, p. 10 (E.C.S.), and an earlier address, "The Chosen Race," December 15, 1878, p. 13 (Col.).

33. See, for example, letters to his daughter Eleanor, December 21, 1932 and December 30, 1932. See, too, Radest, *Toward Common Ground*, p. 137, for a description by Ruth Adler Friess of Christmas in the Ethical Culture Society.

34. "Thoughts Suggested by Christmas," undated in Col.

35. James W. Wise, *Jews Are Like That*, pp. 137–38; also Simenhoff, p. 183.

36. "Jewish Idealism," *Publications of the American Jewish Historical Society,* November 14, 1906, p. 216.

37. See *Dr. Bloch's Oesterreichische Wochenschrift,* February 7, 1908 and June 5, 1908. See also *New York Times* obituary on Adler, April 26, 1933.

38. *American Jewish Chronicle,* May 24, 1918, p. 52.

39. Cf. Adler's lecture "Reformed Judaism," November 22, 1885 (Col.), delivered one week following the Pittsburgh Rabbinical Conference, November 16–18, 1885.

40. "The Recent Persecution of the Jews," December 28, 1879, p. 24 (E.C.S.). Cf. also, "Nationalism and Zionism," November 8, 1918, pp. 2–3 (E.C.S.).

41. Cf. "The Anti-Semitic Prejudice and Its Evil Consequences," December 12, 1897, p. 14 (E.C.S.), and "The Difference Between the Ethical Movement and Left-Wing Judaism," November 9, 1925, p. 10 (E.C.S.).

42. George M. Price, "The Russian Jews in America," *Publications of the American Jewish Historical Society* 48, no. 1 (September 1958): 57–58.

43. Cf. the *New York Post*'s description of the homes, February 8, 1887.

44. Price, p. 58.

45. In 1883, along with Edmond Kelly, he founded the Good Government Club—now known as the City Club—to oppose political corruption in New York City.

46. "Proceedings of the Pittsburgh Rabbinical Conference," *CCARY,* 1923, p. 10.

47. *Jewish Messenger,* December 5, 1884.

48. Myer Stern, *The Rise and Progress of Reform Judaism* (1895) pp. 73–78.

49. See Bernard Martin, "The Social Philosophy of Emil G. Hirsh," *American Jewish Archives* 6, no. 2 (1954).

50. Consult Radest, *Toward Common Ground,* for a chronological table of events and projects in which Adler was involved, pp. 307–14.

51. "Nationalism and Zionism," November 8, 1918, p. 3.

52. Fechheimer's letter is found in the *Jewish Messenger,* May 19, 1882; Schiff's reply in the May 27, 1882 issue. See, too, the editorial of the *American Hebrew,* May 26, 1882, supporting Adler.

53. Taken from Adler's address to the New York Society's Board of Trustees, November 6, 1906, and cited by Radest, *Toward Common Ground,* p. 127.

54. See the letter of Stephen S. Wise to his wife, Louise, 1900, in *The Personal Letters of Stephen Wise* (1956), p. 30.

55. *American Hebrew,* August 10, 1888.

56. A copy of the sermon was sent to Adler by a Mr. J. Judelsohn. Delivered on July 21, 1888, the sermon was hailed by the Jewish press for its moral tone and message. See *American Hebrew,* July 27 and August 10, 1888. The *New York Sun* reported on it July 22, 1888. See Abraham J. Karp, "New York Chooses a Chief Rabbi," *Publications of the American Jewish Historical Society* 44, no. 3 (1955).

57. Undated biographical sketch of Montefiore, p. 7 (Col.); from its tone, probably written shortly after Montefiore's death in 1885.

58. *Ibid.,* p. 21.

59. Radest, *Toward Common Ground,* p. 126.

60. Over the years, this membership was able to pay its leader, Felix Adler, rather handsomely by contemporary standards. Treasury reports of the society show that his salary increased steadily over the years: 1891–92—$6,500; 1894–95—$7,500; 1899–1900—$9,000; 1904–5—$9,500.

61. Radest, *Toward Common Ground,* p. 127.

62. *Ibid.,* pp. 151–53.

63. All of Adler's early associates in the Ethical Culture Movement until the turn of the century were Christian in origin, suggesting that he may have purposely selected Christians to give the society a universal, non-Jewish flavor and representation. Lauterbach charged Adler with that motive in his selection of a Gentile over him as president of the New York Society, and Adler may have been similarly motivated in choosing leaders for his society and for those societies outside of New York. Clearly, the presence of Christian leaders in the movement did project for it a more universal image, and as some of them came, in the 1880s, to lead Ethical Societies with very limited Jewish membership in the United States and Europe (Coit—London; Salter—Chicago; Weston—Philadelphia; Sheldon—St. Louis), Ethical Culture could legitimately claim to be a national, international, and universal movement. All of these developments certainly fulfilled Adler's own aspirations.

Yet in assessing the motive for Adler's selection of Christians, two factors in addition to pragmatic institutional concerns must be seriously considered. All of the Ethical Culture leaders of the 1880s and 1890s emerged from a background that stimulated an intellectual and spiritual direction most in consonance with Adler's own. They were all strongly influenced by Emerson, Channing, and the American freethought movement, which included that liberal Christian intellectual elite with whom Adler had found such spiritual kinship in the 1870s. Indeed, Weston and Salter first met Adler during his term as president of the FRA. The American freethought movement had little impact on young Jews growing up more involved with business than academics. Also, Jews in the last decades of the nineteenth century were reasserting their Jewishness in the wake of continuing European anti-Semitism just when these young liberal Christians were seeking a socially oriented universal religious fellowship. Adler was, therefore, less likely to discover young Jews of a spiritual and intellectual bent suitable to his cause. Then, too, Salter, Weston, and Elliott had come to Adler soliciting aid in career guidance. Few Jews manifesting the requisite social concern and intellectual background similarly sought Adler out.

64. Cf. the very grateful letters of both Hirsch and Sale thanking Adler for having sent them copies of his *Eth.P.L.,* undated in Col.

65. Cf. letters of Adler to Abraham Cronbach, December 27, 1916, November 23, 1925, May 18, 1926, August 25, 1926, and June 19, 1929, in the American Jewish Archives, Cincinnati, Ohio. Also in Col.

66. Cf. Wise's attraction to Adler, in a letter to his wife, 1899, in *The Personal Letters of Stephen Wise,* p. 17. Wise and Adler remained quite friendly in the twentieth century. Cf. Wise's *Challenging Years* (1949), pp. 80, 87, 98.

67. Cf. Adler's letter to Schiff thanking him for his contribution to the Ethical Culture Society, May 17, 1899, in the American Jewish Archives.

68. The first three are all in pamphlet form in E.C.S. as is the 1920 address. The 1897 and 1899 addresses are in Col., but the 1893 and 1922 addresses, which are listed as being in Col., are missing.

69. Cf. "The Recent Persecution of the Jews," December 28, 1879, pp. 23–24; "The Anti-Semitic Prejudice and Its Evil Consequences," December 12, 1897, p. 14; and "The Difference Between the Ethical Movement and Left-Wing Judaism," November 9, 1925, p. 10.

70. Cf. "The Revival of Anti-Semitism," December 5, 1920, pp. 13–14.

71. "The Recent Persecutions of the Jews," December 28, 1879, p. 1.

72. *Ibid.,* pp. 2–20.

73. *Ibid.,* p. 22.

74. Cf. especially "Larger Tolerance," December 26, 1880.

75. "The Recent Persecutions of the Jews," p. 23.

76. *Ibid.,* p. 25. Emphasis is Adler's.

77. *Ibid.,* pp. 23–24.

78. Cf. his two addresses "The Anti-Jewish Agitation in Germany," December 19, 1880, and "Larger Tolerance," December 26, 1880.

79. "The Anti-Jewish Agitation in Germany," pp. 7–8.

80. *Ibid.,* pp. 19–21. Cf., too, "The Revival of Anti-Semitism," December 5, 1920, p. 12.

81. "The Anti-Jewish Agitation in Germany," p. 21. Emphasis is Adler's.

82. *Ibid.,* p. 25.

83. *Ibid.,* pp. 26–27.

84. One might justifiably challenge Adler by contending that his position equally implied the need for Germans to abandon *their* particularism in order to end anti-Semitism. Adler did not take this approach, however, for he was basically committed to the idea that Jews have no further reason for existing as Jews.

85. "The Anti-Semitic Prejudice and Its Evil Consequences," December 12, 1897, p. 6.

86. *Ibid.,* p. 14.

87. "The Revival of Anti-Semitism," December 5, 1920, p. 2.

88. *Ibid.,* p. 11.

89. *Ibid.,* p. 2.

90. *Ibid.,* p. 3. Cf. also an undated MS on one page entitled "Psychological Notes on the Anti-Semitic Movement" (Col.).

91. "The Revival of Anti-Semitism," p. 12.

92. *Ibid.,* pp. 12–13.

93. "The Difference Between the Ethical Movement and Left-Wing Judaism," November 9, 1925, p. 10.

94. See "The Chosen People," December 15, 1878 (Col.).

95. See "Zionism and Its Ideal," November 7, 1915 (E.C.S.).

96. "The Difference Between the Ethical Movement and Left-Wing Judaism," p. 9.

97. *Ibid.*

98. *Ibid.*

99. Adler wrote the text of this message in a letter to his daughters, Eleanor and Margaret, March 29, 1933 (Col.).

100. "Nationalism and Zionism," December 8, 1918, p. 1 (E.C.S.).

101. *Ibid.,* pp. 2–3.

102. *Ibid.,* p. 2.

103. *Ibid.,* p. 3. Cf. Ben Halpern, "Brandeis' Way to Zionism," *Midstream* 18, no. 8 (October 1971): 6.

104. Professor Friess informed me that while Adler and Brandeis discussed American social and labor problems together, they never really talked about Brandeis' Zionism. This seems to be borne out by extant archival material. The archival remains of Adler at Col. contain about fifteen items of correspondence between these two men, none on the Zionist issue. Dr. Alon Gal, who researched the archives of Louis Brandeis at Brandeis University, informed me on September 6, 1973 that the letters between the two men in that collection reflect a cordial, fairly constant relationship primarily dealing with family matters (Brandeis married Alice Goldmark, sister of Helen Goldmark Adler).

105. Unpublished note entitled "Notes in re Zionism," December 13–21, 1930, p. 3 (Col.).

106. "Nationalism and Zionism," p. 1.

107. "Zionism and Its Ideal," November 7, 1915, p. 5 (E.C.S.).

108. *Ibid.,* p. 21.

109. *Ibid.,* pp. 1–2.

110. "Nationalism and Zionism," p. 3.

111. *Ibid.,* p. 4.

112. "Zionism and Its Ideal," pp. 1–2.

113. *Ibid.,* p. 2.

114. *Ibid.,* p. 3.

115. "National Self-Determination and Its Limits," November 24, 1918 (E.C.S.), pp. 1–3.

116. *Ibid.,* p. 6.

117. *Ibid.*

118. *Ibid.,* pp. 6–7. Emphasis is Adler's.

119. "Nationalism and Zionism," p. 5.

120. *Ibid.,* pp. 5, 10.

121. *Ibid.,* p. 9.

122. *Ibid.,* p. 10.

123. *Ibid.,* p. 12.

124. "Zionism and Its Ideal," p. 15.

125. *Ibid.,* p. 16.

126. "Nationalism and Zionism," p. 9.

127. Cf. Morgenthau, *All in a Lifetime,* pp. 385–98.

128. "Zionism and Its Ideal," pp. 5–7.

129. Undated note, "Zionism," p. 3 (Col.).

130. "Zionism and Its Ideal," p. 7.

131. *Ibid.,* p. 8.

132. *Ibid.,* p. 9.

133. *Ibid.,* p. 8.

134. *Ibid.,* p. 9.

135. *Ibid.*

136. *Ibid.,* p. 14. Cf. also, "Nationalism and Zionism," pp. 7–8.

137. *Ibid.,* p. 8.

138. "Zionism and Its Ideal," p. 16.

139. *Ibid.,* p. 16.

140. *Ibid.*

141. "Nationalism and Zionism," p. 13

142. *Ibid.* See also his undated note "The Jewish Question," pp. 1–3 (Col.).

143. "Zionism and Its Ideal," p. 3.

144. *Ibid.*

145. *Ibid.*

146. "Nationalism and Zionism," p. 18.

147. "The Jewish Question," p. 2.

148. "Nationalism and Zionism," p. 18.

149. "The Difference Between the Ethical Movement and Left-Wing Judaism," November 9, 1925, p. 8 (E.C.S.). Since Adler conceived of Zionism as the logical outcome of the repristination of Judaism, he concluded that Zionism was the logical product of Reform Judaism, which led the attempt to repristinate Judaism. Cf. pp. 7–8. See, too, "Zionism," p. 3.

150. "Nationalism and Zionism," p. 14.

151. *Ibid.*

152. *Ibid.*

153. *Ibid.,* p. 15.

154. Undated note "An Examination of the Title of the Jews to a Homeland in Palestine," p. 1 (Col.), and undated note "In Rebus Judaicis," p. 3 (Col.).

155. "In Rebus Judaicis," *loc. cit.*; "Nationalism and Zionism," p. 7.

156. "Nationalism and Zionism," p. 7.

157. *Ibid.,* p. 6; see too, "Notes in re Zionism," December 13–21, 1930, p. 1 (Col.).

158. "An Examination of the Title of the Jews to a Homeland in Palestine," p. 2.

159. "Nationalism and Zionism," p. 6.

160. Undated note "The Palestine Report," pp. 1–2 (Col.).

161. Cf. Morris R. Cohen, "Zionism: Tribalism or Liberalism," in *Faith of a Liberal* (1946). The essay originally appeared in the *New Republic* 18 (March 8, 1919).

162. Cf. Naomi W. Cohen, "The Reaction of Reform Judaism in America to Political Zionism, 1897–1922," *Publications of the American Jewish Historical Society* 40 (July 1951).

163. Cf. I. Levitas, "Reform Jews and Zionism, 1919–1921," *American Jewish Archives* 14, no. 1 (1962).

164. "The Mystery of Life," January 3, 1915, p. 2 (E.C.S.).

165. Cf. "What Should the Ethical Society Mean to Those Who Belong to It and to the Larger Community?" p. 8, October 1922 (E.C.S.). Adler's notion of "worth" as a cement binding society seems reminiscent of Josiah Royce's concept of "loyalty." This topic merits further study.

166. "Nationalism and Zionism," p. 19.

167. "The God in Man," March 21, 1913, p. 6 (E.C.S.).

168. "Nationalism and Zionism," p. 20.

169. "In Rebus Judaicis," p. 2.

170. "Nationalism and Zionism," p. 20.

171. *Ibid.,* p. 20.

172. "Zionism and Its Ideal," p. 17.

173. Cf. L. Brandeis, "The Jewish Problem and How to Solve It" (1915), in Arthur Hertzberg, *The Zionist Idea* (1959), pp. 517–23, especially p. 519.

174. "Zionism and Its Ideal," *loc. cit.*

175. "Nationalism and Zionism," pp. 20–21. Cf. Morgenthau, *All in a Lifetime*, p. 401, for a similar affirmation.

176. "Zionism and Its Ideal," p. 17.

177. *Ibid.*

178. *Ibid.*, p. 18.

179. *Ibid.*

180. "Nationalism and Zionism," pp. 20–21.

181. "Zionism and Its Ideal," p. 21.

182. Cf. "The Palestine Report" and "An Examination of the Title of the Jews to a Homeland in Palestine".

183. "An Examination of the Title of the Jews to a Homeland in Palestine," p. 1.

184. "Zionism," pp. 1–2.

185. Cf. Horace Kallen, *Judaism at Bay* (1932).

186. Cf. Mordecai Kaplan, *Judaism as a Civilization* (1934).

187. "Zionism and Its Ideal," p. 19.

188. Undated note, "Concerning the Perpetuation of the Jewish Race," p. 1 (Col.). Adler's whole outlook on "race" is a topic worthy of study. In 1880 he appears to have held that generalizations about race are invalid; in an 1885 address on "Reformed Judaism," he denied the transmission of racial qualities by heredity. Yet he himself adopted racial generalizations and, in the twentieth century, talked of racial inheritance.

189. "Zionism," p. 4.

190. "Notes in re Zionism," p. 3, December 13–21, 1930 (Col.).

191. *Ibid.*

192. "Zionism," p. 5.

193. *Ibid.*, p. 6.

194. "The Jewish Question," p. 21.

195. Undated note "The Zionist Point of View, The Assimilationist Point of View, The Ethical Point of View," pp. 1–3 (Col.).

196. Undated note "A Variety of Zionism," pp. 1–2 (Col.).

197. "Zionism and Its Ideal," p. 20. Since Adler himself never crossed racial lines, it seems incumbent on him to explain how he arrived at his high ethical ideals without a racial union. He never discussed this point.

198. *Ibid.*

199. *Ibid.*, pp. 20–21.

200. "The Difference Between the Ethical Movement and Left-Wing Judaism," p. 11.

201. "Races and Religions," December 18, 1878, p. 15 (Col.).

202. "The Chosen Race," December 15, 1878, p. 16 (Col.).

203. *Ibid.*, p. 13.

204. *New York Times* editorial, April 26, 1933.

205. Letter in Col.

206. *New York Times* obituary, April 26, 1933.

207. *Ibid.*

208. Letter of Louise Waterman Wise to Adler, March 6, 1933 (Col.).

209. Stephen S. Wise, *Challenging Years*, p. 98. Cf. also, *The Personal Letters of Stephen Wise*, p. 17.

210. A copy of all the eulogies delivered is in Col.

211. *The Personal Letters of Stephen Wise*, p. 44.

212. *Ibid.*, p. 34.

213. *Ibid.*, pp. 113–14.

214. Quoted in Moses Rischin, *The Promised City* (1967), p. 242.

215. *New York Times*, April 27, 1926, as cited by Michael A. Meyer, "A Centennial History," p. 271, n. 26.

216. Cf. James W. Wise, *Liberalizing Liberal Judaism* (1924), pp. 49–52, 129–32, for examples.

217. Meyer, "A Centennial History," pp. 93–94.

218. Letter of Cronbach to Adler, May 15, 1926 (Col.).

219. Letter of Schulman to Adler, September 30, 1931 (Col.).

CHAPTER VII: ADLER'S SIGNIFICANCE FOR JEWISH HISTORY

1. Cf. Michael A. Meyer, "Beyond Particularism: On Ethical Culture and the Reconstructionists," *Commentary* 51, no. 3 (March 1971): 71.

2. *Ibid.*, p. 72.

3. See the *American Israelite*, March 30, 1877.

4. Cf. M. B. Ryback, "The East-West Conflict in American Reform Judaism as Reflected in the *Israelite*, 1854–1879" (Master's thesis for Hebrew Union College, Cincinnati, 1949), pp. 54–60.

5. Jick, p. 190; Meyer, "A Centennial History," pp. 39–40.

6. On the Jew being defined as a Jew by his birth, cf. Kaufmann Kohler, *Jewish Theology Systematically and Historically Considered* (1918), pp. 5–6, and E. Hirsch's lecture to the Sinai Congregation, "Why I Am a Jew" (1895), p. 14.

7. Cf., for example, Ellinger's speech in the *Proceedings at the Second Annual Meeting of the Free Religious Association*, May 27–28, 1869, p. 22.

8. Gottheil, p. 23.

9. Cf. Ellinger's speech in the *Proceedings*, and his *Jewish Times*, December 22, 1876.

10. Speech in *Proceedings at the First Annual Meeting of the Free Religious Association*, May 28–29, 1868, p. 111.

11. Speech in *Proceedings at the Fourth Annual Meeting of the Free Religious Association*, June 1, 2, 1871.

12. Cf., for example, his sermon "Reform Proposition," published in his *American Israelite*, March 16, 1877.

13. Arthur Mann, *Growth and Achievement of Temple Israel, 1854–1954* (1954), p. 58.

14. See his lecture at Beth El, "What Is Judaism?" October 23, 1887, p. 5. Cf. the major controversy precipitated by Max L. Margolis' attempt to place creeds in the forefront of Reform Judaism and the opposition it stirred, led by Kohler. See Margolis, "The Theological Aspect of Reformed Judaism," *CCARY*, 13 (1903), and the ensuing discussion in that volume and volumes 14, 15, and 18 of the *CCARY*.

15. Emil Hirsch, "Why I Am a Jew" (1895).

16. Cf. *CCARY*, 1 (1890): 59.

17. Cf. *Ibid.*, 12 (1902): 154

18. Cf. Adler's "When Are We Justified in Leaving our Religious Fellowship?" March 28, 1886, p. 10 (E.C.S.). Adler consistently opposed the idea of Jewish election and mission following his break with Judaism. And as his own religious ideology developed, so too did the nature of his opposition to this concept. One can trace his opposition to the idea of election in "Liberal Judaism," April 8, 1877 (Col.), "The Chosen People," December 15, 1878 (Col.), "Races and Religion," December 18, 1878 (Col.), "Reformed Judaism," November 22, 1885 (E.C.S.), "The Ethical Culture Society as the Meeting Ground of Gentiles and Jews," December 5, 1897, "The Essentials of Judaism," November 22, 1913 (E.C.S.), *Eth.P.L.*, 1918, and "The Difference Between the Ethical Movement and Left-Wing Judaism," November 9, 1925 (E.C.S.).

19. Cf. articles II and VI of the Pittsburgh Platform, Plaut, *The Growth of Reform Judaism*, pp. 33–34.

20. Article VI, *Ibid.*, p. 34.

21. See Kallen's critique of Reform's universalist pretensions in his essays "Universality of Judaism" (1910) and "Judaism, Hebraism, Zionism" (1910), both published in his *Judaism at Bay.* Cf. also, Morris Jastrow's rejection of the possibility of a universal religion in his *The Study of Religion* (1901), pp. 89, 122–24.

22. Cf. Adler's "Reformed Judaism," November 22, 1885, p. 17 (E.C.S.), and Gottheil's rejoinder in a Tuesday evening lecture at Emanu-El, January 12, 1886. Adler's lecture was published in the *American Hebrew*, December 4, 1885, and Gottheil's response was serialized in issues of the same paper from January 15 through February 26, 1886.

23. "Reformed Judaism," p. 17.

24. *Proceedings at the First Annual Convention of the Free Religious Association*, p. 111.

25. Jastrow, p. 89.

26. *American Hebrew,* February 26, 1886.

27. On Fleischer and Schindler, consult Mann's *Growth and Achievement: Temple Israel.* Schindler's recantation is found in the *Jewish Advocate,* March 31, 1911.

28. Jastrow, p. 89.

29. *Jewish Times,* December 24, 1869.

30. See, for example, articles II, III, and IV of the Pittsburgh Platform; E. Schreiber, "How to Teach Biblical History in Our Schools," *CCARY* 1 (1890); Sheldon H. Blank, "Bible," in *Hebrew Union College–Jewish Institute of Religion at One Hundred Years* (1976), for a survey of the teaching and teachers of Bible at Hebrew Union College.

31. Solomon Schechter, "Higher Criticism—Higher Anti-Semitism," in *Seminary Addresses* (1915). First delivered as a speech in 1903.

32. See, for instance, Kohler, "The Four Ells of Halakhah," *Hebrew Union College Annual* 1 (1904).

33. Cf., for example, Hirsch, "Judaism and the Higher Criticism," in *My Religion.* First delivered as a speech in 1903.

34. See Sale, "The Bible and Modern Thought," *CCARY* 12 (1902).

35. Cf. Morgenstern, "The Significance of the Bible for Reformed Judaism in the Light of Modern Scientific Research," *CCARY* 18 (1908).

36. Kohler did object to ideas which he thought injurious to Jewish religious uniqueness, such as those developed in Franz Delitzsch's lectures on "Babel and Bible" in 1902. Cf. Kohler, "Assyriology and the Bible," *CCARY* 13 (1903). In general, not all Reformers assented to the thrust and content of Bible studies. Cf. the comments of Rabbis H. Barnstein and H. W. Ettelson to the lectures of Sale and Morgenstern, in the yearbooks cited above.

37. Sale, p. 162.

38. Morgenstern, "The Significance of the Bible," p. 238.

39. Compare Geiger's views to Kohler's *Jewish Theology,* pp. 36–38, and to those of Emil Hirsch, "Is Revelation a Jewish Concept?" in Plaut, *Growth,* p. 206, and Morgenstern, *op. cit.*, p. 234.

40. Plaut, *Growth,* p. 224. Plaut, in fact, concluded that "Reform Judaism has not as yet found a satisfactory approach to the Bible."

41. Cf., for example, Emil Hirsch, "In What Does the Originality of Judaism Consist?" *Hebrew Union College Annual* 1 (1904).

42. See undated note entitled "Interview with Eleven Students and Graduates of Hebrew Union College on Request of Mr. Isoermann" (Col.), in which Adler offered the grounds for his dissent from Reform Judaism. Isoermann probably refers to the student Ferdinand Isserman, chairman of the Literary Society for a time, and supporter of the cause to expose HUC students to all points of view, even those not consistent with Reform ideology. My thanks to Michael Meyer for this. See Meyer, "A Centennial History," pp. 77–78 and p. 260, n. 83.

43. James W. Wise used this same thought in criticizing Reform Judaism. See James W. Wise, *Liberalizing Liberal Judaism,* pp. 49–50, 58.

44. Morgenstern, "The Significance of the Bible," pp. 225–26, n. 6.

45. *Daily Graphic,* December 4, 1877.

46. *Stephen S. Wise: Servant of the People,* ed. Carl H. Voss (1970), p. 34. See, too, Meyer, "A Centennial History," p. 147.

47. Cf., for example, Kohler's lecture at Beth El, "What Is Judaism?" October 23, 1887, and his *Jewish Theology Systematically and Historically Considered* (1918); cf. also, for example, Emil Hirsch's address at the Sinai Congregation, 1895, "Why I Am a Jew," and his paper the *Reform Advocate.*

48. Cf. Bernard Martin, "The Social Philosophy of Emil G. Hirsch," *American Jewish Archives* 6, no. 3 (June 1954), and "The Religious Philosophy of Emil G. Hirsch," *ibid.,* 4, no. 2 (June 1952).

49. Unpublished typescript of letter of Emil Hirsch to Adler, June 6, 1918 (Col.). Emphasis added.

50. Cited in D. Einhorn Hirsch, *Rabbi Emil G. Hirsch: The Reform Advocate* (1968), p. 84.

Bibliography

This bibliography is not intended as an exhaustive bibliographical guide to the Adler archival material or to the extensive Adler literature. It simply seeks to help the reader become aware of the general material used and to clarify some of the references employed in this study.

ARCHIVAL SOURCES

Adler Archives

When the original research for this book was done, the vast body of material comprising the Adler archives was in considerable disarray—and to a large extent still is—thus militating against archival specification of individual items. The material was initially found at three New York City locations: the New York Society for Ethical Culture, abbreviated as E.C.S. in this work; the Rare Book and Manuscript Library of the Columbia University Libraries, abbreviated as Col.; and the home of the late Professor Horace Friess, Adler's son-in-law and literary executor. Over the summer of 1977, the Adler material in the Friess home was transferred to the Columbia collection, and the Friess family intends to have all of the E.C.S. material eventually transferred there as well.

At present, twenty boxes of material with no really useful system of organization are housed at the New York Society for Ethical Culture. Over one hundred boxes of material are housed at Columbia, only some of which have been indexed. The index, in fact, was the work of Adler's last personal secretary, Mr. Ernest Jacques, who attempted to order the increasing volume of transcripts and typescript drafts and who laid the foundations for an inventory of the accumulated material. Columbia simply adopted the Jacques index. Unfortunately, when I did my research, I discovered the index to be not totally reliable; frequently, material was listed incorrectly, many items from indexed boxes were missing, and material was all too often juxtaposed in haphazard fashion.

In general, both archival collections contain four broad categories of material: Adler's Sunday addresses and other miscellaneous lectures, either in manuscript, typescript, or pamphlet form, some published, some unpublished; hundreds of letters to and from Adler, either in manuscript or typescript form; a multitude of Adler's fragmentary notes, mostly undated and almost always in typescript; incomplete diary selections in MS, and numerous autobiographical jottings, all in typescript form, with the exception of one manuscript. All four types of material were used extensively.

Other Adler archival materials or materials relating to him are found in: the Department of Manuscripts and University Archives, John M. Olin Library, Cornell University, abbreviated as C.U.; the "Felsenthal Papers" at the American Jewish Historical Society, Waltham, Mass.; and the American Jewish Archives in Cincinnati, Ohio. Material pertaining to Adler in these archival collections was also used in this study.

ADLER'S PUBLISHED MATERIAL

Books

An Ethical Philosophy of Life. New York: D. Appleton and Company, 1918.
Creed and Deed. New York: G. P. Putnam's Sons, 1877.
Incompatibility in Marriage. New York: D. Appleton and Company, 1930.
Life and Destiny. New York: McClure, Philips and Company, 1903.
Marriage and Divorce: Three Addresses. New York: McClure, Philips and Company, 1905.
Our Part in This World. Selections by Horace L. Friess. New York: King's Crown Press, 1944.
The Essentials of Spirituality. New York: James Pott and Company, 1905.
The Moral Instruction of Children. New York: D. Appleton and Company, 1892.
The Punishment of Children. New York: Abingdon Press, 1920.
The Radical Pulpit: Discourses by Felix Adler and Octavius Brooks Frothingham. New York: D. M. Bennet, 1876.
The Reconstruction of the Spiritual Ideal. New York: D. Appleton and Company, 1924.
The Religion of Duty. Addresses edited by L. W. Sprague. New York: McClure, Philips and Company, 1905.
The World Crisis and Its Meaning. New York: D. Appleton and Company, 1915.

Articles

"A Critique of Kant's Ethics." *Mind,* New Series 11 (October 1902).
"A New Type of Religious Leader." *Ethical Addresses* 17 (1910).
"Ethical Development Extending Through Life." *Ethical Addresses* 20 (1913).
"Freedom of Ethical Fellowship." *Ethics and Religion: A Collection of Essays.* Edited by the Society of Ethical Propagandists. London: Swan Sonnenschein and Company, 1900.
"Memorial Exercises in Honor of Octavius Brooks Frothingham." *Ethical Addresses,* Series 2, 10 (1895).
"The Moral Ideal." *International Journal of Ethics* 20 (1910).
"The Problem of Teleology." *International Journal of Ethics* 14 (1904).
"The Relation of the Moral Ideal to Reality." *International Journal of Ethics* 22 (1911).

SECONDARY SOURCES ON ADLER

Published

Bacon, Samuel Frederick. *An Evaluation of the Philosophy and Pedagogy of Ethical Culture: A Dissertation.* Washington: Catholic University of America, 1933.

Bridges, Horace J., ed. *Aspects of Ethical Religion: Essays in Honor of Felix Adler on the Fiftieth Anniversary of his Founding of the Ethical Movement, 1876.* New York: American Ethical Union, 1926.

Felix Adler Memorial Number. The Standard, Journal of the American Ethical Union, vol. 20, no. 2 (1933).

Fite, Warner. "Felix Adler's Philosophy of Life." *Journal of Philosophy, Psychology and Scientific Method* 16 (1919).

Friess, Horace L. "Felix Adler." *Columbia University Quarterly* 26, no. 2 (1934).

———. "Felix Adler's Conception of Education." *Standard* 20, no. 4 (1934).

———. "The Relation of Religion and Philosophy for Felix Adler," *Standard* 20, no. 2 (1933).

———. *The Vision of Felix Adler.* Pamphlet of the New York Society for Ethical Culture, n.d.

Guttchen, Robert S. *Felix Adler.* New York: Twayne, 1974.

———. "Felix Adler's Concept of Worth." *Journal of the History of Philosophy* 11, no. 2 (1973).

Muzzey, David S. *Ethics as a Religion.* New York: Frederick Ungar Publishing Co., 1967 ed.

———. *Felix Adler—Historian.* Pamphlet of the New York Society for Ethical Culture, 1945.

Neumann, Henry. *Spokesman for Ethical Religion.* Boston: Beacon Press, 1951.

Olan, Levi A. "Felix Adler: Critic of Judaism and Founder of a Movement." *Union Anniversary Series,* 1950.

Radest, Howard B. *Toward Common Ground.* New York: Frederick Ungar Publishing Co., 1969.

Reich, Walter. "The Philosophic Status of Adler's Ethical Ideal," *Yavneh Review,* Spring 1966.

The Fiftieth Anniversary of the Ethical Movement: 1876–1926. New York: D. Appleton and Co., 1926.

Unpublished

Hartnett, J. R. "The Origin and Growth of the Ethical Culture Movement in the United States." Doctoral dissertation, St. Louis University, 1958.

Klein, Adolph. "Dr. Felix Adler's Contribution to Experimental Education." Doctoral dissertation, New York University, 1935.

Lawson, David. "Changing Modes of Thought in Moral Education." Doctoral dissertation, Teachers College, Columbia University, 1959.

Radest, Howard B. "Toward A Philosophy of Culture." Doctoral dissertation, Columbia University, 1971.

Rodwin, Richard. "Ethical Religion in America." A copy of this unpublished essay, 1952, was made available to me by Jacob R. Marcus, American Jewish Archives, Cincinnati, Ohio.

NEWSPAPERS

American Hebrew, New York, 1879–1885.
(American) Israelite, Cincinnati, 1869–80.
Chicago Daily Tribune, 1878.
Daily Graphic, New York, 1876–78.
Independent Hebrew, New York, 1876.
Index, A Weekly Paper Devoted to Free Religion, Boston, 1876–82.
Jewish Advocate, Boston, 1911.
Jewish Messenger, New York, 1857–85.
New York Herald, 1876–80.
New York Times, 1875–1933.
New York World, 1869–78.
(Reformer and) Jewish Times, New York, 1869–80.

SUPPLEMENTARY PRIMARY AND SECONDARY LITERATURE

Abell, Aaron, I. *The Urban Impact on American Protestantism, 1865–1900.* Cambridge: Harvard University Press, 1943.

Adler, Samuel. *A Guide to Instruction in the Israelitish Religion.* Translated by M. Mayer. New York: Thalmessinger, 1868 edition.

———. Autobiography, given title "Prelude to America" by Stanley F. Chyet, in his *Lives and Voices.* Philadelphia: Jewish Publication Society, 1972.

———. *Kovets al Yad.* New York: Cherouny Printing and Publishing Co., 1886.

Ahlstrom, Sidney E. *A Religious History of the American People.* New Haven: Yale University Press, 1972.

———. "Theology in America." In *The Shaping of American Religion,* edited by J. W. Smith and A. L. Jamison. Princeton: Princeton University Press, 1961.

Arnold, Matthew. *Culture and Anarchy.* Edited by J. Dover Wilson. Cambridge: Cambridge University Press, 1932.

———. *Literature and Dogma.* London: Smith, Edler and Co., 1873.

Baillie, J. B. "Ethical Idealism." In *Encyclopaedia of Religion and Ethics,* edited by James Hastings, vol. 6, 1955.

Barnard, Frederick A. P. "Inaugural Discourse." *Proceedings at the Inauguration of Frederick A. P. Barnard as President of Columbia College, October 3, 1874.* New York: Hurd and Houghton, 1865.

Blank, Sheldon. "Bible." In *Hebrew Union College–Jewish Institute of Religion at One Hundred Years,* edited by Samuel E. Karff. Hebrew Union College Press, 1976.

Blau, Joseph L. "An American-Jewish View of the Evolution Controversy." *Hebrew Union College Annual* 20 (1947).

———. *Men and Movements in American Philosophy.* Englewood Cliffs: Prentice-Hall, 1952.

———. "The Spiritual Life of American Jewry." *American Jewish Year Book* 56 (1955).

———, ed. *Reform Judaism: A Historical Perspective.* New York: Ktav, 1973.

Burgess, J. W. *Reminiscences of an American Scholar.* New York: Columbia University Press, 1934.

Caspari, Otto. *Die Urgeschichte der Menschheit.* Leipzig: F. A. Brockhaus, 1873.

Catalogue of the Officers and Students of Columbia College, 1866–1867.

Cohen, Julius H. *They Builded Better Than They Knew.* New York: Julian Messner, 1946.

Cohen, Morris R. *A Dreamer's Journey.* Boston: Beacon Press, 1949.

———. *Reflections of a Wandering Jew.* Boston: Beacon Press, 1950.

———. *The Faith of a Liberal.* New York: Henry Holt and Co., 1946.

Cohen, Naomi W. "The Reaction of Reform Judaism in America to Political Zionism, 1897–1922." *Publications of the American Jewish Historical Society* 40 (1951).

Cohn, Bernard N. "David Einhorn: Some Aspects of His Thinking." In *Essays in American Jewish History.* Cincinnati: American Jewish Archives, 1958.

———. "Early German Preaching in America." *Historia Judaica* 15 (1953).

Cohon, Samuel M. "Kaufmann Kohler." In *Great Jewish Thinkers of the Twentieth Century,* edited by Simon Noveck. Clinton: Colonial Press, 1969 ed.

Cohon, Samuel S. "Reform Judaism in America." *Judaism* 3, no. 4 (1954).

Cole, A. C. *The Irrepressible Conflict, 1850–1865.* New York: Macmillan Co., 1934.

Columbia University Alumni Register, 1754–1931. New York: Columbia University Press, 1932.

Cowen, Philip. *Memories of An American Jew.* New York: International Press, 1932.

Cronbach, Abraham. "Autobiography." *American Jewish Archives* 11, no. 1 (1959).

Davis, Moshe. "Jewish Religious Life and Institutions in America." In *The Jews*, edited by L. Finkelstein. New York: Harper and Brothers, 1960.

———. *The Emergence of Conservative Judaism*. Philadelphia: Jewish Publication Society, 1963.

———. *Yahadut Amerika Behitpathuta* (Hebrew). New York: Jewish Theological Seminary of America, 1951.

Eisler, Robert. "Freethinkers." In *Encyclopaedia of the Social Sciences,* vol. 3. 1937.

Ellis, E. R. *The Epic of New York City.* New York: Coward-McCann, 1966.

Ernst, R. *Immigrant Life in New York City, 1825–1863.* New York: King's Crown Press, 1949.

Felsenthal, B. "Some Remarks Concerning Zionism." *Hebrew Union College Journal* 4 (1899).

Felsenthal, Emma, ed. *Bernhard Felsenthal: Teacher in Israel.* New York: Oxford University Press, 1924.

Feuerbach, Ludwig A. *The Essence of Christianity.* Translated by Marian Evans. London, 1854.

Fiske, John. *Outlines of Cosmic Philosophy.* Boston: James R. Osgood and Co., 1875 ed.

Frank, Waldo. *Our America.* New York: Boni and Liveright Publishers, 1919.

Freedom and Fellowship in Religion. Edited by a Committee of the Free Religious Association. Boston, 1875.

Frothingham, O. B. "Attitudes of Unbelief." Lecture in 1878.

———. *Creed and Conduct.* New York: G. P. Putnam's Sons, 1877.

———. "Faith and Morals," Two Lectures, March 5 and 12, 1871.

———. *Knowledge and Faith.* New York: G. P. Putnam's Sons, 1876.

———. *Religion of Humanity.* New York: G. P. Putnam's Sons, 1877 ed.

———. "The Gospel of Today." Lecture, April 16, 1871.

———. "The Inward Guide." Lecture in 1868.

———. "The Scientific Aspect of Prayer." Lecture in 1872.

———. "The Victory Over Death." Lecture, March 31, 1872.

———. "What Is It to Be a Christian?" Lecture in 1868.

———. "Why Go to Church?" Lecture in 1874.

Fuchs, Richard. "The Hochschule für die Wissenschaft des Judentums in the Period of Nazi Rule." *Yearbook of the Leo Baeck Institute* 12 (1967).

Fulton, J., ed. *Memoirs of Frederick A. P. Barnard.* New York: Macmillan and Co., 1896.

Gardiner, Patrick. "The German Idealists and Their Successors." In *Germany,* edited by M. Pasley. London: Methuen and Co., 1972.

Gartner, Lloyd P. *Jewish Education in the United States: A Documentary History*. New York: Teachers College Press, 1969.

Geiger, Abraham. *Judaism and Its History*. Translated by Charles Newburgh. New York: Bloch Publishing Co., 1911 ed.

Gilmore, George W. "Comparative Religion." In *The New Schaff-Herzog Religious Encyclopedia*, Vol. 3. 1969.

Glanz, R. "German Jews in New York City in the Nineteenth Century," *Yivo Annual of Jewish Social Sciences* 11 (1956–57).

————. "Notes on Early Jewish Peddling." In *Studies in Judaica Americana*, edited by R. Glanz. New York: Ktav, 1970.

————. *Studies in Judaica Americana*. New York: Ktav, 1970.

————. *The German Jew in America*. Cincinnati: Hebrew Union College Press, 1969.

————. "The German Jewish Mass Emigration: 1820–1880." *American Jewish Archives* 22, no. 1 (1970).

————. "The Immigration of Jews Up to 1880." In *Studies in Judaica Americana*, edited by R. Glanz. New York: Ktav, 1970.

Glazer, Nathan. "Social Character of American Jews, 1654–1954." *American Jewish Year Book* 56 (1955).

Goldmark, Josephine. *Pilgrims of '48*. New Haven: Yale University Press, 1930.

Goldstein, Israel. *A Century of Judaism*. New York: Congregation B'nai Jeshurun, 1930.

Gompers, Samuel. *Seventy Years of Life and Labor*. New York: Augustus M. Kelley, 1967.

Gottheil, Gustav. "Zionism." *Hebrew Union College Journal*, 4 (1899).

Greenberg, Gershon. "Samuel Hirsch's American Judaism." *American Jewish Historical Quarterly* 62, no. 4 (1973).

————. "The Dimensions of Samuel Adler's Religious View of the World." *Hebrew Union College Annual* 66 (1975).

————. "The Historical Origins of God and Man: Samuel Hirsch's Luxembourg Writings." *Yearbook of the Leo Baeck Institute* 20 (1975).

Grinstein, Hyman B. "Reforms at Temple Emanuel of New York, (1860–1890)." *Historia Judaica* 6, no. 2 (1944).

————. *The Rise of the Jewish Community of New York, 1654–1860*. Philadelphia: Jewish Publication Society, 1945.

Grollman, Jerome W. "The Emergence of Reform Judaism in the United States." *American Jewish Archives* 2, no. 2 (1950).

Halpern, Ben. "Brandeis' Way to Zionism." *Midstream* 17, no. 8 (1971).

Handlin, Oscar. *Adventure in Freedom*. New York: McGraw-Hill Book Co., 1954.

————. "Judaism in the United States." In *The Shaping of American*

Religion, edited by J. W. Smith and A. L. Jamison. Princeton: Princeton University Press, 1961.

―――. *The Uprooted*. Boston: Little, Brown and Co., 1951.

Handlin, Oscar, and Handlin, Mary F. "The Acquisition of Political and Social Rights by the Jews in the United States." *American Jewish Year Book* 56 (1955).

Haney, John D. *Lessing's Education of the Human Race*. New York: Teachers College, Columbia University, 1908.

Hecht, Emanuel. *Biblical History for Israelitish Schools*. Revised and corrected by Samuel Adler. Translated by M. Mayer. New York, 1874 ed.

Hellman, George S. "Joseph Seligman, American Jew." *Publications of the American Jewish Historical Society* 41, no. 1 (1951).

Hirsch, D. Einhorn. *Rabbi Emil G. Hirsch: The Reform Advocate*. Chicago: Whitehall Co., 1968.

Hirsch, Emil G. *My Religion*. New York: Macmillan Co., 1925.

―――. "The Philosophy of the Reform Movement in American Judaism." 1895 address in *Reform Judaism: A Historical Perspective*, edited by Joseph L. Blau. New York: Ktav, 1973.

―――. "Why I Am a Jew." Address at the Sinai Congregation, Chicago, 1895.

Hirshler, Eric E., ed. *Jews From Germany in the United States*. New York: Farrar, Straus and Cudahy, 1955.

―――. "Jews From Germany in the United States." In *Jews from Germany in the United States*, edited by Eric E. Hirshler. New York: Farrar, Straus and Cudahy, 1955.

Hofstadter, Richard. *Social Darwinism in American Thought, 1860–1915*. Philadelphia: University of Pennsylvania Press, 1945.

Hopkins, Charles H. *The Rise of the Social Gospel in American Protestantism, 1865–1915*. New Haven: Yale University Press, 1940.

Humboldt, Alexander von. *Cosmos*. London: George Bell and Sons, 1882 ed.

Jamison, A. Leland. "Religions on the Christian Perimeter." In *The Shaping of American Religion*, edited by J. W. Smith and A. L. Jamison. Princeton: Princeton University Press, 1961.

Jastrow, Morris. *The Study of Religion*. London: Walter Scott, 1901.

Jick, Leon A. *The Americanization of the Synagogue 1820–1870*. Hanover: Brandeis University Press, 1976.

Johnson, Samuel. *Oriental Religions and Their Relation to Universal Religion*. Boston: Houghton Mifflin Co., 1885.

Kalisch, Isidor. *A Guide for Rational Inquiries into the Biblical Writings*. Translated by M. Mayer. Cincinnati: Bloch and Co., 1857.

Kant, Immanuel. *Critique of Practical Reason.* Translated by Lewis W. Beck. Chicago: University of Chicago Press, 1949 ed.

———. *Critique of Pure Reason.* Translated by F. Max Muller, New York: Macmillan and Co., 1957 ed.

———. *Religion Within the Limits of Reason Alone.* Translated by Theodore M. Greene and Hoyt H. Hudson. New York: Harper and Brothers, 1960.

Karff, Samuel E. *Hebrew Union College–Jewish Institute of Religion at One Hundred Years.* Hebrew Union College Press, 1976.

Karp, Abraham J. "New York Chooses a Chief Rabbi." *Publications of the American Jewish Historical Society* 44, no. 3 (1955).

———, ed. *The Jewish Experience in America.* New York: Ktav, 1969.

Kisch, Guido. "The Founders of 'Wissenschaft des Judentums' and America." *Essays in American Jewish History.* Cincinnati: American Jewish Archives, 1958.

Kober, Adolf. "Aspects of the Influence of Jews from Germany on American Jewish Spiritual Life of the Nineteenth Century." In *Jews From Germany In the United States,* edited by E. E. Hirshler. New York: Farrar, Straus and Cuhady, 1955.

———. "Jewish Religious and Cultural Life in America as Reflected in the Felsenthal Collection." *Publications of the American Jewish Historical Society* 45, no. 2 (1955).

Kohler, Kaufmann. "Assyriology and the Bible." *Yearbook of the Central Conference of American Rabbis* 13 (1903).

———. *Jewish Theology Systematically and Historically Considered.* New York: Ktav, 1968 ed.

———. "What Is Judaism?" Lecture on October 23, 1887, Beth El, New York.

Korn Bertram, W. *American Jewry and the Civil War.* Philadelphia: Jewish Publication Society, 1951.

———. "German Jewish Intellectual Influences on American Jewish Life, 1824–1972." In *The B. G. Rudolph Lectures in Judaic Studies.* Syracuse University, April 1972.

———. "I. M. Wise and the Civil War." In *Eventful Years and Experiences: Studies in Nineteenth Century American Jewish History,* edited by B. W. Korn. Cincinnati: American Jewish Archives, 1954.

———. "Isaac Leeser: Centennial Reflections." *American Jewish Archives* 19, no. 2 (1967).

———. "The First American Jewish Theological Seminary: Maimonides College, 1867–1873." In *Eventful Years and Experiences: Studies in Nineteenth Century American Jewish History,* edited by B. W. Korn. Cincinnati: American Jewish Archives, 1954.

———. "The Temple Emanu-El Theological Seminary of New York

City." In *Essays in American Jewish History.* Cincinnati: American Jewish Archives, 1958.

————, ed. *Eventful Years and Experiences: Studies in Nineteenth Century American Jewish History.* Cincinnati: American Jewish Archives, 1954.

Lange, F. A. *The History of Materialism.* Translated by E. C. Thomas. New York: Harcourt Brace and Co., 1925 ed.

Lee, Basil Leo. *Discontent in New York City, 1861–1865.* Washington: Catholic University of America Press, 1943.

Die Lehranstalt für die Wissenschaft des Judentums in Berlin. Berlin, 1897.

Levitas, I. "Reform Jews and Zionism, 1919–1921." *American Jewish Archives* 14, no. 1 (1962).

Levy, Beryl H. *Reform Judaism in America.* New York: Bloch Publishing Co., 1933.

Lewis, Harry S. *Liberal Judaism and Social Service.* New York: Bloch Publishing Co., 1915.

Liebman, Charles S. "Reconstructionism in American Jewish Life." *American Jewish Year Book* 71 (1971).

Mann, Arthur, ed. *Growth and Achievement: Temple Israel.* Cambridge: Riverside Press, 1954.

————. *Yankee Reformers in an Urban Age.* Cambridge: Belknap Press, 1954.

Marcus, Jacob R., ed. *Critical Studies in American Jewish History.* New York: Ktav, 1971.

————. *Studies in American Jewish History.* Cincinnati: Hebrew Union College Press, 1969.

————. *The Americanization of I. M. Wise.* Cincinnati: Printed privately, 1931.

Margolis, Max L. "The Theological Aspects of Reformed Judaism." *Yearbook of the Central Conference of American Rabbis* 13 (1903).

Martin, Bernard. "The Religious Philosophy of Emil G. Hirsch." *American Jewish Archives* 4, no. 2 (1952).

————. "The Social Philosophy of Emil G. Hirsch." *American Jewish Archives* 6, no. 2 (1954).

Matthews, B., et al. *A History of Columbia University, 1754–1904.* New York: Columbia University Press, 1904.

May, Henry F. *Protestant Churches and Industrial America.* New York: Octagon Books, 1963 ed.

Mayer, L. "Eulogy on the Late Dr. S. Adler." *Yearbook of the Central Conference of American Rabbis* 2 (1892).

Mead, Sidney E. "American Protestantism Since the Civil War: From Denominationalism to Americanism." *Journal of Religion* 36, no. 1 (1956).

Mervis, Leonard J. "The Social Justice Movement and the American

Reform Rabbi." *American Jewish Archives* 7, no. 2 (1955).

Meyer, I. S., ed. *Early History of Zionism in America*. New York: American Jewish Historical Society, 1958.

Meyer, Michael A. "A Centennial History." In *Hebrew Union College–Jewish Institute of Religion at One Hundred Years*. Hebrew Union College Press, 1976.

————. "Beyond Particularism: On Ethical Culture and the Reconstructionists." *Commentary* 51, no. 3 (March 1971).

————. "Jewish Religious Reform and Wissenschaft des Judentums: The Positions of Zunz, Geiger, and Frankel." *Yearbook of the Leo Baeck Institute* 16 (1971).

————. "Universalism and Jewish Unity in the Thought of Abraham Geiger." In *The Role of Religion in Modern Jewish History*, edited by Jacob Katz. Cambridge: Association for Jewish Studies, 1975.

Mill, John S. *Three Essays on Religion*. London: Longmans, Green, Reader and Dyer, 1874.

"Minute Book of the Temple Emanu-El Trustees," 1858–90. Housed at Temple Emanu-El, New York.

Mirbt, C. "Deutsch-Katholicismus." In *Encyclopaedia of Religion and Ethics*, edited by James Hastings, vol. 4. 1955.

Morais, Henry S. *Eminent Israelites of the Nineteenth Century*. Philadelphia: Edward Stern and Co., 1880.

Morgenstern, Julian. *All in a Lifetime*. Garden City: Doubleday, Page and Co., 1922.

————. *As A Mighty Stream*. Philadelphia: Jewish Publication Society, 1949.

————. "The Attitude to the Bible." In *Aspects of Progressive Jewish Thought*. London: Victor Gollancz, 1954.

————. "The Significance of the Bible for Reform Judaism in the Light of Modern Scientific Research." *Yearbook of the Central Conference of American Rabbis* 18 (1908).

Nevins, Allan. *The Emergence of Modern America, 1865–1878*. New York: Macmillan Co., 1928.

Panitz, Esther L. "The Polarity of American Jewish Attitudes Towards Jewish Immigration (1870–1891)." In *The Jewish Experience in America*, edited by A. Karp. New York: Ktav, 1969.

Perilman, N. A. "One Hundred Years of Congregation Emanu-El." In *Moral and Spiritual Foundations for the World Tomorrow*. New York: Congregation Emanu-El, 1945.

Persons, Stow. *American Minds: A History of Ideas*. New York: Henry Holt and Co., 1958.

————. "Evolution and Theology in America." In *Evolutionary Thought in America*, edited by Stow Persons. New Haven: Yale University Press, 1950.

————. *Free Religion: An American Faith.* New Haven: Yale University Press, 1947.

————. "Religion and Modernity." In *The Shaping of American Religion,* edited by J. W. Smith and A. L. Jamison. Princeton: Princeton University Press, 1961.

Philipson, David. "Some Unpublished Letters of Theological Importance." *Hebrew Union College Annual* 2 (1925).

————. *The Reform Movement in Judaism.* New York: Macmillan Co., 1931 edition.

Plaut, W. Gunther. *The Growth of Reform Judaism.* New York: World Union for Progressive Judaism, 1963–65.

————. *The Rise of Reform Judaism.* New York: World Union for Progressive Judaism, 1963–65.

Polier, J. W., and Wise, J. W., eds. *The Personal Letters of Stephen Wise.* Boston: Beacon Press, 1956.

Price, George M. "The Russian Jew in America." *Publications of the American Jewish Historical Society* 48, no. 1 (1958).

Proceedings at the First . . . Twelfth Meeting of the Free Religious Association, 1868–1879, 9 vols.

"Proceedings of the Pittsburgh Rabbinical Conference, November 16–18, 1885." *Yearbook of the Central Conference of American Rabbis* 33 (1923).

Rabinowitz, Benjamin. "The Young Men's Hebrew Associations, 1854–1918." *Publications of the American Jewish Historical Society* 37 (1947).

Randall, John H., Jr. "The Churches and the Liberal Tradition." *Annals of the American Academy of Political and Social Science* 256 (1943).

Report of Address at a Meeting Held in Boston May 30, 1867, to Consider the Conditions, Wants and Prospects of Free Religion in America.

"Report of the Committee on Prof. Margolis' Paper on 'The Theological Aspects of Reformed Judaism,' and on His Motion to Have a Creed Prepared for Final Adoption by a Synod." *Yearbook of the Central Conference of American Rabbis* 15 (1905).

"Report of the Committee on the Elaboration of a Systematic Theology." *Yearbook of the Central Conference of American Rabbis* 18 (1908).

Riis, Jacob A. *The Making of an American.* New York: Macmillan Co., 1901.

Rischin, Moses. "The Jews and the Liberal Tradition in America." *American Jewish Historical Quarterly* 51, no. 1 (1961).

————. *The Promised City.* Cambridge: Harvard University Press, 1962.

Rivkin, Ellis. "A Decisive Pattern in American Jewish History." In *Essays in American Jewish History.* Cincinnati: American Jewish Archives, 1958.

Robertson, J. M. *A History of Freethought in the Nineteenth Century.* London: Watts and Co., 1929.

Ryback, M. G. "The East-West Conflict in American Reform Judaism." *American Jewish Archives* 4, no. 1 (1952).

————. "The East-West Conflict in American Reform as Reflected in the *Israelite*, 1854–1879." Master's thesis, Hebrew Union College, Cincinnati, 1949.

Sale, Samuel. "The Bible and Modern Thought." *Yearbook of the Central Conference of American Rabbis* 12 (1902).

Schappes, Morris U., ed. *Documentary History of the Jews in the United States, 1654–1875.* New York: Citadel Press, 1950.

Schechter, Solomon. "Higher Criticism—Higher Anti-Semitism." In *Seminary Addresses.* Cincinnati: Ark Publishing Co., 1915.

Schindler, Solomon. *Dissolving Views in the History of Judaism.* Boston: Lee and Shepard, 1888.

Schlesinger, Arthur M. "A Critical Period in American Religion, 1875–1900." *Proceedings of the Massachusetts Historical Society* 64 (1932).

————. *The Rise of Modern America, 1865–1951.* New York: Macmillan Co., 1951.

Schneider, Herbert W. *A History of American Philosophy.* New York: Columbia University Press, 1946.

————. "The Influence of Darwin and Spencer on American Philosophical Theology." *Journal of the History of Ideas* 6, no. 1 (1945).

Schreiber, E. "How to Teach Biblical History in our Sabbath-Schools." *Yearbook of the Central Conference of American Rabbis* 1 (1890).

Silver, A. M. "Jews in the Political Life of New York City, 1865–1897." Doctoral dissertation, Yeshiva University, 1954.

Silverman, Joseph. "Samuel Adler." *Yearbook of the Central Conference of American Rabbis* 19 (1909).

Simenhoff, H. *Saga of American Jewry.* New York: Arco Publishing Co., 1959.

Smith, J. W. "Religion and Science in American Philosophy." In *The Shaping of American Religion,* edited by J. W. Smith and A. L. Jamison. Princeton: Princeton University Press, 1961.

Smith, James W., and Jamison, A. Leland, eds. *The Shaping of American Religion.* Princeton: Princeton University Press, 1961.

Steinthal, Heymann. "The Original Form of the Legend of Prometheus" and "The Legend of Samson." In *Mythology Among the Hebrews in Its Historical Development,* by I. Goldziher. New York: Cooper Square, 1967.

————. *Über Juden und Judentum.* Berlin: M. Poppelauer, 1910.

————. *Zu Bibel und Religionsphilosophie.* Berlin: George Reimer, 1890.

Stern, Myer. *The Rise and Progress of Reform Judaism.* New York: Myer Stern Publisher, 1895.

Stern-Taeubler, Selma. "The Motivation of the German Jewish Emigration to America in the Post-Mendelssohnian Era." In *Essays in American Jewish History.* Cincinnati: American Jewish Archives, 1958.

Strauss, David F. *The Old Faith and the New.* Translated by M. Blind. New York: Henry Holt and Co., 1873.

Tarshish, Allan. "The Rise of American Judaism." Doctor of Divinity dissertation, Hebrew Union College, Cincinnati, 1938.

Thwing, C. F. *The American and the German University.* New York: Macmillan Co., 1928.

Voss, Carl H. *Stephen S. Wise: Servant of the People.* Philadelphia: Jewish Publication Society, 1970.

————. "The Lion and the Lamb: An Evaluation of the Life and Work of Stephen Wise." *American Jewish Archives* 21, no. 1 (1969).

Wallach, Benno M. "Dr. David Einhorn's Sinai, 1856–1862." Master's thesis, Hebrew Union College, Cincinnati, 1950.

Warren, Sidney. *American Freethought, 1860–1914.* New York: Columbia University Press, 1943.

Weinryb, Bernard D. "The German Jewish Immigration to America." In *Jews from Germany in the United States,* edited by E. E. Hirshler. New York: Farrar, Straus and Cudahy, 1955.

Weinstein, Gregory. *The Ardent Eighties.* New York: International Press, 1928.

White, Andrew D. *A History of the Warfare of Science with Theology in Christendom.* New York: D. Appleton and Co., 1896.

Wiener, Max. *Abraham Geiger and Liberal Judaism.* Philadelphia: Jewish Publication Society, 1962.

————. "Abraham Geiger's Conception of the Science of Judaism." *Yivo Annual of Jewish Social Studies* 11 (1956–57).

Williams, Daniel D. "Tradition and Experience in American Theology." In *The Shaping of American Religion,* edited by J. W. Smith and A. L. Jamison. Princeton: Princeton University Press, 1961.

Wise, James Waterman. *Jews Are Like That.* New York: Brentano's Publishing, 1928.

————. *Liberalizing Liberal Judaism.* New York: Macmillan Company, 1924.

Wise, Stephen S. *Challenging Years.* New York: G. P. Putnam's Sons, 1949.

Zafren, H. C. "Samuel Adler: Respondent." In *Essays in Honor of Solomon B. Freehof,* edited by Walter Jacob et al. Pittsburgh: Rodef Shalom Congregation, 1964.

Zinsser, Hans. *As I Remember Him.* Boston: Little, Brown and Co., 1940.

Index

Abbot, Francis E., 158, 159
Aberheim, Max, 110
Achad Haam, 200
Adler, Abraham (brother of Samuel), 1
Adler, Eleanor (daughter of Felix), 9, 16, 17, 32, 78, 85, 227n16
Adler, Felix: early education, 7, 8, 10, 11, 12; attracted to Reform Judaism, 7, 18, 19-20, 21, 22, 24, 29-31; early character and personality, 10, 12, 13, 17, 18, 28, 29, 65, 228n17, 233-234n115; as intellectual elitist, 12, 101, 166, 167, 184; on Christmas, 29-31, 176; on Jesus, 30, 68, 89, 90, 172; on Christianity, 30, 31, 68, 99, 105, 170, 173, 209; religious doubts increased by scientific thinking, 32-33, 33-35, 35-37, 39, 40, 41, 52-56 passim, 63, 67, 88, 119, 120, 121, 232n78; studies in Germany, 45-49 passim; loyalty to America, 45, 66, 174, 188, 196, 204, 205-206; relationship with Geiger, 48-49, 58-61 passim; rejects Reform Judaism, 55-63 passim, 74, 119, 120, 170, 171; critique of Reform Judaism, 55, 56, 58, 81, 118-126 passim; new religion of Ethical Culture, 66, 69, 70-74 passim; as social reformer, 70, 130, 132, 147, 179, 180, 202, 203, 215; and religious universalism, 77, 78, 81, 83, 84, 125, 162, 165, 187, 192, 208, 209, 210, 214; reactions to his Temple Sermon, 78-82 passim; as president of the Free Religious Association, 83; and his Jewish identity, 84, 85, 89, 105, 119, 132, 134, 162, 165, 174, 175, 176, 177, 178, 206, 208, 209, 210, 214, 223, 224, 225; departs from Judaism, 85, 163; college appointments, 95, 98, 100-105 passim, 102; as threat to American Judaism, 107, 138-149 passim, 215, 216; dismissed as a Jew, 119, 135, 142, 144, 147; as religious emancipator 123-124; on continued Jewish existence, 123, 186, 187, 189, 191, 192, 193, 207-210 passim; interest in and reverence for Judaism, 124, 169, 173-175 passim, 184, 186; as apostate, 124-125, 144, 165, 175, 214;

attracts following, 126; opposes Jews returning to Judaism, 131, 186, 187, 189, 191, 194, 196; controversy with Kohler, 153-161; relationship to Felsenthal, 161-165; estranged from Society for Ethical Culture, 165-167 passim; critique of prophetic ethics, 169, 170, 171, 172, 200, 201; on intermarriage and racial union, 175, 176, 208-210 passim; aid and concern for East European Jews, 179-185 passim, 198, 199; impact on (Reform) Jews and Judaism, 181, 211-213, 215, 216, 217, 218; on racial anti-semitism, 189-193 passim; on Jews as a nation, 197, 198, 206; wins respect of Jews, 210-213 passim
Adler, Isaac (brother of Felix), 2, 8, 10, 11, 14, 15, 19, 39, 44, 49, 50, 74, 85
Adler, Henrietta (mother of Felix), 1, 8, 9, 46, 74
Adler, Jacob (brother of Samuel), 1
Adler, Lawrence (son of Felix), 176
Adler, Liebman, 154, 155
Adler, Margaret (daughter of Felix), 85
Adler, Nathan (cousin of Felix), 1
Adler, Nathan Marcus (cousin of Felix), 1
Adler, Ruth (daughter of Felix), 176
Adler, Samuel (father of Felix): leaves Orthodox Judaism, 1, 168; contributes to development of Reform Judaism, 1, 2, 5, 6, 7; accepts Temple Emanu-El pulpit, 2, 3, 5; wants a son to succeed him as rabbi, 7, 8, 49-50; major ethical and religious influence on Felix, 8, 9, 18, 47, 71, 72; religious values and theology, 22-26 passim, 34, 116; impatient with Felix's interest in philosophy, 72, 73, 74; sorely disappointed that Felix doesn't succeed him, 85; great love and regard for Felix, 85, 160; revered by Felix, 85, 86; mentioned passim
Adler, Sarah (sister of Felix), 7
Adler, Sirig (father of Samuel), 1, 168
Adler, Waldo (son of Felix), 176
Agassiz, Jean Louis, 99
Alzey: birthplace of Felix Adler, 1

279